CHAUCER ALOUD

BELL'S EDITION.
The POETS of GREAT BRITAIN
COMPLETE, FROM
CHAUCER to CHURCHILL.

CHAUCER VOLUME XIV.
Pilgrimage to Canterbury.

Stodhart del: Delattre sc.

London Printed for John Bell British Library May 29th 1783.

THE MIDDLE AGES
a series edited by
EDWARD PETERS
Henry Charles Lea Professor of Medieval History
University of Pennsylvania

A complete listing of the books in this series
appears at the back of this volume

FRONTISPIECE: *Pilgrimage to Canterbury,* drawn by Stothard and engraved by Delattre, from frontispiece to vol. 14 of John Bell's edition
of *The Poets of Great Britain* (Edinburgh: Apollo Press, 1782–83).
Reproduced by courtesy of Robert N. Essick. Actual size, 2⅝″ × 4¼″.

Library of Congress Cataloging-in-Publication Data

Bowden, Betsy.
   Chaucer aloud.

   (University of Pennsylvania Press Middle Ages series)
   Bibliography: p.
   Includes index.
   1. Chaucer, Geoffrey, d. 1400. Canterbury tales.
2. Oral interpretation of poetry. I. Title.
II. Series.
PR1875.073B68   1987   821′.1   87-10792
ISBN 0-8122-8059-8

CHAUCER ALOUD

The Varieties of
Textual Interpretation

BETSY BOWDEN

UNIVERSITY OF PENNSYLVANIA PRESS
Philadelphia

For Sally Soppitt
of Grove City, Pennsylvania
and every other
unsung
high-school English teacher

CONTENTS

ILLUSTRATIONS

Frontispiece: Stothard's *Pilgrimage to Canterbury* (1783)

ACKNOWLEDGMENTS

If I were to begin at the beginning, I would first speak at length of my mentor Charles Muscatine, the only person in the world whose advice I nearly always follow, who has seen me through every step of the way, and next speak of the approximately nine and twenty Chaucerians who gave of their time and expertise to create the Chaucer tapes. As I finish this book, however, let me address immediate gratitude to my editor, Zachary Simpson, and to others who helped me finish. Ken Garson assisted in many ways, including preparation of my index. Ida Levin typed nearly the entire manuscript three times, inadvertently learning Middle English in the process; Rita Lorang and Jeannette Molinaro typed the rest. Edwin Fontanez made tape copies. Among many helpful librarians up and down the East Coast and elsewhere, Norma DiStefano at Rutgers and the staff of the Rare Books Room at University of Pennsylvania deserve particular thanks.

I appreciate early encouragement to undertake this project from the late Bertrand Bronson; E. Talbot Donaldson; Elizabeth Hatcher; and Wayne Shumaker, who spent part of his first retirement year reading a first draft of this book as carefully as he would have a dissertation under his jurisdiction. In my heartfelt expression of appreciation to the Chaucerians who taped the readings, without which this book would not exist, I will have to be a bit sneaky. A few readers-aloud wish to remain anonymous. In the following list, therefore, I have cunningly intermingled medievalists who made Chaucer tapes, medievalists who helped in ways other than taping, nonmedievalists who provided other assistance including general moral support, and some of my friends' kids who would like to see their names in print. Thank you, each and every one: C. David Benson, Marie Borroff, Edward and Ruth Bowden, Erika Brady, Derek Brewer, Saul Broudy, Emerson Brown, Jr., John Buck, Robert Burlin, John Burrow, Tom Burton, Kathy Campbell, Michael D. Cherniss, Howell D. Chickering, Jr., Anthony Cicariello, Mary Ellen Cohane, Marie Cornelia, Susan Crane, Alfred David, Judith Davidoff, Blanche DeVaney, Graham Drake, Joe Duggan, David Dunaway, Alan Dundes, Peter Elbow,

Eleanor Ely, John H. Fisher, Hardy Long Frank, Robert Worth Frank, Jr., John Ganim, Alan T. Gaylord, Catherine Gjerdingen, Kenneth S. Goldstein, Mel Greenlee, Bill Hayes, Donald R. Howard, V. A. Kolve, J. Saul Korey, Hilda Kring, Elizabeth Liebert, Ron Loewinsohn, Bill Lutz, Marjorie Malvern, Priscilla Martin, John McGuigan, Miriam Youngerman Miller, J. Clare Milofsky, Chauncey Mirer, Alice Miskimin, Jo Mugnolo, Ted Newman, Charles A. Owen, Morton Paley, Derek Pearsall, Alice P. Radin, Florence Ridley, D. W. Robertson, Jr., Jeff Rosen, Bruce Rosenberg, Joan Rosenberg, Paul Ruggiers, Bob Ryan, Lily Schatz, J. Ian Schwartz, Geoffrey Sill, Daniel Silvia, Anthony C. Spearing, Martin Stevens, Paul Strohm, Ken Thigpen, Hannah Thomas, Bonnie Wade, R. L. and Sallie Wadsworth, Nina Wallerstein and Jie Wang.

For financial assistance I thank Dean Thomas Magner of Pennsylvania State University and the Research Council of Rutgers University. I quote Chaucer thanks to the Houghton Mifflin Company, and reproduce illustrations with gratitude to Robert N. Essick and to the following libraries: Bancroft (University of California), Houghton (Harvard), Huntington, Pattee (Pennsylvania State University), Van Pelt (University of Pennsylvania), and the Victoria and Albert Museum.

All mistakes and omissions in this book are my own. There may well be some, as I am treating four complicated centuries of print sources as well as the Chaucer tapes. While checking page proofs, in fact, I have just come upon a seventeenth-century reference to the Prioress that is not cited in Caroline Spurgeon's index—a reference that certainly ought to have been discussed in my Chapter 1, "The Prioress on Paper." After a while I stopped banging my head on the desk, and decided that I had better just let you know that in ca. 1608–44 Bryan Twyne regarded the *A* on the Prioress's brooch as evidence of her religious devotion. I can only beg indulgence for my book, a pioneering effort on (as Bob Dylan says) a whole lotta levels.

ABBREVIATIONS

For Chaucer's works, I have in some cases adapted the abbreviations provided in F. N. Robinson's second edition of *The Works of Geoffrey Chaucer* (Boston: Houghton Mifflin, 1957), 647. Full citations for other works listed can be found in the bibliography. Since the bibliography is divided into three sections, I provide the section number in which each work occurs.

BD	*Book of the Duchess*
C.I.A.	Central Intelligence Agency
CkT	*Cook's Tale*
ClT	*Clerk's Tale*
DNB	*Dictionary of National Biography*, edited by Leslie Stephen and Sidney Lee (2)
FrkT	*Franklin's Tale*
FrT	*Friar's Tale*
GP	*General Prologue* to the *Canterbury Tales*
HF	*House of Fame*
J&M	*January and May; or, The Merchant's Tale: From Chaucer,* by Alexander Pope (1)
KnT	*Knight's Tale*
MancT	*Manciple's Tale*
MctT	*Merchant's Tale*
MED	*Middle English Dictionary*, edited by Hans Kurath (2)
MkT	*Monk's Tale*
MLA	Modern Language Association of America
MlrT	*Miller's Tale*
MLT	*Man of Law's Tale*
NPT	*Nun's Priest's Tale*
OED	*Compact Edition of the Oxford English Dictionary* (2)
PardT	*Pardoner's Tale*
PLGW	*Prologue* to the *Legend of Good Women*

PMLA	*Publications of the Modern Language Association*
PriT	*Prioress's Tale*
PTB	*Prologue* to the *Tale of Beryn*, edited by Frederick J. Furnivall and W. B. Stone (1)
RvT	*Reeve's Tale*
ShipT	*Shipman's Tale*
S.P.C.A.	Society for the Prevention of Cruelty to Animals
SqT	*Squire's Tale*
SumT	*Summoner's Tale*
TB	*The Tale of Beryn*, edited by Frederick J. Furnivall and W. G. Stone (1)
Thop	*Tale of Sir Thopas*
Tr	*Troilus and Criseyde*
WBP	*Wife of Bath's Prologue*
WBT	*Wife of Bath's Tale*

CHAUCER ALOUD

Introduction

Reception aesthetics comes as no surprise to Chaucerians. By 1925 Caroline Spurgeon, having collected *Five Hundred Years of Chaucer Criticism and Allusion,* had already pointed out that each age applies its own ideals and standards to Chaucer's text: "at any given time . . . [readers] feel that the way we regard an author . . . is the truest and only possible way."[1] Neither Spurgeon's admonition nor her three dense volumes of evidence for subjective interpretation, however, did much to budge academia's new but not quite articulated assumption that the text itself matters most, its context less, the critic's culture-bound expectations not at all. Furthermore, partly because nearly all were in real life college professors, New Critics tended to proclaim rather than proffer their own interpretations. Conflicting ways of understanding a passage, which might have been termed evidence for the versatility and resultant longevity of Chaucer's text, were often termed wrong.

Nowadays, after a century of "English" as a university-level subject and half a century of New Criticism as its predominant methodology, newer questions and issues are being formulated. Is it not the case that every reader brings his or her own subjective experiences and expectations to a text? Is it not the case that interpretive agreement is based on shared education and culture, and that critical disagreements constitute evidence that a text can sustain more than one valid interpretation?

Literary theorists have lately been bombarding New Criticism with annoying but often hollow shells of self-referential jargon. Armed with actual evidence for varying interpretations of Chaucer's text, instead, I come not to bury New Criticism but to appraise its value as careful description of each critic's imagined performance of the text.

In this book I offer three types of evidence supporting the contention that equally well-prepared and sensitive readers may have divergent yet valid responses to three Canterbury pilgrims: Prioress, Pardoner,

Merchant. The most familiar and accessible type of evidence, which I merely skim, is that of varying interpretations within published twentieth-century criticism.

A second, neglected type of evidence, which I treat fully, using Spurgeon as springboard and reception aesthetics as impetus, is that of readers' responses to these three pilgrims through four centuries. (I stop short, pragmatically, of the prolific Victorians). I discuss the rare direct commentary on Chaucer's text, as well as authors' use of Chaucerian images and characters in their own creative works, hints of readers' imagined visualizations of characters and scenes, and artists' actual visualizations. Art historians provide a vocabulary to describe this last form of interpretation. We as close readers know how to analyze an author's reworking of his source and are able to spot passages that convey mental pictures.

To understand more precisely how early readers and current ones understand Chaucer, however, we must also borrow a shiny new tool from the folklorists' shed: performance analysis. Besides twentieth-century commentary and pre-nineteenth-century interpretations, thus, as a third type of evidence I offer data collected especially for this book: the Chaucer tapes. Between 1979 and 1983, each of thirty-two British and Canadian and American Chaucer scholars read aloud onto cassette tape the same set of *Canterbury Tales* passages. Their oral performances provide data unprecedented in literary studies, provide audible proof that Chaucer's text does indeed sustain widely divergent interpretations by equally qualified readers. Just as no paraphrase can replace a poem or musical score a symphony, so also no mere description, however detailed, can substitute for the experience of hearing this evidence itself on the cassette tape accompanying this book.

By providing these performances I hope to help shift critical issues toward critical cooperation. Hearing Professor A's furiously angry Host, Professor B will perhaps cease saying, "The Host is mildly annoyed at the Pardoner, but not furious," and will begin to ask, "How is it that Geoffrey Chaucer assembled words on paper that allow for such a remarkable variety of aesthetically appropriate performances and imagined performances?"

Performance analysis was conceived along with sound recording and finally born in the 1970s, attended by an assortment of folklorists, rhetoricians, musicologists, actors, and linguists. It is still in its infancy, its methodology in flux. In this book I test ways of analyzing taped performances, therefore, starting with scientific objectivity to make it entirely clear that science has no final solution. Indeed, I suggest that we have not far to go for a viable, well-developed vocabulary to describe aural effects:

New Criticism. Caught in the cross-glare between performance analysis and subjectivist literary theory, New Criticism stands exposed for what it often is: description of the performance each critic hears while silently reading the text.

Regarded as carefully described performance, New Criticism also proves a useful tool for analysis of early Chaucer modernizations. John Dryden was the first to publish modernized Canterbury tales, in 1700; he was soon followed by Alexander Pope and Pope's imitators. (See Appendix B: Canterbury Tales Modernizations, 1700–1775.) While taking into account each modernizer's artistic and commercial motivations for changing certain aspects of Chaucer's text, one can treat a modernization as that author's articulated performance of the Middle English text. Pope adds audiovisual effects—stage directions, almost literally—throughout his *Merchant's Tale* modernization, for instance. His projected performance of the pear-tree scene can thus be compared directly to oral performances of it these 275 years later.

The juxtaposition of aural with historical evidence discloses yet another seldom-investigated issue: punctuation and paragraphing as embodiment of each editor's imagined performance. I barely scratch the surface of the problem when I show that two major twentieth-century critical controversies can be traced respectively to a paragraph first indented in 1775, which demands a change in tone after the Christ's-pardon benediction, and quotation marks first inserted in 1847, which demand that the Merchant maintain a bitterly sarcastic tone of voice for 125 lines.[2]

Performance analysis, then, not only can illuminate its own subject matter, sound recordings, but also can light up unexpected corners of traditional literary scholarship and the newly opened realms of reception aesthetics. In addition, relating aural to historical data can show how literary theorists might well be asking the right questions but nonetheless be ignoring potential complexities when they pose theoretical answers. Examination of evidence makes two theoretical flaws in particular stand out: the fiction of virgin experience and the pretense of historical uniformity.

It is true that some reader-response critics collect samples of nonuniform responses to a text by unprepared readers, usually the critic's students, who are encountering a work for the first time and are unaware of its history of critical controversy.[3] Most theorizing about a reader's process of literary response, however, depends instead on the theorist's imagined reconstruction of how one might respond were one reading a work for the first time. It is only as an aside that Wolfgang Iser, for example, notes that one's "second reading of the text will never have the same effect as the first, for the simple reason that the originally assembled meaning is bound to influence the second reading."[4] He continues to analyze the process of reading a text for the first time, although he is in point of fact reading it for the umpteenth time, pretending to be ignorant of established critical issues.

Musicologist Paula Johnson terms this analytic Catch-22 the "fiction of virgin experience," in her critique of Leonard B. Meyer's theories of "listener response," which predate and parallel "reader response" but apparently remain uncredited.[5] The Chaucer tapes furnish audible evidence that established critical issues cannot be ignored.

Oral interpretations vary widely on tape, but not in the way I had anticipated when I began collecting data. I had chosen *Canterbury Tales* passages famed for ambiguity, about which critics have argued in terms that may be regarded as imagined performance. Is the Pardoner sincere when he invokes Christ's pardon? Is the Merchant bitter about his own marriage? Is the Host goaded to rage at the Pardoner, or mildly irritated, or joking by pretending to be angry? Is Chaucer in some guise amused by the Prioress's lapses, or delighted or disgusted or oblivious?

I had expected to analyze the range of possible performances of each critical crux. Instead, I found that at these points the smoothest of readers-aloud is likely to stumble, stutter, skip, or at best stop performing and start reciting a self-consciously correct exercise in Middle English pronunciation.

But all was far from lost. Even self-conscious performances vary in articulable ways. Besides, unexpectedly rich variety appears in performances of passages about which no one has argued directly. The *Nun's Priest's Tale,* for example, offers a startling range of voices in which Pertelote scolds or cajoles or urges Chaunticleer to overcome his cowardice, in which Chaunticleer convinces or seduces or commands Pertelote to stint of her medical advice, in which the fox talks Chaunticleer into staying and Chaunticleer talks the fox into speaking. Furthermore, it is possible to identify the points at which a particularly spontaneous variety of oral interpretations is likely. Just before or just after an established critical crux, readers are thinking about the problem rather than about what they are reading at that moment.

Thus, as will be shown throughout, the Chaucer tapes provide audible evidence that previously defined critical issues affect interpretation. And who among us, after all, comes undefiled to *Canterbury Tales?* Our horizons of expectation have long since been set by whichever translation or glossed edition we read in secondary school, and by whether our teacher chose the *Miller's Tale* or the *Pardoner's,* and by whether our sophomore-survey professor loved Chaucer and read him aloud or rushed past the unit while wishing the whole course were on novels, and by a host of other influences that shape our critical ideas and attitudes toward this much-studied text.

As an experiment in reader response, one might seek out students who have never read a Canterbury tale in translation, educate them so thoroughly in Middle English and medieval literary conventions that they understand Langland and Lydgate and Gower, and then analyze their responses as they read through the *Tales* or *Troilus* for the first time. Unfortunately, the experimental subjects would long since have left to major in accounting.

In this analysis, it is an advantage that readers have fully developed and potentially articulable understandings of Chaucer; their responses are not those of an imaginary virgin reader experiencing just a glimpse of the Wife's red stockings and the distant crash of the Miller's head against a door. Taped oral performances can project at least some of the complexities in each nonvirgin reader's relationship with this accommodating text.

In earlier centuries, readers' responses to Chaucer's text were influenced by experiences at least as complex and individualized as those of the thirty-two readers-aloud in 1979–83. No standard critical or educational approach existed, and early readers' occupations and their motivations for treating Chaucer varied greatly. Logically, these artists and courtiers and monks and writers and clergymen would display an even wider range of interpretations than do thirty-two late-twentieth-century English professors. Yet theorists do not acknowledge a major discrepancy in their theoretical assumptions about readers now and readers in previous centuries. This is the second theoretical flaw I wish to address.

While maintaining that every reader in the 1980s responds differently to a text, theorists fail to project a comparable range of responses from readers in the 1680s or 1780s. Iser, for example, treats as a unit the responses of all readers living under a particular set of sociohistorical conditions. *Pilgrim's Progress,* he says, reacts against "the religious despair of the Calvinists. . . . Thus the literary text offers a solution which had been explicitly excluded by the doctrine of predestination."[6] But all readers surely did not feel equal despair, or grasp with equal relief the same solution.

During a given sociohistorical period, responses to a text may initially appear uniform because so little evidence survives. Until this century, only a few readers had access to print, vellum, canvas, or engraving plates, and none of them set out to provide evidence useful for our analysis of responses to a text itself. Instead, each was imaginatively recreating Chaucer's characters (in this case) for his or her own purposes.

Occasionally historical evidence does enable us to compare directly several interpretations. Thomas Stothard, born in 1755 in London, painted in 1807 a portrayal of all the pilgrims along the road to Canterbury. William Blake, born in 1757 in London, painted a quite dissimilar representation of the same subject in 1809. An investigation of these men and their two paintings reveals a melodrama of broken friendship, bribed art critics, and treacherous agents.[7] The strikingly different views of the pilgrims from artists with parallel lives furnish proof that reader response to a text must not be assumed uniform at any given time and place in the past.

To a medievalist considering reception of Chaucer's text in other centuries, the sheer amount of available material at first looks daunting, and the sources themselves tangled and impenetrable. More information seems to survive from one week of the eighteenth century than from entire decades of the fourteenth.[8] But gradually shapes emerge, shapes not of amorphous sociohistorical processes but of individual men and women reading particular texts of Chaucer—in bulky black-letter folios, at first—and making particular artistic decisions, which transform their initial understandings into the evidence now extant.

In this book we will see an adolescent Alexander Pope teaching himself Middle English by modernizing Chaucer from his 103-year-old Speght edition. He interprets each pilgrim quite differently than does the artist who is then engraving their portraits for the elegant, but textually absurd, 1721 Urry edition—engraving them at the very art academy where Pope would soon take painting lessons. As we will see, near Chaucer's time a Canterbury monk features the pilgrims in a pun-filled slapstick comedy; three centuries later a Frenchman converts Chaucer to Lollardry at the same time that a cool-headed Elizabeth Cooper questions authority while reading for herself what Chaucer actually wrote. And of course we will see William Blake building New Jerusalem on Albion's eternal shore, populating it with pilgrims significantly different from those of his contemporaries or of anybody else before or since.

What right did Blake have to do that? That is, are there limits on valid interpretation? Blake's Wife of Bath is Whore of Babylon, radiating active energy, eager to seduce the Parson, as Blake's Urizen or rationality, who would suppress the very artistic genius that created him. Many readers now, and nearly all prior to the nineteenth century, can share Blake's attitude toward Alysoun's enthusiastic evil. Yet who among us dares dislike the Parson? Now that Terry Jones has pinpricked the Knight,[9] the Parson remains the one tale-telling pilgrim for whose *General Prologue* portrait no critic has yet claimed irony in the voice of Chaucer-the-pilgrim.

Irony, or sarcasm, is an aspect of silent reading that, when expressed orally, may be captured on tape and analyzed. Saint Augustine defined it thus: "In irony we indicate by tone of voice the meaning we wish to convey, as when we say to a man who is behaving badly: 'you are doing well.'"[10]

There is no neat solution to this problem of aesthetic limitations on oral and thereby imagined performance. Any text can be read aloud with any degree of irony. It is certainly possible to read "A bettre preest I trowe that nowher noon ys" (*GP* l. 524) and "A bettre felawe sholde men noght fynde" (*GP* l. 648) with identical inflections.[11] Why has no one claimed for the Parson the sarcastic tones many hear the narrator use for the Summoner?

Among scholars currently contributing ideas and techniques to performance analysis, only those in oral interpretation have tugged at the knotty problem of aesthetic limitations on performance. This academic field, with ancestry traceable to the old schools of elocution and thence to orally-delivered rhetoric itself, investigates how vocal inflections give meaning to a text. Theorists in oral interpretation assume that "a poem-script always has alternative potentialities of sounding."[12] They go on to discuss whether such alternatives must be resolved or may be preserved, and to what extent any newly developing aesthetics of oral performance and aural understanding can cast light on the more usual experience these past few centuries of "mental soundings," a.k.a. silent reading.[13]

They ultimately avoid saying what would make a reading-aloud wrong, however. The potential range of "Right Readings and Good Readings" remains widely defined in oral interpretation theory. Monroe C. Beardsley says that "criteria of judgment may also be reformulated as aims of the performer," who should keep in mind unity, complexity, and regional intensity of the presentation, so that "we can have different, although equally admirable, performances [of the same text]—one in which some potential complexities are sacrificed to keep the unity tight [and so on]." He raises but leaves unanswered a final issue: whether the performer as artist is obligated "to choose soundings that will maximize truth and wisdom as well as maximize aesthetic value."[14]

Oral interpreters presumably would shudder at a suggestion that machines be used to analyze truth and wisdom. Yet linguists, buoyed by tape recorders and computers, are also investigating how the human voice can give identical phonemic clusters different perceived meanings. Using the speech synthesizer, a machine that instantly prints out pitch contours and phrasing of a taped voice, a linguist can readily run the sort of experiment that Grant Fairbanks did in the 1930s. Going from wax record to film to paper, he laboriously analyzed readings-aloud of the same passage by trained actors, each expressing in turn grief, contempt, anger, fear, and indifference. Machine-aided analysis has since produced distinctions no more precise than Fairbanks's general ones—anger is higher-pitched than grief, for instance.[15]

In 1980 Paul Zawadski of the Speech Department at Pennsylvania State University put through a speech synthesizer several performances of line 150 of the Prioress's description in the *General Prologue,* as will be discussed, and the Host's reply to the Pardoner, "They shul be shryned in an hogges toord" (*PardT* l. 955), read eight times in tones that I had described on first hearing as respectively "contempt," "vicious," "joking," "teasing by pretending to be mad," "mocking," "angry," "calm insult," and "thoughtful distaste." Each voiceprint does indeed look different. But not even such general distinctions as Fairbanks's account for for the differences, which instead show simply that each Chaucerian's voice has its own distinctive characteristics, including pitch.

The speech synthesizer, linguists' most advanced technology, may compare two readings by the same person, but it simply does not display similarities in two readings when the same emotion is conveyed by different readers. One Chaucerian had done two of the readings of *PardT* l. 955, as it happens, proposing them as alternatives. His two voiceprints of what I hear respectively as "calm insult" and "joking" resemble each other far more than his "calm insult" does another reader's "contempt," or his "joking" does another's "teasing."

Wishing to give science and technology a fair chance, I attempted to describe or verify meanings conveyed in oral performance by means of another linguistic experiment. To determine objectively what emotion is being conveyed by a sound pattern, linguists conduct polls. The sounds are played to no more than thirty listeners at a time, so that no one is too far from the speaker; the participants' understandings are then tabulated.

Accordingly, I played half a dozen performances each of *GP* l. 150 and *PardT* l. 955 to four freshman-composition classes at Penn State—thus to over a hundred listeners unfamiliar with Middle English—and then to a group of scholars at the 1980 New Chaucer Society conference. Each listener indicated his or her impressions on the chart given in table 1.

Tabulated, the results tend to confirm my own descriptions of the voices' inflections. But one clear statistic made me decide against search-

TABLE 1. Listening Poll.

GP l. 150: This character is describing a woman who cannot overhear him. Is he praising her sincerely or not?

| sarcastic, insincere | character is not sure | sincere | other (please specify) |

PardT l. 955: This character is speaking directly to another, using words that look insulting. What is he expressing with his tone of voice?

| contempt, scorn, disgust, viciousness (he's calm) | anger, fury (he's upset) | teasing, joking | other (please specify) |

---

ing for more than a rough correlation. This experiment, like the one using voiceprints, included two performances by the same reader of the Host's reply to the Pardoner—one performance angry, the other joking. This reader had specified that he considered the second reading aesthetically inappropriate: "Now some people think the Host is just joking there. I don't think so. I think he's really angry and insulted. But if you *did* think he was joking, you could read it like this." His second reading was the only performance on which the hundred-odd listeners all agreed. Every one marked "teasing, joking" for what the scholar considered a wrong interpretation.

At this point we must stop and ask, What have polls to do with Chaucer? Technology is leading us astray in our quest for the textual grail that will reveal how one man, six hundred years ago, was able to assemble words that have meant so much to so many very different people. Scientific, objective techniques provide scientific, objective results. Aesthetic preferences and limitations, being neither scientific nor objective, reveal human minds understanding human expression. Science and technology, like Wade's boat, can carry us only so far. As literary critics we must stay in sight of shore, of aesthetic appropriateness to the given text and maybe even truth and wisdom.

As literary critics we have more immediate responsibilities, besides. It is we who must decide where to set practical limitations on textual interpretations, day by day. "Oh. OK, can you say why you think of the Prioress as a high-society lady who gets talkative when she drinks? Ah.

Well, 'charitable' is indeed related to that sort of charity, but I'll want to tell you more about the term at Chaucer's time. Oh, and . . . I see. 'Amyable of port.' Now, are you sure you looked up 'port'?"

Of all the issues raised by subjectivist literary theory, I regard as most valuable the demand that we all stop pretending to be analyzing literature in a vacuum. At worst we are writing criticism to keep our jobs as college professors. At best we are writing criticism in order to do better what really is most important: teaching. Making sure Chaucer does not die when we do.

Teaching modern languages, including Chaucer, at the college level is an innovation this past century. I will discuss further the extent to which our teaching techniques, as well as very many critical issues including the Pardoner's sincerity and the Merchant's bitterness, can be traced directly to the same source: George Lyman Kittredge's lectures at Harvard. He lectured; most of us now convey information to students in a less formal style, like mine in this book. But our intent is the same.

Kittredge's own copy of W. W. Skeat's 1894 Chaucer edition, now at Houghton Library, makes clear what interests he passed on to his students. Its margins overflow with references to analogous stories and proverbs from nineteenth-century folklore collections.

In 1846, fourteen years before Kittredge was born, William Thoms coined the term "folklore" to replace "popular antiquities." Also in 1846, Thomas Wright, justifiably the first medievalist in our present scholarly tradition, issued his *Essays on Subjects Connected with the Literature, Popular Superstitions and History of England in the Middle Ages,* which harmoniously melded all three fields.[16] Half a century later, medievalists were busily producing follow-up volumes to *Originals and Analogues of Some of Chaucer's Canterbury Tales.*[17] In their respective classrooms, too, they were almost certainly emulating Kittredge in his. During the first third of this century, in teaching the medieval portion of the modern languages curriculum one would naturally draw on folklore scholarship.

As soon thereafter as 1941, however, in the now-standard *Sources and Analogues of Chaucer's Canterbury Tales,* even the contributors best known as folklorists (Stith Thompson, Archer Taylor) let drop hardly a hint that plots analogous to Chaucer's still enjoy lively oral circulation. Francis Lee Utley, true to his mentor Kittredge, expressed his disappointment over this deficiency and issued a "hortatory" call for assembly of modern folktale analogues—a call still largely unheeded two decades later, according to his 1963 Modern Language Association address.[18]

Medievalists' abrupt abandonment of folklore material and techniques was due in part to the black-marks-on-paper focus of New Criticism and in part to what could be termed the deHarvardization or de-Kittredgization of Chaucer scholarship. But in largest part they scorned folklorists' offering of what was, in point of fact, an invalid thesis. We know now that it is simply not possible to prove that a modern folktale is analogous to a medieval folktale which was never written down. (From this knowledgeable "we" I exclude some literary scholars, untrained in folklore, who still make this mistake, often while mumbling something about "archetypes.")

I term this impossibility the Folklore Dilemma. It shares its unresolvable problem with the Marxist Dilemma and the Women's Studies Dilemma: for any era, what official authorities deem worthy of preservation is primarily what remains. Even with indirect evidence from documents that take for granted that people speak, an unbeliever can never be finally convinced by irrefutable evidence that anybody said anything out loud before Thomas Edison did in 1877 in Menlo Park, New Jersey.

Folklorists always suspected that words on paper could convey very little of the significance of their subject matter. More than any other discipline, folklore scholarship was waiting like a coiled spring for the appropriate recording technology to be invented. Within the past two decades, as sound and video equipment have rapidly become more accessible, more affordable, more portable, folklorists just as rapidly have turned from organization of transcribed texts toward analysis of the performance and function of each variant in its particular social context among "folk," which refers to any group that shares aspects of unofficial culture—for example, college professors exchanging Kittredge anecdotes.[19] Folklore theory and methods, like Pandarus, "hoppe alwey byhynde" the latest developments in technology itself (*Tr* 2.1107). Folklorists are still struggling to represent on paper the vocal complexities of an oral performance, knowing full well that they can capture and should analyze the visual dimension, and knowing too that even the most accurate sound film reproduces only a portion of an outside observer's live-audience experience, and even less of an insider's feelings and responses. Furthermore, the presence of an observer, or even just a microphone, affects the performance situation—a parallel to the Heisenberg Uncertainty Principle, as similarly noted by David Bleich with regard to a silent reader's subjective interpretation.[20]

Modern Chaucerians' taped readings-aloud fall far short of any live fourteenth-century performance context. But for present purposes the variables are manageable: each scholar reads exactly the same text (reproduced in the accompanying pamphlet, *Texts Read Aloud*) from F. N.

Robinson's second edition of *The Works of Geoffrey Chaucer,* and the comparison is of vocal inflections alone—not of those plus body movements, facial expressions, eye contact, audience response both overt and implied, and all the other creators of meaning in a live performance.

Beryl Rowland shows the extent to which Chaucer could have known that Cicero and medieval rhetoricians advise using all these techniques of oral delivery (*pronuntiatio*) to affect an audience.[21] But voice alone will do for now. Past and present folklore investigations combine to teach that we cannot gather nonexistent evidence from times past and that we cannot gather all the evidence from a performance at which we are present, but that we can elicit evidence in an experiment manageable in size, concerning the effects of actual performance on a given text.

Readers of this book can consider the oral evidence itself, which is provided on the accompanying tape. As author, however, I am left with the far from simple tasks of describing the taped voices, demonstrating the ways in which the sounds create variant meanings, and saying how these performance variations relate to interpretive disagreements during this century and previous ones. In defense of my methods I can only point out humbly that the surveyed linguists, folklorists, and oral interpreters offer the merest hint of precedent for what I am doing. Performance analysis is busy being born. No agreed-upon methodology or vocabulary links describable vocal inflections to projected meaning.

Several questions loom large in performance analysis, ones I do not pretend to answer here. A tape emits a pattern of sounds, put there by one human mind and voice and understood by a different human ear and mind. What about the potential gap between intention and execution, or the one between product and description? In the first case, the performer may intend one meaning but convey another; in the second, two listeners, each with different expectations, may construe what they hear differently.

In this book I occasionally return to the first problem, that of a performer's intention. Acute readers will already have noticed a discrepancy in my description of the alternative readings performed by the same person in the two linguistic experiments. I originally described his first reading as "calm insult"; on the listening poll I would have checked the first column, "contempt, scorn, disgust, viciousness (he's calm)." The reader himself—a trained actor, as it happens—would have checked the second column, "anger, fury (he's upset)," for he reveals his intention by stating, "I think he's really angry and insulted."

Listening again, knowing the performer's intention this time, I might well reconsider: "Yeah, he does sound pretty upset." Or the performer, hearing the tape played back, might decide, "I'll do that one over—I sound calmer than I wanted to." Performed meaning is no simpler than human emotion itself, and no likelier to be solved by this book, the first on performed literature to use solicited data. Having permission from these thirty-two Chaucerians to analyze the readings as received, without further consultation, I have no more desire than they do to enter the trackless quagmire of possible discrepancy between meanings intended and meanings perceived.

That dead-end scientific poll of listeners' perceptions represents one approach to the second problem, to wit, that someone else's understanding of a vocally projected meaning may differ from Betsy Bowden's. I will return to this issue in discussing the Knight's intervention in the quarrel between the Host and the Pardoner, and of course I provide the aural evidence on tape in order to confront, not evade, the problem.

I know that this issue, variant listener response, cannot be readily resolved because I deal with it directly in my book *Performed Literature: Words and Music by Bob Dylan.* There the artistic object under analysis is the recorded performance itself, rather than a text. Bob Dylan does not provide texts of his own songs; the music publisher hires someone to listen to his recordings and to write down words and music. The performance, not the text, is primary. It is possible for two equally prepared, experienced listeners to disagree not only on the overall impact of a recorded performance (is it sincere or cynical?) but even on actual words. No matter how often rock critic Greil Marcus and I were to listen to the cut "Isis" on the album *Desire,* for example, Marcus would continue to hear "blinded by sleep and in need of a bath" where I hear "lightly asleep and in need of a bed." Each line fits interlocking patterns of imagery in the song, but each contributes to a slightly different characterization of the narrator and Isis.

Contemplating these and other practical problems of performance analysis, one may be tempted to retreat gracefully back to the printed page. If so much literary criticism contains careful descriptions of mental soundings, what are the advantages of analyzing actual taped performances? After all, critics have developed a fairly extensive and precise vocabulary, agreeing on shared meanings of words including not only "merchant" and "married" and "shrew," but also "bitter" and "resigned" and "joking" and "viciously sarcastic" and "mildly sarcastic."

Furthermore, a critic may be able to imagine and describe a performance more accurately than he is able to produce it out loud. All classroom teaching calls for some degree of acting ability, true, but years of practice do not necessarily carry over when a lone professor faces a familiar text and an unfamiliar microphone. In this book I analyze at length only performances that sound good to me, that is, ones that are appropriate to the text. I hereby deflect inquiry about bad performances to the numerous commercially available ones described in my forthcoming *Teachers' Guide to Chaucer Read Aloud: An Annotated Discography*. Still, might it not be better to analyze performances only by professors with training or natural ability in acting, and to extend to others the option of explaining on paper what meanings they would intend to project?

Obviously, I think not. The agreed-on vocabulary for literary analysis is less precise than it may seem. Philosophically, they say, we can never be certain that the green you see is the same green I see. But surely we can approach the problem more efficiently when we both actually look at a patch of something combining blue and yellow tones. Similarly, does "bitter" sound (or taste?) the same to you as to me?

The effort to describe actual performances forces us to define terms and refine that older, still-useful vocabulary of literary criticism. It prevents us from snuggling back lazily into fuzzy abstractions. Just what do you mean by "agonized sincerity," Professor Kittredge, and just why can't *PardT* ll. 916–18 be performed as an automatic closing formula? Are you quite sure, sir, that your own agonized questioning of the Christian faith is not affecting your response to the passage? You, sir, were raised on Darwin and *Dover Beach*. We were raised on Hitler and Watergate. And as Alexander Pope was raised Roman Catholic, therefore forbidden a formal education, he took revenge by almost single-handedly converting the Father of English Literature from a gloomy proto-Protestant to a jolly teller of lightly satiric, witty tales. Pope was a brilliant man, Professor Kittredge, as you are. Do you feel it quite fair to insist that Chaucer's text be performed only one way for six hundred years?

But soft. In the background of all these new issues, audible over the dull buzz of subjectivist literary theory and the garbled exclamations of performance analysis, a small stern voice still insists: What would Chaucer himself have thought of all this? Are we not seeking, ultimately, Chaucer-the-man's intended performance of Chaucer-the-author's text, which creates the voice of Chaucer-the-pilgrim?

Just as both ends of the political spectrum meet at the goal of income-tax evasion, so too subjective and objective critical theorists bump backs while evading the question of author's intention. Reader-response critics tend to justify methodologically their neglect of what New Critics had sternly labeled for dismissal as "The Intentional Fallacy," although in the last hurrah of the objective-analysis movement F. R. Leavis mutters testily that "some presence of the force of 'intend' is necessary to the meaning of 'means.'"[22] Some theorists term the entire issue bunk, while Marxist critics point out that most authors nowadays intend to make money by selling books.[23]

Everybody talks about author's intention. No one does anything about it except for those medievalists, stretching in the great chain from C. S. Lewis to D. W. Robertson, Jr., and beyond, who maintain that every medieval author must intend church dogma, often ingeniously disguised. They interpret an author's text to convey meanings that he ought to have intended, according to documents preserved by the dominant culture.

Consideration of author's intention brings us right back to the Folklore Dilemma. Fourteenth-century ecclesiastical and political authorities used expensive writing materials only for what mattered to them. They did not bother to record all that might help us understand more fully Chaucer's avowedly secular, apolitical fiction.

Nor did anybody write the biography or preserve the letters and diaries of Chaucer-the-man. Without his fictional works we would know of him only what is collected in the *Life-Records*:[24] that Chaucer saw the Black Death as a youth and Jack Straw's rebellion as an adult; that he married the sister of the wife of John of Gaunt, who kept giving generous gifts to the Chaucers' child born soon thereafter; that Chaucer served Richard II as clerk of the works; that he nonetheless stayed on good terms with the new king, Henry IV. To seek authorial intent in Chaucer's sketchy personal history, outside his literary works peopled with unreliable narrators, is to re-invoke the kind of psychological speculation—Shakespeare must have been depressed while writing tragedies, and the like—that bothered and indeed set into motion New Critics.

Concerning author's undeterminable intention, in analysis of the Chaucer tapes, we would ask specifically, "Did Chaucer intend that his works normally be read out loud?" and then "Did he intend that the same passage read aloud produce strikingly different effects?" The first question draws on historical research under way since Ruth Crosby. Although medievalists are now reinterpreting written records with their eyes open to hints of oral culture, they are not likely to discover dramatic new historical evidence proving that secular works were always read aloud or never read aloud in the fourteenth century.[25]

As to Chaucer's own attitude toward potential variation of meaning in oral performances of his set texts, a few passages could be understood to reveal his own interests, as distinguishable from those of his fictional narrators who purposely divert just such inquiries. The *House of Fame* hints at Chaucer's interest in language spoken aloud: words up above take on "hys lyknesse / That spak the word," for example.[26] Or again, when the Host chimes in with the Knight's objection to the *Monk's Tale*, perhaps he is implying that style of delivery as well as content puts him to sleep (*NPT* ll. 2780–2805). It could also be noted that Bob Dylan does intend that the same set of his words take on different meanings in performance.

But internal evidence and modern analogies would convince no one that Chaucer consciously intended to put together words that would allow for variant oral performances. Chaucer does of course make strong statements urging prevention of variant texts. No advocate of the folkloristic process of change—individual creation and communal re-creation[27]—Chaucer, like his editors five centuries afterward, wants one correct text:

> And for ther is so gret diversite
> In Englissh and in writyng of oure tonge,
> So prey I God that non myswrite the,
> Ne the mysmetre for defaute of tonge.
> And red wherso thow be, or elles songe,
> That thow be understonde, God I biseche!
>
> (*Tr* 5.1793–98)

Having borrowed from the liturgy, probably, the formulaic contrast of singing to reading aloud,[28] Chaucer would be as surprised as anyone else to learn that the sixteenth-century Bodleian manuscript Ashmole 48 and the seventeenth-century Percy folio manuscript both contain ballads indeed based on his "lytel bok," the earlier one sung "To the tune of Fayne woold I fynd sum pretty thynge to geeve unto my lady":

> Tyll at the last he cam to churche
>   Where Cressyd sat and prayed a,
> Whose lookes gave Troylus such a lurche,
>   Hys hart was all dysmayde a.
> ....
>
> But, humbly kneelynge on hys knee,
>   With syghes dyd love unfolde a;
> Her nyght gowne then delyvered she
>   To keepe hym from the colde a.[29]

The Father of English Literature himself had not the power to halt the folklore process. Still less could he control future visualizations, oral interpretations, and mental soundings of his set text. If Chaucer intended to create a text interpretable in only one way for the next six centuries, he has demonstrably failed. I prefer to analyze the evidence to prove instead that Geoffrey Chaucer is a successful author.

CHAPTER 1

The Prioress on Paper

During the past sixty years, a mere one-tenth of the span since Chaucer wrote, critics armed with accurate texts and an established canon have launched a barrage of varying interpretations of the Prioress. By the 1920s her complexities had been marshaled. G. L. Kittredge told of her "thwarted motherhood"; J. L. Lowes listed the romance conventions by which her portrait conveys "the engagingly imperfect submergence of the feminine in the ecclesiastical"; Eileen Power confided the convent rules she was breaking; and Sister Mary Madeleva tried staunchly to defend her piety by mustering elderly nuns she knows who keep pets.[1]

Although by 1841 Isaac D'Israeli had already noticed Chaucer's "fine irony . . .[, which] sometimes left his commendations . . . in a very ambiguous condition," it was not until over a century later that Arthur Hoffman specified for ll. 118–62 of the *General Prologue* just how ambiguity and irony affect the "seesawing . . . critical interpretation of the [Prioress's] portrait in which the satiric elements are sometimes represented as heavy, sometimes as slight, sometimes sinking the board, and sometimes riding light and high." Jill Mann's study of neglected analogues now shows just how unresolvable is the textual ambiguity in the portrait, to contemporaries even more than to us.[2] (See *Texts Read Aloud*, Chapter 2.)

It is evident from the briefest glance at criticism that scholars believe that the narrator's tone of voice may convey irony or some other attitude toward the Prioress. Consider *GP* l. 150, "And al was conscience and tendre herte"—in 1826 "a favourite quotation" in Leigh Hunt's circle. In this one line Charles Muscatine hears delight where D. W. Robertson, Jr. hears "unmistakable sarcasm," R. M. Lumiansky hears "gentle raillery," and E. Talbot Donaldson hears "one last defiant assertion" followed by "obvious relief."

Some critics even try to label a particular tone of voice impossible. To prove that any irony in the portrait does not extend to the Prioress's sincerely religious *Prologue* and *Tale,* for instance, G. H. Russell claims that "the text does not seem to allow of such a reading." He hears the Host invite her *Tale* "with some anxiety and a great deal of deference . . . . It is pointless to read the text in any other way."[3] Pointless or no, it is certainly possible to perform the text with any degree of sarcasm or, for that matter, with grief, contempt, anger, fear, indifference, or any of a vast array of vocal inflections other than those conveying "anxiety" and "deference." Russell, like other critics who make less overt assertions, cannot prove his own imagined performance right by simply stamping all others wrong.

Constituting actual evidence, the Chaucer tapes provide a wide range of different meanings conveyed in performance by equally prepared British and American readers. All but one of the readers-aloud teach, or have retired from teaching, Chaucer at the university level. (That one exception, whose acting ability more than compensates for her unusually frequent slips into Modern English vowels, will be heard in the last reading in the book and elsewhere.) No single reading of the Prioress's portrait is the right one; all are possible.

Some people, after listening to the tape accompanying this book, may take exception to that statement. "All readings are possible," they may say, "but some are more possible than others." Interpretation aside, some scholars may object to certain readings-aloud because of features not analyzed in this book, particularly pronunciation and prosody. So far Chaucerians have been trying to discuss these two issues on the printed page. Now that technology allows for exchange of oral evidence, books as long as this one can be written on pronunciation and prosody alone.[4]

Other books can be written on aesthetic issues, as defined by the field of oral interpretation or other criteria; their authors can argue that only talented or trained actors, using professional-quality recording equipment, should perform for tapes accompanying those books. Such has not been my procedure, however. The accompanying tape contains the equivalent of anthropological field recordings, made on home or institutional equipment. The professional equipment used to make copies could not remove background noise or otherwise improve the originals' sound quality. Some of the many short excerpts from the Prioress's portrait, in particular, are chosen for audible details such as vocally-created punctuation rather than for sound quality or aesthetic effectiveness.

Sometime in the future, perhaps not long after this book is published, recording engineers may well develop a way to produce second- and third-generation tapes that sound as good as the original. Now, for example, a background buzz becomes amplified in each tape generation, increasingly engulfing the voice. I do not wish to delay publication, however, until someone else invents something.

In order to investigate what textual features allow such a variety of readings-aloud, I will analyze *GP* ll. 118–62 in more detail than will afterward prove useful in the chapters on the Pardoner and the Merchant. I will argue that one such feature—ambiguity—is not just a New-Critical catchword. Certainly, we should continue to refine and define our perceptions of ambiguity, especially in its relationship to irony. But in part— a part too large to discount—ambiguity on the page allows flexibility in performance and imagined performance, by readers both present and past. Because of its potential flexibility in performance, Chaucer's text has outlived its sociohistorical context; it has always been regarded as great literature, always for different reasons.

In this first chapter I will treat diachronic evidence for varying interpretations through those centuries; in the following chapter I offer synchronic evidence from the Chaucer tapes. Before the nineteenth century, according to Caroline Spurgeon's accounts, only two people commented on the Prioress: John Dryden, who used one adjective, "mincing," and John Ferne, who indirectly referred to her bad French.[5] Thus, this chapter will introduce basic interpretive sources other than pre-Victorian commentary: the modernized *General Prologue* and the illustrated Urry edition from the early eighteenth century, John H. Mortimer's drawings and William Lipscomb's modernization from the late eighteenth century, and Blake's and Stothard's rival paintings from the early nineteenth century.

This dearth of diachronic evidence for the Prioress's reputation stands in contrast to the wealth of it generated by the other principal female pilgrim. The sacred female may outrank the secular in estates literature, but Alysoun's popularity far surpasses Eglentyne's. For five centuries the Wife of Bath prances through commentary on Chaucer; she has all to herself a full seventeenth-century commentary by Richard Brathwait, Dryden's modernization of her *Tale* and Pope's of her *Prologue,* a play by John Gay, and a ballad collected by Samuel Pepys and published, then deleted, by Thomas Percy. In the ballad, which was fruitlessly condemned for over two centuries, she talks her way into heaven by bluntly pointing out the faults of Biblical figures already in residence there.[6]

The Prioress does appear occasionally, walking in the Wife's shadow. In about 1450, a Canterbury monk wrote into the *Prologue* to the *Tale of Beryn* his interpretation of Chaucer's characters including, as protagonist, a silly heterosexual Pardoner. This near-contemporary author has Wife and Prioress stroll arm in arm admiring the herb garden and then join the innkeeper's wife for wine until the male pilgrims return variously from exploring the town of Canterbury, examining its battlements, drinking with an old school chum of the Monk's, and so on.

In 1700, at more of a distance from Chaucer's language and intentions, Dryden still pairs "the mincing Lady Prioress, and the broad-speaking gap-tooth'd Wife of *Bathe*." In 1721, artist George Vertue places the two women together, at the center of the procession of pilgrims leaving Canterbury. (See figure 1.) In 1804, Sir Walter Scott praises Chaucer's characterization in "the affected *sentimentality* of the Abbess, the humour of mine Host, and [of] the Wife of Bath." That same decade, William Blake centers a cruciform Host in the cavalcade of Canterbury pilgrims, one arm spread toward the Wife of Bath as Whore of Babylon, at midpoint of the rear half of the procession, and the other toward the Prioress riding primly at midpoint of the front half. Stated oversimply, the Host's arms spread toward the female keystones of unrepressed, active "evil" (Blake's heaven) and repressed, passive "good" (Blake's hell).[7] (See figure 2.)

Blake's interpretations are, in a word, idiosyncratic. Yet we will see that his creation of a sinister Pardoner, one no longer comic as in centuries before, has lasted in ways that would have appalled him. Nor does Blake's problematic Prioress much resemble Prioresses before or after him. Even a Prioress at his time, as depicted by Leigh Hunt in the earliest direct discussion of her *General Prologue* portrait, differs decisively.

Leigh Hunt in 1826 is first to articulate that he hears *GP* ll. 118–62 as "a good-natured banter of the poet's upon the mode of singing the service in nunneries, their boarding-school French, and . . . the importance they attached to nicety of behaviour at dinner." A century of hard textual scholarship was to pass before Lowes said of her brooch, "I think she thought she meant love celestial." Hunt makes this point nearly as succinctly: "the lines about the crowned A and the motto . . . are to let us understand, that there was more love in her heart than she was aware of."[8]

Indeed, chatty essays by Hunt and others have had more influence than has been recognized on our century's scholarly interpretation of Chaucer—influence by way of George Lyman Kittredge addressing the first generations of college students to study Chaucer. Although a secondary-school edition, Charles Cowden Clarke's *Riches of Chaucer,* had appeared by 1835, before the 1870s university students studied ancient literature and philology, not literature written in the language they already spoke. Harvard, in the forefront, first founded a chair of English in 1876. The great ballad scholar Francis James Child, for twenty-five

FIGURE 1: Departure scene, from p. 1 of John Urry's edition of *The Works of Geoffrey Chaucer* (London: B. Lintot, 1721). Reproduced by courtesy of the Bancroft Library, University of California at Berkeley. Actual size, 6¼" × 3".

FIGURE 2: *Chaucers Canterbury Pilgrims*, engraved by William Blake in 1810. Reproduced by permission of the Huntington Library, San Marino, California. Actual size, 37½″ × 12″.

years a professor of rhetoric and oratory, thereupon became the professor of English until his death in 1896.[9]

At that time Oxford University Press, spotting a new market while publishing W. W. Skeat's seven-volume *Complete Works of Geoffrey Chaucer*, brought out a one-volume *Student's Chaucer*. A copy of this latter—recently found in a Harvard Square bookstore marked "o.p. ed., beat up & written in"—was owned by one Ernest Bernbaum on 11 February 1902. Bernbaum has left indications of the attitudes of his professor—probably Child's student Kittredge—such as "take as much of that as you like," which he wrote by the Retraction to *Canterbury Tales*. What Kittredge said between 1888 and 1936, to classrooms of Harvard students, can be further inferred from extensive marginal notes in his own Skeat edition, as well as from *Chaucer and His Poetry: Lectures Delivered in 1914 on the Percy Turnbull Memorial Foundation in the Johns Hopkins University*, published by Harvard University Press.

Kittredge's readings often respond directly to the only previous commentary on Chaucer, that of Hunt and other essayists in nineteenth-century periodicals and then, as publishing uncopyrighted material became increasingly profitable, in Chaucer editions that reuse Thomas Tyrwhitt's text. Introducing *Selections from . . . Chaucer* in 1847, for example, Charles Deshler claims that, for Chaucer, woman

> is ever as mild, patient and submissive, as she is beauteous; and is always accompanied and adorned by the fireside virtues. . . . How perfect and yet how gentle, is Chaucer's ridicule of that artificiality of her nature, which caused the "tender-hearted Prioresse" to dignify trivialities and formalities into a high importance, at the expense of real perfections and accomplishments; and which led her to lavish upon insignificant objects, affections that are based upon deep and abiding principles of humanity.

In his next paragraph, Deshler declares Chaucer's

> passionate fondness for birds, and flowers, and . . . . scenes of rural enjoyment and innocence . . . . His writings may be called a continuous poem in praise of Woman, Flowers, Rural pleasures and the Spring.[10]

Kittredge disagrees vehemently with Deshler, albeit without naming him. Indeed, he says, "her gentleness and sweet dignity are her best protection." But the Prioress is "fond of society . . . . pleasant and amiable . . . . As to her table manners, which often make the uninstructed laugh, they are simply the perfection of mediaeval daintiness. Nothing is farther from Chaucer's thought than to poke fun at them." In his next paragraph, Kittredge declares, "You do not care to hear from me that Geoffrey Chaucer took pleasure in birds and flowers and running brooks," for these are "matters of every day" and Chaucer's genius is that of characterization.[11]

Kittredge's insistence on the Prioress's perfection has remained rare, almost unique. Besides her table manners, her bad French has made commentators chuckle through the centuries from 1586 to an 1841 essay on "The French of Stratford atte Bowe."[12]

Her Stratford French is also the image most expanded in the earliest modernization of the *General Prologue,* in 1712, published first in Lintot's miscellany along with a modernized *Reeve's Tale* and the early short version of *Rape of the Lock.*[13] There and in most republications, the two works *Chaucer's Characters, Or The Introduction to the Canterbury Tales* and *The Miller of Trompington, Or, The Reve's Tale from Chaucer* are attributed to the actor Thomas Betterton, who had died in 1710. (See Appendix B.) Betterton had been friend and mentor to Alexander Pope, who in 1709 at age twenty-one had published his first work, his modernized *January and May; or, The Merchant's Tale: From Chaucer.*

The two Betterton pieces have long been assumed to be Pope's, an attribution I discuss in reference to the *Merchant's Tale.* Briefly, no one except Pope has ever bothered to claim that Betterton wrote them. Yet despite stylistic similarities, contextual evidence including Lintot's account book, and Pope's well-documented love of anonymity, Pope scholars in their startling neglect of his Chauceriana have not come to consider the modernized *General Prologue* and *Reeve's Tale* for his canon. Since Pope certainly at least completed the two works, I will refer to their author as Pope/Betterton.[14]

Whether partly by Betterton or wholly by Pope, the 1712 portrait of the Prioress can be analyzed for expansions, contractions, and adjustments that indicate the modernizer's understanding of the text, combined inextricably with his artistic awareness of eighteenth-century readers' tastes. This analysis will supply evidence that ambiguity or binary irresolution, under whatever name, does figure in readers' responses before the twentieth century. Pope/Betterton does understand two auras of meaning in the Prioress's portrait. As a poet, furthermore, he responds not by resolving but instead by developing both possibilities.

The two auras of meaning in 1712 differ from those in the twentieth century, however. Nowadays the two involve the Prioress's heartfelt religiosity as opposed to the conventions of "courtly love," a term invented by Gaston Paris in 1883 and seized upon by C. S. Lewis and others eager to systematize medieval sexuality.[15] Pope/Betterton develops no such idealization of secular medieval love. To him, the Prioress is both a woman whose religious vocation commands respect, personal sincerity being not at issue, and a woman inoffensively pretentious about social graces and sincerely fond of pets—the latter resembling Belinda in *Rape of the Lock,* published in the same volume as this Pope/Betterton modernization.

Pope/Betterton first adds a line to emphasize the Prioress's dignity, then breaks up the phrase "symple and coy," which now echoes medieval French romances:

> There was with these a Nun, a Prioress,
> A Lady of no ord'nary Address.
> Her Smiles were harmless, and her Look was coy.
> She never swore an Oath but by Saint *Loye.*[16]

In Pope's time, "coy" looks were either shy or disdainful; they took on sexual overtones only by analogy with the verb. "Address" referred not to her residence but rather to her attire, her preparedness, or her courteous manner of speaking.[17] Thus Pope/Betterton downplays potential sexuality in the portrait's opening. Instead he implies a contrast between this ladylike figure and other possibilities: apparently prioresses somewhere exist with harmful smiles, brash looks, and ordinary addresses.

Pope/Betterton deletes from her face the Prioress's entuning nose, but he amplifies the sounds of her French:

> Known by the Name of Lady *Eglantine:*
> She sung the Office with a Grace Divine;
> She spoke the *French* of *Stratford*-School, by *Bow,*
> The *French* of *Paris* she did never know:
> For *French* of *Paris* did to her appear
> Strange, as our *Law-French* to a *Frenchman's* Ear.

Next, Chaucer's ten-line paean to her table manners is cut back and combined with the abstractions that follow it:

> At Meals she sat demure, carv'd neat, and well,
> No Morsel from her Lips unseemly fell.

She never dipp'd her Finger in the Mess;
Nor with one Drop defil'd her holy Dress.
With a becoming Grace, and smiling Eye,
She gain'd Respect from all the Company.
Easie and free, still pleasant at her Meat;
And held it no small Pain to counterfeit;
She hated Stateliness, yet wisely knew
What fit Regard was to her Title due.

In modernizing "peyned hire to countrefete cheere / Of court, and to been estatlich of manere," Pope/Betterton renders the verb as if the two attitudes cause her pain, even though the transitive sense of "to take pains or trouble . . . to endeavour, strive" was current then, as it still was in 1841 when the *General Prologue* was next modernized (*OED,* s.v. "pain"). In 1835 Clarke would gloss the lines accurately: "she strove to assume a courtlike and stately countenance and manner." [18] Yet in 1841 Richard Horne, like Pope/Betterton, chooses the intransitive verb, such that courtliness causes pain to the Prioress:

It gave her pain to counterfeit the ways
Of court; its stately manner and displays;
And to be held in distant reverence. [19]

The 1841 sense is far sloppier than is Pope/Betterton's in 1712. Unlike Horne, Pope/Betterton makes sense of an intransitive "pain." With it he clarifies the textual contrast he sees between a religious authority figure and a weeper over small hounds, combined in the same body. By inverting the syntax of *GP* ll. 139–41 so that pain hurts the Prioress—so that, despite this woman's natural inclinations toward warmth, she must act with dignity befitting her office—Pope/Betterton has invested her with the respect due a nun for the sake of her holy vocation.

Few twentieth-century critics respond to her vocation with much respect at all. Muscatine does suggest that "the mere statement of the Prioress's occupation has such strong connotations that a large number of courtly traits can be played against it." He cites "conscience" as a trait that fits both medieval systems, religion and romance. Robertson would disagree: he attacks "editors" for "misglossing the text. . . . the word *conscience* means just what it says, 'conscience.' The meaning 'concern' or 'sensibility' was rare in the fourteenth century, if indeed it existed at all." [20]

Pope/Betterton has eased out this now-controversial "conscience" and replaced it with visual details. Critics including Donaldson and Bernard Huppé point to the moment of suspension between connotative worlds. We think we are at last about to learn of her religious conscience, at *GP* l. 142, but we learn instead of her charity toward "vermin rather than suffering humanity."[21] Pope/Betterton creates a similar suspension between human and animal worlds, for his term "Creature" evokes both. He goes on to make beast-directed her certainly Christian pity, devoutness, charity, tender heart, and compassion, this last term apparently his rendering of "conscience":

> She pity'd every Creature in Distress,
> Devout, and charitable to Excess.
> Her tender Heart with such Compassion fill'd,
> She'd weep to see a poor *Mouse* caught, and kill'd.
> Her Lap-dogs still with her fair Hands she fed,
> With Milk, and roast Meat, mixt with Crumbs of Bread.
> In her own Chamber, on her Bed they slept;
> If any dy'd, most bitterly she wept.

On Cut D of the tape we will hear how narrators' varying attitudes toward whipped dogs contribute to their varying interpretations of the Prioress. We will see later, also, that Alexander Pope loved dogs. Eighteenth-century audience and artistic intention aside, Pope personally would have sympathized with the Prioress's feeding, weeping over, and even sleeping with her dogs.

By adding this last image, perhaps Pope/Betterton meant to hint at the Prioress's thwarted sexuality, just as Kittredge would find thwarted motherhood in the text. But Pope/Betterton's authorial voice does not condemn the Prioress for directing some of her affections to snuggling little bodies who love her as purely and selflessly as her husband, Christ, is said to do.

Pope/Betterton renders the rest of the portrait nearly line by line. He does condense Chaucer's two clauses concerning her forehead "broad, smooth and shining," thus de-emphasizing possible impropriety to allow for an extra visual detail of "Eye-brows, neat and small."

Chaucer's first-person narrator here—"I trowe . . . . as I was war"— similarly steps aside for the sake of more visual details. The narrator's backhanded compliment or insult, "she was nat undergrowe," becomes external description: "A slender Waste, inclining to be tall." Pope/Betterton pictures her quite differently, and more respectfully, than do several modern critics. To Edgar Duncan she is "stylish stout," to Gordon Harper "bulbous," to Charles Moorman "portly," to John Gardner "somewhat overweight."[22] On Cut B we will hear how voices likewise create various possibilities for "nat undergrowe."

For Pope/Betterton the Prioress's brooch with crowned A transmutes to an "Ornament of beaten Gold," engraved with "a circling Wreath" above its "*Amor vincit Omnia.*" The wreath is presumably one of victory. So precise and discrepant a visual image impels a search for a pre–1712 picture of the Prioress holding such an ornament. The evidence is finite, for until the late eighteenth century, the only pictured pilgrims illustrate editions of the *Tales.*

Among manuscripts that picture pilgrims, only the Ellesmere includes the Prioress, carrying no wreathed ornament. The fourth illustrated book printed in England was William Caxton's second edition of Chaucer (1484?); its woodblocks of the pilgrims were reused until 1542 by three other printers. Richard Pynson's first edition (1491/2) likewise launched a set of woodblock pilgrims, some of which reappear as late as 1561. Several portraits from both sets and elsewhere are reproduced and accounted for in Muscatine's *Book of Geoffrey Chaucer.*[23]

I must bypass woodblock pilgrims as potential evidence, despite charming details that peep through the unavoidable roughness of the prints—a winking Friar, a Miller's mule, a flamboyant Squire. (See figure 3.) Their origins are unfortunately but irreversibly as vague as their outlines.[24] The folio-buying public expected each pilgrim to appear in the *General Prologue* or beside his *Tale* or (only in Pynson's first edition) in both places. But as decades pass, the illustrations become less appropriate. More and more frequently a noticeably worn woodblock does double duty. In William Thynne's 1532 edition, for instance, one woodblock indiscriminately portrays Summoner, Merchant, Franklin, and Manciple. And in John Stowe's 1561 edition the Wife and the Prioress— differing damsels to any reader—are pictured by the same woodblock. She carries no wreathed ornament.

The pilgrims are not portrayed in Thomas Speght's seventeenth century editions, the last in black-letter type. And by 1712, John Urry had barely begun work in Oxford on the textually irresponsible edition that would appear nine years later, six years posthumously. In the small world of eighteenth-century British intellectuals, though, it seems possible for Pope/Betterton to have had a preliminary peek at the elegant engravings under way for this edition, which show each pilgrim on horseback in a medallion heading his *Tale.*

The artist might be George Vertue, who did the frontispiece portrait of

FIGURE 3: The Squire, from folio 29 of William Thynne's edition of *The Workes of Geffray Chaucer* (London: T. Godfray, 1532). Reproduced by courtesy of the Pattee Library, Pennsylvania State University. Actual size, 2¾″ × 3¾″.

Chaucer and the departure scene from the Tabard Inn for Urry's edition. (See figure 1.) But the pilgrim portraits are unsigned, and by 1711 Vertue was associated with the art academy at Lincoln's Inn Fields headed by Sir Godfrey Kneller, among whose artists another might have portrayed the pilgrims.[25]

Pope went to this academy regularly for painting lessons, beginning in 1713/14. His art instructor, Charles Jervas, had Pope copy, among other portraits, Chaucer's from "Occleve" (i.e., from Harleian ms. 4866, or more likely from a presumed copy of it) and his late friend Betterton's

portrait from Kneller's rendering (this latter being the only extant paint-
ing by Pope). Jervas, who remained Pope's lifelong friend, replaced
Kneller as chief portrait painter to British royalty after Kneller's death at
Twickenham in 1723.[26]

I provide these particulars of intertwining lives, however, merely to
foreshadow the half-century during which Pope's often-anonymous hand
seems omnipresent. Like Satan in *Paradise Lost* I have led the reader
astray, past an introductory gallery of early visual interpretations which
go to show that the 1712 modernizer of *GP* ll. 118–62 did not in fact
take the detail of a wreath over the motto from the engraving under way
for Urry's edition, for in it the Prioress carries no such ornament. (See
figure 4.) From her long string of beads instead dangles a Christian cross
atop a heart—an effective visual representation of two kinds of Amor,
and one that will reappear nestled in the cleavage of Blake's Wife/Whore
of Bath/Babylon. Although not a source for Pope/Betterton's wreath,
then, the Urry engraving can indicate how another careful reader of
Chaucer's text, within the same few years in London, understood the
Prioress.

As in the Ellesmere manuscript and the rougher woodcuts, the Urry-
edition Prioress looks severe. Lips pursed, feet firmly together on a side-
saddle platform, she gazes directly at the reader. Perhaps her cloak could
be fastened tighter; perhaps her headpiece is pushed slightly higher than
need be. But she is clearly someone commanding "fit Regard . . . to her
Title due," as she is for Pope/Betterton.

If we look only to her person, we see merely the stern nun. To interpret
the artist's interpretation, however, we must also observe how she
handles her horse. With careful details the Urry-edition artist shows character traits—control, daring, timidity, indiscretion, aggressiveness, and
so on—by each pilgrim's interaction with his mount. "The characters of
Chaucer's Pilgrims are the characters which compose all ages and nations," says Blake, echoing Dryden; "some of the names or titles
are altered by time, but the characters themselves for ever remain un-
altered."[27] Blake's point, debatable in regard to human nature, certainly
applies to equine nature. Horses never change. I write this chapter with
an arm muscle strained thanks to Darcy who, just like Bucephalus 2350
years ago, bolted in terror at the sight of his own shadow.[28]

The Urry-edition Prioress has been given a docile horse who will keep
moving with the herd whether or not signaled to do so. Some inexperienced riders would be tense, holding the reins too tightly; quite the opposite, this novice lets the reins droop far too loosely, trying too hard not
to hurt its mouth. It takes advantage of her by looking aside instead of

FIGURE 4: The Prioress, from p. 142 of John Urry's edition of *The Works of Geoffrey Chaucer* (London: B. Lintot, 1721). Reproduced by permission of the Van Pelt Library, University of Pennsylvania. Actual size, 5¾″ × 4¼″.

ahead, hoping to spot leaves within grabbing distance. (The Nun's Priest likewise rides inexpertly, in Urry's edition, while his horse looks toward the viewer with conspiratorial amusement.)

This artist, like Pope/Betterton, conveys the ambiguity of the *General Prologue* portrait principally as control over humans versus sentimentality toward animals. Unlike Pope/Betterton, however, the Urry-edition artist uses images of cross and heart, combined in the Prioress's brooch, to suggest in addition a religious/romantic ambiguity.

Pope, as will be discussed, was shunned for his Roman Catholic upbringing and so would have been motivated to downplay a nun's potential sexual irregularity in favor of the text's more overt and less loaded images of her pampered pets and pretentious French. Pope/Betterton's use of the classical image of a wreath, appropriate for the similar phrase occurring in Virgil's tenth *Eclogue,* seems to be an attempt to deflect attention from "amor" to "vincit"—from an "amor" apparently ambiguous to the Urry-edition artist in the same way it was to Hunt over a century later. Pope/Betterton, therefore, might intentionally be altering the interpretation usual at his time. We cannot be sure, though, because we have only these two earliest pieces of evidence to work from—two that provide different interpretations.

One cannot generalize about reception aesthetics for Chaucer even when considering the second decade of the eighteenth century in Twickenham and Lincoln's Inn Fields. I propose that the picture might represent a standard response at its time, and the modernization an intended change, primarily because I can guess Pope/Betterton's motivation for change but know nothing about the Urry-edition artist. The reverse could be true: given that we lack earlier evidence, the Urry-edition interpreter could have been first to emphasize the double meaning, religious and romantic, of "amor" in *GP* l. 162.

By 1779, however, still a century short of "courtly love" and its subsequent domination of responses to *GP* ll. 118–62, the Prioress has already become decisively man-oriented, rather than dog-oriented, in her deviation from a nun's ideals. In John H. Mortimer's *Departure of the Canterbury Pilgrimes* she looks young and pretty, in striking contrast to the haglike Wife of Bath.[29] (See figure 5.) But the two women enjoy equally gallant treatment. The Wife's horse is being held by the Friar, with whom she certainly flirts (*WBP* l. 855). Their mutual gaze is mirrored by that between the Prioress and the fat Squire, who has just helped her to mount. He may simply be explaining earnestly how one uses reins, which she is holding up. Knowing the Squire's way with the ladies, though, we might well wonder.

Like her Urry-edition counterpart, Mortimer's Prioress holds the single reins of her calm horse loosely. Its elegant tail cascades, matching the folds of her wimple. Mortimer's Knight rides a horse as large and solid and well-groomed as hers, but his in contrast prances and fights for its head despite taut double reins. (A double bit provides firmer control.) Mortimer's ugly Wife of Bath sits "esily" on her likewise lively "amblere" (*GP* l. 469), which turns its delicate muzzle and betasseled ear as if to flirt with the Miller's flat-footed, droopy-eyed, scraggly-maned nag.

Having observed carefully the Urry illustrations and Mortimer's work, Blake says of his own painting that "the Horses he has also varied to

FIGURE 5: *Departure of the Canterbury Pilgrimes,* drawn by John H. Mortimer and engraved by J. Hogg, on p. 22 of *Mortimer's Works: A Collection of Fifty Historical Designs* (London: Thomas Palser, 1816). Reproduced by courtesy of the Victoria and Albert Museum, London. Actual size, 7¾″ × 10¼″.

accord to their Riders." Commentators remark on the horses in Thomas Stothard's painting, too. For example, Walter Scott says that "if the procession were to move, the young squire who is prancing in the foreground would in another minute be over his horse's head."[30] Stothard has hidden most of his Prioress's mount, unfortunately, although the uprightness of its neck makes it seem more energetic than those she rides in previous depictions.

For our analysis of implied characterization and understanding in Stothard's 1807 *Pilgrimage to Canterbury,* we have a valuable guide in self-effacing art critic William P. Carey. In 1808 he published his *Critical Description of the Procession of Chaucer's Pilgrims to Canterbury, painted by Thomas Stothard,* for readers who had not yet seen the picture during its tour of British cities. Carey repeatedly denies that Stothard's art agent Robert Cromek paid him to praise his client's painting. Carey even prints in his second edition purchase receipts from Cromek for the first edition. If we are to believe Blake, who bitterly accused Cromek of stealing his idea for the painting and passing it to Stothard, Cromek's business practices would not preclude such a payoff.[31] At any rate Carey, whatever his motivation, describes Stothard's Prioress as one

> in the flower of life. Her profile is pleasing. Her complexion fair; but the tints of her cheek show more of the paleness of the lily than the lustre of the rose. . . . [She shows] pensive character. There is a happy affectation, a sort of demure elegance, in her downcast look and action.

Her open cloak shows that she "allows herself more license" than does the Second Nun, and she has brought along her "favorite dog."[32]

Carey does not note her apparent indifference to the danger of that dog's skittering toward flaying hooves beneath the Squire and Yeoman; and he brushes past other potential complexities that I see in Stothard's painting. My visual interpretations are influenced overmuch by Blake, however. I will assume Carey's description is true enough to Stothard's intention that I may cite it in comparison with my own description of Blake's painting and of Blake's sources, Mortimer and the Urry edition, because I cannot pretend neutrality in my strong aesthetic preference for Blake.

Neither can I pretend that my immersion in Blake's other visual and verbal art makes it possible to summarize neatly his interpretation of the Prioress, nor of the other pilgrims he painted and then engraved. (See figure 2.) "As he stems from no tradition, so he established none," says Bertrand Bronson. Illustration of texts embodies the common sense of its age, "a kind of sense to which Blake never cared to lay claim."[33] For one thing, Blake very intentionally sets visual representation of each pilgrim at odds with each one's verbal description in the *Descriptive Catalogue* for his exhibit, in order to force superficial readers to become thoughtful viewers.

Using the abstract words he so distrusts and despises, Blake calls the Prioress "of the first rank, rich and honoured. . . . truly grand and really polite," then later equates her with the Wife of Bath as "also a scourge and a blight." He uses similar terms for the Pardoner, who is "sent in every age for a rod and scourge, and for a blight," and who like the Summoner is "grand, terrific, rich and honoured in the rank of which he holds the destiny." In his painting Blake links the Prioress visually with the Wife, Pardoner, Second Nun, Summoner, and Knight; each pairing has a resoundingly different significance. Her visual attributes, notably the net on her horse, also link her to Tirzah, a terrifying figure of repressed female sexuality found elsewhere in Blake's works. What seems to ordinary readers like Carey to be the "demure elegance" of the Prioress, seems to Blake to be the net of false religion, which lures, smothers, and finally snuffs out the potential poetic/artistic genius in every human soul.[34]

Art patrons who did not understand Blake's intentions—nearly all of them, in fact—stayed away in droves from Blake's 1809 exhibition of *Canterbury Pilgrims* and other works.[35] Stothard's painting, in contrast, enjoyed immense popularity throughout the century. Thus, concerning these two London artists at work a century after the Urry edition and Pope/Betterton modernization, we can say with a certainty impossible for the earlier pair that Stothard's is the standard interpretation, Blake's the aberration.

The same year as Blake's exhibition, there also appeared in London art circles the first reproduction from the Ellesmere manuscript: Chaucer-the-pilgrim, published then by F. C. and J. Rivington and again in 1810 as frontispiece to Henry John Todd's *Illustrations of the Lives and Writings of Gower and Chaucer.* The manuscript itself had recently arrived in London, amidst some fanfare.[36] It may well be that established artists were allowed to examine it at Bridgewater House, although neither Blake nor Stothard seems definitely influenced by Ellesmere details.[37]

These early-nineteenth-century Chaucer-related activities were surging in the wake of Thomas Tyrwhitt's 1775 edition of the *Tales,* in five volumes octavo, the first Chaucer that was smaller and cheaper than the previous folio editions. Tyrwhitt neglected to copyright his text amidst the legal confusion of the Booksellers' War.[38] John Bell—"indisputably the most versatile member of the London printing trade at any period"[39]—promptly used the apparatus and text of Tyrwhitt's *Tales,* along with Urry's text for *Troilus* and Chaucer's other poems, in his

British Poets series (Edinburgh, 1782–83). Other inexpensive reprintings soon followed. Some credited the editor; others did not. After a polite protest against Bell in *Gentleman's Magazine*,[40] Tyrwhitt died in 1786, having left as a legacy a Chaucer text not only accurate but also affordable, at last, by masses of readers.

Tyrwhitt does get full credit nine years posthumously from the first modernizer of the *Prioress's Prologue* and *Tale*—the Reverend William Lipscomb—who was ensconced far from London with only Tyrwhitt's edition and George Ogle's 1741 *Canterbury Tales . . . Modernis'd by several Hands* (as Lipscomb explains in order to excuse himself for not expanding Tyrwhitt's notes). Lipscomb's *Canterbury Tales . . . completed in a Modern Version* adds twelve more *Tales* to nine *Tales* from Ogle's collection and the Pope/Betterton *Chaucer's Characters* (with substitutions). Lipscomb omits the oft-reprinted *Tales* of Miller and Reeve (see Appendix B) and even their *General Prologue* portraits, although he leaves *GP* l. 542 as "There was beside a Miller and a Reeve."[41]

Modernizing Canterbury tales for the first time, a century earlier than Lipscomb, Dryden had set a precedent by changing the text in three ways: "I . . . often omitted what I judg'd unnecessary, or not of Dignity . . . . added somewhat of my own where I thought my Author was deficient . . . . [and restored] the Sense of *Chaucer,* which was lost or mangled in Errors of the Press."[42] Of Dryden's three kinds of changes—omission, addition, restoration—Lipscomb practices only the first. Thanks to Tyrwhitt, a modernizer need worry less about printing errors. Furthermore, says Lipscomb, "exhibiting . . . [Chaucer] free from stains has been effected scrupulously by the omission of the offensive passages, and not by the presumption to substitute fresh matter. . . . [The omitted parts would have] operated as a just bar against their general reception" (1:viii–ix).

Rev. Lipscomb's expurgations would seem to result not from any deep repugnance toward Chaucer's bawdiness, but instead from a desire to produce what he and his publisher believed could be sold to the reading public, ninety-five years after Dryden and eighty-six years after the first Copyright Act. Lipscomb trims offensive passages only from the *Tales* he himself modernizes: although he is hard put to keep his *Shipman's Tale* free of innuendo, he does prevent Chaunticleer from feathering Pertelote in public. From Ogle's collection he leaves intact Pope's Wife and Merchant and the pseudonymous *Summoner's Tale.* (See Appendix B.) And he refrains from modernizing the *Parson's Tale,* "because I did not wish to swell the work with what was dry and unentertaining" (1:xi).

Lipscomb likewise seems uninterested in the *Prioress's Tale.* He shrinks it by a third, to 186 lines, and converts it to couplets so that its verse form no longer sets it apart (3:195–203). He condenses or eliminates passages that do not advance the narrative—skipping, for example, the stanza beginning "0 martir, sowded to virginitee" (*PriT* ll. 579–85).

Aside from such laudatory interludes, Lipscomb retains most elements of the *Tale* that have been brought to bear on interpretations of the Prioress as a character. He makes the Prioress's allusions to childhood slightly less specific than Chaucer does—her "powers so mean, so infantine" replace those of Chaucer's child "twelf month oold, or lesse"—and he assigns no age to the widow's son (3:195–96, for *PriT* ll. 484, 503). His references to Jews are slightly more specific than Chaucer's, but no more compassionate: the "murderer vile" in the alley "watch'd the victim with impatient look," for example (3:198, for *PriT* ll. 567–69). Lipscomb's Prioress does refrain from repeating the excremental image, saying just that the Jews "in a sewer his mangled body threw" (3:199, for *PriT* ll. 571–73). She slightly expands the possible slur on male clergy:

> The holy abbot then, for such was he,
> (At least such rev'rend abbots ought to be)
> (3:201, for *PriT* ll. 642–43)

All in all, though, the teller of the 1795 *Prioress's Tale* does not emerge as a strongly defined character.

We will see that Lipscomb's modernization of the Pardoner's sermon closing, sales pitch, and interaction with the Host—the exact object of modern critical controversy—can be analyzed for implied tones of voice and thus compared to readings-aloud and published commentary. It is more difficult to detect the voice of Lipscomb's imagined Pardoner behind his modernized *Tale* of three seekers after death. Analogously, only one reader-aloud even attempts to deliver the entire *Pardoner's Tale* in the goatlike voice of the Pardoner imitating himself preaching to gullible churchgoers.

Similarly, our object of study here is the Prioress's character, not much of which is discernible in her retelling of a widely distributed legend. Critics strain to find hints of her personality imbedded in the traditional material. Lipscomb, who seems less interested in this *Tale* than in some of the others, does not even try.

Lipscomb does term the Prioress "meek," in the transition from the *Shipman's Tale*. He reduces to a couplet the five-line request for a tale by Chaucer's Host, who to Lipscomb is "mild and courteous, as a modest maid." Lipscomb also adds, "I'll please you, if I can" to the "gladly" with which the Prioress replies to the Host (3:194, for *PriT* ll. 445–51).

Presumably she speaks the line meekly, then, rather than in a flirtatious simper or in grit-teethed exasperation or in trembly eagerness or . . .

Meanwhile in Dorsetshire, cozy by the fire, Dorothy Wordsworth was reading aloud to her brother from an inexpensive reprint of Tyrwhitt's text. On December 4 and 5 of 1801, according to her journal, William modernized the *Prioress's Tale.*[43] Wordsworth states his goal in modernizing: "no further deviation from the original has been made than was necessary for the fluent reading and instant understanding of the Author," with "no other object but to tempt the mere modern Reader to recur to the original."[44]

From the *Prioress's Prologue* and *Tale* Wordsworth retains Chaucer's thirty-four rhyme royal stanzas and indeed many of the same rhymes and lines. Like Lipscomb he softens the harsh image of a pit where "Jewes purgen hire entraille" to one "whence noisome scents exhale," probably for reasons of publication more than of characterization.[45]

Wordsworth diverges twice from rhyme royal. Instead of *a b a b b c c,* he makes his last verse *a b a c d d c* for no reason his editors can suggest.[46] More significantly, Wordsworth adds an entire line to Chaucer's stanza that compares the boy to St. Nicholas, making eight lines rhymed *a b a b c d d c.* Wordsworth's line is inserted between Chaucer's lines, "For sely child wol alday soone leere. / But ay, whan I remembre on this mateere":

> For simple infant hath a ready ear.
> Sweet is the holiness of youth: and hence,
> Calling to mind this matter . . . .[47]

Furthermore, a year after first publishing his *Prioress' Tale,* he quotes his own line as if it were Chaucer's:

> "Sweet is the holiness of Youth"—so felt
> Time-honoured Chaucer speaking through that Lay
> By which the Prioress beguiled the way,
> And many a Pilgrim's rugged heart did melt.[48]

His stated goals as a modernizer aside, Wordsworth thus both responds subjectively to the Prioress and authoritatively attributes his own feelings to Chaucer.

Wordsworth's response to her resembles Hunt's and Stothard's, at his time, but certainly not Blake's. It resembles also those of a great many twentieth-century critics. "Everyone has always been charmed by the portrait of the Prioress," says Donald Howard, before pointing out some of her faults. However, "women [critics] are harder on Madame Eglantine . . . than are the men," Edgar Duncan noticed thirty years ago in a footnote, hastening to add in full-size type, "Obviously the Narrator was charmed by her, and so are we."[49]

Although post-Spurgeon researchers might discover evidence in Victorian letters and diaries, at present we do not know how female readers responded to the Prioress before the twentieth century. Wordsworth's correspondence, though, can indicate what he and fellow-modernizers and publishers thought about the question, "What do readers most desire?"

Besides the *Prioress's Tale,* in December of 1801 Wordsworth modernized *The Cuckoo and the Nightingale* (now considered spurious), *Troilus and Criseyde* 5.519–686, and the *Manciple's Tale.* All but the last he published in 1820 and again in 1827 as *Selections from Chaucer, modernised.* In 1840 he offered all four modernizations to Thomas Powell and Richard H. Horne for what would become *The Poems of Geoffrey Chaucer modernised,* of which "20 years ago I would have undertaken the Editorship." But three weeks later the seventy-year-old poet "yielded to the judgments of others" and withdrew his two *Tales.* He adds:

> The large and increasing instant demand for literature of a certain quality, holds out the strongest temptation to men, who could do better, writing below themselves, to suit the taste of the superficial Many. What we want is not books to catch purchasers, Readers not worth a moment's notice . . . but profound or refined works comprehensive of human interests through time as well as space.[50]

A worthy sentiment, but not one to convince the collaborators, including Wordsworth's near-contemporary Hunt, who modernized a replacement *Manciple's Tale* for this volume. The collection, far odder in its assortment and arrangement of works than Ogle's compilation, which was published exactly a century earlier, contains a *General Prologue* by Horne, *Cuckoo* by Wordsworth, three *Legends of Good Women* by Powell, Hunt's *Manciple's Tale, The Rime of Sire Thopas* by "Z.A.Z.," Wordsworth's *Troilus* extract, the *Reeve's Tale* by Horne, Powell's *Flower and the Leaf,* Hunt's *Friar's Tale, The Complaint of Mars and Venus* by the Robert Bell who published Chaucer in his poets series of 1854–56, *Queen Annelida and False Arcite* by Elizabeth Barrett, the *Squire's Tale* by Hunt, and the *Franklin's Tale* by Horne.

It would be interesting to investigate whether exposure to these, by any

standards the worst modernizations ever published, inspired the young
Skeat and Furnivall and Child to commit their lives to providing their
intellectual progeny with accurate texts and information. It is better to
laugh, now, than to despair at the motivations of the contributors and
the execution of the work—better to pick out favorite bits such as
Horne's solemn news that Absolon, to re-attract Alison's attention after
the serenade, "brings a small scaffolding or stage (probably drawn by a
mule) before her window,—mounts it, and enacts the part of *Herod*." [51]
It is better to appreciate scholars' work that followed the 1841 modernizations and to be glad that no one a century hence can possibly accuse
us of writing about Chaucer in hopes of making lots of money.

Horne's stated intention in modernizing Chaucer echoes Wordsworth's: "preserving as much of the original substance as can be rendered
available." [52] Despite his own more accurate modernizations, Wordsworth remains untroubled by the compilation. He deems Hunt's *Manciple's Tale* "not failed" and Horne's *General Prologue* and *Franklin's Tale*
"very well done." He disapproves of the *Reeve's Tale*, however, because
"by indispensably softening down the incidents . . . [Horne] has killed
the spirit of that humour, gross and farcical, that pervades the original." [53]
Like Lipscomb, then, Wordsworth as reader and poet is not offended by
Chaucer's bawdiest. He presumes it will not sell, and he wishes authors
did not have to care what sells.

Withdrawing his own *Manciple's Tale,* which he never did publish,
Wordsworth sounds like no one so much as the dreamer/author in *PLGW*
ll. G452–64, trying fruitlessly to tell Queen Alceste "myn entente":

> Tell Mr. Quillinan, I think he has taken rather a *narrow* view of
> the spirit of the Manciple's Tale, especially as concerns its *moral-
> ity*. The formal prosing at the end and the selfishness that per-
> vades it flows from the genius of Chaucer, mainly as
> characteristic of the narrator whom he describes in the Prologue
> as eminent for shrewdness and clever Prudence. The main
> lesson, and the most important one, is inculcated as a Poet ought
> chiefly to inculcate his lessons, not formally, but by
> implication. [54]

Doubtless Quillinan like the Queen replied, "Lat be thyn arguynge."

As to why Wordsworth withdrew the *Prioress' Tale* as well as the *Manciple's* from the 1841 collection, we have one clue. For the 1827 publication of his own *Selections from Chaucer, modernised,* he adds to his

1820 preface a sentence praising binary irresolution in the *Prioress's Tale*. He sounds defensive: "The fierce bigotry of the Prioress forms a fine back-ground for her tender-hearted sympathies with the Mother and Child; and the mode in which the story is told amply atones for the extravagance of the miracle." [55] In this direct comment on the *Prioress's Tale*—the earliest Spurgeon found—Wordsworth's use of "fierce big-otry" shows that, whatever the attitude of Chaucer toward fourteenth-century Jews, our responses to blatant anti-Semitism are not merely the post-Auschwitz ones that some critics imply. [56]

The tale itself—child murder by an ethnic minority—has a long life. As folktale motif V361, "Christian child killed to furnish blood for Jew-ish rite," it occurs widely with or without V254.7, "Murdered boy still sings 'Ave' after his death." [57] Carleton Brown provides thirteenth- to fifteenth-century texts of close analogues to the *Prioress's Tale;* Bill Ellis finds earlier, less exact analogues; Gavin Langmuir has thoroughly re-searched an early incident that looks to a nonfolklorist like the origin of the legend. Cecil Roth, editing an eighteenth-century report by the car-dinal who became Pope Clement XIV, traces accusations from 1144 to 1934 that Jews bake Christian children's blood into unleavened bread; his appendix on the ritual-murder issue of the Nazi organ *Der Stürmer* (1 May 1934) includes a protest against that issue by the president of the Folk-lore Society. [58]

Barre Toelken analyzes the analogous current urban legend: "A young boy . . . is attacked and mutilated by thugs belonging to the local feared minority group." In the 1970s Toelken traced the always "true story" of a white boy's castration (which had occurred just hours or days previ-ously, in the restroom of a certain shopping mall or drive-in theater) by Indians in Idaho, Hispanics in Utah and Los Angeles, blacks in Philadel-phia, and hippies in Portland. Janet Langlois adds that during the 1967 race riots, Detroit blacks told the story about whites, and Detroit whites told it about blacks. [59]

By 1986 in New Jersey, the castration image had taken a symbolic twist. According to my Rutgers students, mall shoppers everywhere were being earnestly warned to watch their children because in that very mall, just hours or days previously, a group of thugs had abducted a girl by cutting off her hair in the restroom to disguise her as a boy. The core of the *Prioress's Tale* lives on, Toelken says, "because it provides a succinct and usable traditional experience for any majority group that wants to rationalize and vivify its symbolic fears of the minority group . . . . an important clustering of culture-specific ideas, performed in what can only be called a culturally pleasing way." [60]

So there is the Prioress: not undergrown, smiling coyly, conscience-befilled, telling her version of a legend that your neighbors or students or you might well tell tomorrow. Each reader of her portrait brings to it an impenetrable mass of personal experiences, inclinations, intentions, limitations, and attitudes toward women, nuns, Christians, Jews, jewelry, dead mice, small dogs, white bread, and bad French. Each personal mass will remain unpenetrated in subsequent chapters.[61] Though I investigate personal and artistic motivations for Blake and Pope and other early interpreters, I will for overwhelming practical and professional and for that matter personal reasons ignore the private life of each Chaucer scholar who has kindly provided aural data for investigation of varying interpretations of Chaucer's text. For the historical record, as induced by my publisher (*pace* Wordsworth), I provide in Appendix A the names of readers-aloud who wish to be identified. In my analyses, however, I use cut numbers in lieu of individuals' names, and I refer to personal circumstances only to point out audible cases of teacher-student influence.

The readings-aloud of the same text thus can provide directly comparable evidence for the variety of possible interpretations by readers who share a definable number of traits. All readers-aloud were exposed to Chaucer scholarship first in a classroom and then in a tradition of published commentary traceable to Kittredge. Thirty-one share in addition their profession; some share gender; and all, while reading aloud, share the sociohistorical context of the Anglo-American 1980s, which has become nearly as small a town as Pope's London because of media technology.

I have suggested, with more caution than have theorists of reception aesthetics, that a reader's response stems in part from sociohistorical context—from Victorian desires for virtuous women, for example, or from now-faded respect for a nun's vocation. I will suggest in several chapters the role that gender plays in interpretation, regardless of sociohistorical context. Although no evidence survives of women's responses to the Prioress before this century, I suspect that Elizabeth Cooper in 1737 was no more charmed by her prissiness than I am.

One distinction between twentieth-century interpreters of Chaucer and those of the five preceding centuries looms clear and large, however: occupation. A monk wrote *Prologue* to the *Tale of Beryn*. Dryden was an author, and Pope became the first author ever to earn a living from book sales (thanks to Britain's Copyright Act of 1709, the first in the world). Other extant responses come from clergymen, artists, essayists, gentleman scholars. Nowadays, however, we who interpret Chaucer are nearly all teachers.

Succinctly, but perhaps more cynically than need be, Richard Levin posits a cause-and-effect relationship between the shift to teaching "modern languages" and the rise of New Criticism. It used to be that a professor really knew what his students really did not know: how to read literature in Latin or Greek. Now, according to Levin, to maintain classroom authority a professor must pretend that only he has the key to interpretation of a work. This bluff carries over into his publications. Karl Kroeber, tracing a hundred years of literary study by the Modern Language Association, likewise notes the development of a "magisterial mode of written discourse" adapted from the classroom; "this lecture style has set the tone for all critical writing."[62]

In university studies it was first Child and then Kittredge who applied folklore scholarship to medieval literature, as I am still doing in this book. It was Kittredge most of all who developed techniques to teach the "modern languages," techniques that we all still use. The effect of one classroom teacher on thousands of students who themselves never saw print can be estimated from prefaces to the folklore-related Chaucer studies published during the decades between *Originals and Analogues of Some of Chaucer's Canterbury Tales* (1872–87, Chaucer Society) and *Sources and Analogues of Chaucer's Canterbury Tales* (1941, Chaucer Group of the MLA).

1898: Kate O. Petersen, compiling *Nun's Priest's Tale* analogues, is "deeply indebted" to Kittredge for "valuable references and suggestions ... for revising the entire text in proof, and, in short, for help of every description."

1901: Kate O. Petersen, writing on the *Parson's Tale*, remains "under constant obligation to Professor Kittredge."

1901: Gustavus H. Maynadier thanks Kittredge for "suggesting the subject of my investigation [*Wife of Bath's Tale*], for his invariable readiness to help me with advice, and for his kindness in reading the proofsheets."

1908: Karl I. Young dedicates his study of *Troilus and Criseyde* sources to Kittredge, who suggested the subject, directly guided every step, and gave "constant generous advice ... [plus] most of the training without which I could never have undertaken the investigation at all."

1910: Carleton Brown, "acting on a suggestion made by Professor Kittredge ... proposed to Dr. Furnivall to print" as Chaucer Society publications his *Prioress's Tale* source study.

1927: Margaret Schlauch, who collected *Man of Law's Tale* analogues for her dissertation at Columbia, thanks Kittredge for his especially helpful comments as a reader for New York University Press.

1930: John W. Spargo dedicates his study of *Shipman's Tale* analogues to Kittredge's student Archer Taylor, then at the University of Chicago.

1931: Dudley D. Griffith owes primary gratitude for his *Clerk's Tale* study to John M. Manly, then at the University of Chicago, who had been in the same seminar of Child's as was Kittredge.

1934: Bartlett Jere Whiting did his Harvard dissertation under Kittredge, who now at age 74 "also has read the proof" on *Chaucer's Use of Proverbs*. Whiting declares a debt almost as resounding, besides, to "encouragement which a Freshman in Harvard College gave me, perhaps unwittingly, in 1927," a spontaneous insight which he then quotes.[63]

And so it goes. It is no longer gentleman scholars or general readers, but instead teachers and students who in this century read Chaucer. What would happen if Chaucer critics were to drop the pretense of proclaimed authority in print while maintaining it in their own classrooms in whatever manner they chose? What harm could come of our writing about Chaucer in the tones that we use to talk about him? Scholars, writing for an audience of others with less or more teaching experience, could then relax and present their own ideas, their textual interpretation and historical research, their perceived structural patterns and imagined performances, as what they really are for nearly every one of us: our best efforts to nudge Chaucer up off the page and into the hearts and minds of one more generation.

Each reader, each teacher, each generation, each epoch has its own way of interpreting Chaucer. Many scholars would claim that only a late-fourteenth-century understanding matters, but they then unavoidably choose which late-fourteenth-century evidence to emphasize based on their late-twentieth-century convictions and expectations, whether for irony or dogmatism. The oral readings of Chaucer's set text will allow us to confront the problems of modern interpretation of medieval texts and to return to their historical context wary of our own unarticulated prejudices.

It would be far easier to read aloud a valid fourteenth-century interpretation of Lydgate's text than of Chaucer's, for Lydgate speaks only to his own age. One is forced to learn the expectations and experiences of Lydgate's particular culture secondhand in order to make any sense of his text. But Chaucer's text speaks directly, in human voices that we can recognize.

Furthermore, Chaucer's text treats experiences not limited to any one culture's time and space—birth and death, men and women, self and others. Chaucer does not pass judgment or dictate what to think about these and other topics. Instead, he presents at least two sides to each situation, so that a reader must bring his or her own experiences to bear on the text's ambiguity, on its binary irresolution. The reader must use personal experience to hear and picture a calm or disapproving or delighted or despairing narrator emphasize some aspect or another of characters who resemble people known to the reader.

Potential flexibility in performance can be expected in a text containing unresolved binary oppositions, but ambiguity is neither sufficient nor necessary to ensure a text's success. Unresolved binary oppositions, such as Lydgate's lists of paired culture-bound abstractions, do not necessarily result in great literature that will continue to make living sense through the centuries. At the risk of reiterating Dryden, who responded to that text three centuries after Chaucer and three centuries before us, I would maintain that portrayal of living people, not culture-specific ideas, is what ultimately allows Chaucer's ambiguous text to live on in our respective minds' eyes and minds' voices:

> *Chaucer* follow'd Nature every where; but was never so bold to go beyond her . . . . Some of his Persons are Vicious, and some Vertuous; some are unlearn'd, or (as *Chaucer* calls them) Lewd, and some are Learn'd. . . . We have our Fore-fathers and Great Grand-dames all before us, as they were in *Chaucer*'s Days; their general Characters are still remaining in Mankind, and even in *England*, though they are call'd by other Names than those of *Moncks*, and *Fryars*, and *Chanons*, and *Lady Abbesses*, and *Nuns*: For Mankind is ever the same, and nothing lost out of Nature, though every thing is alter'd.[64]

CHAPTER 2

The Prioress on Tape

Is mankind ever the same? We agree with Dryden every time we remark a lawyer who seems busier than he is or a physician who especially loves gold. Yet by nature mankind creates technology, which technology may well alter the outward manifestations of human nature.

For the first two millennia after writing was reintroduced into Western culture, only the wealthy could afford writing materials. After the technology of paper-making reached Europe in the twelfth century, a far larger amount and variety of literature came to be preserved for the future. The invention of printing, not long after, gradually led to our present custom of owning numerous books, which we read alone, silently. Because of one basic human characteristic, the urge toward technological development, silent readers' responses to Chaucer's text now differ from predominantly aural understandings of it in earlier centuries.

Technology of paper and print came to affect writers' motivations as well as readers' experiences, for eventually profit became possible. As recently as 1775 Thomas Tyrwhitt, the reincarnation of Chaucer's Clerk, could simply forget to copyright his edition of *Canterbury Tales*. But the Romantic poets, two generations beyond Tyrwhitt and one beyond Blake and Wordsworth, found that they could demand large sums of money from publishers.[1]

As profit penetrated poetic ideals, the 1840s saw attempts to mass-market Chaucer with slipshod modernizations and editions that overlaid Chaucer's text with a Victorian image of female perfection.[2] Wordsworth, dying, pointed and despaired. Finally, half a century later, Kittredge seized Chaucer by the shoulders and steered him firmly toward the non-profit classroom, where he remains.

Not everyone in the 1840s regarded Chaucer primarily as a source of money, though. Thomas DeQuincey, still fighting the Battle of Ancients and Moderns, in comparing him to Homer remarks that Chaucer's language is easy to understand given *"the benefit of an oral recitation . . .* [with] pauses in one place, the hurrying and crowding of unimportant words at another, and . . . distribution of emphasis everywhere."[3]

DeQuincey here names several of the aural characteristics accounted for in musical transcription: phrasing (or pauses), tempo (or speed), duration (or stretching and cutting short), stress (or volume or loudness), rhythm (or meter), and pitch. In our own century, sociolinguists and others have tried to transcribe the speaking voice by adapting a musical vocabulary.[4]

Such transcription systems have proven minimally useful. Musicologists know well that the best-annotated song on paper looks not at all the way it sounds in any given performance. Similarly, attempted representations of speech become hopelessly bulky or idiosyncratic, or both. Analysts in performance fields more and more often simply exchange tapes, thanks again to technology, rather than attempt some unavoidably inadequate transcription. And to one philosopher grappling with how performed music conveys meaning, the literary vocabulary can provide a role model: "The language of criticism by which we assimilate and assess literature was not found ready-made. It had to be invented, phrase by phrase and term by term. And so it must be for music."[5]

I will be showing that the standard vocabulary of literary criticism can provide a fairly solid basis for performance analysis, because so many commentators have in fact described their imagined performances. I will suggest further—keeping the negative example in mind of New Criticism's never-stated premises—that this literary vocabulary be cautiously expanded to include sounds certainly shared by the present interpretive community.

This community agrees on what sounds Muscatine must mean by "delight," Robertson by "unmistakable sarcasm," Lumiansky by "gentle raillery," and Donaldson by "defiant assertion" in the narrator's voice concerning the Prioress's conscience and tender heart.[6] Could I see a show of hands, please. How many readers of this book would really truly have no idea what I meant, were I to say that a particular voice sounds like Donald Duck in trouble?

In this chapter's initial approach to performance analysis, however, I will restrict myself to sounds describable in a relatively objective vocabulary. Considering the potential impact on literary analysis of the earliest phonograph recordings, Raymond Alden long ago spoke of the subjectivity of mental soundings of a poem's meter, especially in regard to pauses:

> Metrical form is based on certain relations of sounds . . . [which]
> are not accurately represented by the symbols used in the print-
> ing of verse. . . . with anything like the clearness which the musi-
> cian attains through the symbols available for his art. . . . the
> rhythm of verse may be dependent on silences . . . . the pause
> which might be registered phonetically does not correspond
> exactly with the temporal unit which it is conceived to represent
> . . . . here we have a relatively simple example of the possibility
> of divergence between rhythm conceived and rhythm expressed.[7]

It is indeed a bit easier to say what pauses can do to meter than what they can do to meaning. But at a pause let us first begin, for a silent moment in a reading-aloud is at least there or not there. Furthermore, the earliest commentator on *GP* ll. 118–62 mentions phrasing. Leigh Hunt in 1826 begins his *Dictionary of Love and Beauty* with the A on the Prioress's brooch. In requoting the line, he pointedly changes its punc-tuation:

> And after, *Amor vincit omnia.*

> By the way, what a pretty majestic couplet is this, with its flowing
> line followed by the pause at *after:*—

> On which was first ywritten a crowned A,
> And after,—*Amor vincit omnia.*[8]

Like many commentators before and after him, Hunt regards punctua-tion as a system to indicate oral features on the page.[9] Future investi-gations, perhaps using oral data, may come to define more precise relationships between theories of oral performance (i.e., rhetoric) and theories of punctuation. For purposes of my own nontheoretical study, I will simply regard editorial punctuation as at least partly an attempt to capture on paper a bare few of the rich modulations by which the human voice conveys meaning with silence (ellipsis, period, semicolon, dash, comma), loudness (exclamation point, italics), and pitch shifts (question mark, colon, parentheses, quotation marks), combined variously with other inflections.

All participants in the Chaucer-tapes project read aloud from the punc-tuation in F. N. Robinson's second edition. (See *Texts Read Aloud*, Chap-ter 2). None follow it exactly. With examples from the forty-five-line portrait of the Prioress, I will show how oral interpretations vary because of vocal inflections, including but not limited to those describable as orally inserted punctuation. But let us first investigate the issue of punctuation. Without implying that graphic representation and head-counting can replace hearing the taped performances, I will first demonstrate the range of possibilities for two lines, the one repunctuated by Hunt at the very end of the portrait, and then *GP* l. 156, "For, hardily, she was nat undergrowe."

I have thirty-three readings of *GP* l. 162, including four by the same person, who helpfully read the entire portrait "in a reportorial and unemotional style," then "as if I were making fun of her," then as if "breathless with admiration," then (after taping other passages) "as a friend might describe her and certainly as I describe her after a long evening drinking Scotch and reading Chaucer." For ease of reference, I count these readings as if they were by four different readers. In the quoted lines that follow, ellipses indicate pauses and italics indicate loudness.

Robinson's edition italicizes the foreign-language motto in *GP* l. 162 and places no comma before it. Ten of the thirty-three readers-aloud do observe editorial punctuation by not pausing. Including the reader who intended to sound "reportorial and unemotional," none of these ten projects a strong opinion about "amor." With no pause before it, the motto flows on in a tone of voice similar to the descriptive "and after." One of the ten readers does speed up a bit for the motto. Another says it a bit more firmly, perhaps performing the italics, thereby seeming to dare someone to criticize the Prioress.

But these hints are slight compared with the array of meanings projected by readers who pause at one or more places in the line. Seventeen of the readers, like Hunt, pause before the motto but nowhere else. The vocal tones to which they shift vary greatly. One reader rushes the motto, for example, creating a narrator who hopes no one will notice the impropriety. Two instead shift to a foreboding tone of voice, invoking the Prioress's probable fate for letting love conquer her. With tones of exaggerated affection, another reader puts the Prioress in her childlike place: "Isn't she a silly little goose, to let love conquer her?" Yet another uses that same phrasing to imitate (as that reader's stated intention) "a little girl at the side of the road, perhaps one who hopes to become a nun someday, and breathless with admiration." A childish nun, a childish narrator, or one of many adult attitudes may emerge following a non-editorial comma inserted orally before "amor."

Of the six readers who pause even oftener, two phrase the line "And after . . . Amor . . . vincit omnia." They both create the same effect—an effect that editorial punctuation could not convey except by a disruptive-looking dash or ellipsis. With the pause after "amor," both imply that completing the motto is going to do what it then does not do: resolve the ambiguity of "amor." These two readers provide evidence that textual ambiguity can indeed be retained in oral performance.[10]

The remaining four readers phrase the line "And after . . . Amor . . . vincit . . . omnia." Among them, the reader who provided four alternatives conveys by this phrasing a narrator's mockery of the Prioress. Neither punctuation nor a literary-critical vocabulary can quite account for other features of this reader's vocal tone. It does satirize the Prioress's ignorance, but not as Augustinian irony in which the narrator would mean the opposite of "And after Amor vincit omnia."

I have gone on at some descriptive length so that you, gentle and responsive reader, will become irritated enough at the inadequacy of graphemes on paper that you want to hear the evidence. No amount of theoretical justification can replace comparing your comprehension of what you just read to what you will hear. From now on, I will arrange my discussion with headings according to cuts on the tape. Concerning this chapter's minute details, also, a summary will end each section. Remember to expect the sound quality of anthropological field recordings.

Cut A, GP l. 162

A1:   "And after Amor vincit omnia"—neutral, untroubled (following Robinson's punctuation).

A2:   "And after . . . Amor vincit omnia"—shift to affectionate motto ("Isn't she a silly little goose, not to see the ambiguity?").

A3:   "And after . . . Amor vincit omnia"—shift to breathless admiration ("All that, and she knows Latin too!").

A4:   "And after . . . Amor . . . vincit omnia"—"amor" remains ambiguous in performance.

A5:   "And after . . . Amor . . . vincit . . . omnia"—mockery, stated as intention by same reader as A3.

Among objectively audible features, pauses have occasionally been specified by critics reading silently—usually longer pauses than those just heard, such as the momentary hush that G. G. Sedgewick experiences after the Pardoner's benediction (to be discussed). Somewhat more often, critics describe their imagined performances with respect to another relatively objective feature, stress or loudness. Concerning *PardT* l. 918, "I wol yow nat deceyve," we will see that several critics argue meanings requiring that either "yow" or "I" be emphasized by loudness. In another example to be discussed, critics' arguments for the Merchant's honesty or dishonesty depend in part on their silently hearing a louder "wiste" or a louder "no" in *GP* l. 280, "Ther wiste no wight that he was in dette."

Moving such issues toward the aural arena, Florence Ridley has pointed out that the opening of the *Nun's Priest's Tale* may be read in a neutral storytelling tone. But, if one instead stresses more loudly each pronoun that in the text refers to the old widow—"No deyntee morsel passed thurgh *hir* throte . . . . Repleccioun ne made *hire* nevere sik . . . . No wyn ne drank *she*"—the passage becomes the Nun's Priest's criticism of his superior, the Prioress, for her overindulgent ways.[11]

Cut B, GP *l. 156*

Each of these examples—*PardT* l. 918, *GP* l. 280, and several *Nun's Priest's Tale* lines—contains both a personal pronoun and a negative particle. So does *GP* l. 156, which Robinson punctuates, "For, hardily, she was nat undergrowe." I have thirty-four performances of this line, by twenty-eight readers (including practice runs by two readers, as well as the four alternatives by the same person). Of the thirty-four, only three follow Robinson's punctuation by pausing exactly twice, before and after "hardily." These three convey attitudes of gentle tolerance toward the Prioress. They sound much like the ten (including A1) who follow editorial punctuation for *GP* l. 162.

Six of the seven readers who pause only at Robinson's second comma likewise sound gentle and tolerant. The seventh reader, however, sounds accusatory instead by making "nat" louder. To this narrator, who will be heard in context in Cut D7, the Prioress seems something far worse than undergrown.

A louder "nat" does not in itself create an accusatory line, however. Among the three readers who pause at both of Robinson's commas, one (who will be heard in context in Cut D5) uses a louder "nat" to help express his continuing toleration of Eglentyne's external appearance. In addition, among eleven readers who phrase the line with no pauses at all, five sound gently approving while making "nat" louder, including the one who intends (and conveys) breathless admiration.

The other six, among these eleven, neither pause nor stress any particular word. Two of them disapprove of the Prioress's physical appearance, however, while four simply report her size (including the one intended to sound "reportorial").

To sum up so far, twenty-one readers pause early in the line or not at all. They project several narrators: most are so fond of or indifferent toward the Prioress that her size does not matter; a few carry over their disapproval of her too-charming face to the rest of her body. A louder "nat," then, may convey attitudes ranging from admiration to accusation, but these and other attitudes may be conveyed by inflections other than stress on "nat."

None of these twenty-one readers is amused. The remaining thirteen of the thirty-four readers, in contrast, make fun of the Prioress. They all do so with pauses later in the line, sometimes combined with stress or other features that can be objectively labeled.

Laughter may signal mockery, of course. B1 pauses at neither of Robinson's commas but instead after "she," as if thinking up a joke; then he chuckles while pausing again before "nat."

The other twelve of these thirteen all mock the Prioress while inserting just one pause into the line, before "undergrowe." Four of them say the exact opposite of what they mean. They project Augustinian irony by stressing the first half of the last word: "For hardily she was nat . . . *under*growe." To B2 and three others, she is overgrown instead, perhaps "bulbous" or "stylish stout" as she is for those several published critics.[12]

The other eight of these twelve pause, then deliver "undergrowe" with even stress. Three sound simply amused. The other five all hold the pause in such a way that the entire word "undergrowe" becomes an ironic substitute for what that narrator is really thinking about her and her facial features. B3, as an example, even inserts "uh" to hold off stating the alternative. For hardily she was not supposed to show her forehead? For hardily she was not much of a nun? For hardily she was not bad looking at all? Each of these five readings projects something not in the text, something left unsaid by the narrator. A pause here can evoke an unpredictable multitude of nontextual elements, thus, in addition to the precise ironic opposite of "undergrowe."

A stressed word can do the same. In a final example, B4 stresses "she," then pauses. In doing so B4 brings to the text some woman other than the Prioress, a woman too small in size: "For hardily *she* . . . was nat undergrowe" the way *some* women are.

For the subjective-criticism record, let me note that I grew to five foot eleven in the early 1960s, when girls were supposed to be little and cute and cuddly, and that I like B4's reading best of all. Having realized the source of my preference for B4's reading, I would not try hard to argue its validity in terms of the text. A critic should be wary of a search for textual and even extra-textual evidence to argue the exclusive validity of what is his or her favorite imagined performance.

Cut B, GP *l. 156*

B1: "For hardily she . . . was . . . nat undergrowe"—narrator thinks up joke.

B2: "For hardily she was nat . . . *under*growe"—she's overgrown.

B3: "For hardily she was nat . . . undergrowe"—narrator starts to say something else but decides not to.

B4: "For hardily *she* . . . was nat undergrowe"—the way *some* women are.

GP l. 156 contains both a personal pronoun and a negative particle. Stress on either one, or on another syllable, plus strategically placed pauses, may create meanings including Augustinian irony. The combination in one line of pronoun and negative creates potential flexibility in performance, both here and elsewhere, and specifically may do so by summoning to the text someone not in it, such as the Prioress to the opening of the *Nun's Priest's Tale*.

Cut C, GP ll. 118–21, 127–32, and 142–43

Elsewhere in the Prioress's portrait, the description of her care at table includes several lines in which occur both a personal pronoun (she/hir) and a negative (no/ne). Audible features involving pitch, along with stress and pauses, affect their oral meanings.

Eglentyne's table manners are analogous, of course, to those advised by the Duenna in *Romance of the Rose*. As for Chaucer critics, "none of them ever wore a religious habit, nor had the least idea of what real distress a Sister feels at getting a spot on her habit, especially at table";[13] critics differ only as to tone of satire in *GP* ll. 127–36. Is the narrator just amused at her daintiness, or is he implying sternly that her mind ought to be elsewhere than on her lips, her fingers, and her breast? Do her manners seem overdone only after the apparent closing line 132 (as in Dorigen's list of suicidal wives, *FrkT* ll. 1419–25), or are they overdone from the start?

In the first half of this passage, *GP* ll. 127–32, C1's satire sounds harsher and more serious, more didactic, than does C2's. Differing stress on personal pronouns and negative particles helps create the differing effects. C1 tends to stress the negatives, especially in "*no* morsel." His narrator thereby seems to be watching the Prioress and remarking on her foolishness. C2 instead imitates Eglentyne's own thoughts, as if the lines were indirect discourse. His stress on personal pronouns summons to the text the messy eaters with whom she is contrasting herself. "Ne wette *hir* fyngres in *hir* sauce depe" particularly seems thought by a prim nun who considers herself a cut above all those fingerwetters.

C1's harsher satire also involves pitch-related punctuation created in performance, for C1's voice inserts quotation marks around "curteisie" in *GP* l. 132. The pitch change and pauses create sarcastic or ironic quotation marks, like those often found in student compositions, indicating "so-called curteisie."

The distinction is difficult to describe, but easy to hear, between sarcastic quotation marks and ones that set apart direct discourse. As examples of the latter, consider three readings of *GP* ll. 120–21. C3 quotes the Prioress's saying "but by Seinte Loy" but does not quote her name. C4 quotes "by Seinte Loy" and not her name. C5 quotes both "by Seinte Loy" and also the Prioress calling herself "madame Eglentyne." None is sarcastic; they simply quote what she said.

In audible contrast, two other readers insert ironic quotation marks into *GP* ll. 120–21, each around only the "madame" half of her name. To both C6 and C7, her French title is pretentious and undeserved. C7's satire sounds milder than C6's because of performance features other than the "so-called madame" that they share. Neither quotes the oath. But C7 pauses before "by" and then drops in pitch, so that the oath sounds anticlimactic and the narrator playful: "Did you *really* think she was going to *curse?*"

Many examples of sarcastic quotation marks occur in readings-aloud of *GP* ll. 142–43. A number of Chaucerians convey the Prioress's shortcomings by ironically quoting one or both of the loaded abstractions that can be made to name her so-called "conscience" and (C8 being an example) her mistaken belief that she is "charitable."

Sarcastic quotation marks can be orally conveyed or imagined by a silent reader, that is, as varying combinations of pauses, pitch shifts, and stresses. Insofar as they can be distinguished from quotation marks that signify direct discourse, they reliably convey Augustinian irony. Yet the oral effect is hard to sustain for more than a word or two. As I will show in a discussion of *MctT* ll. 1267–1392, the panegyric on marriage assigned since 1847 to the Merchant rather than to January, it is difficult even to imagine a voice saying the exact opposite of what it means for a long stretch of text.

A final example, too, shows that pinpointing sarcastic quotation marks brings us only a small step closer to the billowing issue of imagined and performed irony. C9 opens the Prioress's portrait not charmed in the slightest by her simple coyness. From the start C9 condemns her; this very harsh irony brings to the entire portrait the ideal nun who is Eglentyne's diametric opposite.

C9 creates Augustinian irony, however, not by using techniques noted so far. Long pauses after "nonne," "prioresse," "symple," and "cleped" allow time for the narrator's condemnation to sink in—allow enough time, indeed, for each listener to begin contemplating his or her own deviation from ideals. Thus slowness of tempo, with pauses not describable as oral punctuation, can help create direct, unamused, didactic irony.

C9's strongest effects are not ones that adapted musical terms can label, however. Instead, they are best described using visual images. C9's nostrils seem to flare on "nonne"; he sneers "symple"; and his narrator snorts with disgust at "madame Eglentyne."

Insofar as extended irony can be performed or imagined, it is best described using a range of visual, aural, and other comparative terms— by using metaphor, that is, not objective language. Metaphor works as long as everyone reading the commentary pictures and understands a sneer, for example, in the same way. Conceivably, at some distant time and place the gesture of raising one's upper lip over closed teeth, like a canine threat, could convey something pleasant—something flirtatious, perhaps, rather than a sneer. Desmond Morris and others have begun to show that a certain gesture (and, by extension, vocal tone) might well convey different meanings in different cultures.[14] But I am not talking here about different cultures. I am not even talking about whether someone in fourteenth-century England, listening to C9, would picture a sneer. I am simply developing ways to describe the aural evidence which you, the reader of an analytic book on Chaucer, hear.

Cut C, GP ll. 118–21, 127–32, and 142–43

ll. 127–32

C1: harsh, didactic satire conveyed by stress on negatives, especially "no" in line 128, and by sarcastic quotation marks around her so-called "curteisie."

C2: milder, amused satire conveyed by stress on personal pronouns, especially in line 129, such that narrator imitates nun's own self-satisfied thoughts.

ll. 120–21

C3: "but by Seinte Loy" quoted as direct discourse.

C4: "by Seinte Loy" quoted as direct discourse.

C5:   "by Seinte Loy" and "madame Eglentyne" quoted as direct discourse.

C6:   direct, disapproving satire: "madame" quoted ironically, implying that she is not one.

C7:   milder, amused satire: "madame" quoted ironically, implying that she is not one; teasing pause before oath.

ll. 142–43

C8:   ironic quotation marks: she was so "charitable" (so *she* thought, but we know better) and so pitous.

ll. 118–21

C9:   harshly ironic, didactic disapproval conveyed by slow tempo, long pauses, and various tones of antipathy not describable in musicological terms or translatable into punctuation.

Cut D, GP ll. 146–56

The Western-European system of musical transcription gradually expanded in scope from neumes indicating relative pitch, in the ninth century, to staffs showing absolute pitch by the twelfth, then eventually to indications of duration, mensuration (or rhythm), tempo, and relative volume. Is it right for analysts of the speaking voice to regard a millennium of musical transcription as primarily a negative example, as a stopgap method during the centuries before recording technology would allow one musician to hear another without face-to-face contact?

Rather than reject once and for all the possibility of describing performance in terms of objectively measurable elements, let us investigate two near-identical readings of a passage. D1 and D2 can be partially described in terms of similar pitch, pauses, duration, rhythm, tempo, and volume. If one were to describe the two only in terms adapted from a musical vocabulary, however, one would be cataloguing some similarities while ignoring most differences. Labels for objective qualities are useful as a common ground, as a base from which to focus and refine for discussion our experiences of the rich variety of meanings conveyed in performance. Musicologists would agree.[15]

To tell what the Prioress feeds her dogs in *GP* l. 147, readers D1 and D2 pause mid-line, at Robinson's comma. At that point each switches from a rougher to a smoother tone of voice, thereby imitating the textures of the two types of food. D1's contrast is more emphatic, because the rolled *r* growls: "With rrrrosted flessh . . . or milk and wastel-breed."

D1 and D2 here exemplify what I have elsewhere termed "oral onomatopoeia." With surprising frequency a singer will imitate a word or phrase in a song's lyrics. Examples of oral onomatopoeia would include a voice that falls in pitch on the word "fall" or "ground," rises in pitch on "up" or "hope," pauses after "break" or hurries past "rush." Complexity can increase if the vocalist sings the word "hard" softly, say, or if singer and instrument(s) contradict each other: the voice might fall abruptly while the keyboard part rises in joyful loops. I have shown too that overt imitation of lyrics often characterizes a playful or satiric version of a song.[16]

Indeed, following their oral onomatopoeia in the dogfood line, both D1 and D2 go on to satirize the Prioress's concerns. Both do so by speeding up *GP* ll. 148–49; then both slow down and insert pauses at the same two points in line 150.

The two narrators convey quite different attitudes, however. In *GP* ll. 148–49, D1 briskly lists two additional examples of the Prioress's improper behavior regarding pets (including dead ones). Then he slows the tempo to phrase the oft-discussed line 150 as "And *al* . . . was conscience . . . and tendre herte" with disapproval verging on disgust.

D2 instead imitates what would be the Prioress's own voice pitying hurt puppies (cf. C2). To D2's narrator she is silly, not wrong. Mock sympathy in D2's voice occurs especially in the drawn-out vowels of "soore" and "al." By speeding up *GP* ll. 148–49, D2 imitates the nun's increasing eagerness to tell a trapped listener about the horrid things that nasty men do to poor helpless doggies. D2, like D1, slows down and phrases *GP* l. 150 as "And aaal . . . was conscience . . . and tendre herte." D2 thereby imitates, with affectionate mockery, Eglentyne's opinion of her own tender-heartedness.

D2 stretches rather than stresses "al," and D2's first pause is briefer than is D1's. Might these very small differences in phrasing, duration, and volume of *GP* l. 150 be making D1 sound offended and D2 gently mocking? A monstrous issue looms again: potential measurability of emotions projected in oral performance.

In an attempt to analyze variant readings of *GP* l. 150 with a speech synthesizer, which measures pitch contour and duration, I chose sixteen distinctive deliveries, including this D2 representing "fake pity" and others that sounded to me "condescending," "careful not to offend her," "disgusted," and so on. Because of background noise or vocal idiosyncrasies, the speech synthesizer was unable to process ten of the tapes, including D2 and all four of the variant readings by one person. My ear divides the six readings of *GP* l. 150 for which the machine did provide printouts into more and less sympathetic camps. For three I had originally noted "impressed by her elegance," "wants to think so but isn't sure," and "genuine sympathy." For the other three I had noted "yeah, sure," "and al was . . . something else," and "Don't believe it for a minute!"

Allowing for the individual differences in reading speed and pitch range that make reader-to-reader comparison so difficult, still these six vocal printouts divide into two groups according to the relative pitch of "al was." Three printouts show pitch rising from "al" to "was"; three show it falling.

The falling-pitch faction includes "genuine sympathy" plus the two most sarcastic readings, however; the rising-pitch faction has the rest. No correlation here. Back to your lair, science. Technologically-enhanced objectivity offers no solutions. It can supply mistakes to learn from and some musical terminology that, adapted (not adopted) and combined with metaphorical and other descriptions, can be used to begin analysis of orally-conveyed meaning.

Hold it. Science, please lurk a moment longer at the entry to your lair. Sound recording technology can help us sharpen the analytic tools fashioned by humanists. For example, ever since E. Talbot Donaldson proposed layers of voices in the text, Chaucerians have been making finer distinctions among these layers and tracing the technique to medieval rhetorical theory.[17] On tape, now, we can hear Chaucer-the-pilgrim, Chaucer-the-author, and Chaucer-the-man. While complexities still abound, the issue can be addressed using oral evidence for what were previously silent possibilities.

D1 represents one way of understanding Chaucer-the-author. As a Christian teacher in the tradition of St. Augustine, he describes lapses in human behavior primarily to urge his students to behave otherwise. D2 represents a different conception of Chaucer-the-author. He describes human fallibility in order to amuse us—not by making us laugh outright at absurd pilgrims, however, but rather by making us laugh a little at ourselves. Just as D2 fondly imitates the Prioress, we realize, so too will he tease us should we start acting so silly. D1 and D2, two Chaucers-the-authors, employ different pedagogical techniques.

Chaucer-the-pilgrim, in contrast, is no educator. He takes all that he sees at face value and believes all that he hears. He would echo the Monk's tone of voice while passing on that good opinion:

What sholde he studie and make hymselven wood,
....

Lat Austyn have his swynk to hym reserved!

(*GP* ll. 184, 188)

Similarly, Chaucer-the-pilgrim would enter Madame Eglentyne's moral world, would project her own serious sentiments about dead and smitten dogs.

D3 represents an oral possibility for Chaucer-the-pilgrim. Regarding petfood selection as nobody's business but the Prioress's own, D3 waxes indignant at the horrifying scene of *GP* ll. 148–49. In line 150, "conscience" presents no problem at all. D3's narrator has no doubt whatsoever that humans ought to direct their conscience downward toward beasts as well as upward toward God.

At this puppy-bashing passage, let me reiterate my purposes in factoring out personal lives of the readers-aloud. D4 and D5 respectively express indifference to and glee over suffering dogs. If we were to leap to conclusions about each reader's personal life, as do some subjectivist critics—if we were to urge that the S.P.C.A. keep D4 and D5 under surveillance—we would miss the quiet voice of Chaucer-the-man.

D4's overall tone of toleration resembles D2's tone of mock sympathy. D5's tone of disapproval, though less didactic, resembles D1's. Thus, the fine line between author and man is here marked by dogges.

Dogs, like horses, do not change character as millennia pass. In any time, some humans like dogs for their affectionate fidelity; others find them servile and constantly underfoot. Nineteenth-century scholars used to posit two different authors for the *Odyssey* and *Iliad* based partly on these two attitudes.

Alexander Pope loved dogs. Chaucer apparently did not. In modernizing, as will be noted, Pope changes or eliminates Chaucer's images of dogs that cringe, fight mindlessly over bones, piss on rosebushes, whine, grovel, eat their dead masters, and so on. Perhaps subconsciously, as suggested by P. D. Juhl, D4 and D5 both work Chaucer-the-man's apparent antipathy into their own oral interpretations.[18]

Except D3, most readers inject into *GP* l. 147 an awareness that convent rules forbid pets. No rule insists that illegal pets be beaten, though, and many readers pass the images in lines 148–49 without particular notice. D1, for example, uses the couplet as brisk transition from stern disapproval of the nun's rule-breaking to stern disapproval of her misuse of abstract moral categories.

D4, instead, is aware of the cruelty toward animals but decides not to intervene. Similarly, he makes a conscious decision not to be troubled by the term "conscience." D4, in fact, may seem almost too tolerant. Indeed, Chaucer-the-man did manage to stay on good terms with both royal factions, no mean feat.

D4, minding his own business (without D3's defensiveness), merely describes meat and milk. With a stretched "soore" he expresses momentary sympathy for Eglentyne's feelings. In a pause between "men" and "smoot," however, he shrugs aside the chance to take a stand on behalf of cowering curs. D4's line 150 I had originally noted as "And al was . . . something else but why not just call it 'conscience'—*she* sure doesn't know the difference." With a pause resembling B3's pause before "undergrowe," D4 starts to say something other than "conscience" but decides not to.

D5 is less tolerant toward both dogs and disobedient nuns than is D4. As he continues reading *GP* ll. 146–56, though, D5 delineates the precise target of his disapproval: nuns should not break rules. They cannot help how they appear to men, though.

D5's narrator has no sympathy for foibles involving dogs. At their first appearance in *GP* l. 146, with a combination of slightly lower pitch, slightly louder volume, and a slight pause afterward, D5's voice manages to frown at the "houndes." D5's narrator, perhaps Chaucer-the-man, seems almost to relish the images of *GP* ll. 148–49. On "yerde smerte," particularly, his inflections imply something like "damn yapping mutts get what they deserve."

Pausing at the same two points in *GP* l. 150 as does D4, D5 instead projects firm, calm Augustinian irony: "yeah, sure," according to my initial notes. The entire line means its opposite. Unlike D1's, though, D5's narrator is not trying to teach anybody a lesson with line 150. What do you expect, he implies, from someone who's bothered by what I'd sure like to do to all those creatures that bark at night and defecate in my yard?

Chaucer's text can allow for both yapping mutts and whimpering pups. Perhaps Chaucer-the-man intended the former and would have performed the passage as does D5, or perhaps he would have shrugged aside hurt dogs as does D4. But the *Life-Records,* unlike Pope's biography, provide no external evidence about the man's interaction with dogs. Critics should be wary of arguing their own likes and dislikes as if they were Chaucer's, and should focus on textual issues that can be legitimately investigated given our limited knowledge of Chaucer's personal attitudes.

One such issue is the text's potential for flexibility in performance. To what extent does a text control or put any limits at all on readings? Can a range of meanings be predicted, or must they be merely catalogued after the fact? The next passage, especially *GP* l. 151, is one in which meter and assonance at least nudge readers toward certain vocal inflections.

The narrator in D5's reading, moving on to describe the nun's facial features and apparel, backs off from his calm disapproval of her actions (ll. 146–49) and her misuse of moral abstractions (l. 150). D5 reads *GP* l. 156 with stress on "nat," pausing at both of Robinson's commas (cf. Cut B). Although similar phrasing and stress will accuse the Prioress in Cut D7, D5 makes the line convey a narrator comparatively tolerant toward Madame Eglentyne's appearance. He condemns her breaking of rules but does not condemn her attractive physical features, which she did not choose. She wears a habit, after all, and was born with her nose shape, eye color, and small, soft lips. Speeding up in *GP* ll. 154–55, D5 then hesitates at "ffffair fffforheed," which he knows is no neutral description. But it is the state of her soul, not her face, for which she should be blamed.

Does content alone cause the audible shift in attitude of D5's narrator after *GP* l. 150? Perhaps not. No matter how offensive a narrator finds the Prioress's claim to conscience and a tender heart, a reader is hard put to maintain dignified indignation past a line of text so cheerfully onomatopoetic as "Ful semyly hir wympul pynched was." Ordinary scansion marks, along with the relevant consonants noted below, can show some of what happens orally in D6's reading.

```
    ´   ´  ˘ ˘      ˘    ´   ˘  ´    ˘  ´
Ful semyly . . . hir wympul pynched was
    s              w    p    p       w  s
```

After a pause early in the line, most readers including D6 begin folding the sounds, slowly. The two pinched-then-exploded *p* sounds create a "tra la tra la," as might the Prioress at her dressing table. Then, D6 neatly presses the line flat, with the *s* and *w* now together but reversed. That is, meter and consonance encourage a reader to imitate the action of folding, pinching tight, and smoothing flat a pleat in one's wimple.

Seated with Eglentyne before her mirror, D6 particularly relishes her soft red lips in line 153. He thus joins the many readers who over the years have fallen prey to the charms of the Prioress—have fallen, thanks in part to the meter and consonance of *GP* l. 151. That is, the text itself here makes it easy for readers to create a lightly mocking Chaucer-the-author who imitates the nun's own thoughts (cf. Cuts C2, D2).

It is possible, however, to phrase *GP* l. 151 such that its onomatopoeia is less striking. D7, for example, pauses after "wympul" rather than earlier. D7's condemnation, which slides to mere disapproval on this line 151, then shifts to foreboding. As he lists her facial features, D7 grows louder, faster, more eager to arrive at that fair broad forehead that will seal her self-induced doom. His stretched "ffffair," unlike D5's hesitant one, draws particular attention to the forehead's inappropriateness. D7's line 156, despite stress on "nat" and phrasing that resembles that of D5 and of other tolerant narrators not heard here, directly accuses the Prioress of being something much worse than undergrown (cf. Cut B). An intolerant Chaucer-the-author has again spoken, legitimately, from the text.

In sum, at a few points one can spot the potential for flexibility in performance. Although future studies may come to show otherwise, I would say that although we can predict that potential, we cannot predict what meanings readers will project. A line that contains a personal pronoun and a negative particle, like *GP* l. 156, may well allow varying meanings in performance; we cannot anticipate what they will be. A line with potentially onomatopoetic meter and consonance, like *GP* l. 151, may likewise allow varying, but unpredictable, meanings in performance.

Some passages of Chaucer's text allow intricate performances in which a narrator's attitude shifts in every line. Many readers convey such rapid-fire emotional changes for the Wife of Bath, especially during *WBP* ll. 453–80 about her lost youth. For *GP* ll. 151–56, the possibility is demonstrated by D8, the only reader-aloud on the tape who is not a Chaucer professor.

D8 so far has remained untroubled by the Prioress's table manners and pets, conveying only a twinge of conscience with a pause before "tendre herte" in *GP* l. 150. During lines 151–56, the quick shifts in emotion can be described partly—but only partly—in terms of stress, pitch, tempo, and other scientifically verifiable features.

Unlike the case of *GP* l. 151, at which point a number of readers shift tone, no textual characteristics such as meter or rhyme seem to motivate the many audible shifts in lines 152–56. And no reader other than D8 shifts moods quite so abruptly and articulately in this passage. Thus, Chaucer's text allows but does not require D8's complex characterization.

D8 sounds quite cheery throughout lines 151–52 but slows down while phrasing "Hir mouth ful . . . smal, and . . . therto . . . softe and . . . reed" with frequent rising pitches that signal questioning. During this line the narrator is becoming increasingly aware that these are really not the sort of terms with which one should praise a Prioress. With a deep breath and renewed briskness D8 returns to the description, only to arrive (with a pause) smack up against the fairness of that forehead. Hastening with a stutter to say something about it free of sexual innuendo, D8 realizes during an intake of breath after line 155 that it is nothing to get so upset about after all. The chuckle during "undergrowe" is directed not at the Prioress, as was B1's, but rather at the pilgrim-narrator's own momentary fluster.

Cut D, GP ll. 146–56
ll. 146–50

D1: Chaucer-the-author as stern, moralizing teacher.
  l. 147—onomatopoetically contrasting foods, with rolled *r*; pause after "flessh."
  ll. 148–49—faster tempo as brisk list of additional faults.
  l. 150—slower, disapproving "And *al* . . . was conscience . . . and tendre herte."
D2: Chaucer-the-author as genial, teasing teacher.
  l. 147—onomatopoetically contrasting foods; pause after "flessh."
  ll. 148–49—faster tempo as amused narrator's imitation of nun's eagerness to tell of canine suffering; stretched "sooore."
  l. 150—slower tempo; narrator imitating nun's opinion of her own pity: "And aaal . . . was conscience . . . and tendre herte."
D3: Chaucer-the-pilgrim conveying Eglentyne's feelings.
  l. 147—petfood selection is owner's business, no one else's.
  ll. 148–49—sympathetic indignation.
  l. 150—of course "conscience" applies to hurt dogs.
D4: Chaucer-the-man indifferent to dogs.
  l. 147—petfood selection not my business.
  l. 148—momentary sympathy, with stretched "sooore."
  l. 149—hesitation, then shrug, at dog beating.
  l. 150—"And al was . . . something else" (cf. B3).

ll. 146–56

D5: Chaucer-the-man actively disliking dogs.
  l. 146—vocal frown at "houndes."
  ll. 148–49—yapping mutts get what they deserve.
  l. 150—entire line means the opposite, as Augustinian irony.

    ll. 151–55—don't blame her for physical appearance; "ffffair
        fffforheed" as hesitation to mention it (cf. D7).
    l.   156—stress on "nat" helps create tolerant narrator (cf.
        D7).

ll. 151–56

D6:   l.   151—onomatopoeia induced by meter and consonance pat-
         terns in the text.
      ll. 152–56—relish for charming appearance, especially on
         "softe and reed" in line 153.
D7:   l.   151—phrasing "Ful semyly hir wympul . . . pynched was"
         interrupts onomatopoetic pleating effect.
      ll. 152–55—increasing indignation conveyed as increasing
         tempo and volume; "ffffair" as condemnation (cf. D5).
      l.   156—stress on "nat" helps create accusatory narrator
         (cf. D5).
D8: line-by-line mood shifts as described.

The analysis so far shows the remarkable range of attitudes and emotions conveyed by the human voice, distinctions as fine as that between
chuckling at the Prioress (B1) and chuckling, in the exact same spot, at
oneself (D8). Our inner voices must convey ranges even wider, nuances
even subtler. Our task as scholars is to describe our inner voices, and
justify them, as precisely as possible—not to demand that all other Chaucerians hear the same ones.

Our task as teachers, however, is in part to justify the limits we set on
interpretation. We can of course step outside the text in order to provide
information that the Latin "amor" has senses as wide-ranging as English
"love," and that fourteenth-century nuns were supposed to keep their
foreheads covered. But such information is just as apt to amplify textual
ambiguity as to resolve it.

Furthermore, as students ourselves we were told to seek ambiguity,
irony, and satire in Chaucer's text. To what extent are we passing on
issues unquestioningly, without wondering what new ones ought to be
raised and which old ones are still worth cultivating?

In the previous chapter I demonstrated that interpreters before the
twentieth century found ambiguity in *GP* ll. 118–62. In Cut D I have
demonstrated that *GP* l. 151 itself can easily sound lightly satiric on
account of meter and consonance patterns. My continuing investigations
will likewise suggest how irony and ambiguity can be found partly in the
text itself, rather than solely in New Critics' expectations for the text.

I proceed with more caution than do many recent subjectivist critics, therefore, who reject everything New Criticism has to offer. While I reject its authoritative tone, I retain much of its vocabulary and findings, though with a different spirit and a more clearly articulated goal: that of showing students what is so great about great literature. It would be a shame to turn our backs on two millennia of literary criticism and talk only about each other, and an especial shame to ignore the thoroughly justified criterion that literary criticism ought to concern literary texts.

In adapting the New Critical vocabulary to describe performance, I do not pretend to use the terms "irony," "ambiguity," and "satire" much more precisely than have my predecessors. I do provide aural evidence that may help theorists articulate why relationships are so complex among the three principles. Satire may ridicule directly or may involve subtle ambiguities or implied ironies; textual ambiguity may allow for irony or may create effects other than irony.

Schematizing scholars rely heavily on the force of mystical numbers. William Empson splits hairs to distinguish seven types of ambiguity, for example; and a standard reference article claims to discuss two main categories of irony but promptly falls under the charm of the very powerful number three: "*Naïveté* is a special form of irony half way between verbal and dramatic." Ancient rhetoricians distinguish at least fifteen types of irony, including litotes and hyperbole and mycterism ("the sneer") as well as sarcasm, this last being the type emphasized by St. Augustine and a type sometimes audible in oral delivery of satire.[19]

Rhetorical terms became increasingly blurred during the gradual shift to silent reading of printed paper. Perhaps modern rhetoricians, using tape recorders, will come to investigate each such rhetorical figure in terms of its origin in vocal tones. Meanwhile, however, I approximately use "irony" as the bringing to the text of unstated elements, whether mocking or not, and "satire" as some form of ridicule. "Ambiguity" I tend to use for a potential plurality of meanings in the text itself, sometimes specifically as unresolved binary oppositions like those to be discussed concerning the *Merchant's Tale*.

Cut E, GP ll. 122–23 and 137–41

In *GP* ll. 122–23, as for *GP* l. 151, potential for satire stems from textual ambiguity rooted in meter and consonance patterns. By use of phrasing to manipulate the meter of *GP* l. 151, D7 was able to avoid joining the Prioress at her morning toilette. E1 and E2, however, demonstrate that satire-inducing ambiguity lurks behind their two alternative ways of phrasing the metrically irregular line 123.

As before, scansion marks and consonance/assonance patterns can indicate how the text itself encourages a satiric reading:

Ful weel she soong the service dyvyne
            soon   s   n

Entuned in hir nose ful semely
    oon   noos   s

The very regular meter of *GP* l. 122, with its easy lilt at the end and its orderly repetition of consonants *s* and *n,* compels one to sing the line onomatopoetically. But a reader is hard put to render *GP* l. 123 at all smoothly. Some readers including E1 stress "ful," creating three strong accents in a row. Others, like E2, let implied accent fall instead into a pause after "nose."

By smoothing the meter, E2 makes *GP* l. 123 sound less irregular, in contrast to line 122, than does E1. By pausing, however, E2 draws attention to that so nasal-sounding "nose," its phonemes the reverse of the smooth "soong" before. Both readers, thus, make her entuning nose sound silly: E1 by making her stumble on the meter, after a smooth start, and E2 by staring at her nose.

Cuts E1 and E2 again demonstrate that the potential for satire may be detected in Chaucer's text itself, but only the potential. Like that old philosophers' tree that falls unheard in the forest, satire fulfills its potential only in a human mind—a mind that, by definition, has ideas of its own.

None of my close friends, for example, would ever pain herself to "countrefete cheere / Of court" or to act "estatlich of manere." Such women still exist, but I have never had much interest in making their acquaintance. My antipathy toward this aspect of the Prioress's behavior is reinforced, though, by potentially satiric features of repetition, rhyme, syntax, and meter in *GP* ll. 137–41.

Let us first hear a reading that shares none of my prejudices. The sound of a passing automobile, in the background of E3's sympathetic reading, can symbolize the modern setting in which we are all trying to understand Chaucer's people, who both resemble and differ from people we know.

Throughout *GP* ll. 137–41, E3 sounds primarily kind and respectful toward the Prioress. In lines 140–41, however, her tone edges toward exasperation. Stress on "estatlich" and "digne" implies that this is all getting to be a bit much. In this sentence the seeming praise builds up and up until it sounds silly in spite of a narrator's sympathetic attitude. The two most obvious causes are the word "and" repeated six times in five lines, four times as first word, and the internal rhymes.

One line begins with "of" instead of "and." This enjambed "cheere / Of court" completes both internal rhyme sets, hire/cheere and desport/ port/court. The enjambed phrase echoes the three "abstraction-of-noun" phrases before and after it, and less directly the phrase "of greet desport." The progressively out-of-kilter triple rhyme sounds quite silly, as if reducing desport to only one's externally apparent port might squeeze one an enjambed entry into a not-quite-rhymed court.

The Prioress's efforts to get others to take seriously her courtly port become increasingly ineffectual, for syntax reinforces repetition and rhymes. Each of the three infinitives that tell what she "peyned hire" to do becomes longer and more passive. "To countrefete" requires her conscious and perhaps ingenious actions; "to been estatlich" one need mostly hold shoulders back and chin up, and not talk much; "to ben holden digne of reverence" transfers active effort to those who behold her. Step by step, Eglentyne loses control of her infinitives.

Along with repetition, rhyme, and syntax, meter too creates a tailspin. The lines start out confident and regular until the Prioress arrives at "court." Then, as if she has tripped on the threshold, accents increasingly tumble toward the line-ending abstract phrases.

⏑ ´ ⏑ ´(⏑) ⏑ ´ ⏑´⏑ ´(⏑)
And peyned hire to countrefete cheere

⏑ ´ ⏑ ⏑ ⏑ ⏑´⏑ ⏑ ⏑ ´(⏑)
Of court, and to been estatlich of manere,

⏑ ⏑ ⏑ (´) ⏑ ´ ⏑ ⏑⏑´ ⏑
And to ben holden digne of reverence.

Four weak syllables intervene before the accented syllable in "estatlich." Discounting a technical stress barely detectable in any performance, five weak syllables precede "digne." The two final adjectives of pretentiousness demand at least stress, as in E3. Many readers here also convey oral onomatopoeia with a stately-sounding "estatlich" and a "digne" that sounds snobbish, nose held high, perhaps linked in a reader's mental concordance to Symkyn's wife "as digne as water in a dich" (*RvT* l. 3964).

Before hearing E6's oral onomatopoeia, which shifts line by line, let us consider the two alternative ways of phrasing the passage by E4 and E5. Like E1 and E2, E4 and E5 project satire through their phrasings, but in slightly different ways. Both E4 and E5 arrive at line 141 using tones of mockery directed at a silly little girl, tones similar but not identical to those with which C2 and D2 imitate the nun's own childish thoughts about herself.

While initially listening to the material in these four cuts—C2, D2, E4, E5—for each I had jotted down the same comment "awwww." In relistening to the tapes and writing this book, I have come to make finer distinctions among the narrator's amused imitation of the Prioress and the varieties of his amused condescension toward her. From experience with this and other performed literature I offer one solid item of authoritative advice. Write down everything that pops into your head as you listen. If a passage seems interesting but you cannot articulate why, rewind the tape and listen again and again. Write something, however vague. You can always refine your perceptions later, relisten and decide that compared to other readings this one is not so vicious, say, after all. Or, you may decide that your first aural perception was accurate but that, to discuss the passage for a wider audience, you will need to rearticulate initial descriptions such as (for readings of *GP* ll. 137–41 not heard here) "thinks she's the cat's pajamas" or "oh, lay off it, bitch."

Preliminary aural analysis takes a long long time—at least five hours to listen for the first time to less than an hour of tape, I find. If you write down nothing about a passage, you will never return to it.

Besides changing or adapting one's perceptions, one must analyze far more evidence than is eventually referred to. I had initially noted many performance features that have turned out to be not particularly relevant to the points I am here making about Cut E4. For example, a colon not in Robinson's text follows "sikerly" in E4's line 137. Elsewhere too, readers orally insert colons by raising the pitch and breaking off abruptly. But, unlike sarcastic quotation marks, a colon seldom seems to affect aural meaning when added to Robinson's text.

E4's non-Robinsonian phrasing does, however, affect aural understanding of *GP* l. 139. Midway through the line, E4 introduces a firm pause, perhaps an intended caesura. Doing so spotlights the midline rhyme: "And peyned hire . . . to countrefete cheere." E4 again pauses firmly where nearly all readers do, at Robinson's comma after "court." He has doubled the effect of the silly rhymes, though, by exposing the Prioress's fussy hire/cheere as fully as her forced-rhyme desport/port/court. E4's voice then drops slightly in pitch on line 141, as if confiding to someone behind her back, so as not to hurt Eglentyne's feelings, how undignified her supposed dignity really is.

E5 instead, like most readers, does not bisect *GP* l. 139. Having passed hire/cheere without particular notice, E5 comes down hard on "court," then with a pause draws attention to the inappropriateness of that locale. Overall he sounds more disapproving than E4, and not amused. Hearing the edge of sarcasm, almost meanness, that cuts into line 141, we must remind ourselves that Eglentyne really ought not to be trying to make her desport and her port rhyme with "court," really ought to grow up. E5's reading, like C9's, makes us examine our own behavior.

E5's line 138 begins not with the text's "and" but with an intake of breath, which disrupts neither sense nor meter, nor even the list's cumulative effect. As I will mention again later, such oral evidence can demonstrate how readers of manuscripts and early printed editions were able to appreciate Chaucer fully in spite of what, to W. W. Skeat and his progeny, look like unbearably corrupt texts.

E4 and E5, the final pair of readings I will compare in line-by-line detail, demonstrate what previous pairs have shown: that we can find ambiguity in Chaucer's text, can find in it the potential for flexibility in performance, but we cannot predict what will happen when a mind or voice or mental voice interacts with that text. Almost certainly, E4 did not plan in advance just how he would manipulate phrasing to make the Prioress sound childishly silly. Nor would every reader necessarily create that effect by inserting a caesura into *GP* l. 139. Having noted the effect, though, we can seek the cause partly in the text's midline rhyme and other features.

Besides readings reflecting respect or amusement or disapproval, demonstrated by E3–5, this passage also allows line-by-line shifts in mood as complex as those heard in Cut D8. Although this potential is there, again only one reader, E6, realizes it orally.

E6, differing from D8, changes moods by performing oral onomatopoeia. With his voice, E6 imitates the image in each line. D8's shifts project the narrator's changing attitude toward stances he maybe ought to be taking toward the Prioress's facial features. E6's shifts instead convey consistent light mockery on the part of a narrator who is focused on the nun's description rather than on himself.

Playfully imitating what the text says, in *GP* l. 137 E6 sounds certain, in line 138 pleasant and amiable, and in line 139 pained but then cheerful in spite of the meaning of "cheere" in this context, which the reader certainly knows. E6's line 140 sounds stately, then, and line 141 mock-dignified. The teasing term "digne" is enclosed in mildly sarcastic quotation marks: "She's childishly happy pretending dignity, so why should we spoil her illusion by telling her it's the opposite?"

If there is such a creature as "Chaucer-the-poem," which itself creates many voices, it is brought to life only by E6 among the thirty-two Chaucer scholars who made tapes for this project.[20] That is, E6's voice here does exactly what the text says. E6's is certainly a possible reading and an interesting and valid one, I would say, but it is not the only one.

Cut E, GP ll. 122–23 and 137–41
   ll. 122–23

   E1:   three accents together on "nose ful sem . . ." make line 123 sound very irregular compared to line 122.
   E2:   phrasing "Entuned in hir nose . . . ful semely" smooths the meter but draws attention to her nose.

   ll. 137–41

   E3:   respectful narrator yields to slight exasperation on "estatlich" and "digne."
   E4:   amused narrator doubles Prioress's silliness with phrasing "And peyned hire . . . to countrefete cheere," which highlights the less obvious internal rhyme set; pitch drop on line 141 keeps satire indirect. Notice also orally-created colon after "sikerly" in line 137.
   E5:   disapproving narrator calls attention to inappropriateness of "court," with stress and pause after it, then edges toward open sarcasm in line 141. Notice also intake of breath replacing "and" in line 138.
   E6:   line-by-line oral onomatopoeia might be said to create "Chaucer-the-poem," who sounds lightly amused.

In this passage, GP ll. 137–41, occur examples of most vocal effects noted so far: orally-created punctuation including sarcastic quotation marks; oral effects more clearly described in metaphorical than in objective terms; meter and other textual features that allow or even encourage, but do not demand, satire; line-by-line mood shifts; oral onomatopoeia; "Chaucer-the-x"; ambiguity on the page and flexibility in performance. This passage would therefore seem an ideal terminus for this analysis, were it not located midway through the Prioress's portrait.

I refuse to go on. Rather than fulfill readers' culture-bound expectations of linear progression from beginning to end of the passage, I will not summarize what I already said about *GP* ll. 142–62.

Linear movement forward toward a goal figures heavily in what subjectivist critics term our "horizon of expectations" regarding a text, an idea that folklorists and anthropologists discuss in concrete terms as "worldview."[21] Imposition of this evolutionary worldview, of development toward the present as goal, has caused neglect and even scorn of earlier Chaucer commentary. Each critic feels impelled to prove that this, the most recent interpretation based on the best of all possible texts, must be the best interpretation ever proposed.

It certainly helps to have a text not mangled by errors of the press, as Dryden knew perfectly well his was. Is our understanding of Chaucer superior to Dryden's or Pope's or Blake's or Kittredge's, though, just because we have technological advantages? Yet over and over scholars who deign to deal with earlier centuries have guffawed at details such as the "bows," rather than "boughs," that Dryden's knights carry in *The Flower and the Leaf,* which we in our fully evolved wisdom know to be spurious.

Most Chaucerians' idea of their predecessors comes from Caroline Spurgeon's introduction. She knew that her understanding was influenced by her own time but not precisely how; she was unaware of her rolling the centuries into a vast snowball to be used as base for the greatest interpretive snowman ever constructed. For example, she underrates the unabated seventeenth-century interest in Chaucer. With texts so terrible, she seems to assume, how *could* they have appreciated him? The scope of commentary is much more accurate in the work's magnificent index, which brings together from centuries apart opinions on such issues as Chaucer's "Indecency: Frivolity . . . . Piety . . . . Impiety . . . . Sublimity . . . . Want of sublimity . . . . Prolixity . . . . Brevity."[22]

I would certainly urge that we in this century take advantage of laboriously collated texts, and also of facsimiles, photocopying, easy travel to distant libraries, telephones, mail, computers, and of course tape recorders, in our efforts to understand how it is that someone who died in 1400 can mean so much to us and, if we try, to our students. But technological inventions do not change human nature, only its manifestations. I would certainly never claim that we are superior to our tapeless predecessors because we live in a post-deconstructionist, post-intentionalist, post-textual, post-modern world. What I suggest is just what DeQuincey urged in 1841, as quoted more briefly above:

> Some ninety or one hundred words that are now obsolete, certainly not many more, vein the whole surface of Chaucer; and

thus a *primâ facie* impression is conveyed that Chaucer is difficult to understand: whereas a very slight practice familiarises his language. . . . And observe—*had Chaucer's Tales enjoyed the benefit of an oral recitation,* were they assisted to the understanding by the pauses in one place, the hurrying and crowding of unimportant words at another, and by the proper distribution of emphasis everywhere . . . there is no man, however unfamiliar with old English, but might be made to go along with the movement of his admirable tales, though he might still remain at a loss for the meaning of insulated words. . . .

Review [orig. Revise] those parts of Chaucer which at this day are most obscure, and it will uniformly be found that they are the *subjective* sections of his poetry; those, for instance, in which he is elaborately decomposing a character. A character is a subtle fugacious essence which does, or does not, exist according to the capacity of the eye which is applied to it. . . .

Chaucer also, whom Dryden in this point so thoroughly misunderstood, was undoubtedly a most elaborate master of metre, as will appear when we have a *really* good edition of him.[23]

CHAPTER 3

The Pardoner on Paper, After and Before the Eighteenth Century

Using a better edition, a century later than Thomas DeQuincey, Garnett Gladwin Sedgewick employs linear evolution to present his own "mostly 'subjective interpretation' of the Pardoner and his behaviour"[1] as the end point of "The Progress of Chaucer's Pardoner, 1880–1940." In his oft-reprinted article Sedgewick describes how he, as opposed to George Lyman Kittredge and Walter Clyde Curry, would perform key passages, especially *PardT* ll. 916–18, the transition from addressing an imaginary audience to addressing the pilgrims. (See *Texts Read Aloud,* Chapter 5.) For a hushed pause of "a second or two" after *PardT* l. 918, he even admits there is "no basis . . . in the text except that a shift is plainly indicated there" and except "frankly . . . my own experience in reading the poem."[2]

Sedgewick does not specify that the plain indication of a shift consists of a paragraph indentation first made by Thomas Tyrwhitt in 1775, one that was eliminated immediately by modernizer William Lipscomb and later by editor Thomas Wright, but was reinstated by W. W. Skeat and by editors thereafter. Neither does Sedgewick specify that his experience in reading the poem is in large part pedagogical.

Clearly Sedgewick, Curry, and Kittredge read the passage differently to their classes and have influenced students and grandstudents to do the same. Kittredge and Sedgewick would each read a genuinely sincere benediction. Kittredge would follow this with an out-of-control, wildly jesting sales pitch in what Sedgewick calls Kittredge's "doctrine of benedictory paroxysm." Sedgewick, instead, would follow it with an "impudently ironic joke," the Pardoner in control of his emotions and tempted to "get some fun out of their embarrassment."[3]

Thus arose the sincerity issue. In the less chummy postwar world, critics became testy in their efforts to describe and to prove the exclusive validity of a precise shade of genuine or pretended sincerity in the voice that evokes Christ's pardon.

Several recent commentators still understand at *PardT* ll. 916–18 "momentary sincerity (we cannot mistake it)" or a moment of "pure and untainted" good or a "wistful" tone.[4] Others argue for a tone of fake sincerity, in which the Pardoner parodies himself "by grotesquely exaggerating [both] his rascality . . . . [and] his decency," or in which "this traditional, expected, devout, and apparently sincere wish" is followed by the last half-line "as a last clinching blow in his preparation for the attempted sale."[5] Likewise hearing "an imitation of sincerity, a covert appeal for social acceptance by claiming the pilgrims as fellow members of an in-group who know what pardons are really worth," Malcolm Pittock would stress the second-person pronoun in *PardT* l. 918, as did Curry: "I wol *yow* nat deceyve." By stressing the first-person pronoun instead, one hears Charles Mitchell's Pardoner, who is proving himself morally superior. "*I* wol yow nat deceyve," he says to Mitchell, "for those who buy his pardon must first deceive themselves into believing that it is genuine."[6]

Without evoking his own training in radio drama, Donald Howard points out that whether the Pardoner's "utterance is sincere or part of his game" would be determined by a subtle tonal distinction, and that following *PardT* l. 918 "the hiatus is in us, not in the scene: the Pardoner could speak that second line so hard upon the first as to swallow up 'deceive.'" Howard would disallow, however, a "formulaic or perfunctory" performance of the benediction.[7] In this, Howard's Pardoner differs from Eric Stockton's, who forgets "he is not really preaching but telling a story" and so proceeds through "his usual closing formula." He differs from Ralph Elliott's Pardoner, who gives a perhaps spurious "ring of sincerity" to one of "the many conventional medieval formulas . . . often uttered without much thought for their content or relevance," and differs from Paul Beichner's, whose sincere-sounding "minstrel prayer for the audience" ends this "exposition of his fund raising technique."[8]

Alone among commentators on the benediction, Felicity Currie argues for no change in vocal tone after *PardT* l. 918, because the Pardoner has been insulting the pilgrims all along. But Currie also makes the startling claim that the Pardoner "has elicited identical reactions from his fellow-pilgrims and from decades of critics."[9]

Fortunately, as happened somewhat earlier in the case of the Prioress's portrait, critics at last have begun retreating from Sedgewickian proofs—

"I'm right; therefore, you're wrong"—toward an implicit recognition that Chaucer's text is worth studying for those very qualities that can elicit such varying responses from equally prepared readers. At least in the classroom one can feel responsible to the text by asking, as if naively, "How could the Pardoner start trying to sell relics to pilgrims who already know they're false?" With only slight prodding, students spontaneously re-create major critical positions: he's carried away by his own eloquence and forgets; he's such a sleazy used-car-salesman type that he thinks he has them fooled; he's just joking; he's drunk. In my classes the faction who, unbeknownst to them, share G. H. Gerould's belief that the Pardoner "is in the talkative stage of intoxication" tend to be the most vociferous in presenting textual evidence.[10]

Among publishing critics nowadays, skirmishes break out over interpretations of the Merchant more than they do over the Pardoner. And the Wife of Bath still regularly makes hackles rise. A recent introduction for British secondary-school students, for example, uses the phrase "coarseness and vulgarity" three times in the two pages discussing just her *General Prologue* portrait.[11] But about the Pardoner, critics have almost agreed to disagree.

They have agreed perhaps over-hastily, however, that the narrator's "I trowe he were a geldyng or a mare" (*GP* l. 691) means that the Pardoner was a *eunuchus ex nativitate,* a homosexual, or perhaps a hermaphrodite.[12] From this point of assent critics take divergent paths. The Pardoner arouses our sympathies with his "actual physical innocence," for we know "that the Pardoner's alienation and bitterness are partly caused by a congenital sexual deficiency." Or else we confront the "definitely evil . . . . false eunuch who stands and points the way of cupidity, malice, impenitence, spiritual sterility."[13] In short, twentieth-century critics accept the truth of the Pardoner's boast in *PardT* l. 452, "Nay, I wol drynke licour of the vyne." They reject, however, the following line as a sinister or pathetic attempt to claim sexual normalcy: "And have a joly wenche in every toun."

Modern readers thus keep the wench standing in the shadows, shunted aside almost as completely as she was for "those ornaments of this civilized age, and patterns to the civilized world, the ingenuous, intelligent, well informed, and artless young women of England" who in 1835 found lines of asterisks in lieu of both the jolly wench and the gelding/mare. In 1841 the inept modernizer Richard Horne inserted nearly as titillating a line, by a narrator so ingenuous he does not know where one looks to figure out which one: "He fitly rode a gelding or a mare."[14]

At a recent MLA session on "The Sexuality of Chaucer's Pardoner,"

panelists neglected both the wench and the Pardoner's incipient wedding
(*WBP* ll. 164–68) in order to question extensively whether "mare" was
ever slang for "homosexual male." Also given short shrift was the only
clear evidence we have for a near-contemporary understanding of Chaucer's Pardoner, evidence that shows him thoroughly heterosexual, pur-
suing a wench, quite undaunted by second-century Latin medical
treatises or millennium-old slurs on spiritual eunuchry.[15]

About half a century after Chaucer's death, in what became Northumberland ms. 455, occurs an untitled work first published in John Urry's
1721 edition as *The Prologue* [to the *Tale of Beryn*], *Or, the mery adventure of the Pardonere and Tapstere at the Inn at Canterbury.* Set during
the pilgrims' day and night at Cheker of the Hope Inn, before they resume
tale telling en route home, the 732-line interlude recounts the amorous
attempts of a Pardoner who much resembles Absolon of the *Miller's Tale,*
yearning ineffectually for the tapster who tricks him with another man.

I do not imply that the *Prologue* to the *Tale of Beryn* (hereafter *PTB*)
closes the case on the Pardoner's sexuality. Something is strange indeed
in his *General Prologue* portrait. The *PTB* author has made certain
choices among all the possibilities in Chaucer's text in order to create a
dupable character for his own imaginative work. A century later, John
Heywood likewise creates his own works in which comic Pardoners compete with other men to sell sham relics and insult women. Through the
eighteenth century, past Pope/Betterton's modernized *General Prologue*
and other works in which sexuality is not at issue, the Pardoner remains
in various ways a comic character. Thomas Stothard's 1807 painting still
shows "a ludicrous species of effeminacy" who is "fashioned to provoke
risibility."[16] Enter Blake.

The progress of Chaucer's Pardoner, if truth be told, follows a road
lined with laughter for four full centuries. Then Blake arose in the path
scowling, declaring the Pardoner a scourge and a blight. Without pausing
to look at the painting or read carefully the *Descriptive Catalogue,* commentators wheeled on their heels. For nearly two centuries now they have
been retracing the road in the dark, frowning with disapproval, proving
the Pardoner wicked. "A humbug, living on the credulity of the people,"
says Charles Dickens. "The one lost soul among the Canterbury Pilgrims," says Kittredge.[17] To Blake, however, truly lost souls were precisely those unaware that

> Without Contraries is no progression. Attraction and Repulsion,
> Reason and Energy, Love and Hate, are necessary to Human
> existence.

> From these contraries spring what the religious call Good &
> Evil. Good is the passive that obeys Reason. Evil is the active
> springing from Energy. . . .
> Energy is the only life, and is from the Body; and Reason is
> the bound or outward circumference of Energy. . . .
> Energy is Eternal Delight.
> Those who restrain desire, do so because theirs is weak enough
> to be restrained.[18]

Blake's misunderstood moral stance is not solely responsible for two centuries of stern disapproval, of course. I will show that he interpreted the Urry-edition Pardoner as evil. Besides, the time has lately been ripe for stern disapproval, albeit on ordinary, non-Blakean moral grounds. The time had been ripe before, in the seventeenth century. But then, instead of labeling this complex character wholly evil, sober Protestants simply extracted bits from the Pardoner's sermon on gambling and gluttony, and included them in commonplace books printed for the middle classes during a "Vogue of Chaucer as a Moral Teacher."[19]

No such vogue troubled the Canterbury monk who wrote the *Prologue* to the *Tale of Beryn*.[20] Whole-heartedly borrowing Chaucer's racier lines, scenes, and images, he has the Pardoner sigh to the tapster Kitt, for example, "Allas! that love ys syn" (*PTB* l. 48; *WBP* l. 614). He tones down other images slightly. When they first meet, the Pardoner grabs Kitt by her "myddill," not her "queynte"; and after he says "sith yee be my prisoner, yeld yewe now," we need not stand there like Pandarus and watch (*PTB* ll. 25, 317; *MlrT* l. 3276; *Tr* 3.1207–8).

Like so many readers through the centuries, too, this *PTB* author is inspired by Chaucer's puns to create his own. In the scene most evocative of the *Miller's Tale*, for example, the *PTB* Pardoner approaches Kitt's bedroom "as glad as eny goldfynch . . . [suspecting] no gyle," since he has paid in advance for her favors. Within, Kitt whispers to her paramour, "dischauce yewe nat til this chek be do." F. J. Furnivall translates "don't take off your lower garments"; the *Middle English Dictionary* confirms that the verb occurs only here.[21] Its pun neatly combines Chaucer's ancestral name and his most memorable scene.

In addition, Kitt refers to the tricking of the Pardoner as a "chek." Modern tourist maps still mark the location of Canterbury's best-known hostelry, the Cheker of the Hope, even though the last in a long series of inns by that name burnt down over a century ago along with its signboard, which displayed a checkerboard in a hoop. But both "cheker" and "hope" had further fifteenth-century connotations such that the inn's

name also advertises this story in which a "chek" indeed checks the
Pardoner's hopes (*MED*, s.vv. "chek," "chekker," "chekken," "hop,"
"hope").

Without noting these puns and other textural features, E. J. Bashe has
shown that the *PTB* author knows Chaucer thoroughly, for he makes
90–95 percent of his characters' actions and words fully appropriate to
the pilgrims as Chaucer characterizes them.[22] The *PTB* protagonist particularly exemplifies this technique of development rather than alteration
of character. Of the details about the Pardoner that appear in his *General
Prologue* portrait, his interruption of the Wife, and the *Pardoner's Prologue* and *Tale*, the *PTB* author chooses and develops several traits besides the "joly wenche in every toun." The *PTB* Pardoner associates with
other lower-class pilgrims, sings a great deal, loses his temper too easily,
has sober second thoughts about trusting women, and takes part in petty
thievery—stealing successfully from street peddlers but unsuccessfully
from Kitt. Even his hood figures in the story, the hood that en route to
Canterbury "for jolitee . . . was trussed up in his walet" (*GP* ll. 680–81).
As the pilgrims prepare to ride for home, on the morning after the slapstick battle, the Pardoner hides his facial wounds

> with the typet of his hood,
> And made lightsom cher, for men shuld nat spy
> No thing of his turment, ne of his luxury [i.e., lust].
> (PTB ll. 662–64)

He rides out of the gates "a-mydward the route," singing as usual. Only
a pilgrim with perfect pitch could have detected that "his notis wer som-
what lowe, for akyng of his hede" (*PTB* ll. 670, 672).

No direct mention appears in *PTB* of the Pardoner's head of fair hair,
shoulder-length or longer, streaming flaxen waxen in the *General Prologue* and rivaled only by Absolon's in the *Miller's Tale*. Nor do his rab-
bity, glaring eyes appear, except to peer longingly at Kitt from beneath

> both eyen liddes,
> And lokid hir in the visage paramour a-myddis;
> And sighid there-with a litil tyme, that she it here myghte,
> And gan to trown & feyn [i.e., croon and say] this song, "now,
>   love, thou do me righte!"
> (PTB ll. 67–70)

The Pardoner sings to Kitt, not to the Summoner, with whom he twice
interacts with no hint of homosexuality. Leaving the cathedral, the Miller

and Pardoner steal some Canterbury brooches. No one notices except the
Summoner, who

> seyd to ham "list!
> Halff part!" quod he, pryvely rownyng on hir ere:
> "Hussht! pees!" quod the Miller, "seist thowe nat the frere,
> Howe he lowrith undir his hood with a doggissh ey?
> Hit shuld be a pryvy thing that he coude nat a-spy."
> <div align="right">(<i>PTB</i> ll. 178–82)</div>

Successfully distracted, the Summoner raves of the even worse tale he
will tell about the Friar on their way home (as indeed he does, *SumT* ll.
2162–2294). Perhaps they split the take nonetheless, for the Summoner
readily joins the Pardoner to serenade Kitt:

> And when the Pardoner hem aspied, a-noon he gan to syng,
> "Doubil me this bourdon," chokelyng in his throte,
> ffor the tapster shuld here of his mery note.
> He clepid to hym the Sompnoure that was his own discipill,
> The yeman, & the Reve, & the Mauncipill;
> And stoden so holowing; for no thing wold they leve,
> Tyl the tyme that it was wel within eve.
> <div align="right">(<i>PTB</i> ll. 412–18)</div>

So, sometimes a bourdon is just a bourdon. Fond as he is of puns, the
PTB author here ignores possibilities projected by Thomas Ross concerning the two songsters in *GP* ll. 672–73:

> Ful loude he soong "Com hider, love, to me!"
> This Somonour bar to hym a stif bourdoun;
> ....

The musical meaning of the word is certainly here in this passage,
but Baum thinks (and I agree) that there is yet a third (and maybe
a fourth) very obscene sense. A "bourdoun" was a stick, a staff:
a stiff bourdoun between these two possibly homosexual person-
ages has an unmistakably libidinous sense. Finally, the word also
meant a mule, a hinny (recall the Pardoner's sexual shortcomings).[23]

The sexual shortcomings of the *PTB* Pardoner are, however, all directed
at Kitt. They include his staff, never termed a "bourdon," for he first

meets this town's jolly wench when he "toke his staff to the Tapstere" (*PTB* l. 22).

Despite tangled syntax in *PTB* ll. 19–20, the opening scene is surely one of thirty or so sundry folk famished for breakfast, having ridden since sunup, and the Canterbury innkeeper "so halowid from o plase to a-nothir" that the pilgrims get unequal treatment, which the Pardoner attributes to class privilege. By suppertime such problems will fade: the Knight makes sure all get served the same food at the same price, while the wealthier treat for wine. At breakfast, however, only the Pardoner is so irritated at poor service to lower estates that he stalks off to the tap-room with his staff, hungry for food but finding instead Kitt, "al redy for to kys," who promptly shows him the bed where she now lies alone

> al nyght al nakid
> Without mannys company, syn my love was dede:
> Ienkyn Harpour ∔ yf ye hym know,

Jenkyn so lusty from head to admirable feet (*PTB* ll. 23–30; *WBP* l. 598). With copious sobs she collapses. Comforting her, the Pardoner wishes he could love her as well as she did the dear departed. He wonders further whether he will still be smarting "this month hereaftir, for yeur soden disese," with a pun not available now to would-be amorous adventurers concerned about herpes (*PTB* l. 51; *MED*, s.v. "disese").

Leading him by the nose throughout, Kitt keeps him supposing he is making the moves. "Ienken . . . . Is that yeur ∔ name, I yow prey?" she offers an alias (*PTB* ll. 62–63). Like the Wife of Bath she tells a dream. In hers "the Preest & the clerk . . . put me out of the chirch," for which the Pardoner has a cocksure interpretation: "Now, seynt Danyel . . . . comynly of these swevenys the contrary men shul fynde" (*PTB* ll. 104–8). The dream means she will find a new lover, he concludes, but like Chaunticleer he fails to follow up the implications: the lover could be somebody else.

After dinner the Pardoner returns. He had tossed Kitt a coin, saying "ye list be my tresorer; for we shull offter mete" (*PTB* l. 98), and now he wants

> To make his covenaunte in certen, that same eve
> He wold be loggid with hir; that was his hole entencioun.
> (*PTB* ll. 300–301)

Whole/hole creates not a "perfect pun," in which each homophonic word functions fully in its context, but rather a "bad pun" in which the suggested word differs in spelling, pronunciation, or grammatical part of speech from the word in context. Bad puns are far commoner than perfect ones, throughout the history of English and other languages. ("All peoples pun."[24]) Loose spelling conventions in the fifteenth century allow this to be a closer pun than it would be now, although the term evoking Kitt's orifice remains a noun not an adjective (*MED*, s.v. "hole").

Larry Benson analyzes *MlrT* l. 3276 wherein "queynte" becomes an adjective used as a noun to mean "precious little thing" and so functions as a pun on "cunt."[25] The *PTB* author, in another bad pun, likewise uses the adjective "queynt" to evoke the noun. Kitt uses an apparent compliment for the Pardoner's wit to deny him access, in her neat evasion of his direct query as to "who shall ligge here / This nyghte":

> "Iwis it is grete nede to telle yew," quod she:
> "Make it nat ovir queynt, thoughe yee be a clerk!
> Ye know wele I-nough I-wis, by loke, by word, by work!"
> "Shal I com then, Cristian, & fese a-wey the Cat?"
> "Shul yee com, sir? benedicite! what question is that?"
> (*PTB* ll. 346–52; *MlrT* ll. 3275–76; *SumT* l. 1775)

Chaucer's "queynte" pun, though not nearly so lonely as Benson implies, is certainly his best known through the centuries. Although the noun first appears in a glossary in 1778 (where Tyrwhitt just says "See *Junii Etymolog.* in v"), earlier readers notice the pun with gusto. In *The Shepherd's Week*, footnoting "I queintly stole a Kiss [from Buxoma]," John Gay unconvincingly claims he means it only as in *MlrT* l. 3275, "*Arch* or *Waggish* . . . not in that obscene Sense wherein . . . [Chaucer] useth it in the Line immediately following." And a half century before Gay, in 1661, one J. T. likewise footnotes the word in dedicating *The Horn exalted, or Roome for Cuckolds:*

> Read, and beware how that ye firk,
> Least the repentance stool o' th' Kirk,
> Prove the reward of your queint* wirk.   *Chaucer[26]

Two centuries after *PTB*, that is, J. T. still ignores grammatical part of speech in order to pun, as Kitt does, on queynt clerks; an English-speaking audience then would laugh at Shakespeare's *Henry V*, act 3, scene 3, wherein the French princess is shocked to learn the English word for "la robe": "de coun." As Kitt further tricks the Pardoner, "con" works as just such a bilingual bad pun. The English verb evokes the

French noun and also echoes the Wife of Bath's slurs on clerks' book-learning:

> "I-wis I trowe, Ienkyn, ye be nat to trust to!
> ffor evir-more yee clerkis con so much in book,
> Yee woll wyn a womman, atte first look."
>   Thought the Pardoner, "this goith wele"; & made hir better chere.
>   (PTB ll. 342–45; WBP ll. 706–10)

In other places too we learn from the Pardoner's own thoughts that he really is as dopey as he acts. Kitt hugs him goodbye with the skill of one who has learned from an old friar how to curry a horse or curry favor (PTB l. 362; MED, s.v. "fauvel"). Nonetheless the Pardoner walks away thinking

>   many a mery thought by hym self a-loon:
> "I am I-loggit," thought he, "best, howe-so-evir it gone!
> And thoughe it have costid me, yit wol I do my peyn
> ffor to pike hir purs to nyghte, & wyn my cost ageyn."
>   (PTB ll. 373–76)

It is not until he actually hears the voice of Kitt's paramour that he thinks, "A! . . . I trow my berd be made! / The tapster hath a paramour" with whom she has probably already eaten "the Cawdell that I ordeyned for me" (PTB ll. 485–87). During the battle his thoughts are practical—"A! ha ha! . . . beth there pannys a-ryn?" as he gropes for a helmet (PTB l. 569). Afterward the narrator reports the Pardoner's rumination that he has had "strokis ryghte I-nowghe; / Witnes on his armys, his bak, & his browe" (PTB ll. 597–98). And at last the Pardoner painfully deduces a lesson:

>   remembryng his foly,
> That he [never again] wold trust a tapster of a comon hostry:
> ffor comynly for the most part they been wyly echon.
>   (PTB ll. 653–55)

Chaucer sometimes tells his characters' inner thoughts, notably Criseyde's. Sometimes he refrains from doing so: "God woot what that May thoughte in hir herte" about January in bed (MctT l. 1851). At one oft-noted point he makes Absolon's inner thoughts audible: "'A berd! a berd!' quod hende Nicholas" (*MlrT* l. 3742). With its more straight-forward report of inner thoughts, the *PTB* author's characterization provides valuable evidence as to what passes through the medieval mind of a chump.

In other techniques besides puns and character development, the *PTB* author likewise emulates his model. Chaucer employs characterized narrators, predictable folktale plots, and proverbial language. The *PTB* narrator steps forward several times to assure his audience that the beguiler will be beguiled, the same as in the *Reeve's Tale* and ever so many other stories (*RvT* l. 4321; *PTB* ll. 119–29, 302–8, 394–98, 433–46; to this last compare also *Tr* 5.1772–78 and other expressions of that narrator's attitude toward Criseyde's shortcomings). In addition, from the Pardoner's first appearance we can predict that the character flaw of a quick temper, not just the wiles of a woman, will make his beard—the proverbial phrase in *PTB* ll. 436, 485, and 622 echoing *GP* l. 689 and *NPT* l. 2920.

The *PTB* author has also learned from Chaucer to use images that foreshadow his climactic scenes. For example, Chaucer works an elaborate pattern of holes and smells into the *Miller's Tale*. Similarly, the *PTB* author makes sure to introduce early his Pardoner's fiery temper, mawkishly doglike behavior, and non Chaucerian staff.

In the *Reeve's Tale* Chaucer mentions no staff until the miller's wife finds one (*RvT* ll. 4295–96, echoed in *PTB* ll. 555–56) and baps her husband's glinting skull. Preparing for his own slapstick-in-the-dark, the *PTB* author has his angry, hungry Pardoner first meet Kitt with his staff and then accidentally leave it behind in her room while his amorous expectations grow. There, later, Kitt and her paramour and the Canterbury innkeeper ("a shrewid company") discuss it as they devour what the Pardoner has sent up for a romantic late supper:

> [Kitt:] "yf he com & make noyse, I prey yew dub hym knyght."
> "Yis, dame," quod hir Paramour, "be thow nat a-gast!
> This is his owne staff, thou seyist; thereof he shal a-tast!"
> (*PTB* ll. 464, 456–58)

The three are giggly, though, not villainous; the Pardoner brings the beating on himself. Though as persistent at seeking vengeance as is Absolon, he does not succeed. Foreshadowing the night's outcome, for he will huddle until dawn just out of reach of a snarling "grete Walssh dogg," the Pardoner invents a signal when he finds Kitt's door locked:

> [He] scrapid the dorr welplich, & wynyd with his mowith,
> ....
> "Away, dogg, with evil deth!" quod he, that was within.
>   (*PTB* ll. 633, 481, 483)

Realizing as promptly as Absolon what the score is, the Pardoner's hot love cools just as quickly. (And after the battle, he is "in grete dispeyr; / ffor aftir his hete he caughte a cold, thurh the nyghtis eyr" [*PTB* ll. 629–30].) His psychological burning "ffor pure verry angir, & for gelousy" is developed in far more detail than Absolon's (*PTB* l. 500; *WBP* l. 488; *MlrT* ll. 3754–59). The *PTB* Pardoner takes no action, though. He scratches again on the door only to get a better idea of his adversary's size:

> So feyn he wold have herd more of hym that was with-in.
> "What dogg is that?" quod the Paramour; "Kit! wost thou ere?"
> "Have God my trowith," quod she, "it is the Pardonere."
>   (*PTB* ll. 508–10)

The Pardoner reviles Kitt with a string of names that the narrator refrains from repeating. Then his temper flares:

> He axid his staff spitouslich with wordis sharp & rowc.
> "Go to bed," quod he within, "no more noyse thow make!
> Thy staff shall be redy to morow, I undirtake."
> "In soth," quod he, "I woll nat fro the dorr wend
> Tyll I have my staff, thow bribour!" "Then have the todir end!"
> Quod he that was with-in; & leyd it on his bak,
> Righte in the same plase, as Chapmen berith hir pak.
>   (*PTB* ll. 520–26)

The same trait that leaves Chaucer's Pardoner tongue-tied before the Host (*PardT* l. 957) makes the *PTB* Pardoner foolishly insist on immediate repossession of his gratuitous staff. Why is there a staff at all? No Pardoner before or after him carries a staff. In his Ellesmere portrait, and four centuries later in Blake's, he carries his "croys of latoun ful of stones" (*GP* l. 699). In the fifteenth-century Cambridge ms. Gg.4.27 the Pardoner carries the "sholder-boon . . . that was of an hooly Jewes sheep" (*PardT* ll. 350–51), which he would clutch still in a mid-seventeenth-century letter, if the writer had not confused the Pardoner with the Friar. Converted in 1641 to an antipapal "Scots Pedler," he carries a sack full of such items as "Romish Gloves perfum'd" and "the scull of a damn'd Jesuite."[27] And he is certainly a young man, needing no staff emblematic of old age, as it is for the old man in his *Tale* (*WBP* l. 187; *PardT* l. 730). Why a staff?

In reference to the pear-tree scene of the *Merchant's Tale*, I will suggest the extent to which "Freudian" (in its popular sense) overtones may be conveyed or disregarded in performance. In several readings-aloud, May's vocal inflections make clear that the "peres" dangling overhead are those connected to Damyan's body (*MctT* ll. 2331–33). Less subtly than his model would have done, the *PTB* author keeps the Pardoner's non-Chaucerian staff present in scenes of potential and frustrated sexuality. His carefulness in doing so indicates artistic intention to use this attribute as a phallic symbol.

Wielding this concrete symbol of the Pardoner's thwarted heterosexuality, the paramour lands a second blow "oppon his browe" (*PTB* l. 530). The inkeeper wakes and demands to know what is going on, although they "knew hem both wele" (*PTB* l. 535). And the chase is on for a supposed thief through the pitch-dark passageways of Cheker of the Hope. It is the *Reeve's Tale* finale writ large, full of detail as to where fifteenth-century innkeepers stored pans and water cans and kitchen keys and large vicious dogges. The collaborators call a halt when they start getting hurt, then whisper loudly that they will lock the gates and catch the thief in the morning. In addition to all his bruises and the cold he has caught, the Pardoner's cheeks run with blood; the innkeeper has gashed his shin by tripping over the Pardoner's just-fallen pan-helmet; the paramour's eyes will water for a week because the Pardoner did land one ladle blow "on the grustill on the nose." Only "she that cause was of al," like Alison, escapes unscathed (*PTB* ll. 577, 580; *MlrT* ll. 3850–53).

As we perhaps pity Absolon or carpenter John or January, so also we might pity the Pardoner as he slinks at last toward his bed—praying to St. Julian that the devil take them "so to disseyve a traveling man of his herbegage"—only to be forced to spend the rest of what was "trewly for the Pardonere . . . a dismol day" hunkered out of reach "in the doggis littir," wishing over and over for a bit of bread "the dogge for to plese" (*PTB* ll. 625–50). But despite such possibilities for sympathy he is clearly a buffoon, one whose temper may cause his silver tongue to fail him entirely, as it did Chaucer's Pardoner, or to burst out with just the wrong demand.

Had Elizabeth Cooper not been so conscientious a scholar as to reject John Urry's 1721 edition in favor of Thomas Speght's older but reliable ones, and had she read Urry's beyond page 594, where the questionable provenance of *Tale of Beryn* is noted, perhaps Cooper would not have passed on the fifteenth century the harsh judgment we still live with:

> Poetry . . . had like to have been bury'd in . . . [Chaucer's] Grave;
> For War, and Faction, immediately after restor'd Ignorance, and
> Dulness almost to their antient Authority. Writers there were;
> but Tast, Judgment, and Manner were lost.[28]

Say what you will of the last three elements, one fifteenth-century writer cannot be accused of Dulness, nor of Ignorance concerning Chaucer's works.

By the sixteenth century, still two centuries short of this first direct commentary on the Pardoner as a literary creation, by Cooper, writers were becoming more lively—or more accurately, people with livelier things to say were gaining access to writing materials.[29] One of them, John Donne's grandfather John Heywood, wrote scripts for court interludes while a musician for Henry VIII. A friend of Sir Thomas More and resembling him in "his combination of steadfast orthodoxy with exuberant gaiety and zeal for reform,"[30] Heywood adapts Chaucer's text in order to exaggerate into absurdity some abuses of the true Church at Rome.

In *A mery Play betwene the Pardoner and the frere, the curate and neybour Pratt* (1533), Heywood gives portions of the *Pardoner's Prologue* to his character, who competes for offerings with a friar whose fund-raising techniques echo the *Summoner's Tale*. The Friar first enters to advise the audience of their financial responsibilities toward his voluntary poverty. He kneels to pray; "in the meanwhile entreth the pardoner with all his relics" and announces his own sermon, transposing into direct address most of *PardT* ll. 335–76 with appropriate deletions. For example, references to gulling the audience are eased out of *PardT* ll. 339–52:

> That no man be so bold, be he priest or clerk,
> Me to disturb of Christ's holy wark;
> Nor have no disdain nor yet scorn
> Of these holy relics which saints have worn.
> First here I show ye of a holy Jew's hip
> A bone—I pray you, take good keep
> To my words and mark them well.[31]

After the mitten that increases grain, Heywood's relics outdo Chaucer's: the great toe of the Holy Trinity that cures toothache, the Virgin Mary's sunbonnet that eases childbirth, St. Michael's brain-pan that alleviates headaches. Then he switches to his "trick of declaring that great sinners, especially adulterous women, must not make offerings to his relics." [32] Heywood clarifies the situation by having the Pardoner address not "goode men and wommen" but exclusively "ye women all," with "she" referring to "wight" (pp. 7–8; *PardT* l. 377).

Heywood's Friar and Pardoner start their sermons in alternate lines on the page, forming rhymed couplets and sometimes juxtaposing meanings to comic effect. Thrice they accuse one another of caring only for money, not souls, then return to their respective sermons that display fund-raising rhetoric in all its glory. At last the brewing fight breaks out:

> FRIAR. Our Lord in the gospel showeth the way how—
> PARD. Ye shall now hear the Pope's authority.
> . . . .
>
> FRIAR. But I shall leave thee never an ear, ere I go:
> PARD. Yea, whoreson friar, wilt thou soe—
> > *Then they fight.*
> FRIAR. Loose thy hands away from mine ears—
> PARD. Then take thou thy hands away from my hairs:
> Nay, abide, thou whoreson, I am not down yet;
> I trust first to lay thee at my feet.
> FRIAR. Yea, whoreson, wilt thou scrat and bite?
> PARD. Yea, marry, will I, as long as thou dost smite—
> > *Enter the Curate.*
> > (p. 22)

To the Parson who enters, Pardoner and Friar elaborate their accusations, sounding equal in comic greed and selfishness as well as in shortness of temper (albeit not in length of hair). Unimpressed, the Parson calls neighbor Prat to help oust the two: "Take ye that lay knave, and let me alone / With this gentleman" (pp. 23–24). The play ends abruptly as the would-be ousters get the worst of it—"The red blood so runneth down about my head," cries Prat—and the rivals instead become cohorts:

> FRIAR. Will ye leave then, and let us in peace depart?
> PARSON AND PRAT. Yea, by our lady, even with all our heart.
> FRIAR AND PARD. Then adieu to the devil, till we come again.
> PARSON AND PRAT. And a mischief go with you both twain!
> > (p. 25)

Later, probably in 1544, Heywood features another Pardoner in *The Playe called the foure PP*. Pardoner, Palmer, Potycary, and Pedlar praise their respective professions. This Pardoner boasts even more relics, including the bees that stung Eve as she tasted the fruit, the "buttock-bone of Pentecost," and a slipper of one of the Seven Sleepers, which the apothecary refuses to kiss because that sleeper "trod in a turd" (p. 44).

From an atmosphere becoming as fetid as some of Chaucer's, Heywood swings the group of men to a scene familiar to folklorists, a liars' contest:

> 'POTH.   Now if I wist this wish no sin,
> I would to God I might begin.
> 'PARD.   I am content that thou lie first.
> PALMER.   Even so am I; now say thy worst.
> Now let us hear, of all thy lies,
> The greatest lie thou mayst devise.
> And in the fewest words thou can.
>
> (p. 48)

The Potycary tells of curing a "wanton [who] had the falling sickness" by using the relevant orifice for a cannon. The Pardoner tells of seeking a female friend in hell; the devils express great relief at being rid of her. The Palmer's lie wins hands down, though, the other contestants agreeing to promptly and discussing heartily the Pedlar's judgment. In his life of travel he has met five hundred thousand women, the Palmer says,

> Yet in all places where I have been,
> Of all the women that I have seen,
> I never saw nor knew in my conscience
> Any one woman out of patience.
>
> (pp. 49, 57)

Overall Heywood's two Pardoners are amiable fellows. Neither sinister nor sexually aberrant, comically exaggerating their relics, they compete with other men only long enough to discover common interests in money and misogyny. A century and a half after Chaucer, the Pardoner has recovered from his humiliation at Kitt's hands enough to find security as a comic satire on Roman Catholic abuses.

He still satirizes Rome's "Babylonish Rites" in 1641, if indeed Chaucer's Pardoner lurks behind the sadistic *Scots Pedler*, which shares a pamphlet with an antipapal *Canterbury Tale, Translated out of Chaucers old English Into our now vsuall Langvage* but in fact unrelated to any plot in genuine or spurious Chauceriana. One might claim severely repressed eroticism in the Scots Pedler's delight at his sackful of

> Conspiring heads, and hearts and tongues, and feete
> Of Popes, of Prelates, Cardinalls and Priests,
> Who living were in their bloodthirsty feasts,
> Drunke with the gore of Protestants and Kings,

and in his eagerness to

> macerate the bulke of that base slut [i.e., the Church at Rome],
> With all the crew of th' Antichristian cut;
> A whip, a whip to mortifie her skin,
> And lash her soundly like an arrant queane,
> From place to place, and so sign her passe
> To Rome from whence she came, with all her trash.[33]

But the possibly Pardonerlike narrator is the positive ideal in this gruesome poem. His own sexuality is by no means subject to mockery and will not become so again until Stothard's painting. The eighteenth century had other concerns.

CHAPTER 4

The Eighteenth-Century Pardoner(s)

In 1587 the once-exuberant John Heywood died in exile, sent abroad by Protestants' persecution after Queen Mary's death. Alexander Pope was born 101 years later, born Roman Catholic. Among other sorts of religious oppression, he was denied access to formal education including the universities. Schooling himself with a vengeance, he discovered Chaucer by age thirteen, when he neatly inscribed his copy of the 1598 Speght edition "Ex Libris ALEXANDRI POPEI; Ac è Dono GABRIELIS YOUNG. 1701."

I will suggest that Pope used his immense influence to reverse for a century, almost single-handedly, the see-saw of Chaucer's reputation. Many earlier responses to Chaucer were probably inaccessible during Pope's boyhood. The adventures at Cheker of the Hope were buried in one manuscript; works by Heywood and other Catholics were seldom printed; and the genial commentary on Chaucer by Richard Brathwait had been published one year before the Great Fire of 1666 devastated the London book industry. Although Chaucer's oral reputation at this or any other time cannot be ascertained, the printed sources probably available to the young Pope portrayed Chaucer as a gloomy or snarling moralist, a Puritan before the Reformation.[1]

Thanks to Gabriel Young (a neighbor) and to Dryden, however, Pope found on the page a witty and wonderful Father of English Poetry and of limitless possibilities—possibilities excluding proto-Protestantism, though. By far the most frequent marginal ticks in Pope's Chaucer folio occur throughout the antipapal *Plowman's Tale*, its spuriousness easily detectable after Speght's overdefensive Argument:

> A complaint against the pride and couetousnesse of the cleargie: made no doubt by Chaucer with the rest of the Tales. For I haue seene it in written hand in Iohn Stowes Library in a booke of

such antiquity, as seemeth to have beene written neare to Chaucers time.[2]

Having satisfied himself that this work was not Chaucer's, Pope proceeded to modernize what he wanted to. As he grew rapidly rich and famous for *Rape of the Lock,* Pope secretly edited miscellanies and in other ways nudged wit, including Chaucer's, into popular print. Once again Chaucer became "jovial, facetious, merry."[3]

It is artistic and interpretive genius that throws a monkey wrench into neat socioeconomic analyses of reception aesthetics. The jolly Chaucer whom William Blake knew and rejected vehemently, setting off repercussions still felt, differs radically from the dour Chaucer whom Pope knew and rejected. They differ precisely because of Pope.

Presumably without foreknowledge of his power-to-be, Pope used the Betterton *Chaucer's Characters* and other modernizations to impose his own understanding of each pilgrim onto eighteenth-century readers— onto readers except the very few who with Elizabeth Cooper still sought out the closest texts to Chaucer's own, those in hard-to-read black-letter folios printed the century before. Everyone else read modernizations by or inspired by Pope. They encountered most frequently by far the *Miller's Tale* (eleven appearances in print, 1700–1775, in two different modernizations), the *Reeve's Tale* (fourteen appearances in three versions), the *Summoner's Tale* (four appearances under different titles of the same pseudonymous modernization), the *Shipman's Tale* (five appearances in three versions), and Pope's two acknowledged modernizations as well as Dryden's, all conveniently available in inexpensive periodicals and miscellanies. (See Appendix B.)

The 1712 Pope/Betterton Pardoner fits right into this fabliau atmosphere, which Pope would help create. While other lower-class characters cavort sexually, however, this one sings hymns at the top of his lungs while picking the pockets of his companions. He shows no sign of a hot temper, these several centuries after he demanded back his staff from Kitt, and he certainly shows little potential for sincerity in regard to Christ's pardon.

What manner of man is this modernized Pardoner, the only one known to most readers in the eighteenth century? He is a manly man, built like the Miller. He hails from the lower classes, as he does in the reworkings by the *PTB* author and Heywood, the latter distinguishing the "lay knave" Pardoner from the "gentleman" Friar. (See previous chapter.) He sings for the sake of money at the end of his *General Prologue* portrait but not at the beginning for the sake of love. This love song, sung in harmony with the Summoner, is the longest segment that Pope/Betterton omits (*GP* ll. 670–74). If with anyone, the Pardoner hobnobs with the money-loving Reeve, who "rode hindmost of the Company" too.[4]

Thus, as he did in the Prioress's portrait, Pope/Betterton focuses the reader's questions elsewhere than on the Pardoner's potentially irregular sexuality. A bare hint of bisexuality in the Pope/Betterton Summoner may appear at the end of his portrait, instead, replacing his still problematic cake-shield:

> To him all Wenches in the Bishop's See
> Paid publick Tribute, or a private Fee.
> Boldly he rode, a Garland on his Head;
> Of all unmarried Men and Maids, the Dread.

> *The Pardoner.*

> A *Pardoner-monger* last brought up the Rear,
> With Patriarchal Face, and Holy Leer:
> His Hair was of the Hue of yellow Wax,
> Straight and unequal as a strieke of Flax.
> Yet long, and thin it grew from his large Head,
> And all his brawny Shoulders over-spread.[5]

Only in the word "leer," which refers to sideways glances including but not limited to wanton ones, does Pope/Betterton allow carefully modified sexuality to enter the Pardoner's picture (*OED,* s.v. "leer").

To this picture, as he did for that of the Prioress, Pope/Betterton adds observable aural and visual details that clarify the narrator's viewpoint. The first of these link the Pardoner with another working-class maker of music, the Miller. Pope/Betterton's Miller appears "short shoulder'd" with "brawny Flesh, large Sinews . . . . hard Head . . . . huge Nose."[6] He therefore resembles the Pope/Betterton Pardoner, except for his hair and the latter's "Patriarchal Face, and Holy Leer." These two images use theological abstractions as if they were visual adjectives, a stylistic trait we will note in the modernizations of the *Tales* of Reeve and Merchant.

The Pope/Betterton narrator avoids reporting characters' inner thoughts, or their actions that take place elsewhere than before his eyes, without providing evidence for his knowledge.[7] He omits, for example, *GP* l. 682—how could an observer know that the Pardoner considers himself "of the newe jet"?—and after mention of the goatlike voice adds aural evidence adapted from *PardT* l. 332: "Aloud he said his Orisons by rote." The narrator does not pretend to hear over hoofbeats or across time what the Pardoner says about his relics: instead of "he seyde" twice, the modernized *GP* ll. 694–98 display

> a Pillowbere,
> Which *piously was thought* our Lady's Veil;
> He kept, beside, a *Gobbet* of the *Sail*
> Which *Peter* had (and now this Pard'ner hath)
> When Christ rebuk'd him for his little Faith.

The parenthetical comment nudges syntax forward as well as back, implying a narrator fully aware of religious sham and a bit amused. But he refrains from imposing his opinions: without a first-person pronoun, *GP* l. 691 becomes "He might have been a Gelding, or a Mare." And the narrator's knowledge of the Pardoner's income is based on accounts, not hearsay:

> In one poor Village would collect more Pence,
> (As by Record too plainly does appear)
> Than a poor Parson lab'ring all the Year.

In the last segment, for *GP* ll. 707–14, Pope/Betterton switches the scene to a village church. He does so with a space and paragraph break before line 707:

> Howe'er, to tell the Truth just as it stood;
> He seem'd in Church, *Ecclesiastick good.*

By changing "was" to "seem'd" in line 708, Pope/Betterton makes the narrator less naive. He thereby smooths away some of the textual ambiguity later so important to Blake, for whom the Pardoner as scourge, blight, and trial of men also "is in the most holy sanctuary . . . suffered by Providence for wise ends."[8]

Undaunted by Blake's future plans, the Pope/Betterton Pardoner tries to outdo the Monk's "Gingling of his Bridle, loud and clear . . . as any Chappel Bell,"[9] for he closes both the village-church service and *Chaucer's Characters* itself by singing

> best of all an Offertory . . .
> So loud, so chearful, that the Chappel rung;
> This gain'd him Pence from the deluded Crowd;
> *Therefore* he sung so chearful, and so loud.

FIGURE 6:   The Pardoner, from p. 132 of John Urry's edition of *The Works of Geoffrey Chaucer* (London: B. Lintot, 1721). Reproduced by permission of the Van Pelt Library, University of Pennsylvania. Actual size, 5¾″ × 4¼″.

A loud, cheerful singer, brawny and leering with holiness, this rough-built charlatan may fool his rural audiences, but the Pope/Betterton narrator sees right past the Pardoner's tricks even while claiming to see only what passes before his own eyes. Such a Pardoner seems no threat at all to the educated. It is with a shudder, then, that we turn to the Urry-edition Pardoner, created in the same decade and the same metropolitan area as Pope/Betterton's.

A viewer might well tense up like the Urry-edition Pardoner's horse, its neck arched and eyes dead ahead despite slack reins. (See figure 6.)

Though totally obedient, it will soon be jabbed again by the Pardoner's huge spur, prominently framed between horizon and soft underbelly. This Pardoner is certainly young and beardless, perhaps verging on effeminate. He is almost as certainly not to be trusted. His straggly hair frames a fine-featured, weaselly face. Slit eyes peer sideways as if sizing up viewers, examining us without making eye contact. Heavy eyebrows and eyelids align with the small straight mouth to suggest smugness. This Pardoner would sooner murder an infant in its cradle than sing so cheerful, and so loud.[10]

Thus, again, the Pope/Betterton pilgrim differs markedly from the concurrent Urry-edition one. For the Prioress no earlier evidence survives; for the Pardoner it does, although it is distant. We do not know whether this evidence was available to the Urry-edition artist and Pope/Betterton. We can say, however, that the earlier conceptions resemble the latter's slightly and the former's not at all. Previous Pardoners are comic to various ends, never sneaky or evil as in the Urry-edition engraving. As anticipated, then, in this case it could just as well be Pope/Betterton who is adapting a more common interpretation—the Pardoner as comic figure in some way attacking Roman Catholic corruption—and the Urry-edition artist who is fully innovative.

Blake certainly knew the Urry illustrations. Nearly every one of Blake's pilgrims can be analyzed partly as Blake's response to the Urry artist's portrayals; he responds sometimes with imitation, sometimes with opposition, but most often in a way inarticulable in such Urizenic terms.[11]

For his own purposes, for example, Blake borrows the net from the Urry-edition Prioress's horse, but he passes her heart-and-cross symbol of ambiguous Amor instead to the pilgrim Whore of Babylon. (See figures 2 and 4.) Thus Blake removes from the Prioress what would soon become her best-loved attribute. On the other hand, however, he follows Urry's artist to pass on devious villainy as a primary attribute of the Pardoner, as can be seen particularly in the fearfully arched necks and strained mouths of both Pardoners' horses.

Rather than overleap the century between Urry and Blake quite so fast, though, let us pause halfway to examine a verbal interpretation that more resembles earlier ones. Thanks largely to Pope, Roman Catholicism rapidly lost popularity as a topic for British satire. In eighteenth-century France, however, it is precisely in order to demonstrate one of those "fraudes pieuses, qui dans ces Siecles d'ignorance défiguroient la Religion," that part of the *Pardoner's Prologue* becomes the first passage of Chaucer ever translated into French. Not to be outdone, within two years the Wife of Bath crossed the channel also, along with *Palamon and Ar-*

cite—both works translated from Dryden's modernizations, however, rather than directly from Middle English.[12]

The translator—probably the Abbé Prévost, editor of *Journal Étranger* during the first half year of 1755—gives biographies, comments, and sample passages for a series of English poets. He chooses the *Pardoner's Prologue* to illustrate that Chaucer "avoit adopté, si non ses opinions [of his contemporary Wycliffe], du moins sa haine & ses invectives contre les Moines." To Prévost, Chaucer presents the Pardoner as "un de ces Vagabonds, qui couroient les Campagnes, pour sémer la superstition & recueillir de l'argent. . . . Le Cafard explique lui-même sa méthode de prêcher, & l'art avec lequel il débite ses . . . . Reliques supposées, d'une espece fort singuliere."[13]

This introduction (especially the term "cafard," translatable as "sanctimonious cockroach") shows again that concern for the Pardoner's ethics need not be serious in tone. Prévost's loose translation of *PardT* ll. 350–76 begins with the elsewhere-displayed "os d'épaule de Mouton." Mark Twain would have delighted in re-Englishing it: "if any horned beast becomes inflamed on account of having swallowed a venomous insect," and so on.

In *PardT* ll. 366–71, the section most altered, Chaucer's Pardoner addresses "sires" but in fact goes on to give their wives a recipe for jealousy-preventive soup. Prévost's Pardoner begins with a straightforward sales pitch to the ladies:

> Bien plus, Mesdames, cette Relique guérit aussi de la jalousie. Quand un mari est dans l'accès de ce mal dangereux; qu'on lui fasse seulement son potage avec cette eau miraculeuse: vous verrez disparoître toutes ses inquiétudes & ses défiances. Il laissera sa femme sur sa bonne foi: eut-il tout vû de ses propres yeux? Il prendra désormais la réalité pour une illusion.[14]

The *Merchant's Tale* or its optical-illusion analogues may be inspiring this last image. The translation ends with a very loose paraphrase—that I thus gain their confidence so that they come forward, kiss the relics, "& moi j'empoche leur argent."[15]

Half a century later, pocketing money, though not that of gullible Catholics, is one cause of Blake's outrage at the painting by his colleague and erstwhile friend Stothard:

> he has done all by chance, or perhaps his fortune,—money, money. . . . When men cannot read they should not pretend to

paint. To be sure Chaucer is a little difficult to him who has only
blundered over novels, and catchpenny trifles of booksellers.
Yet a little pains ought to be taken even by the ignorant and
weak. . . . he has jumbled his dumb dollies together and is praised
by his equals for it; for both himself and his friend are equally
masters of Chaucer's language. They both think that the Wife of
Bath is a young, beautiful, blooming damsel.

He goes on to criticize Stothard's Knight, Squire, Reeve, Plowman, and
inaccurately labeled three Monks, Goldsmith, and Sea Captain. Furthermore, says Blake, Stothard's background shows the

Dulwich Hills, which was not the way to Canterbury; but perhaps the painter thought he would give them a ride round about,
because they were a burlesque set of scare-crows, not worth any
man's respect or care.[16]

Blake does not directly censure Stothard's Pardoner. Blake doubtless
would. In William Carey's description, Stothard's Pardoner appears as

a sort of jointless, nerveless, compound of youth and imbecility,
half-made and loosely-put-together; a limber, herring-backed
"Popinjay," fashioned to provoke risibility. . . . a ludicrous species
of effeminacy. . . . [With a] strange roll of his large gogling
eye. . . . he looks with a whifling simper at the wife of five husbands, as if sure of meeting with one who stood in need of a
pardon in her.[17]

Carey says further that Stothard has created a contrast between the Pardoner and that "ratling, roaring, fiery . . . boisterous Son of Bacchus,"
the Summoner.[18]

In his painting likewise, Blake pairs Pardoner and Summoner as differing physical types, each of whom incorporates "a Devil of the first mag-
nitude, grand, terrific, rich and honoured in the rank of which he holds
the destiny."[19] Blake balances the two visually against the good Parson,
whom he seems to praise effusively in his next paragraph, but whose
portrait much resembles Blake's portrayals elsewhere of Urizen, the ultimate represser of natural desire.[20] (See figure 2.)

The appearances of Pardoner and Summoner call into question the
superficial good of the two pilgrims whose pose and physical types mirror
theirs, the Prioress and Second Nun. Blake creates intricate visual links
between Prioress and Pardoner—from their pointed headpieces and hair,

past their spidery right hands clutching symbols of religious hypocrisy, to her curlicue dogs and his curlicue shoes. Repressed by heavy net and scalloped double reins, the Prioress's horse arches its neck as does the Pardoner's. The latter, with similar but less elaborate tack, is kept in line instead by active fear: it strains as if ducking a blow from the bejeweled cross, the symbol of established, repressive Christianity as opposed to Jesus's desires. Blake, in short, makes the Pardoner a key figure in his grandiose portrayal of all Mankind as manifestations of poetic genius in ever-shifting constellations of binary oppositions, with no one figure being good or evil except insofar as Urizenic, stifling rationality terms it so.

The gender of Blake's Pardoner does show a "species of effeminacy," as in Carey's description of Stothard's Pardoner. But hermaphrodism by no means always indicates evil, or always good, in its many occurrences throughout Blake's visual art. On the title page of *Marriage of Heaven and Hell,* for example, the embracing hermaphroditic figures represent an angel from Blake's Hell of creative energy and a devil from Blake's Heaven of repressed obedience—or vice versa. For Blake, a body neither male nor female can give visual form to his antirational ideas. Thus, Blake's verbal description of the Pardoner is one that his painting can gradually be seen to illustrate, not contradict:

> But I have omitted to speak of a very prominent character, the Pardoner, the Age's Knave, who always commands and domineers over the high and low vulgar. This man is sent in every age for a rod and scourge, and for a blight, for a trial of men, to divide the classes of men; he is in the most holy sanctuary, and he is suffered by Providence for wise ends, and has also his great use, and his grand leading destiny. . . . The uses to Society are perhaps equal of the Devil and of the Angel, their sublimity, who can dispute.[21]

Blake, going beyond the Urry-edition artist, tried to both show and tell what he meant by the Pardoner. He died thinking that no one had learned a thing. Perhaps that was true. Perhaps even if Blake had never lived, the nineteenth century would eventually have looked to Chaucer's text itself, found there more complexity than in Stothard's jollified painting, and pushed back into use the serious end of the see-saw, which Pope had thought to leave airborne once and for all. I personally prefer to believe that Blake balanced on the fulcrum and jumped up and down to unjam men's minds.

Chaucer's text itself contains problematic sexual imagery referring to the Pardoner. The two paintings by Blake and Stothard demonstrate reader response to the Pardoner's questionable sexuality, at this one point during the span of time between his Absolonian ineptness in the fifteenth century and his eunuchry or homosexuality now. But the two artists' responses could hardly differ more. Stothard makes him the silliest-looking among the nine male pilgrims who gaze goo-goo-eyed at the Wife of Bath, whereas Blake uses the hints of hermaphrodism in Chaucer's text to give visual manifestation to this male/female, whose greatest evil exists for the sake of greatest good.

Meanwhile, William Lipscomb was having enough problems caused by his own sexuality to fret much about the Pardoner's, for he found himself no longer able to support his rapidly growing family on graduate-student income. In 1789, after fourteen years spent earning his M.A. at Oxford, during which time his *Beneficial Effects of Innoculation* won the 1772 prize for English verse, he accepted at age thirty-five the rectorship at Welbury, North Riding, Yorkshire. Sermons occupied little of his time, apparently, since by 1792 he had published his modernization of the *Pardoner's Tale* and three years later his *Canterbury Tales of Chaucer, completed in a Modern Version*, which includes twelve *Tales* not in Ogle's 1741 collection.[22]

Lipscomb's modernization provides valuable evidence of one man's understanding of Chaucer's Pardoner, an understanding not adapted to other artistic ends, and that one man being an overeducated rector recently isolated "in a remote village, near 250 miles from London" (1:x). Cynicism about his own rural congregation seems to color Lipscomb's rendering of the end of the Pardoner's sermon. Otherwise, the alterations he makes from Tyrwhitt's text are those of one who has "imposed it on myself, as a duty somewhat sacred, to deviate from my original as little as possible in the sentiment" that he perceives as Chaucer's (1:vii).

My analysis of Lipscomb's modernization will incorporate the technique that critics after Kittredge developed for Chaucer's text and others, that of describing one's own imagined performance of vocal tones implied by the printed page, but with awareness of the method's limitations. Analysis of the modernizer's imagined performance can provide evidence directly comparable to that of readers-aloud attempting to project their own imagined performances, whereas visual art or an original work with a Chaucerian character can supply indirect evidence at best.

Because Lipscomb's modernization has never been reprinted, I provide here the end of his Pardoner's sermon and interaction with Host and Knight, which are the passages most subject to twentieth-century controversies. For ease in discussion I provide some line numbers referring to equivalent lines in Robinson's text, since Lipscomb gives no line numbers and since those in Tyrwhitt's text are distractingly different from Robinson's.[23] To begin, notice that Lipscomb's expansion of "that oon" in the first line quoted distinguishes this instigator of the murder from his reluctant and frightened fellow riotour:

> This done, the one whose hard and ruthless heart   (882)
> First urg'd his friend to play a murderer's part,
> Thus silence broke—"Away with coward fear!
> "Now with gay wine," he says, "and jovial cheer,
> "Let first our hearts be warm'd, and then the grave
> "The corpse its destin'd prize may duly crave."   (884)
> Then takes the wine, and (so just fate ordain'd)
> The poison'd flask into a bowl he drain'd;
> Quaff'd the dire beverage, and with heart'ning smile
> Gave it his friend, his terrors to beguile.
> But soon they both its noxious vapours found,
> And lifeless sunk extended on the ground.
> Thus fell they all (so will'd Heaven's just decree)
> The victims of their deep-laid villainy.   (894)
> Ah! what is man? when his corrupted soul
> Yields to debasing sin's uncheck'd controul!
> First senseless drunkenness his passions fires,
> Then rise tumultuous strong and fierce desires;
> These urge him on to each atrocious deed,
> Till to fell murder's crime at length they lead.
> The slave of sin, his heart no mercy knows,
> Him he ne'er thinks of to whom all he owes,
> From whom health, strength, and life, and every blessing flows.
> Now, gentle sirs! may Heaven your faults amend!   (904)
> But chief from avarice' baleful sin defend!
> Let each bring spoons or rings with grateful heart,
> And to your Pardoner of your hoards impart!
> Let each gay wife, if she would save her soul,
> Bring me her wool, and instant in my roll
> In fairest characters her name I'll place,   (911)
> And she shall sure receive forgiveness' grace.
> Come then! your offerings bring, and here as clean
> As if ye ne'er by sin had tainted been,
> I'll straight absolve you from the guilty load,   (913)
> And lead you safe to Heav'n's all bless'd abode;   (912)
> For in my tale, good sirs, I this forgot—   (919)

Pardons and relics in my pouch I've got;
Myself receiv'd them from the sacred hand
Of th' holy Father; nor does England's land
Produce a fairer shew: ye then that please,
Here on the ground devout with bended knees,
If sins your wounded consciences aggrieve,
Sweet absolution from my hands receive!
Unless ye better like, as on ye go,
(For in so long a journey sins will grow)
Careful to take a pardon fresh for each,
At every town that in our way we reach:
But then forget not, friends, if this ye do,
Each time fresh pence to give both good and true.   (930)
Great is your comfort, that among you here
Ye have so good and kind a Pardoner;
Who's still at hand as on your way ye ride,
At each mishap that may by chance betide.
Who knows but from his horse, of wine o'erfull,
Some hapless wight may fall, and break his skull?   (936)
And then what blest security 'twould be,
'Mongst you to have a friend assur'd like me!
If right I guess, our Host shall first begin,   (941)
For surely he's envelop'd most in sin.
Come then, sir Host, your humble offering bring,
And every relic, every holy thing.
Give me one groat, and for a price so small
Shall your unholy lips e'en kiss them all.
    "Nay," quoth the Host, "no relics, I beseech;   (946)
"As well might I salute thy reverend breech;
"And thou a relic of some saint might'st name,
"The part which modest nature hides in shame.
"But by the sacred Cross St. Helen found,
"Would that my purse with coilons did abound!
"Then holy relics would I all despise,
"And the dear current coin alone I'd prize."
    Not one word more the Pardoner deigns return,   (956)
But his fierce eyes all wild with anger burn.
Then said the Host, "No longer will I jest
"With one whose captious temper's so confess'd."
    On this the Knight, a mild and worthy man,   (960)
Anxious to heal dispute, to speak began.
    "Pardoner," he says, "let soft forgiveness swage
"The warm effusions of thy causeless rage:
"Mirth to promote is all our Host intends;

"Give each his hand then, and again be friends!"
Thus did they each salute in friendly mood,   (968)
And cheerful all their destin'd way pursu'd.

                                        (3:175–78)

Before discussing Lipscomb's omission of the Christ's-pardon benediction, let us note some less startling alterations, such as the use of quotation marks. Tyrwhitt had used no quotation marks, depending as did previous editors on syntax and on parentheses around an occasional "quod he." Most reusers of Tyrwhitt's text reproduce it exactly, except Charles Cowden Clarke, who adds quotation marks to his 1835 school edition along with modernized spelling and other pedagogical aids. Thomas Wright in 1847, followed by the influential W. W. Skeat, was first to impose quotation marks on an edition for adults. Among modernizers, Pope uses no quotation marks; Ogle adds them when reprinting Pope and others in 1741.

Lipscomb sets apart the closing speeches of Host and Knight. His Pardoner and narrator, however, both speak unenclosed by quotation marks and are thus relatively undifferentiated. In Robinson's edition the Pardoner's speech ends decisively at *PardT* l. 945—a useful guide, it seems, until one discovers that Robinson never opened the Pardoner's speech with quotation marks at *PardT* l. 463, and that he uses double rather than single marks for quotations within the *Tale*. It is not a typographical error at line 463, for Larry Benson has retained Robinson's punctuation in reediting the text for *The Riverside Chaucer,* published in 1987 just in time for mention here. Skeat's prototypical quotation marks create problems in a slightly different way. Chaucer's text was never meant to have quotation marks. When they are imposed, it fights back and sloughs them off.

This lack of differentiation between the speeches of Lipscomb's Pardoner and narrator suggests, as does his most altered passage, Lipscomb's authorial tendency to identify himself with this deliverer of sermons to dull-witted churchgoers. While de-emphasizing the ethics of cheating, Lipscomb emphasizes the Pardoner's mocking of his audience. In Tyrwhitt's text, Lipscomb found and altered a rather elaborate conclusion reinvoking earlier warnings against "glotonie, luxurie, and hasardrie." [24] The moral of Lipscomb's modernized sermon is greatly simplified: use of alcohol leads straight to pointless murder.

The Pardoner drinks. That Lipscomb thinks we should laugh at his hypocritical stance, rather than condemn it, is indicated by Lipscomb's addition of a light-hearted image of intoxication to *PardT* ll. 935–36.

Shortly after condemning strong drink as evil in and of itself, Lipscomb's Pardoner takes for granted that anyone might well take a tumble from his horse—just as the Cook will in *MancT* ll. 46–55, at which point even the peevish Manciple soon admits that imbibing a wee drop too much is no grounds for condemnation. (Lipscomb expands this *Manciple's Tale* scene in his modernization, 3:380–81.)

By evoking the *Manciple's Prologue* at this point in the Pardoner's speech, Lipscomb implies on paper a joking tone of voice like those to be heard reading these lines on Cut F. Several readers set out to perform one possibility that critics have proposed: the Pardoner, surprised to see the pilgrims caught up in his rhetoric, launches into his pitch actually hoping to sell a few pardons. Most such readers' serious voices break into amusement by *PardT* l. 928, at the image of fresh new pardons piled at every mile's end. A few manage to keep sounding serious, though, until this image linked by Lipscomb with the comically drunken Cook. Here the staunchest collapse. Aural evidence and Lipscomb's adaptation both indicate the near impossibility of uttering "ther may fallen oon or two / Doun of his hors, and breke his nekke atwo" with a straight face.

Lipscomb's Pardoner need not change his tone from serious to mocking at any point at all, however, for nowhere is this his actual sermon. It is his mocking imitation of a sermon, throughout, free from Kittredge's pronouncement that the fate of the three riotours be considered "so moving that no one could tell it flippantly."[25] Consistently, Lipscomb's Pardoner demonstrates to his intellectual equals how

> I view the gaping crowd collected round,
> Aloud I rant, as ye have heard before,
> And tell a thousand idle stories more;
> ....
>
> 'Tis not to check foul vice my words are meant,
> But gain, ungodly gain 's my sole intent.
> And when I once have earth'd them in the grave,
> Little I care whether their souls they save.
> 　　　　　　　(3:157, for *PardT* ll. 392–94, 403–6)

Lipscomb specifies his immense respect for Tyrwhitt's edition (1:x). That respect does not extend to paragraphing, which he often changes. For example, Tyrwhitt separates the Pardoner's silent wrath from the Host's refusal to play, more decisively than Lipscomb wants, by a paragraph break at *PardT* l. 958. Lipscomb also eliminates the 1775 edition's indentation at *PardT* l. 919, after "I wol you not deceive."[26]

Paragraphing, unlike punctuation, was imposed by all early editors of Chaucer. No edition before Tyrwhitt's begins a new paragraph after the Christ's-pardon benediction. All readers of the many publications of Tyrwhitt's text, however, saw the shift in tone indicated there. In Wright's mid-century edition of *Canterbury Tales,* directly based on Harleian ms. 7334, he like Lipscomb lets the Pardoner's sermon blend into the sales pitch. Skeat's paragraphing, however, following Tyrwhitt's, was destined to hold the field and, in this case, to help define a major critical controversy about tones of voice in Chaucer's silent text.

Uninfluenced by Kittredge's response to Skeat's edition, Lipscomb perhaps eliminated simply as inessential Tyrwhitt's indentation at *PardT* l. 919, along with the Christ's-pardon passage. It may be instead, however, that Lipscomb dropped the passage motivated by a discomfiture similar to that which Kittredge would articulate. To Lipscomb too, perhaps this particular blasphemy cast a pall over an otherwise lighthearted demonstration of gulling techniques.

For these or other reasons, Lipscomb has made the Pardoner's transition from addressing the imaginary church audience to addressing the pilgrims a gradual, not abrupt, one. Before either audience, he could claim to have forgotten relics in his pouch and could bid sinners to kneel (for *PardT* ll. 920–25). By the next line he is clearly addressing these pilgrims on the move—but addressing them in the joking manner implied by Lipscomb's treatment of two images that nearly all readers-aloud likewise make amusing (*PardT* ll. 927–30, 935–36). Then he turns to the Host.

What precisely is going on between Lipscomb's Host and Pardoner? Why does the Pardoner bid the Host bring forth not only his offering but also his—the Host's—relics and holy thing? Certainly "thing" could have many many referents other than "penis," for which it has been continually a slang term—as it is in one exactly contemporaneous example, a folksong quoted by Robert Burns on 8 March 1795.[27]

As Lipscomb's Pardoner does not invoke Christ's pardon, so also his Host does not call down Christ's curse. Omission of the curse and of the scatalogical image (*PardT* l. 950) imply a less harsh tone of voice than that argued by some modern critics. Lipscomb's added couplet, in which the Host coyly refrains from naming (presumably) a flaccid penis, also implies teasing rather than fury. The joke in the next two couplets eludes me, however; slang dictionaries provide no relevant entries to clarify the Host's apparent pun on "coilons" and "coin."[28]

Whatever the exact insult, Lipscomb's Pardoner responds with a display of his "captious temper"—fault-finding or carping, that is, not sophistical (*OED*, s.v. "captious"). Instead of reiterating the Pardoner's wordlessness, for *PardT* ll. 956–57, Lipscomb adds his "fierce eyes," which reflect from *GP* l. 684 his "glaring eyes, like a new started hare" (1:177). A hare does not glare in anger; Pope/Betterton's rendering bypasses the term's double meaning. By linking the two eye images, Lipscomb makes the Pardoner's quick temper a deeply embedded character trait, such that the mock sermon's abrupt conclusion fulfills the *General Prologue* hint. By proposing a handshake rather than a kiss of peace, then, Lipscomb's mild and anxious Knight successfully calms the Pardoner's "causeless rage," credits the Host, and ensures a happy ending.

For Lipscomb, as for the author of the *Prologue* to the *Tale of Beryn*, the Pardoner loses his temper over trifles. This hapless comic figure wants other people to like him. But he cannot take a joke here and cannot take a hint in *PTB*. Overall, then, Lipscomb's Pardoner shares more traits with his fifteenth-century counterpart than with either of his contemporaries.

Lipscomb, Stothard, and Blake were born respectively in 1754, 1755, and 1757. Lipscomb had a full university education, then moved to the provinces, while Blake and Stothard both were apprenticed as artists and then lived their lives in London's cultural maelstrom. These three interpreters would have had similar contact with Chauceriana. Their responses, in a word, differ.

Again, theorists of reception aesthetics should take heed. Textual interpretations do vary extensively within the identical sociohistorical context. Furthermore, interpretations similar to each other can occur at distant times and places, motivated by disparate ideas and intentions.

Blake, reworking the Urry illustrations, made the Pardoner essential to his own imaginative attack on repressive rationality. Stothard made the Pardoner just another clown infatuated with the Wife of Bath. Lipscomb made the Pardoner express his own mild disdain toward uneducated churchgoers. An amused Abbé Prévost made the Pardoner display Chaucer's alleged antipathy toward Roman Catholicism; the *Scots Pedler* author did the same, but viciously. Pope/Betterton made the Pardoner's portrait express his educated narrator's mockery of such a lower-class charlatan. Heywood made the Pardoner a light satire on corruption within the one true Church. The *PTB* author made the Pardoner a short-tempered fool in search of love. Chaucer made the Pardoner.

How did Chaucer make the Pardoner? asked Elizabeth Cooper in 1737, calmly, with a clear head thanks to her involvement with primary texts and her uninvolvement with running battles of the scholarly establishment. Because no one else has, I will discuss not only Cooper's comments on the *Pardoner's Prologue* but also her entire approach, which has set such precedents for our own.[29] Without insisting that source-hunting as a valid tool for literary analysis is necessarily better—just because more recent—than such scholarly activities as proving everybody Protestant, I would insist that it has proven fruitful these two and a half centuries. Cooper invented it.

I exaggerate. At Cooper's time Pope was providing footnotes with sources for his own poetry, for example, and Cooper's anthology would appear the same year as Thomas Morell's edition containing exhaustive notes on Chaucer's possible sources and analogues.[30] But as far as I have found, Cooper is what she claims to be: the first anthologist of English literature to see her duty as providing analytic commentary on texts rather than panegyric biography.

Cooper praises Chaucer, as is common. She also praises William Langland, as is not common. But her purpose in quoting them both is to show parallel stylistic features and thereby to investigate the writing process:

> *Chaucer* seems to have this Model [*Piers Plowman*] in his Eye; and, in his *Pardoners Prologue,* particularly, has a Feature or two nearly resembling the Speech and Character of *Sloth* hereafter quoted.[31]

Faux-Semblant has replaced Langland's Sloth as a source, now, but the methodology has remained.

Cooper also quotes from *Piers Plowman* the passage in which Conscience calls forth Kinde, Death, and Age to devastate the world (B20.79–100), because "I think [it] seems to have given a Hint to *Milton*" for the lazar-house in hell passage of *Paradise Lost,* which she then quotes. In a current standard edition of Milton, the editor footnotes the lazar-house passage:

> Godwin, in his *Life of Chaucer* (II, 412) suggested that Milton got the "first hint of a lazar-house from *Piers Plowman,* Passus XX," but the spirit of Milton's scene is rather like that of Du Bartas. . . .[32]

William Godwin in 1803/4 credits "preceding commentators" with the idea.[33] Twentieth-century footnotes do not remark on Milton's rightful place in the Battle of Ancients and Moderns or on other major critical concerns of the male literary establishment at Cooper's time.

In context, Cooper's typical-sounding praise of the "Morning-Star of the *English* Poetry" (p. 23) fits into the overall plan for her book:

> to constitute a *Series of Poetry* (which has never been aim'd at
> any where else) and compleat one of the most valuable Collec-
> tions, that ever was made publick. . . . few People suppose there
> were any Writers of Verse before *Chaucer,* but, as it appears there
> were many, 'tis absolutely necessary to give a Specimen from a
> few of them, both as Curiosities in themselves, and to manifest
> from what a low and almost contemptible Original, that happy
> Genius rais'd his Profession at once. (pp. xv, 1)

Writers before Cooper published lives of the poets and selections of their
work, but Cooper points out the major differences between her work and
theirs. Instead of just repeating what the last anthologist said, Cooper
has actually read what each author from Edward the Confessor through
Samuel Daniel wrote. After acknowledging the collected biographies
published by Jacob, Winstanley, Phillips, Wood, and Blount,[34] she says
pointedly:

> What use I have made of all, or any of these Circumstances, will
> be obvious; as well as what is peculiarly my own. — This, how-
> ever, I may, with Modesty, hint, that many Mistakes in Facts
> are rectify'd, several Lives are added, the Characters of the Au-
> thors are not taken on Content, or from Authority, but a serious
> Examination of their Works. (p. xv)

Examining Chaucer's contemporaries, for example, Cooper reports
that Thomas Hoccleve is by some authorities "highly applauded, by others not so much as mention'd" (p. 31). Because she has not succeeded in
finding a copy of *De Regimine Principum,* she herself refrains from judg-
ing an author whom she knows only from his epitaph on Chaucer.[35] John
Gower, whom authorities praise and whom she has read, "does not appear to have much Genius; his whole Work being little better than a cool
Translation from other Authors" (p. 19). Her strongest praise goes to
Langland who "is not so much as mention'd either by *Philips* or *Win-
stanly;* though, in my Judgment, no Writer, except *Chaucer,* and *Spencer,*
for many Ages, had more of real Inspiration" (p. 7).

Cooper expresses her harshest disappointment over the much-touted
Lydgate. The longstanding concern over Chaucer's irregular meter had
been intensified after 1614 by a publication of Lydgate's *Troy Book* with
its meter regularized, presented as if it were the original language. Thus
Lydgate came to be called the better versifier. Sometimes the praise is as
reluctant as in 1707: "Let the Wit of this Monk be what it will, his
English, and his Numbers, are more polish'd than his Master's."[36]

William Winstanley, however, joins those literary authorities whose rhetorical flourishes replace reading. In language and sample verse copied word for word from Thomas Fuller, he says that Lydgate

> both in Prose and Poetry was the best Author of his Age, for if *Chaucer*'s Coin were of greater Weight for deeper Learning, *Lydgate*'s was of a more refined Standard for purer Language; so that one might mistake him for a modern Writer. But because none can so well describe him as himself, take an Essay of his Verses, out of his *Life and Death of* Hector . . . .
>
> I am a Monk by my profession,
> In *Berry*, call'd *John Lydgate* by my name.[37]

Cooper may have regarded Winstanley as a particularly pretentious authority, for her introduction to Lydgate (quoted below) and her book title *The Muses Library* both quietly mock his first compilation of biographies and poetry, *The Muses Cabinet* (1655). Reworking its material to publish two more compilations besides much else, Winstanley expanded the final work by his usual practice of borrowing "freely . . . without acknowledgment," this time from the *Theatrum Poetarum* published by Edward Phillips, Milton's nephew. Winstanley began as a barber, according to the *Dictionary of National Biography,* and as a scholar he retained the scissors. His occasional independent judgments express Royalist sympathies. For example, Phillips mentions Milton's "Fame . . . to all the Learned of Europe," adding "how far he hath reviv'd the Majesty and true *Decornm* [sic] of Heroic Poesy and Tragedy: it will better become a person less related then [sic] my self, to deliver his judgement."[38] Winstanley, however, assures readers that Milton's "Fame is gone out like a Candle in a Snuff, and his Memory will always stink."[39]

Cooper, like Winstanley or any literary scholar, lets personal preferences affect her opinions. Unlike most, she states outright the circumstances and evidence that have led her to pass negative judgment on Lydgate:

> Many Authors are so profuse in his Praise as to rank him very little below his Master, and, often, quote them together; which rais'd my Curiosity so high, that I gave a considerable Price for his Works, and waded thro' a large Folio, hoping still to have my Expectation gratified. — But I must, either, confess my own want of Penetration, or beg Leave to dissent from his Admirers. — Modesty, indeed, he has to a very great Degree; ever

disavowing all Pretence to Merit, speaking of *Chaucer* with a
religious Reverence, and pleading the Command of Princes for
following his Track. — But, as to the Compliments that are made
him, of deep Scholar, Logician, Philosopher, *&c.* let his own
Words answer, in the Close of his *Fall* of *Princes;* which will, at
once, illustrate my Idea both of the Poet, and the Man.

> Out of the *French* I drough it of Entent,
> ....
>
> Have me excused! my Name is *John Lidgate,*
>   Rude of Language, I was not born in *France,*
> Her curious Miters in *English* to translate!
> Of other Tong I have no Suffisance.[40]

Cooper also read the whole of *Piers Plowman.*[41] Although some authorities contemporary with Cooper believe Langland lived later than
Chaucer and do not even know his name, she has found three "Historical
References. . . . [which] place him in the Reign of *Edward* III. or that of
Richard II" (p. 8). The poem is greatly defective in rhyme and meter, she
says. Otherwise her critical opinions resemble recent ones; this very long
poem

> does not appear to me of a Piece; every Vision seeming a distinct
> Rhapsody . . . . [But] if the Poetical Design is broken, the Moral
> is entire; which is, uniformly, the Advancement of Piety, and
> Reformation of the *Roman* Clergy. (p. 9)

For sample passages she chooses, as do modern anthologists, the wedding
of Lady Meed (B2.141–236), the lines on St. Truth as lead-in to two
Deadly Sins (B5.57–58, 76–124, 392–418a, 420–25), and the apocalyp-
tic attack by Kinde, Death, and Age (B20.79–100).

It is in the context of the growing rowdiness of Chaucer's reputation,
because of his fabliaux modernized for readers including scholars who
never bother with the originals, and in the context of her own Alysounian
attitude toward Authority, that Cooper offers her own balanced judgment concerning Chaucer:

> But his own Works, are his best Monument. In those appear a
> real Genius, as capable of inventing, as improving; equally suited
> to the Gay, and the Sublime; soaring in high Life, and pleasant
> in low: Tho' I don't find the least Authority in History to
> prove it. (p. 23)

CHAPTER 5

The Pardoner on Tape

We now lack Elizabeth Cooper's opportunity for a virgin experience with Chaucer's text.[1] We cannot brush aside, as she did, a small amount of generalized panegyric on Chaucer. Instead our teachers point out, orally, specific passages; eventually we propose our own interpretations in response to published criticism, which often describes imagined performance.

Partly because the Pardoner orates for a living, Kittredge and later commentators on the Pardoner's "astonishing performance"[2] specify his tones of voice even more frequently and precisely than they do those of other characters. For example, without stating that she is articulating a range of possible mental soundings or imagined performances, Penelope Curtis says of the Pardoner's sermon,

> We hear many tones, of confidential intimacy, a prurient excitement, pulpit-loud indignation, but all these tones are at play in the one swelling of the voice. The conceit is sharp enough—
> "Oure blissed Lordes body they totere": its tone *could* be sober, or an indirect attack, or a lament, or it might be a jibe.[3]

While questioning, as I do, the absoluteness with which authorities label the tones of a text, Curtis continues to use the functional vocabulary of New Criticism—functional, as long as everybody reading the article agrees on the sound of a jibe.

In addition to descriptive words and phrases such as these, twentieth-century critics regularly bring metaphor and simile to bear on analysis. They assume that the interpretive community of Chaucerians, like their own students, will understand literary criticism couched in comparisons.

Usually this assumption is valid. Changes in technology and social conditions can dim an analogy, however. As usual, Kittredge set precedent in his published lectures. He explains, for example, that the pilgrims' stories resemble "the soliloquies of Hamlet or Iago or Macbeth," and their self-revelations those in the "smoking-room of a small steamship with only three or four dozen passengers. . . . keep them at sea for an extra week, and, if they are n't careful and if the cigars hold out, they will empty their hearts to one another with an indiscretion that may shock them to death when they remember it ashore."[4]

The references to Shakespeare still evoke direct responses from those who share Kittredge's culture, but the steamship image is fading. We now understand his point by imagining, say, airline passengers held hostage, though not at gunpoint. A half century after Kittredge, as one example, Paul Beichner explains the Pardoner's fundraising in terms of income-tax deductions and the Ford Foundation—images meaningless at Kittredge's time but effective for Beichner's readership, now and for an indeterminable stretch of the future.[5]

Performance analysts may make additions to the stock of analogies to present-day situations. They must do so cautiously, though, ever questioning which experiences readers of Chaucer criticism certainly share. Thus, rather than awaiting arrival of a technological vehicle like the speech synthesizer, which might someday objectify communication from one human brain to another, we can take immediate advantage of technology from another platform: that of the global village. The increasing homogeneity of world culture—formerly bemoaned by folklorists not yet reassured that cockroaches and folklore will survive the nuclear holocaust[6]—can allow a careful expansion of comparative vocabulary in academic writing.

One tempting source for analogies should be handled gingerly: the mass media. References to characters in particular films or television programs will not last. Comparison to character types can be effective, however. Anyone likely to read Chaucer criticism would have aural images of a tough detective, a cold seductive bitch, a country bumpkin, a hero to the rescue. And media aside, the real world offers a wealth of shared experiences: sullen teen-agers, tough meter maids, bored waitresses, glad-handing politicians, officious ushers, and (let us hope) a few caring friends and respected colleagues.

As of this chapter I abandon, as promised, minute examination of individual lines. Hereafter I primarily use visual and aural analogies to describe longer passages. An objective vocabulary, adapted from musicology, brings us no nearer to the meaning of speech than it does, ultimately, to the meaning of music. Although such features as pauses and pitch shifts can help shortcut description, no given combination of them projects a predictable meaning. Musicologists have tried and found wanting their own vocabulary. Certainly we ought not to expect more of it than it has ever offered before.

> The peculiar experience of an individual may . . . cause a
> "happy" tune to be associated with images of a sad occasion. . . .
> For example, the image of a triumphal procession might within
> a given culture be relevant to the character of a piece of music;
> but the association might for private reasons arouse feelings
> of humiliation or defeat.[7]

That is, even if each of us were to hear Kittredge perform *PardT* ll. 916–18 in his way, we each might well respond differently to a paroxysm of agonized sincerity—respond with cynicism or sympathy, perhaps, or with self-satisfied amusement or condemnation. And someone a century hence might respond in yet another way.

A century before Kittredge, William Lipscomb simply eliminated the Christ's-pardon benediction, whether for reasons of artistic consistency or book sales or antipathy to blasphemy or all of the above. Without pushing the unprovable assumption too far, let us note a few major changes in sociohistorical conditions since 1795 with relation to imagined performance of *PardT* ll. 916–18.

Lipscomb wrote at a time of British expansionism, when few questions were being asked as to whether technology, commerce, and Christianity ought to be imposed on persons presumed uncivilized. By Kittredge's time, though, many such questions had to be asked, for Christianity was clearly running short of answers. If all Christian nations would sincerely believe in Christian values, it seemed, World War I would not happen.

Then along came an utterly sincere Christian, Adolf Hitler. With rhetoric as spellbinding as the Pardoner's, Hitler convinced gullible churchgoers of what he sincerely believed: the killers of Christ deserve no pardon. Educated people now must live with the result, though few would articulate its effect on their responses to medieval literature. Incited by legends like that told by Chaucer's Prioress, for example, Christians in Lincoln in 1255 killed nineteen Jews. Christians of the same generation as many present-day scholars, sharing our same cultural milieu, killed six million.

Sincerity about Christ's pardon has become a weak beam indeed with which to illuminate the darkness and smoke of the ultimate implications of Christian morality. Sincerity about any ethical question is becoming less and less reliable, too. "I wol yow nat deceyve," says the Pardoner. "I am not a crook," says Richard Nixon sincerely, looking a television audience straight in the eye, a few days before resigning rather than face impeachment charges. "I knew nothing of illegal arms shipments," says Ronald Reagan, oozing sincerity.

I have noted that bland, self-conscious readings-aloud occur at long-argued critical cruxes. Among all my data, this phenomenon is most noticeable at *PardT* ll. 916–18. Very many readers-aloud stumble and repeat portions of the benediction. Several reverse pronoun and negative into "I wol nat yow deceyve," including Robert Ross on his brilliantly executed recording.[8] One of the twenty-four readers-aloud, thanks to leader tape, even ends side A of the cassette with line 916 and begins side B midway through line 920.

Readers' audible discomfort indicates not only intellectual awareness of this crux, I would say. It implies in addition their lack of personal commitment to the issue defined by Kittredge—a lack of personal conviction, after World War II, that a sincere tone of voice could in any way prove that the "Pardoner has not always been an assassin of souls," such that at mere mention of Christ "his cynicism falls away."[9]

Cut F, *PardT* ll. 895–906 and 913–36

Fortunately for this comparative study, a volunteer recorded the benediction passage three times, before a live audience in Kalamazoo, Michigan, on 8 May 1982, stating intentions and aesthetic judgments for each. (See *Texts Read Aloud*, Chapter 5.) This reader presents his preferred oral interpretation of *PardT* ll. 913–36 as F1. By means of a strong caesura followed by a tone shift in line 915, states F1, the Pardoner makes the pilgrim audience "feel a bit like fools for getting so caught up in his rhetoric."

Indeed, F1 shifts from quavering sincerity to a smirking benediction, which after line 915 incorporates a chortle so stage-villainous as to evoke laughter from F1's Kalamazoo audience. Thus the twentieth-century audience's response resembles, but does not duplicate, the fictional pilgrims' response to the doubly fictional church audience's response. The pilgrims would laugh partly at themselves, F1 intends, whereas the Kalamazoo audience laughs with the Pardoner at his skillful manipulation of both in-text audiences. The aural distinction would resemble that between B1, who in *GP* l. 156 chuckles about the Prioress's overgrown size, and D8, who chuckles there at the narrator's own fluster.

F1 continues the teasing tone of the benediction, mocking as pretentious even the "popes hond" and "devocion" in *PardT* ll. 922–23. F1's line 919 evokes the "oh no!!" of a cartoon character slapping his forehead while falling backward on his heels. F1's Pardoner consistently makes fun of the church audience, not the pilgrims, as he pretends to peddle pardons like ice-cream bars in lines 925–30. By lines 935–36, wherein he enthusiastically contemplates the economic benefits should one or two take a tumble, F1's Pardoner has crossed the line to full parody. Even beyond imitating the mad scientist in a horror film, eager to bear body parts of the fallen to his basement laboratory, F1 takes on the voice of the fang-clad host who rises from his coffin at 2 A.M. Sunday to introduce this week's Creature Feature, *The Tomato That Ate Cleveland.*

Note that this reader, F1–3, each time delivers line 913 as a self-confident declaration. Performances by other readers, however, vary markedly. "I yow assoille, by myn heigh power" may be smirked or shrugged or declaimed, confided to the chosen few, or even intoned in a chant like the Roman Catholic mass. *PardT* l. 913 offers such a wide range of oral interpretations partly because of its proximity to a major critical crux. Readers, all thinking ahead to the benediction, perform line 913 with complete spontaneity—an issue to be investigated further in the discussion of Cuts F6–7 and G.

Most readers of *PardT* l. 913 are thinking about how to make lines 916–18 something other than a paroxysm of agonized sincerity. As F2, however, our same reader demonstrates for the Kalamazoo audience how Kittredge might have performed lines 913–19. Such a paroxysm necessitates a break in tone within line 915, plus another after line 918. The two breaks, while possible to imagine, are difficult to perform and also aesthetically inappropriate to the text, according to the reader. "I like to believe in Kittredge's interpretation," F2 states, "but I really can't make myself do it." Thus, Cut F2 presents an oral interpretation which its reader considers wrong. Note that F2 stresses "yow" in *PardT* l. 918, as did Walter Clyde Curry.[10]

As F3 this reader then performs *PardT* ll. 913–19 in a way he considers aesthetically possible but only up to a point, that point being the image of pardons "newe and fressh at every miles ende." With no strong caesura in line 915, F3 continues in a tone of voice like that of the sermon. The benediction sounds kind and the pardon priceless. The confident inflections in line 919 echo those of line 913. F3 states that he intends to convey a Pardoner who pulls off a "super-trick, trying to get at least some of the dumber pilgrims, maybe even the Host himself, to really unbuckle their purses." This reading with no break in tone creates a less interesting Pardoner, F3 states, and is difficult to sustain past line 926.

Among the other readers-aloud of this line, over half do sound clearly amused in *PardT* ll. 927–30. The ones with comparatively serious voices, however, include those Pardoners trying to trick the pilgrims as well as those jokingly demonstrating a sales technique that uses serious vocal inflections.

F3's perceived limitation applies even better to a passage a bit further on. As mentioned, my data indicate the near impossibility of reading *PardT* ll. 935–36 seriously. Only one other reader approximates F1's horror-film host. The most frequent tone among the rest of the openly joking readers, as exemplified by F4, is one of enforced fun. It is not a tone in which to address actual children, but one in which to pretend to patronize irritating children: "Say, kiddies, let's all go horsie riding and break our little necks."

Other readers do not sound amused or amusing in these two lines. In the context of chuckles or snickers elsewhere, though, here they project images of slick hucksters telling the pilgrims how to sell refrigerators to Eskimos, coals in Newcastle, and property insurance in event of nuclear holocaust.

Unlike them, F5 never snickers at the gullible. He nonetheless jokes with us and with the pilgrims, subtly, flattering our ungulled sophistication by means of oral onomatopoeia. Rather than salesmanship F5 projects reassurance, with the studiously casual tones of a land developer guaranteeing a school board that buried toxic wastes will remain in their barrels. F5's oral onomatopoeia imitates, then playfully contradicts, the action of *PardT* ll. 935–36. F5's vocal pitch falls abruptly, not on "fallen" but rather after the image is completed on the word "hors"; then it rises on "atwo" as if uninjured despite appearances to the contrary.

Does content alone make this equestrian-mishap couplet funny? Can it be read both accurately and seriously? Perhaps not. As in the lines that imitate the Prioress's courtly port and pleated wimple (*GP* ll. 137–41 and 151), metrical patterns in *PardT* ll. 935–36 at least encourage a satiric reading.

The couplet's rhyme is not really rhyme but repetition; thus a neck broken "atwo" seems as casually irrelevant as whether "oon or two" fall. During most of the couplet strong pauses alternate with strong stresses, each of which ends an anapest extended from two to three weak syllables. The effect is one of stumbling, of starting to fall but catching oneself, four times before the last half line. At that point, readers seldom perform what on paper looks like three neat iambs ending the second line. If readers did, the half line's reassuring regularity would contradict the threat of broken necks. In ways too various to indicate with scansion marks, however, readers not performing iambs instead make that half-line echo the four stumbles before it, such that once and for all the rider catches himself before his skull hits the ground. Thus both visual and oral prosody help make the lines those of a joker.

   ˇ ˇ ˇ ´ ˇ ˇ ˇ ´ ˇ ˇ ˇ ´
   Paraventure . . . ther may fallen . . . oon or two

   ˇ ˇ ˇ ´   ˇ (´) ˇ (´) ˇ (´)
   Doun of his hors . . . and (. . .) breke his nekke atwo.

My previous chapter's analysis has demonstrated that two centuries ago William Lipscomb found *PardT* ll. 935–36 funny and perhaps found lines 916–18 too unfunny to fit the scene. Besides adding the *Manciple's Prologue* image and eliminating the Christ's-pardon benediction, Lipscomb changes the content of one other passage. He substitutes a simplistic sermon-ending moral, perhaps from his own experience, for the complex rhetorical flourishes and benediction of *PardT* ll. 895–906. In this passage Chaucer's Pardoner finishes his sermon and invokes God's forgiveness on the imaginary congregation, then tries to sell them pardons.

This first transition from sermon to benediction to sales pitch could affect how a reader understands the next unfolding step of audiences within audiences and voices within voices: the Christ's-pardon crux. Yet no one has argued about the earlier transition.

In *PardT* ll. 895–903, the Pardoner imitating himself addresses first the abstract sins themselves, then someone who would blaspheme Christ, then "mankynde." All three are depersonalized and addressed as "thou." At line 904—"Now, goode men, God foryeve yow youre trespas"—the abrupt switch to address the immediate church audience, with the change in second-person pronoun, could indicate a break in performance almost as clean as that at "And lo, sires, thus I preche." How sincerely do readers-aloud perform this unargued benediction?

Among the spontaneous interpretations on tape, some call the pilgrim audience front and center for ll. 895–906: the Pardoner is demonstrating how to deliver a memorized purple passage followed by a memorized sales pitch. In other readings the imagined church audience remains to the fore, absorbing the full force of persuasive inflections as well as words. Anyone still harboring suspicions that the same set of black marks on paper must convey the same discursive meaning, by the way, should ponder the eight different shades of meaning conveyed by F6 and F7 in the four vocative O's in lines 895–97.

F6, exemplifying a didactic Pardoner, supplies the pilgrims with an oral handbook of rhetorical phraseology, highlighted by rhetorical vocal inflections. A slick professional, F6 coolly delivers the vocatives of lines 895–99 in a despairing tone calculated to arouse guilt and shame. F6's voice, by trembling with weepiness on "allas! mankynde" and "unkynde, allas," neatly frames the balanced appeal of lines 900–903.

Shifting tone at Robinson's paragraph indentation (shared by early editions), F6 makes the benediction a transition to brisk, businesslike inflections. Techniques of oral salesmanship will constitute the next chapter. In *PardT* l. 906 the pilgrims learn how stress on "myn" and a louder "hooly pardoun" can spotlight one's merchandise.

Like several ambiguous lines already noted, *PardT* l. 906 contains a personal pronoun and a potentially negative verb (although not the negative particle of *GP* ll. 156, 128–29, or 280, or *PardT* l. 918). Stress on either "myn" or "may," or on both, can help give *PardT* l. 906 different meanings—but, as usual, not predictably different ones. "May" could sound either hesitant or anticipatory, for example. Kittredge might well have read this line as foreshadowing the Pardoner's doubts about his own pardon, might well have understood "*Myn* hooly pardoun (as opposed to Christ's) may (as opposed to "certainly will") yow alle warice." But that same stress pattern by F6 conveys instead "*Myn* hooly pardoun (don't be fooled by imitations) may (if you do what I'm about to tell you)."

Overall, F6 performs the type of Pardoner who takes the pilgrims into his confidence by demonstrating just how empty language can be—by demonstrating, as promised, that a vicious man can tell a moral tale (*PardT* ll. 459–60). F7 exemplifies the other type of Pardoner, whose fully persuasive tone of voice leaves us listeners less aware of the pilgrim audience existing between us and the church audience than we are while listening to F6. A Pardoner so carried away by his own oratorical skill, or by liquor, that he genuinely tries to sell pardons to the pilgrims might deliver *PardT* ll. 913–20 as F7 does lines 895–906.

F7's voice walks the line—a fine line, indeed—between fake sincerity and genuine sincerity. Except during one intake of breath after *PardT* l. 905, F7's Pardoner expresses fully sincere concern for the souls of the churchgoers, for the souls of the pilgrims, for all our souls. Or does he?

F7's vocal pitch climbs one level higher on each of lines 895, 896, and 897. Then it drops slightly to address "thou blasphemour," whose greatest indignation of all, "pride," will glow atop the solid monument of sins. The passage framed by "allas" is set apart as decisively as F6's, but not by means of weepiness; instead, at line 900 F7 shifts from indignation at sin to compassion for sinners. The pain of "mankynde," unless he ceases being "unkynde," reverberates with the pain felt by Christ-the-man while losing his herte-blood in line 902.

F7 prays the first half of line 904, then builds to a confident declaration of benediction. That is, the tone moves from private to public prayer. The Pardoner's nonreligious confidence wells out, then, for just a moment: F7's intake of breath after line 905 seems to smother a smug smile. Another snow job well done. Only very acute, unspellbound listeners would notice this crack in the Pardoner's holy façade, though, for F7 rushes on to address "yow alle" in trembly eagerness echoing lines 900–903. Eager in fact for nobles, sterlings, spoons, rings, and wool, he nonetheless offers his pardon as if its existence is secondary to his sincere, compassionate concern for the good of his listeners' souls.

Cut F, *PardT* ll. 895–906 and 913–36
ll. 913–36

F1:   reader's preferred interpretation, mocking throughout; stage villain blending into horror-film parody.

ll. 913–19

F2:   Kittredge's interpretation, considered wrong by same reader as F1.

F3:   interpretation in which the Pardoner tries to "pull off a super-trick," considered inferior to F1 by same reader.

ll. 935–36

F4:   pretending to patronize irritating children.

F5:   studied casualness reassures the gullible, while oral onomatopoeia signals the joke to us sophisticated listeners.

ll. 895–906

F6:   didactic Pardoner shows pilgrims how he tricks audiences.

F7:   sincere Pardoner ends sermon at imaginary church.

To propose any further mental soundings of the Pardoner's sales pitch that follows Christ's pardon, commentators should take into account the variety of possible performances of his sermon-to-sales-pitch transition in *PardT* ll. 895–906, which has one more layer of voices within voices than lines 913–20. Instead of simply stepping outside of the church audience, a reader of lines 895–906 must take into account both textual audiences as well as, insofar as possible, the medieval reading and listening audiences, whose responses to an apparent offer of God's forgiveness would differ from ours after World War II and from Kittredge's before it. Proposed mental soundings for the final transition could also be compared to the corresponding transition in the *Pardoner's Prologue,* where he shifts to address the church audience at *PardT* l. 352 and then returns to the pilgrims at line 389.

Another passage that could help critics articulate preferred readings of the Pardoner's tone of voice after *PardT* l. 915—whether he is joking by trying to sell relics to the pilgrims; or seriously trying to sell; or jokingly demonstrating his sales technique, which includes a serious tone of voice; or seriously sharing his sales technique, which includes jollying the customer—is the opening of the *Pardoner's Prologue, PardT* ll. 329–40 and further. At *PardT* l. 340 some readers inject scorn into the word "Cristes," some into "hooly," some into both, some into neither. A few readers sound sinister, even malicious, already in line 329. Other Pardoners begin by mocking themselves. Several sound elegant and dignified in this honored profession of orator. One sounds defiant. One is hoping for sympathy. Quite a few cheerfully explain what they do for a living, sometimes with scorn for "chirches" in line 329 and sometimes not. These blend into the more clearly didactic lead-ins. Two readers project "lordynges" as the call to attention in a potentially unruly lecture hall; one explains his job to grade-school students; others instruct well-behaved classes of pilgrims. And several readers create Ancient-Mariner Pardoners who are eager to tell all, glad at last to find listeners for their trade secrets.

Two different readers happened to tape the *Pardoner's Prologue* at times when, on their respective campuses, midday chimes were recorded in the background of *PardT* l. 331, "rynge it out as round as gooth a belle." That coincidence can represent all the separate but often shared circumstances with which each silent reader understands Chaucer's text, and which each professor conveys in not only vocal inflections but also gestures, facial expressions, and scientifically unverifiable attitudes.

As for the *locus desperatus* of the epilogue, and especially for those furious, indignant, irritated, or joking words of the Host—which Lipscomb in 1795 plus most of my students regard as crude humour, but which need not be heard thus by everybody—the rest is silence. On the Chaucer tapes lurk all possibilities that have been argued by critics and many that have not, for the interaction between Host and Pardoner.

Cut G, *PardT* ll. 960–65

With what precise tone of voice does the Host silence the Pardoner? Who is joking, who angry, how much, and why? Why is the Pardoner speechless? At what exactly do all the people laugh? Is it quite all right for two men to kiss and make up? Sexual innuendo aside, their quarrel precisely involves proposed kissing of the Pardoner's relics and old breech. Can the Knight's proposed kiss of peace be neutral? Does the incident end happily, as in Lipscomb's modernization wherein a hand-shake replaces the kiss? Or do the two ride forth on their way still see-thing, planning scurrilous stories about pardoners and innkeepers?

Readers-aloud, focusing on so many established critical issues, read unselfconsciously and spontaneously the lines containing the Knight's in-tervention in the quarrel. The Chaucer tapes offer a wide variety of oral interpretations for *PardT* ll. 960–65, concerning which lines a very few critics have made only oblique suggestions. Penelope Curtis mentions the Knight's "feudal authority exercised on only this occasion," and Elise Parsigian refers to his "command," whereas John Gardner's Knight ad-dresses the Pardoner as if he were "a foolish, ill-behaved child."[11] In Lipscomb's modernization, also, a mild Knight anxiously soothes a Par-doner who didn't get the joke. In accounting for my data, I will include these four described mental soundings in their appropriate categories.

In reference to *PardT* ll. 960–65, I wish to address several methodo-logical questions that may occur to readers of this book. First, how do you know that I am not picking and choosing evidence that supports my thesis, while suppressing the rest? Second, might I not then be arranging this chosen evidence to validate my perceptions? Third, what if someone else hears a different projected meaning than I do, in the same reading-aloud? Finally, presuming you do trust my choice of evidence and my described perceptions of meaning, why do I not simply abandon any reference to objectively audible features and employ instead completely metaphorical, impressionistic descriptions?

In answer to the first and fourth questions, I hereby involve you the reader in an experiment. I ask not "Which was mooste fre?" but rather "How do they sound to you?" concerning all the available evidence in this one case: the twenty-four spontaneous readings-aloud of *PardT* ll. 960–65, plus two that I solicited for reasons to be discussed.

For each reading I provide completely metaphorical descriptions, based on those that popped into my head as I first listened to each tape. I make no attempt to validate these initial impressions by reference to audible features. Some of these descriptions I would have since modified upon relistening, but I leave my first impressions for the sake of the experiment. In doing so I exaggerate only slightly the pedagogical—and thereby critical—custom of describing a text's tones in terms of comparable modern situations, without adequate reference to its verbal texture and without sufficient regard for differing social contexts of different readers.

If you are interested in joining this experiment, you should play Cut G now, before reading further. Please note what meanings you understand from each reading-aloud, and send me these notes along with brief biographical information including when and with what professor(s) you studied Chaucer.

In answer to the second and third questions, I here present the results of a similar experiment, which show that I do indeed arrange aural data to support my thesis. They show also that someone else may indeed hear the same reading-aloud and understand it differently—the same as happens when listening to Bob Dylan songs, as mentioned in my Introduction. I thus wish to delineate rather than ignore problems of performance analysis, because textual analysts have too long done the latter—have too long pretended that their own responses to a text can be validly arranged to support a thesis in such a way that alternative theses seem false, rather than alternative.

For this experiment Tom Burton volunteered to do what I have just asked you to do. He listened, without preparation, to the twenty-six readings of *PardT* ll. 960–65 in Cut G and noted his understanding of each. A comparison of our responses demonstrates that I had in fact skewed my perceptions in order to support a feminist interpretation of the data.

Critics on paper have recently been investigating the same hypothesis that I was here proposing on tape. They say that a woman's perception of textual issues, and in particular of textual women, differs in fundamental ways from a man's perception. Yet white, middle-class, middle-aged males dominate the current interpretive community. For example, Alice Kaminsky's survey of twentieth-century criticism on *Troilus and Criseyde* confirms that nearly all interpreters blame Criseyde. Kaminsky argues that the variety of men's justifications for blame allows for her own sympathetic interpretation as well, of Criseyde as a "sensual woman with a strong will to survive."[12]

Kaminsky's survey and this chapter's experimental results both indicate that a feminist approach ought to be presented as one possible interpretation, but not the only one. The temptation to do otherwise is perhaps stronger in the classroom than in published criticism.

On the other hand, I find that a shift from tentative to overt cynicism in my classroom presentation of "courtly love" has had little effect on my students' responses to *Troilus*. I used to present "courtly love" as a literary construct possibly useful for understanding Troilus's behavior. Lately, bolstered by comments of Georges Duby and others, I brush past "courtly love" as an inaccurate idea invented by late-nineteenth-century juxtaposers of discrepant material.[13] Regardless of the approach I use when teaching, I find that male and female students both point out extensive textual evidence that all Troilus does is cry, except sometimes when he whimpers, and that Diomede is at least honest about what he wants. (At Cheker of the Hope in Canterbury, Diomede would have gripped Kitt's wrists and chin, looked her straight in the eye, and said, "Before we go to your place, do you have any diseases you want to tell me about?")

For my students, as for anybody else's, responses to the text are not spontaneous. They are shaped by professorial attitudes, which in this case are created only partly by my own research on courtly-love conventions and are relayed only partly in a conscious pedagogic plan. Primarily, any man who has regarded me as a goddess whom he is unworthy to serve has rapidly convinced me that he is indeed unworthy.

No man, including Chaucer, has experienced the receiving end of courtly-love conventions. The genius of Chaucer as opposed to Lydgate, say, is that he put words onto paper that appeal directly and meaningfully to readers whose own life experiences differ as fundamentally as do those of male and female, a gap wider at many points than the gap between fourteenth-century males and twentieth-century males.

For experimental purposes it would be ideal if Tom Burton and I, male and female, also represented opposite extremes of possible life experiences for twentieth-century Chaucerians. We do not, because we are close to the same age—both born after World War II. Also, we share the lack of any high-powered intellectual background. We grew up in rural areas of Shropshire and Pennsylvania, respectively, where few of our contemporaries (not even our siblings) went on to college. Our respective parents encouraged us to go on but remain surprised to have produced Chaucer professors gainfully employed in Australia and New Jersey.

Burton and Bowden differ indisputably, however, as to gender. We also differ in the relative formality of our introductions to Chaucer. At the University of Bristol Burton began specializing in Middle English as an undergraduate, studying with Basil Cottle, who thereafter became his graduate supervisor. He taught school in Africa before starting his Ph.D.; having finished it, he had just accepted a job selling insurance when the University of Adelaide called him. Burton never expected to teach Chaucer, nor did I. Nonetheless Burton's post-secondary education prepared him for that precise eventuality.

I, however, never took a Chaucer course. I argued my way out of that particular English-major requirement, at the University of Wisconsin in 1969, on the grounds that I had already learned Middle English by typing it—by typing notes and glosses to some Canterbury tales for V. A. Kolve, thanks to intervention by R. L. Wadsworth, who had found me down and out, a street hippie in London, with no money for a plane ticket back to finish college. Chaucer rescued me, financially and (if truth be told) emotionally—not a usual motivation for one's turning to medieval literature at the University of California, where at my request Charles Muscatine worked some Chaucer into a seminar on fabliaux.

Coming from a quite dissimilar background, thus, Burton listened to cuts that I had classified and arranged as follows, according to the tone I heard in the Knight's "Namoore of this, for it is right ynough!"

G1–2   (plus Curtis and Parsigian in print):   royal command.
G3–6:   diplomat or professional negotiator.
G7–12:   authoritative, but in a situation to which he is unaccustomed.
G13–18   (plus Lipscomb):   kind and patient.
G19–24   (plus Gardner):   scolding misbehaving children.
G25–26   (on request, as will be discussed):   royal command.

Harboring no preconceptions as to how I must have arranged the data, Burton heard instead three groups: "authoritarian (which takes in your 'royal command' and some of your 'scolding' ones); soothing (which covers your 'kind and patient' and some of the others); combinations of authoritarian 'Namoore's with more soothing words to follow (e.g. G6)."[14]

In each description that follows, I give my own initial response first, followed by Burton's as "TB." Remember that presentation of all the available evidence, this one time, necessarily includes many readings with background buzzes, fuzziness, and other flaws in sound quality.

Cut G, *PardT* ll. 960–65

G1 issues a royal decree, then continues with formal fondness, as a king who loves his subjects. TB: Authoritative.

G2 issues a brisk command, then tries to cheer everybody up. TB: Authoritative (slightly less regal).

G3 is brisk also, accustomed to his role as a professional mediator. Although his is not to command obedience, he has the authority of extensive experience. Notice the textual variants here and elsewhere, like scribal errors: no "for" in line 962, and an extra "ye" to help question the propriety of "kisse" in line 965. TB: Reads too fast! Sounds sort of worldly-wise/bored—"Come on, let's get this over."

G4 also has extensive diplomatic training and experience, but in a more class-structured society; he is talking down to underlings. TB: Soothing. Let's keep the peace.

G5 is less formal, light and cheerful, for he fully expects this proposed mediation to proceed without a hitch. TB: Similar to G4. Cheer up and keep the peace.

G6 is likewise accustomed to success in whatever negotiations he proposes but in addition has learned the value of polite coaxing of the parties in dispute. TB: Combination of authoritarian "Namoore" with peace-keeping formula following.

G7 probably does not arbitrate as a career, but he makes an efficient and self-confident suggestion with no doubt it will be followed. In line 965, the "kisse" suggests not questioning of propriety as did G3's, but rather satisfaction at the solution. TB: Same as G6.

G8 is firm but not quite so certain that this suggestion will create immediate accord. TB: Same as G6, or perhaps more soothing.

G9 was not born into authority nor did he achieve it. Realizing that authority has been thrust upon him, however, he pleads with social equals, then gets louder and more enthusiastic, trying to cheer them up. TB: Very soothing. Most soothing so far.

G10 likewise finds the role thrust upon him of addressing this embarrassing dispute. G10's Knight is compelled to speak up in a gentlemen's club, where two spatting members are about to spill brandy on the leather armchairs or disturb denizens reading the *Times* across by the fireplace. TB: Similar to G6.

G11 takes charge in a sheepish military manner, when two other guys in the barracks start rough-housing: "If you don't cut it out and the sarge walks through the door, we're *all* in trouble." TB: Soothing rather than authoritarian.

G12 is one of the guys also, but one lounging around a pool table. The bartender doesn't even look over. But if these two pull guns, cops might come and then start snooping around the rest of us. TB: Something like G3.

G13 begins the series of primarily kind and patient Knights. Momentarily irritated that they would act this way, in line 962, G13 then makes kind suggestions for healing the breach. TB: Like a 45 record played at 33; conciliatory rather than commanding.

G14 gently coaxes, in a voice so sympathetic that perhaps he remembers what it feels like to lose one's temper. TB: Very soothing.

G15, G16, G17, and G18 are quite similar in their gentle, kind, patient suggestions to the quarrelers. TB: G15 fairly soothing; G17 and G18 soothing; G16 "a bit forced when she speaks as the Knight. I'd say the emphasis is on command."

G19 sounds kind also, but not to other adults. A mother's fond coaxing is addressed to five-year-old twins who both want to sit next to the window. But they played somewhat quietly all morning, and as soon as she drops them at kindergarten she'll meet her best friend for lunch. TB: Soothing.

G20 is also fond of five-year-olds or would not be facing this roomful of them, but when the twins misbehave a teacher's responsibility is to scold them. TB: Soothing.

G21, still expecting obedience, calls out across the playground when they start scuffling. TB: Authoritarian.

G22 is finally starting to lose patience: "Stop this nonsense! Act your ages!" TB: Authoritarian.

G23 is losing track even of ages, just scolding with little hope that anything but the close of the school day will end dispute. TB: Similar combination to G6.

G24 is seeing double, ready to collapse as soon as the door closes behind the last parent come for quadruplets or any of the rest. And today only Tuesday. TB: Weary "Namoore" and fairly soothing "make it up."

Burton and I coincide in our assessments of the extremes, hearing regality in G1 and weariness in G24. In between, though, Burton hears various tones but does not make the distinction to which my feminist hypothesis led: that many of the women's voices sound to me as if they are scolding children. In addition, no woman seems to me to have read the passage in tones of professional political authority; G1–6 are all men. A tone of professional command is spontaneously imagined by Parsigian and Curtis, however, both women. Is it possible that such a tone is physically difficult for a female voice?

In the next chapter, thanks to a very deep-voiced male reader who volunteered the *Pardoner's Prologue* in a goatlike falsetto, I will mention sex-determinate limitations on oral delivery. Just to make sure that women can read the passage as a royal command, I asked two to do so. G25 had spontaneously created a sympathetic Knight as G14, and G26 had not previously done a reading. They sound regal to me. Burton heard both G25 and G26 as "fairly commanding."

Rather than spin out the matter too fine and thereby entangle ourselves in the sticky issue of reader's intention, I will simply conclude that I had subjectively perceived sex-determinate interpretive differences, ones that fade in the light of experiment. I look forward to receiving your notes on your initial understanding of the readings on Cut G.

It still seems to me, as I will investigate further, that the single most audible feature of any given reading—is it a girl or a boy?—must likewise contribute essentially to any one person's understanding of a text. Individually varying experiences, expectations, and attitudes usually involve degree: more or less wealth, more or less religious training, more or less respect for rules. But nearly everyone—let us cautiously say everyone who has ever published literary criticism—is either male or female. One of the very few generalizations made by anthropologists about cultures so far discovered, furthermore, is that all distinguish male from female social roles. In some cultures men provide child care and in some women hunt, but all differentiate, as does ours.

Principally, though, I present the results of this experiment in an admonitory spirit. First, wholly impressionistic descriptions are more interesting to write and to read—more fun, to be honest—than are ones attempting objectivity. Effective communication lurks somewhere in between the musicological extreme and the literary one, though ranging closer to the latter. Descriptions of aural meaning must begin with each listener's comparison of the sounds heard to familiar visual and aural experiences. An analyst then must link analogies to labelable elements in each performance, such as pitch and pauses, without expecting that a given element will predictably create a given meaning.

Second, I have shown that I did indeed arrange the data in order to support my own feminist perceptions. Analogously, should any subjectivist critic look up from theory to gaze at actual evidence for varying interpretations of a text, he should be wary of falling into the New-Critical marle-pit from another direction: that of pretending to be objective while interpreting the range of interpretations.

It is our responsibility as professors (and secondarily as publishing critics) to keep in mind gender and other differences that may be causing each of us to respond to a work in a certain way. Rather than authoritatively impose contextual and aesthetic limitations on interpretation, we should first question the validity of each limitation. Thus we can come to question the unstated assumptions of our cultural context and our personal experiences, which we both share and do not share with the next generation of potential Chaucerians.

CHAPTER 6

The Old Man in the *Pardoner's Tale*

Among the next generation of potential Chaucerians, only a few will have encountered any version at all of folktale motif K1685, "The treasure-finders who murder one another"—those few being film buffs who know *The Treasure of the Sierra Madre* with Humphrey Bogart.[1] Therefore, students need to learn that the story was told thousands of times after and before Chaucer, and furthermore "that the old man in the *Pardoner's Tale* should seek death is a feature not paralleled in any known analogue of the tale."[2]

The multitude of conflicting interpretations of this character by 1951 had led one critic to argue that "the old man is merely an old man" and by 1964 had elicited from another, "not merely *an* old man, but *the* old man."[3] Recent interpreters lack the conviction of Kittredge, though, for whom the old man is "undoubtedly Death in person." Kittredge was passing on the standard nineteenth-century label. Introducing the 1841 collection of modernizations, Richard Horne says that Chaucer "introduces Death in a dramatic scene as a very poor old man, too old to live, yet who cannot escape from life."[4]

Horne, Leigh Hunt, and the other collaborators had planned a second volume of modernizations. In 1846, however, the project having been abandoned unmourned, Hunt includes a remnant from the collection—a still comic *Pardoner's Prologue,* with prose translation at page bottoms—in his *Wit and Humour, Selected from the English Poets.*[5] Then in 1855, for his *Stories in Verse,* Hunt modernizes *PardT* ll. 463–82 and 661–888 as *Death and the Ruffians.*

The title makes Hunt seem almost as certain as are Horne and Kittredge of this allegorical label, Death, for the old man. But Hunt's plot summary preserves some of the ambiguity that twentieth-century readers find:

> Three drunken ruffians, madly believing Death to be an embodied
> person, go out to kill him. They meet him in the shape of an old
> man, who tells them where Death is to be found; and they find
> him accordingly.[6]

Nor does the only earlier plot summary, Thomas Speght's in his 1598
edition, dictate one-to-one allegory: "A company of riotours conspire to
kill Death, who killeth them one after another." As will be discussed,
also, one eighteenth-century reader interprets the old man as not Death
but Time.

Thus, though it may sometimes look as if Kittredge cut from whole
cloth this old man and every other issue in twentieth-century criticism,
here and elsewhere he was reformulating, for Harvard students, problems posed by nonacademic commentators on Chaucer. As another example, in the introduction to *Death and the Ruffians,* Hunt antedates
Kittredge in noting the difficulty of telling the *Tale* of the Pardoner in the
same tone of voice as his *Prologue.*

The Pardoner himself states that a vicious man can tell a moral tale
(*PardT* ll. 459–60), and a mocking huckster tells it for William Lipscomb
in 1793. Hunt, however, finds a discrepancy: "He tells this admirable
story in the tone of a good man, though he has prefaced it (in the original)
with an impudent confession of his knavery." Kittredge authoritatively
converts discrepancy to impossibility. In the *Tale* the Pardoner's voice
must necessarily convey "fervor . . . because the tale is so moving that no
one could tell it flippantly."[7]

Cut H, *PardT* ll. 329–34, 366–71, and 711–75

Would that Kittredge had preserved for us the experiment H1 volunteered to attempt: a performance of a flippant Pardoner's impudent confession in a voice "as smal as hath a goot" (*GP* l. 688) before a shift to
his normal deep pitch to create the old man, riotours, apothecary, tavern-
keeper, and little boy in the *Pardoner's Tale.* H1 shifts from a goatlike
falsetto in lines 366–71 of the *Pardoner's Prologue* with audible relief
to his own voice in lines 711–24 of the *Tale.* (See *Texts Read Aloud,*
Chapter 6.)

This deep-voiced reader's experiment implies possible sex-determinate
limits on oral performance, albeit not on mental soundings. The strain
of maintaining falsetto produces a near-identical up-pitch at the end of
every line (except *PardT* l. 367, on "rage") and in other ways prevents or
veils meaningful vocal inflections. Only in line 369 does H1 create a

specifiable tone, the patently insincere indignation of "And *nev*ere shal he *moore* his wyf mys*triste.*"

When H1 drops to his normal pitch, we meet there a narrator sympathetic to poverty and meekness (on "povre" and "mekely"), then in *PardT* ll. 716–17 one more indignant at the riotours' rudeness than is the old man himself. But H1's old man can take care of himself: in line 715, the tone of greeting shows that as soon as he sees these ruffians he knows to expect trouble. H1's proudest riotour is not as tough or blind-drunk as some to be heard on Cut I, though. The hissed *s* on "sory" and "so," plus pauses, project his hesitancy. The brash words of lines 717–19 mask the fear with which H1's riotours regard this mummified figure risen abruptly in their path. As in Cut I2 to come, H1 projects a particularly visual interpretation. The characters interact in response to actions and appearances we listeners do not see.

Before approaching Cut I's old men, ranging from sternly manipulative to pathetic, and the narrower spectrum of vicious or curious riotours, let me present H2 reading *PardT* ll. 329–34, 366–71, and 711–75. Taking advantage of her higher-pitched female voice, H2 effectively characterizes the Pardoner as orator. Within the *Tale* delivered in his squeaky voice, furthermore, H2 even manages to read lines 731–36 as the Pardoner imitating himself preaching a sermon in which an old man imitates himself calling out to mother earth.

H2's *tour de force* of oral delivery begins with the shrill-voiced Pardoner's call to attention, clearly distinguished from Chaucer-the-pilgrim's "quod he" in *PardT* l. 329. H2's Pardoner compensates for his vocal handicap by sounding loud and authoritative even while confiding trade secrets. Self-satisfied that he has captured everyone's attention by lines 332–33, he launches into a full-performance Latin chant.

For several readers besides H2, the Pardoner breaks into a church-Latin chant from time to time in both *Prologue* and sermon. A quick test with listeners who understand no Middle English shows that those raised Catholic promptly label the inflections here those of the Latin mass. Having been raised Methodist, I had never imagined the Pardoner chanting. Religious upbringing of each reader-aloud, though not obvious like gender, demonstrably figures in oral interpretations and by implication in silent ones.

Basking equally in present or recollected spotlights, H2's Pardoner has made no distinct shift to address the church audience at *PardT* l. 352. On the last segment of the *Prologue* assigned to readers, lines 366–71, H2's inflections differ in degree, not in kind, from those directly addressed to the pilgrims. Self-satisfaction at the pilgrims' full attention has become a professional salesman's satisfaction at the efficacy of his product, jealousy-assuasive soup bones.

H2 maintains what is certainly this Pardoner's voice, not Chaucer's or the scholar's own, throughout the *Tale*. The rest of Cut H2, *PardT* ll. 711–75, demonstrates that the difficulty of doing so is in fact not limited to Hunt, Kittredge, H1, and other males. A goatlike falsetto, projected to a crowd, necessitates straining vowels across high pitches. It thereby limits the potential for variety in characters' voices. They all seem to be calling out to one another across a vast chasm and sometimes seem like robots programmed for human speech. No one could perform this dialogue well in artificial falsetto; H2 is remarkable in performing it at all.

Why is this one aural stage direction so hard to follow? Throughout his works, Chaucer specifies far more details of appearances than of speaking voices. We do know how quite a few characters sing: the Prioress through her nose, Alison loud like a swallow, Nicholas in a blessed voice, Absolon in one "gentil and smal," and so on. But of speaking voices besides the Pardoner's, we know only that the Friar affects a lisp and that the Clerk's rare remarks are short and quick. These vocal traits, habitual but voluntary, help characterize the latter two—just as, for example, a temporary tone of quaking anger helps characterize the Summoner.

Because such vocal habits develop for a particular reason, responsive readers experience them differently than they do the Pardoner's permanently squeaky voice. We think about why the Friar lisps and wonder why the Clerk speaks tersely, just as we think about motivations for a voice that quakes in ire. We think about the Pardoner's voice as well, but we know that he speaks that way in all moods, to convey all emotions. His vocal characteristic is permanent. A reader no more need perform the Pardoner's falsetto than gap her teeth to read the Wife or join her eyebrows to read Criseyde.[8]

Aural evidence, textual consideration, and common sense all weigh against attempting a literal oral manifestation of *GP* l. 688. Kittredge muddied the issue, however, by mixing in morality. Squeakiness became flippancy, and a curt story set in a merciless universe became so moving that not even Kittredge could imagine performing its entire script in the Pardoner's specified voice.

Although Kittredge could not, H2 gives it the old college try (as it were). Despite difficult mechanics of oratorical falsetto, H2 does distinguish the characters' voices from each other and does make them convey labelable attitudes.

As Cut H2 continues, the old man sounds kind and friendly on *PardT*

l. 715, resembling a number of others. As is not at all common, H2's riotour replies in open terror. Perhaps in lines 717–18 his voice cracks from the strain of the Pardoner's falsetto, however, rather than from fear.

H2 uses a tremolo to distinguish the old man's speeches from those of narrator and riotour. After the Pardoner supplies such a tremolo on "olde" in both lines 714 and 720, it recurs throughout *PardT* ll. 721–49 as a signal of advanced age. Thus H2 keeps us aware of the old man's vulnerability, even while he is expressing slight resentment (ll. 721, 747), defiance (midline 741), or other signs of potential strength in the confrontation. He sounds even older when he imitates his own pleas to his mother, in lines 731–36, insofar as words stretched more tremulously make one sound older. Holy Writ speaks in the voice of a very "oold man," also, especially on those two words in line 743.

Maintaining falsetto seems to block certain common readings. Nearly all readers convey some degree of threat with lines 750–59. H2's riotours instead, no longer terrorized after the autobiography, begin with almost a horselaugh followed by a chuckle on line 750. "No way!" says line 752. H2's representative riotour passes through attitudes including amazement at the old man's knowledge (ll. 753–54), honorable pledges by "my trouthe" and by God, a renewed twinge of fear after line 757, and then bravado ending in accusation. His most harsh phrase, "thou false theef," sounds milder than the least harsh parts of most other performances of *PardT* ll. 750–59.

As another instance of H2's unusual interpretation, H2's old man displays none of the smugness or glee common to other readings of *PardT* ll. 760–67. Sounding pitiful, wanting only to be rid of them, he almost weeps in relief as the riotours scamper away in the middle of line 767.

H2's fully characterized Pardoner picks up the tale at this point with heartiness verging on demand that we succumb to his compelling interpretation. He brushes past the famously ambiguous line 772 so that it can sink in later. Instead, his voice forces us to sit down and feel glad like the riotours as they (we) run vocal fingers through the bright gold. A skillful orator, H2's Pardoner makes listeners participate in sin, against our will or better judgment. At story's end, relieved at our narrow escapes, we will give pence generously.

In comparison, other Pardoners on tape make sure that listeners do not miss the heavy irony of line 772. As in Cuts F6–7 and in the many described mental soundings of *PardT* l. 913ff., the issue arises here of the two in-text audiences. In this case either subtle or overt dramatic irony in line 772 could help make the story effective for gullible churchgoers as well as for the pilgrims and for us overhearers.

A naive reading of line 772 encourages purse-unbuckling in the way just described for H2. The use of overt irony on this line, exemplified by H3, in another way can cue even the dumbest churchgoers that death is close and that earthly treasure cannot be taken with them. I make no further attempt to detangle ambiguities here; I simply reiterate that "irony" is an oral issue that for too long has been discussed as if it existed on the silent page.

H3 reads *PardT* l. 772 with definite irony, unlike H2, and does not imitate the Pardoner's falsetto. Otherwise, H3 shares with H2 several features that are unusual compared with other oral interpretations of *PardT* ll. 755–75. H3's riotour does not threaten with lines 755–59, except for slight accusation on "false theef," and like H2's he swears heroic vows by his trouthe and by God. H3's old man then sounds kind, if perhaps a bit brisk at sending unsuspecting boys to secret death. He resembles H2's old man more than he does all the others on the Chaucer tapes, though, who seethe with sinister glee. H3's Pardoner steps in at line 767, slightly bored with the story that he has told so often—but not too bored to pinpoint the irony of line 772 with a decisive chuckle.

H3's reading, though bland in characterization and fuzzy in sound compared to others, deserves a place in this study because H3 is F. N. Robinson, reading his own second edition. As I was examining Francis Lee Utley's papers at Ohio State University, a class handout led me to the language lab where not only Utley and his colleagues but also Robinson had left practice tapes for Ohio State students. Robinson's must date from 1959 when he, twenty years emeritus after his half-century at Harvard, took an L.H.D. at Ohio State.

Kittredge died in 1941, twenty-six years before Robinson did. I have determined to my disappointment that the Harvard language lab harbors no such tape of Kittredge, nor of anyone else prior to Larry Benson. Kittredge's voice lives on only through his publications and his students, including Robinson and, indirectly, all of us.[9] Unfortunately, Robinson at Ohio State read only *PardT* ll. 661–776, thus leaving us no second-generation paroxysm of agonized sincerity.

Cuts I3–4, M1–4, and N1–2 will present teacher-student pairs who eerily resemble one another in details of oral delivery, even while conveying ideas of their own. Perhaps therefore Kittredge, like Robinson, chuckled or otherwise indicated overt irony with the ambiguous line 772. If so, Kittredge was passing on an interpretation that can be traced back another century via the modernized *Pardoner's Tales* of Leigh Hunt in 1855 and William Lipscomb in 1793.

Both early modernizers, however, keep the ambiguity subtle in *PardT*

l. 772. With updated spelling only, "No lenger thanne after Deeth they soughte" could have fit either Hunt's or Lipscomb's poem. Lipscomb's replacement line conveys a slightly different ambiguity than we now perceive in Chaucer's, especially if experienced aurally:

> Charm'd with the view, of Death they think no more,
> But bend in raptures o'er the glittering store.[10]

Lipscomb's comma signals that the phrase "of Death" belongs with the clause that follows it. Nonetheless, for a moment the reader applies "Death" to the gold, as if the line read "Charm'd with the view of Death, they think no more."

In 1855, three decades after his succinct remark on the double meaning of the Prioress's motto, Hunt likewise develops the ambiguity apparent to us now in line 772. His substitute line, stripped of dramatic irony in immediate context, occurs two couplets before the gold itself appears:

> They reach the nook: and what behold they there!
> No Death, but yet a sight to make them stare.[11]

By this point, however, Hunt has long since foreshadowed the irony of the coming discovery. In addition to his plot summary quoted, he plays with the term d/Death as his riotours launch their quest. Hunt's ruffians, from their first speech, gratuitously insult the dead and the innocent:

> They curs'd, and call'd the vintner's boy, and said,
> "Who's he that has been made cold meat tonight?
> Ask the fool's name, and see you bring it right?"[12]

They go on to propose crude tactics for murdering Death:

> "God grant a fig's end," exclaim'd one. "Who's he
> Goes blasting thus fools' eyes? Let's forth, we three,
> And hunt him out, and punch the musty breath
> Out of his bones, and be the death of Death."[13]

Hunt uses his old man to reinforce the ambiguity. His modernized lines 760–67 contain no benediction—be it sincere, grit-teethed, or gloating. Instead, Hunt's old man conveys the dramatic irony of d/Death with terse exasperation:

> "Sirs," quoth the old man, "spare, I pray, your breaths:
> Death ye would find, and this your road is Death's.
> Ye see yon spread of oaks, down by the brook;
> There doth he lie, sunn'd in a flowery nook." [14]

Like Hunt, Lipscomb eliminates the benediction of *PardT* ll. 766–67 and personifies Death more precisely than does Chaucer, picturing him upright under the oak rather than in Hunt's prone position. Instead of sounding exasperated, however, Lipscomb's old man would speak in calm, dignified tones, perhaps edging toward sarcasm or smugness on the last line:

> "Sirs!" then the man replied, "if you to find
> "All-powerful Death so strongly are inclin'd,
> "Let but that crooked path direct your feet,
> "And then the wish'd-for foe ye sure shall meet:
> "For in that grove that rears its head so high,
> "I late beheld him as I passed by.
> "See you yon oak that towers above the wood?
> "Beneath its wide-extended shade he stood;
> "And there he'll wait, my honest word believe,
> "Nor shall th' event your glowing hopes deceive." [15]

Lipscomb's old man replies thus to a riotour's "saucy tone" (for *PardT* ll. 750–51). His riotours earlier, quite unlike Hunt's thugs, reply with "hearty voice" (for *PardT* l. 702) to a stirring vow sealed with a triplet:

> "Shame on your fears," a bravo bold replies;
> "I scorn the caitif, and his pow'r despise;
> "And I will restless hunt each lane and street,
> "So that the dreaded foe at length I meet.
> "Come now, my boys, we three our oaths will plight,
> "Our force against the tyrant to unite,
> "And he shall ne'er survive th' approaching night."
>   "Agreed," with hearty voice, they each reply'd,
> "Nought shall henceforth our cordial souls divide." [16]

Thus, Lipscomb provides both direct and indirect evidence that he hears bold heartiness in *PardT* ll. 692–701, whereas Hunt, as quoted, hears a crude snarl. These alternative possibilities are by no means time-bound, for both can be heard now on commercially available recordings. On a Folkways album, Victor Kaplan has the three youths nobly vow to seek a cure for the plague; on Caedmon, Robert Ross performs them as crude repulsive drunken slobs staggering out the door. Ross's oral characterization then remains the more consistent, for at line 717 Kaplan must convert his fresh-faced lads into brash scorners of a whimpering dotard.[17]

Perhaps because Lipscomb imagines all voices filtered through his Pardoner's mockery of the uneducated, his elegant-speaking riotours remain more consistent throughout than do Kaplan's oral ones. Hunt, like Ross orally, keeps his riotours rude and vicious throughout. They first greet the figure as "old crawler," for "carl" in *PardT* l. 717. Instead of the "saucy tone" Lipscomb imagines in lines 750–59, then, Hunt provides more nasty names and gratuitous cursing.

> "Nay," t'other cried, "Old Would-be Dead and Gone,
> Thou partest not so lightly, by Saint John.
> Thou spak'st but now of that false villain, Death,
> Who stoppeth here a world of honest breath:
> Where doth he bide? Tell us, or by the Lord,
> And Judas, and the jump in hempen cord,
> As surely as thou art his knave and spy,
> We'll hang thee out, for thine old rheums to dry.
> Thou art his privy nipper, thou old thief,
> Blighting and blasting all in the green leaf."[18]

A nineteenth-century dictionary of slang clarifies the insulting names. A "crawler" would today be called a "brown-nose": "A workman who curries favour with a foreman or employer; a 'lick-spittle' or 'bumsucker.'" And "nipper," in association with "thief," evokes a lad in training as a cutpurse or pickpocket.[19] Thus, the latter image foreshadows the hidden treasure, and both images emphasize that Hunt's riotours regard the old man as not Death himself but an agent sent by Death, his "espye" (*PardT* l. 755).

Might Hunt himself think the same about the old man? Or, despite the misled riotours' identification, might Hunt join some modern critics who instead regard the old man as an agent sent by a benevolent force, by God, bringing instant death to disrespectful youngsters so that we good Christians can enjoy eternal life?

Hunt's conception of the old man appears in his exasperated farewell, as quoted, and also in his first exchange with the riotours (for *PardT* ll. 760–67 and 714–20). Like H1's old man, Hunt's knows to expect trouble. He need not sound meek, for Hunt shifts the adverb from his greeting to his physical movement. Then the old man looks the boys straight in the eye. Hunt's ruffians meet

> A poor old man, who meekly gave them way,
> And bow'd, and said, "God save ye, Sirs, I pray."
>
> The foremost swaggerer, prouder for the bow,
> Said, "Well, old crawler, what art canting now?
> Why art thus wrapp'd up, all save thy face?
> Why liv'st so long, in such a sorry case?"
>
> The old man began looking steadfastly
> Into the speaker's visage, eye to eye.[20]

Six decades earlier, Lipscomb likewise shifts the adverb so that the old man need not speak meekly as he steps aside. After Lipscomb's riotours make a sympathetic inquiry, however, his old man raises not a steadfast eye but a feeble one:

> An aged man they met, in mean array—
> "Save you, good lords," he said, and meekly gave the way.
> Him then the boldest of the three address'd,
> "Wretch that thou art, by double griefs oppress'd,
> "By age bent down, not less than carking care,
> "Wherefore so long dost thou such misery bear?"
>
> Then rais'd the aged man his feeble eye,
> And in his visage look'd, and made reply.[21]

Each modernizer's mental picture is thus conveyed partly in terms of eye contact, Hunt's old man seeming more of a match for ruffians than Lipscomb's would be. Analogously, silent and oral interpreters of the passage visualize degree of eye contact and imagine or perform voices appropriately.

Early evidence of such interpretations occurs in the two earliest illustrations of the *Pardoner's Tale*. The first picture appeared a generation before Lipscomb, the second a generation after him. It is the later old man who more resembles Lipscomb's, more resembles the feeble old soul who would meet the riotours' eyes only briefly before dropping his own again.

S. Williams, the artist for C. C. Clarke's 1835 school edition, provides

THE PARDONER'S TALE.

"Now, Sirs, quod he, if it be you so lief
To finden Death, turn up this crooked way;
For in that grove I left him."

l. 465.

FIGURE 7:   *Pardoner's Tale* scene (captioned with lines 760–62), by S. Williams, facing p. 264 of vol. 1 of *The Riches of Chaucer,* ed. Charles Cowden Clarke (London: Effingham Wilson, 1835). Reproduced by permission of the Van Pelt Library, University of Pennsylvania. Actual size, 2¼″ × 3″.

as caption for his picture the directions to the grove, *PardT* ll. 760–62. (See figure 7.) Williams portrays three mean-looking carousers, analogous to Hunt's, in somewhat Elizabethan outfits. One, piratelike in turban and eye patch, pulls a dagger; another swigs from a flask. The third, legs braced and arms akimbo, defiantly confronts a pathetic figure quite unlike Hunt's. Pointing the way wearily with drooping finger, clutching his staff as if needing it to sit upright, Williams's robed and bearded old man does not arise from the hillock or even raise his eyes from his mother earth.

In contrast, the earliest illustration shows the moment at which an undaunted, indeed daunting old man has looked the riotours straight in the eye and sternly sent them up the crooked path to death. (See figure 8.) Robed and bearded, he holds the staff without needing it for support. The three well-dressed Elizabethan courtiers, resembling Lipscomb's riotours, appear neither sinister nor rowdy. One is still regarding with bemused interest the old man's face. The other two—one round-eyed and eager, the other wary—have turned to discuss the route, the way shown them by Time.

Besides his *Departure of the Canterbury Pilgrimes* (fig. 5), John H. Mortimer before 1779 made eight drawings of scenes from the *Tales,* including the one just described, *Three Gamblers and Time.*[22] Indeed, Mortimer's old man resembles the Father Time who still graces New Year's napkins. (One might trace the history of this visual image, comparing it with that of the Grim Reaper.) Was Time the old man's standard allegorical label in the eighteenth century, as was Death in the nineteenth? Perhaps.

In the absence of other evidence, though, we must also consider the possibility that idiosyncrasy—which Blake would term genius—accounts for this representation of the old man. Mortimer, one of the very few artists praised and emulated by Blake, elsewhere creates conceptions out of the ordinary. Within *Departure of the Canterbury Pilgrimes,* for example, Mortimer portrays a plump Squire—one not at all likely to "wel . . . sitte on hors and faire ryde" or to charm the ladies with his even stature, agility, and strength (*GP* ll. 94, 83–84)—and a witchlike Wife of Bath who could much resemble the hag in her *Tale.* (See figure 5.) And we will see that in the eighteenth century only Mortimer questions the cheery amorality of Pope's modernized *Merchant's Tale.* In Mortimer's illustration, the May who climbs toward Damyan sets upon January's back a shoe in the shape of a cloven hoof. (See figure 11.)

These four early interpretations lay out a range of possibilities for the old man's confrontation with the riotours. Before 1779 Mortimer's strong old man, Time, meets genteel riotours; in 1793 Lipscomb's feeble man meets genteel boys; in 1835 Williams's feeble man meets rowdy boys; in 1855 Hunt's strong old man meets ruffians. The differences represent each interpreter's interaction with the text, not that text's changing

FIGURE 8:   *Three Gamblers and Time,* drawn by J. H. Mortimer and engraved
by J. Hogg. Leaf of unknown origin bound into a copy of John Urry's edition of
The Works of Geoffrey Chaucer (London: B. Lintot, 1721), fEC. C3932.C/
721W. Reproduced by permission of the Houghton Library, Harvard University.
Actual size, 7⅜″ × 9⅝″.

significance in shifting sociohistorical conditions, and certainly not a
linear development toward ours as the best of all possible understandings
of the scene. All four of these combinations, and others besides, can be
heard on the Chaucer tapes.

Cut I, *PardT* ll. 713–24 and 737–67

Exaggerated viciousness occurs often, echoing Hunt's or Williams's riotours, as readers-aloud project their confrontations with the multitudinous old men who populate twentieth-century criticism, or with someone even weirder. Most readers make the riotours neither saucy, as does Lipscomb, nor scared, as do H1 and H2, but instead scornful of the old man—who is sometimes irritated at their rudeness, sometimes oblivious, sometimes quavery with fear. That is, the responses of characters to each others' tones vary as widely as do the tones themselves.

Of twenty-four readings-aloud of the Pardoner passages, twenty-two include the confrontation scene. (Two women readers skipped the *Tale* itself, for reasons to be suggested.) Two of these readings have been heard already as H1 and H2. From the remaining twenty, I have eliminated half in which the characterization is less sharply defined; these readers tend to recite rather than enact.

Of those ten readings that do dramatize, however, not all are aesthetically successful. For reasons to be suggested, this is a difficult scene for modern readers. Several, like Kaplan on the Folkways recording, shift characterization midstream. An old man may greet the riotours in a pathetic quaver at line 715, for example, but harden abruptly to viciousness matching theirs at line 721. Cut I therefore includes just four readings, four that differ among themselves, however, as extensively as do the four pre-twentieth-century interpretations.

On Cut I, these four readings are arranged according to the strength of the old man's initial greeting. Beginning with an old man who, like H1's, acts as tough as the punks he faces, Cut I proceeds through a less confident rendering of "Now, lordes, God yow see," to conclude with old men who quaver with fear at the mere thought of riotours. As an example of the complexity conveyed in performance, though, I3's old totterer sounds pathetic until line 761, when his voice slides into smug satisfaction at the success of his ploy. During I3's lines 761–67, we come to realize what the riotours never do: that they have been insulting someone very powerful who has cunningly disguised himself as a helpless old man.

The oral range of possibilities cannot be usefully generalized, however, into a strong or feeble old man confronting genteel or rowdy riotours, as I did for the pre-twentieth-century evidence on paper. Let me unfurl, therefore, the range of possibilities with an account of all ten characterized readings.

Lines 713–15: The old men of three of the ten readers first greet their respective riotours in quavery, pathetic voices. Two are hearty and friendly. Two know to expect trouble, as did H1's. Two, preoccupied, just want to get on past the stile. One is a ghost.

Lines 716–19: The riotour sounds harsh and scornful to seven readers. Two riotours are curious. The one meeting the ghost sounds defiant. None of these ten initially uses brashness to cover fear, as do both H1's and H2's.

Lines 720–24: The old man begins to answer sounding very tired of telling this story, for two of the readers, but to one he seems a delighted Ancient Mariner—"Say, glad you asked!" Four sound resentful or insulted, while two more ghosts briefly join the other one.

Lines 737–42: The figure finishes his tale, in varieties too complex to calculate here, and turns his attention to the riotours' problematic courtesy. One old man is still irritated at them. One lays down firm rules for teen-age behavior, whereas three offer kind advice to kids who obviously have not been properly brought up. Five old men sound fussy, quavery, scared of the riotours.

Lines 743–49: Quoting scripture word-for-word and then paraphrased with proverbial force, one old man sounds smug. The appeal to traditional wisdom bolsters the self-confidence of four of the five fearful ones; they plus one of the kind advisors finish the passage in voices notably firmer than when they began. Four readers do not shift tone, delivering the Biblical injunction with whatever attitude they conveyed in lines 737–42.

Lines 750–59: As a methodological aside, note that the "oother hasardour" who replies could perhaps sound different because he differs in character from the "proudeste," who spoke first. But the text throughout the *Tale* makes it difficult to distinguish among the three riotours. Is "the worste of hem" in line 776, for example, the same riotour as the "proudeste" in line 716 on account of the worst deadly sin? Or is the youngest instead the proudest because the phrase "with sory grace" occurs in both lines 717 and 876?[23] Lipscomb attempts to distinguish them; Hunt does not. For purposes of this analysis, I will assume that we are hearing not two riotours who differ in character but rather a representative riotour who conveys what all three feel.

As suggested, this second speech by a riotour most often sounds angry and threatening, usually becoming more and more so. Six of these ten threaten. But notes of fear now creep into two riotours' voices. Another sounds indignant at being told what to do by a mere ghost, and one requests information.

Lines 760–67: The old man points them up the crooked way in a sly or cunning voice for three readers and in a smug or gleeful voice for six, ranging in degree from subtle to crowing. Only one reader conceives him with any mercy left at this point, but the note of warning in that voice comes too late to stop the riotours' mad dash.

Hunt's old man took his leave from the riotours with terse exasperation, as quoted, and Lipscomb's with calm dignity. The old man's final speech has as much potential for flexibility in performance as does the rest of the passage. Yet, after dialogues that vary so widely, the interpretations of nearly all the readers-aloud converge in the portrayal of a sinister old man expressing some degree of glee at his imminent gory revenge for random insolence.

The variety of dialogues perhaps parallels, without imitating, the variety of readers' classroom techniques. We all face potentially disrespectful youths, after all, whom we must convince of the authority of texts and of our own experience. But few of us would chortlingly lure new students, even openly insolent new students, to secret death. Why such convergence at *PardT* ll. 760–67? Let us hear that oral variety and that convergence in the four readers I1–4, then consider the implications.

I1, lines 713–24: Meeting these young toughs, I1's old man speaks heartily but, like H1's, knows to expect trouble. Sure enough, the riotour answers with scorn. He speaks with generalized scorn to everybody these days, though—to old men, young women, baby sisters, dogs of up to medium size. The old man replies with anger successfully repressed: "They'll soon get what they deserve, or else grow up, so why should I let them think they can upset me?"

I1, lines 737–49: I1's old man ends his tale feeling very sad about his mother's rejection of him. After a long pause for readjustment to the present situation, he begins to list for the riotours certain rules of teenage behavior for which they will be held responsible from now on. In line 741 he explains the one exception to the rule, which he himself, the Bible, and traditional wisdom—three equal *auctoritates*—all state. He expects no back talk, then, for he bids them go their way in tones of satisfaction at his unexpected opportunity to influence kids who obviously lack such influence. With stress on "have" in line 749, he remarks that some of us have better things to do than hang out at stiles.

I1, lines 750–59: The old man's story and firm list of rules put not quite respect but a tinge of scared awe into the riotour's voice. With quotation marks around "Deeth" in line 753, he rushes on to prove his bravery: "Honest, I really am seeking death, or anyhow somebody named 'Deeth.'"

I1, lines 760–67: The riotours had their chance, but that foul language repealed it. The old man's voice as he sends them to death bubbles not with repressed anger as earlier but with politely repressed glee. A pause spotlights the word "abyde" that ends line 763: "Indeed Death will abide; but as I suspected already back in line 747, you will not." The glee becomes overt, no longer repressed, in the second half of line 765. The narrator's pause before "olde man" in line 767 leaves the actual identity of this apparent old man as ambiguous in performance as it is on the page, except that performance ultimately slants him to the sinister.

I2, lines 713–24: An apparently unsuspecting old man enters I2's scene, though a hint of defensiveness is revealed by the pause midway through his hearty greeting. In reply comes scorn—"What right have *you* to live on?"—and three vocal question marks in lieu of the two commas and exclamation point with which Robinson punctuates line 717. Insulted but very much in control of his soft, brisk reply, I2's old man chuckles softly on line 723 and says "youthe" so as to draw attention to theirs. For a moment I2's old man sounds ready to team up with F1's Pardoner, to experiment in their basement laboratory with the exchange of old for young body parts.

I2, lines 737–38: Then I2's old man becomes even more complex. Recounting his search not for anatomical subjects but for his own death has made him very sad. I2 imagines him turning to address the riotours a line earlier than do most readers. "Ful pale and welked is my face," he tells them, "as you can see."

I2, lines 739–47: He has forgotten or forgiven their insult—unless of course his kind tone is part of his ploy to lure them into his clutches. As he explains etiquette, his stress on "old man" in line 740 conveys low expectations for their ability to absorb more than one simple concept at a time. Perhaps next week they will be assigned to memorize the parallel rule for addressing old women. I2's stress on "your*self*" recommends basic literacy as the path to redemption. He loudly delivers the Biblical passage as if it were a policy announcement, its authoritativeness letting him use the word "if" in line 747 to imply that if they continue this uneducated behavior they almost certainly will not abide.

I2, lines 748–49: As in his line 738 and as in H1's reading, I2 visualizes interaction one step ahead of most readers. While I2's old man is still speaking, the insolent riotours sneer or jeer. Thus his resigned farewell, lines 748–49, says that he has done his best but already knows that his advice has been ignored.

I2, lines 750–59: Still, I2's riotours are less obnoxious than some. The hasardour's loud talk partly covers fear. Into line 754 creeps a note of regret for his deceased friends and a note of hope that perhaps this text-quoting codger really does have access to sources of information closed to them. But threats come easy to his mouth. The "or" in line 756 he has picked up from "or else" as snarled by tough cops on American television.

I2, lines 760–67: And it turns out that this sweet old man has held a grudge after all. Slyly, quietly, he directs the seekers to certain death. In line 764 he explains the inexorable workings of death in the same calm tone with which he explained the one exception to the rule in line 741; the inflections relate the two entire lines somewhat as rhyme pulls together two words whose discursive meanings are otherwise unrelated. Even though up to this point he has sounded like someone whose directions will be accurate as well as helpful, he has known all along that he will not just send but righteously condemn the riotours to grisly death.

Of all the old men in cuts H and I, I2 is the one I would least like to meet were I lost in a strange city. He would clearly state helpful-sounding directions, while checking for observers who might interfere with his divine mission to rid the world of scum. Although he could not condemn me for illiteracy, he would find some other implacable reason for murder within his own private system of justice.

I3's old man, though ultimately murderous like I2's, seems less scarey. Upon accosting him on the street, I would assume that he was lost like me and even more fearful. Even if I stayed to chat, I would then have *PardT* ll. 760–67 with his openly maniacal cackling during which to redirect his attention to a cat's moving shadow, let us hope, not to an actual alternate victim, and break and run.

I3, lines 713–14: I3 performs a pathetic weakling who draws strength from *auctoritates*—or so it seems until, as the riotours turn their attention from him to the oak, he reveals to us listeners the true nature of this Old Man cunningly disguised as an old man. Taking special care to establish the critical issue "Who is the Old Man in the *Pardoner's Tale*?" as he hobbles on stage, I3 introduces a lower-case "oold man" in line 713, then shifts to vocal capitals for "Olde Man" a line later. I3 pauses after "povre" so that the picture can register, then projects foreboding with a lengthened vowel in "mekely."

I3, lines 715–24: That I3's o/Old m/Man is far from meek we could never guess from his first greeting—weak, helpless, quavery, even silly. As the riotour answers, our sympathies recoil. His is no scornful adolescent attitude toward the world in general, like I1's, but a vicious spitefulness as if he believes this particular pathetic old soul has done something wrong. For just one half-line then, the old man's otherworldly nature peeps out. But the riotours fail to notice that the ghost of line 721 quickly reassumes his pretended human voice. He pauses after "youthe" in line 724 to peer at them, wondering pitifully whether these young people might volunteer for the exchange.

I3, lines 737–41: The old man presents to the riotours the autobiography of one so helpless, so ineffectual, so likely a victim for their violent attack that he cannot persuade even his own mother to take care of him. His pout on "she wol nat do" then is directed away from mommy and toward the riotours in lines 739–40. It is a charming pout, the self-effacing whimper of someone who has forgotten all methods to get what he wants except for those that worked during his first childhood. His hesitation on "but" in line 741 expresses uncertainty: "Jeepers, I don't *think* I did either of these things."

I3, lines 742–48: I3's "Hooly Writ" rings out like a bell, but the scriptural passage itself sounds fussy and senile. It is the paraphrase of that text, the age-specific Golden Rule, that gives strength to this old man's voice. By line 746, with louder pronouns and a long pause to make clear that "ye" means the second-person not the indefinite pronoun, his slow-burning anger glimmers at last. With lines 747–48 I3 says, "good riddance."

I3, lines 749–59: I3's old man then starts to add a note of warning to line 749 but is rudely interrupted by the hasardour, whose harshly worded threat needs no vicious tone to intimidate this helpless old coot (so he thinks). This hasardour finds the occupation of "espye" distasteful, ending line 755 in the tone of a union organizer saying "fink" or "scab." Along with his bluff in line 759 as he pretends he is not afraid of being "sleen," the hasardour's offended tone on "espye" complicates his character and the *Tale* by hinting that he does have a moral structure, a sense of right and wrong, albeit one not exactly aligned with official policy in which "glotonye, luxurie, and hasardrye" (*PardT* l. 897) are always unforgivable sins no matter in what degree.

I3, lines 760–67: And the moral issues indeed remain unresolved. The old man's last speech reveals what he has kept so thoroughly hidden from the riotours and has revealed even to us more sensitive listeners only in lines 721 and 749. All along I3's old man has been luring them on, into this trap now about to snap shut. Still quavery and cracking in line 760, as he interrupts them in his turn, his voice firms up to say "fynde Deeth" in a tone of foreboding—"Indeed you will, for sure"—and then "croked wey" in a crooked voice, oral onomatopoeia at play. "You'll get yours," say his satisfied inflections in line 762. The vowel of "tree" stretches into a gleeful "heh heh"; he chortles outright at the "no thyng" they can do to save themselves; and he is gleeful, very very glad to direct them to that oak in line 765. A distinct chuckle at the end of his speech, in line 767, seals the benediction's sinister irony, for he knows full well that they are not even listening to his briefly proffered plan for amendment and salvation.

I4, lines 713–19: With I4, reading only lines 713–24 and 760–67, let me make the point that interpretations are passed on in classrooms as well as in published criticism, generation after generation. Reader I4 studied in I3's classroom, some decades ago now. On Cut I4, notice how closely the old man's trembly, pitiful greeting resembles I3's. But the interpretations then diverge. I4's riotours sound far less spiteful than I3's— a bit resentful, perhaps, that the old man knows something they do not, but primarily curious (somewhat like Lipscomb's).

I4, lines 720–24 and 760–67: Although I4's old man totters on stage in I3's footsteps, teacher and student go their separate interpretive ways. Instead of otherworldly, I4's old man sounds simply exhausted as he begins to recite the story that he has told so many many times to so many many people who never really listen. Despite the indifference he expected from the riotours, I4's old man expands what is hinted in I3's line 749. With lines 760–67, in an effect unique among the ten characterized readings, I4's old man tries to warn the boys not to go.

I do not wish to brush past the fact that the only reading truncated on Cut I is the only one in a woman's voice, nor that only a woman tries to warn tipsy teen-agers of the death trap. Certainly female scholars deal with the *Pardoner's Tale* in the same proportion that they teach and publish about the others. But orally, for this project, women have produced decidedly less distinctive performances of this passage than have men. Two even chose to read *Prologue* and closing but skip over the *Tale*.

Among my data here and on the *Merchant's Prologue* to be discussed, a sex-determinate lack of enthusiasm is audible—a sort of oral *occupatio*, or refusal to perform. Women readers certainly do not lack acting ability; they project with gusto and complexity not only the Wife's *Prologue* and Pertelote's advice, but also what might seem the more male-oriented concerns of January's problems or Chaunticleer's heroics. Consider the woman who as D8 creates such precise line-by-line shifts in the narrator's attitude to the Prioress's improprieties, who as O5 will create a remarkably dramatized pear-tree scene parallel to Pope's, and who elsewhere consistently does articulate complex performances. Her *Pardoner's Tale*, sandwiched between her more fully realized *Prologue* and epilogue, is bland and thin in texture. Her old man does send lads to death with a definite chortle of glee—my initial marginal note is "heh heh heh (Hitchcockian)"—but elsewhere he just recites his lines.

The riotours' voices, harsh in most conceptions, may hamper oral delivery by a female. Let me further venture that the less enthusiastic readings-aloud of this *Tale* could parallel women's lesser interest in grounds for justification of surprise murder.

It is, after all, a gruesome little story. Critics have noted the hypocrisy of the Prioress's advocating Old Testament justice over New Testament mercy. But in her terms, Jews who murder children deserve to die. These riotours have done nothing more than drink a bit more than they can handle, set out in hope of preventing more plague deaths, then brag to just the wrong person. They should have gone to medical school.

Although sociohistorical conditions and reader's gender do not supply predictably varying interpretations, both factors do seem applicable in this case. Women consistently avoid the scene, and men consistently end it the same way. Whether confronting vicious scorn or boyish curiosity, nearly all readers' old men—weak, strong, tentative, indignant, whatever—merge toward one, one who with smug sinister glee points the way from the cattlecar to the waterless showers installed by someone who has decided to rid the world of undesirable non-Christians.

Certainly no reader consciously intended to perform the old man in the *Pardoner's Tale* as a caricatured Nazi death-camp guard. And I was certainly startled to arrive at this image. As I received the tapes in 1979–83, I initially listened to each straight through the selections for five pilgrims. Not until I sat down to relisten and write about the Pardoner passages, in 1984, did I notice that for nearly every reading (I4 and H2 being almost the only exceptions) I had jotted next to the old man's final directions something like "smug," "gleeful," "gloating," "sneaky," "sinister," or "chortling." If my image of a Nazi death-camp guard is too specific, I would be glad to entertain alternative suggestions for a shared cultural image so appropriate to the *Tale* and so strong as to create near unanimity among performers whose oral interpretations elsewhere vary so vastly.

My outline of the great variation in the old man's interaction with the riotours barely begins to sort out possibilities for just the old man. It stops far short of the young Pardoner's attitude toward the old man, Chaucer-the-pilgrim's attitude toward the Pardoner's attitude toward the old man, and so on. Personal experiences, cultural expectations, and necessarily secondhand understanding of the Middle Ages all intertwine inextricably also in determining readers' interpretations of lines 725–36, the bulk of the autobiography eliminated from Cut I. Some old men resent "Goddes wille" in line 726; others' heartfelt acceptance of it carries through the rest of the passage; others suppose that God must know what he wants but still hope that Mother can somehow naysay the decision.

And of these old men's projected relationships with their respective mothers and of how her rejection of each might be affecting his rejection of the riotours' need for mercy as well as justice, I can only nod in awe at mathematical possibilities alone.

I nod with the authority of the holder of the Math Award, Grove City High School Class of 1965. A little over a year later, a sophomore-survey exam demanded that I "Name four things that the old man in the *Pardoner's Tale* might stand for." The grader, not responsive to the tone of exasperated sarcasm with which I wrote "Life Death God Satan," gave me three out of four points without marking which of the four was wrong. Sometimes I still wonder.

CHAPTER 7

The Merchant as Character on Paper

The old man in the *Merchant's Tale* would seem to have problems enough of his own. Nonetheless, twentieth-century critics have added to his burden by asking to what extent the Merchant identifies with old January in his *Tale,* and whether that attitude would necessitate a bitter tone of voice in his *Prologue.*[1] January and the Merchant both suffer marital problems—the former with a young, cheerfully adulterous wife who keeps her opinions to herself, the latter with a malicious shrew of unspecified age. Is bad marriage in general, disregarding these and other differences, so powerful a theme that the Merchant as Anyhusband must needs enter his own *Tale?*

During the four centuries to be discussed, the last one completely dominated by Alexander Pope's modernization, this comical story blithely blames January for his foolish attempt to divert the course of nature. Pope states such a moral explicitly, in terms that echo the opening to his other modernization so closely that George Ogle, in his 1741 collection, inserts no link between the *Merchant's Tale* and the *Wife of Bath's Prologue* as he does between other *Tales:*

> Thus ends our *Tale,* whose Moral next to make,
> Let all wise Husbands hence Example take;
> And pray, to crown the Pleasure of their Lives,
> To be so well deluded by their Wives.
> > *End of the* Merchant's Tale.

> > Prologue to the Wife of *Bath*'s Tale.
> > *By the same Hand.*

> Behold† the Woes of Matrimonial Life,
> And hear with Rev'rence an experienc'd Wife!
> To dear-bought Wisdom give the Credit due,
> And think, for once, a Woman tells you true.
> > †*The Wife of* Bath *speaks.*[2]

As did readers of all editions from William Thynne's in 1532 until Thomas Tyrwhitt's, Pope experienced the tale order *SqT-MctT-WBP*. Pope saw the latter two as neat mirror images: old man with young wife, then old wife with young man. A century later William Blake, his artistic spirit not at all kindred to Pope's, also found the juxtaposition inspiring. But Tyrwhitt justified making the Wife of Bath follow the tale of constant Constance, to allay his distress at the "gross . . . . impropriety . . . to an incredible degree" of Justinus's reference to the Wife.[3]

Similarly troubled by "the express mention of *Grisilde*" at *MctT* l. 1224, thereby ignoring her allegorical fame predating the Clerk's turn en route to Canterbury, Tyrwhitt also "changed the order of the three last Stanzas [of the envoy], so as to make it end" with alliterative weeping and wailing like the Merchant's in *MctT* l. 1213.[4] In nineteen manuscripts and in all early editions, it is not the Franklin but instead the Merchant who speaks in despair of his son so unlike the Squire.

Readers before Tyrwhitt thus heard the Merchant bewail both his son and his new wife, then later apologize for his rude inability to glose, while they heard a Franklin with no family problems apologize for his rude speech (*SqT* ll. 673–708; *MctT* ll. 1213–44, 2351; *FrkT* l. 718). Pope merges the voices of these two wealthy bourgeois pilgrims to create his narrator for *January and May*. Other early readers to be discussed likewise regard Merchant and Franklin as similar in their attitudes toward wealth, nobility, and education. One would be hard put to prove that a downwardly mobile son would upset the one more fittingly than the other.

The Ellesmere manuscript has many textual as well as artistic advantages, but I remain unconvinced that the tale order *SqT-FrkT* in lieu of *SqT-MctT* is among them. What jars for a moment—a merchant with a bride of two months and a son the Squire's age running wild—is easily reconciled: this father, who often leaves town on business and was hoping for help controlling the son, has remarried unwisely. This rejected tale order provides a rich backdrop of human drama and motivations. In contrast, we can only shrug aside the Franklin's gratuitously ungrateful son, who behaves so badly despite a secure home life. Perhaps Chaucer did intend the *SqT-FrkT* order, of course, and perhaps he intended to fill in more on the Franklin's family someday, as he would have for other open ends.

I am nat textueel. I do not intend to enter the tale-order fray buffered only by a mass of evidence that the tale order *SqT-MctT-WBP* made good artistic sense to many scribes and all editors of Chaucer for three centuries, to the translator of *Tale of Beryn*, to Pope/Betterton and his contemporary who illustrated the Urry edition, to Blake and his spiritual antithesis Stothard, and especially to Ogle, who created a full-length family drama from the response to the *Squire's Tale* plus the *Merchant's Prologue*.[5] It was not on account of tale order alone, anyhow, that Kittredge heard the Merchant speak in a "despairing echo [of *ClT* l. 1212]. . . . He is a stately and dignified personage, the last man from whom so furious an outburst would be expected; but his disillusionment has been sudden and complete. . . . now that excitement loosens his tongue, he goes all lengths, for he is half-mad with rage and shame" when he tells this "savage and cynical satire."[6]

No, it took more than tale order, more than the stark contrast of two girls who married for money, May and Grisilde, to make the text shriek all that to Kittredge and thence his students. It also took quotation marks. (See *Texts Read Aloud*, Chapter 8.)

As noted, Tyrwhitt cannot be held to blame for quotation marks. First to use them in a scholarly context was Thomas Wright, in his best-text edition of 1847–51, followed by W. W. Skeat in his far more influential manuscript-collated edition of 1894–97. Only in this past century, therefore, has January's foolishly extravagant praise of marriage in *MctT* ll. 1263–65 been followed by the Merchant's foolishly extravagant praise of marriage in *MctT* ll. 1267–1392, the latter in a sarcastic voice as in the last clause of *MctT* l. 1266, "Thus seyde this olde knyght, that was so wys." Kittredge and his lineage face the problem, as did no reader of editions before Wright's, of accomplishing what readings-aloud of the Prioress's portrait show to be very difficult. Readers must sustain or imagine sustained Augustinian irony for much longer than a line or so.

The strain of performing for 125 lines a voice that says consistently the opposite of what it means would be enough to make anybody bitter, regardless of the Merchant's marriage or the reader's own marriage. In future chapters we will hear how readers-aloud deal with such extended irony, including the one line (1318) that seems inappropriate to January's consciousness, and we will see how Pope rendered the passage as the not quite consistent musings of somebody not quite bright.

It is unsettling to think that four flyspecks on paper, two before *MctT* l. 1267 and two after line 1392, might have robbed twentieth-century criticism of its relatively lively debate on the Merchant's bitterness, with subtitles uttered through gritted teeth: "Another Swing of the Pendulum," "Getting beyond Old Controversies." "If thou art not yet an Editor," whines or declares or snaps John Urry, "I beg truce of thee until thou art one, before thou censurest my Endeavours."[7] Rather than meditate on the uses and abuses of editorial power, let us look to the Merchant's life before Skeat.

Throughout the centuries he remains a shrewd businessman. He appears quite dashing in the eighteenth century, when British merchants were regarded as romantic adventurers. Possibly elderly in sixteenth-century editions, at all other times he is old enough to have a grown son but young enough for the hardships of travel. Only in Ogle's *SqT-MctT* link does his wife enter the scene. Elsewhere, his major relationships are with the Franklin, the Host, the Wife of Bath, his money, his son, and his horse.

The first of the Merchant's traits to be portrayed is his superior horsemanship, for he is constantly on the road: "hye on horse he sat" (*GP* l. 271). In the Ellesmere manuscript, as Martin Stevens points out, the two figures with most in common are those of Squire and Merchant. Well able to handle the high-spirited animals needed in their respective professions, the Ellesmere Squire and Merchant each raise one hand to balance their seats on rearing horses. The Squire's horse continues to rear (illustrating *GP* l. 94) in the visualizations of the Urry-edition artist and Stothard and Blake; Stothard even shows its unruliness causing the Yeoman's horse to shy.[8] But the Merchant's steed calms down by 1721. By 1807 and 1809 it stays in line with obedient horses, though still champing the bit in Stothard's picture. (See figures 2 and 9.)

In the *Prologue* to the *Tale of Beryn*, the Merchant would probably know how to handle his horse. Certainly he knows how to handle the animal spirits of drunken fellow travelers who join the Pardoner to serenade Kitt:

> The hoost of Southwork herd hem wele, & the Marchaunt both,
> As they were at a-countis, & wexen som-what wroth.
> But yit they preyd hem curteysly to reste for to wend;
> And so they did, al they route, they dronk & made an ende.[9]

Besides the shrewish wives that bond Chaucer's Merchant and Host (*MctT* ll. 1213–39, 2419–40; *MkT* ll. 1891–1922), this fifteenth-century Merchant and Host have in common their interest in money, their distaste for rowdiness that would disrupt the one good night's sleep on this trip, and their ability to deal diplomatically with behavior that offends them.

The *PTB* Host and the Merchant continue as sensible, seasoned travelers come sun-up. The Host joys in the morning freshness but decides not to draw lots so early. What if it fell to someone too sleepy or hung

FIGURE 9:   The Merchant, from p. 66 of John Urry's edition of *The Works of Geoffrey Chaucer* (London: B. Lintot, 1721). Reproduced by permission of the Van Pelt Library, University of Pennsylvania. Actual size, 5¾″ × 4¼″.

over to tell a tale? And some people just do not like to talk before breakfast:

> ffor who shuld tell a tale, he must have good will therto;
> And eke, som men fasting beth no thing iocounde,
> And som, hir ⊬ tungis, fasting, beth glewid & I-bound
> To the Palet of the mowith, as offt as they mete;
> So yf the lott fell on such, no thonk shuld they gete.
>   (*PTB* ll. 708–12)

Instead, the Host asks for volunteers.

> "By the rood of Bromholm," quod the marchaunte tho,
> "As fer as I have saylid, riden, & I-go,
> Sawe I nevir man yit, to-fore this ilch day,
> So well coude rewle a company, as our hoost, in fay.
> ....
>
> Wher + for I woll tell a tale to yeur consolacioune;
> ....
>
> Ther shall no fawte be found in me; good will shal be my chaunce,
> With this I be excusid, of my rudines,
> All thoughe I can nat peynt my tale, but tell as it is;
> Lepyng ovir no centence, as ferforth as I may,
> But telle yewe the yolke, & put the white a-way.
> (*PTB* ll. 717–20, 724, 728–32)

Chaunticleer could not have put it better. Before the author's joke on *NPT* l. 3443, the next-to-last couplet presents the same Merchant/Franklin combination that will reappear as Pope's narrator, here expressing respect bordering on adulation for the Host's authority.

The author presents as the Merchant's second tale his 3292-line translation from French of the *Tale of Beryn*. Beryn, the only child of an aging couple, is spoiled rotten. On her deathbed his mother asks that her husband remain single for Beryn's sake: "Let hym have no Stepmodir" (*TB* l. 984). She looks around to kiss Beryn, after the priest performs last rites. But he has already left for his dice game, "ffor, as sone as he had ete, he wold ren out anoon" (*TB* l. 1000). Beryn gets back in full what he deserves. His stepmother indeed deprives him of his inheritance, and then his overseas sales career flounders in misfortune until saved by all-powerful father figures: a wise man named Geffrey (as in the French original) and an omnipotent duke in an Ozlike palace.

The *PTB* Merchant displays definite interest in a remarried old man's ne'er-do-well son, who learns how hard it is to earn a living at foreign trade. He himself need not be old, though, just sensibly middle-aged like Franklin and Host. But during the next century, a spurious detail suggesting old age crept into Chaucer editions, including Speght's first one. In 1602 Speght corrected it, restoring the forked beard of the manuscripts, but in 1598 the Merchant's portrait in the *General Prologue* begins, "A Marchaunt was there with a long berd."[10]

Readers of sixteenth-century Chaucer editions, including Pope/Betterton, thus met a Merchant wearing the long beard traditionally associated with old age, like several Januarys to be surveyed, rather than the forked beard that reminds one New Critic of American Indians' cowboy-movie distrust of white men's tongues.[11] In the 1712 modernization, Pope/Betterton chooses to associate the beard with neither old age nor untrust-worthiness—except insofar as a goat image could evoke either one, or lechery besides:

> With these a Merchant, in a motley Coat,
> Well mounted too, and bearded like a Goat.
> A *Flanders-Beaver* on his Head he wore;
> His Boots were neatly buckled on before.[12]

The Merchant of modern editions next spends two lines speaking solemn opinions, "resons," about the increase of his winning. Speght's 1598 Merchant speaks for just one line of his "reasons," a term not in Speght's glossary. Rather than "sownynge" any more, he with quieter dignity shows his wealth: "Shewing alwaye y encrease of his winning" (Speght, for *GP* ll. 274–75).

Here Pope/Betterton confronts the term "reasons," which unbe-knownst to him had shifted in meaning since Chaucer's time. As he does for the Prioress's "pained her for to counterfet chere" (Speght, for *GP* l. 139, as discussed), and as Pope does for January's "face sadde" (Speght 28v, for *MctT* l. 1399, to be discussed), Pope/Betterton manipulates the text so that the misunderstood word helps convey his own thoughtful understanding of the character. In addition, as he does in the *Reeve's Tale* (where, for example, he renames the daughter Grace), Pope/Betterton adds theological imagery. Characteristically, also, in this next couplet he employs an abstraction as if it were a visual adjective, as is the case for the Pope/Betterton Pardoner's "Patriarchal Face" and the "Philosophick Frown" that Pope gives to January's brother Justinus.[13]

> He prov'd with Reasons strong, and formal Face,
> T'increase in Wealth was to increase in Grace.

Pope/Betterton continues the Merchant's portrait with further theological issues of vice and charity. Why? Now, "'Alexander Pope of London Merchant' is the habitual legal description of the poet's father," who traded linens to Virginia successfully enough to retire in comfort at age forty-two. Pope's father, like Chaucer's Merchant at that time, had re-married after his first wife died. His second wife, the poet's mother, was of a higher social rank (unlike May) and "remarkable for kindness and good sense" (unlike the Merchant's wife). Born the year that his father retired to the country to escape Protestant persecution, Pope was denied education by secular authorities. Instead he learned from priests and then books provided by his constantly solicitous father.[14]

To what extent would Pope/Betterton realize, and intentionally downplay, the potentially negative aspects that modern critics point out in the *General Prologue* portrait of a Merchant who maybe withholds the king's taxes and maybe sells French coins at a profit and maybe hides usury behind the terms "bargaynes" and "chevyssaunce," or maybe does none of the above? In Speght's glossary Pope would have found "cheuisaunce" defined "merchandise," and in the section "Corrections of some faults, and Annotations vpon some places" he would have found noted for *GP* l. 278 that "Shieldes in French called *escus,* are French crownes, wherein this Merchant did deale by returne" (Speght Bbbb.iii v).

Unaware of some fourteenth-century linguistic nuances but fully aware of a merchant's concerns, Pope/Betterton does not falsify his source to create a saintly Merchant. Indeed, an adolescent poet might have enjoyed pinpointing a few imperfections in a figure resembling his father, however beloved. Instead, Pope/Betterton uses theological terms to show the Merchant's honest but incomplete effort to observe Christian values in the contradictory world of commerce. Thus, most eighteenth-century readers would come to know Chaucer's Merchant as a morally ambivalent character who neither cheats nor is cheated.

> Greedy of Gold, and popular Esteem,
> He wish'd the Sea were shut to all, but him.
> Traffick in Mony he had studied well,
> Knew where th' *Exchange* would rise, and where it fell.
> In Debt to none, in Bargains strict and nice,
> Thought unprompt Payment was the greatest Vice.
> What he with Pains had got, with Care he'd save;
> Not Charitable, for he seldom gave.

By substituting this antithetical closing couplet for Chaucer's uninformative rhyme line "I not what men him call" (Speght, for *GP* l. 284), Pope/Betterton eliminates one ominous overtone that two centuries later, on the first page of the first issue of *Philological Quarterly,* Thomas Knott would amplify into "Chaucer's Anonymous Merchant [music up]. . . . one whose secret history, when unveiled, discloses a labyrinth of devious practice and scandalous high finance."[15]

Pope/Betterton also interprets for his own artistic purpose *GP* l. 280, in Speght given as "There wist no wight that he was in det." A flurry of twentieth-century essays pose different interpretations for this line, each scholar insisting that his is the only correct reading rather than that Chaucer's line is flexible in imagined performance. Pope/Betterton's "In Debt to none" differs from Richard H. Horne's 1841 modernization— "And no one knew that he was much in debt"—and from Arthur Hugh Clough's 1852 remark on the "merchant so discreet and stedfast / there wiste no man that he was in debt." "Chaucer does not know that he is in debt," proclaims Kittredge. "He merely suggests it as a possibility."[16] After Kittredge, readers have continued to evaluate variously his financial condition:

He was in debt, but no one knew it.
No one knew him to be in debt.
He was not in debt.
He was anything but in debt.
If he was in debt, certainly no one knew it!
It would never have occurred to people that he was in debt.
Whether or not he was in debt, no one knew that he was.[17]

Oscar Johnson, having listed most of these possibilities, says that the line "was not ambiguous for anyone hearing Chaucer recite it, since. . . . the meaning of the line would at once be made clear by the sentence melody." Johnson uses stress marks to show that "ther *wiste* no wight" makes the line mean that he was in debt, whereas "ther wiste *no* wight" makes it mean that he was not in debt. But then he invokes a very pale spectre of "logical stress" to prove that his own imagined performance must be the one that "Chaucer specifically has in mind."[18]

Chaucer did specifically have in mind a Merchant with a forked beard, not a long one. The artist for Urry's 1721 edition must therefore have worked from a draft of that edition itself, or from Speght's 1602 or 1687 edition, for his Merchant wears a forked beard as he ought. (See figure 9.) He also has magnificent boots that hug his calves tightly but cover his knees in loose folds—this style being practical and indeed almost essential for all-day riding (*GP* ll. 270–73).

The Urry-edition Merchant is a professional traveler, like the *PTB* one. He and his means of transportation, who spend most of their days together, understand one another thoroughly. Both in profile, they peer together across a calm sea with ships. They form a matched pair—the horse's high saddle and its master's broad-brimmed hat (*GP* ll. 271–72), the rider's long cavalier ringlets and his mount's lush mane and tail stirred by sea breezes. Over down-turned mouth and hooked nose, the Merchant's eyebrow slants upward in a definitely worried look. His companion looks as worried as a horse can, with eyes and alert ears pointed exactly where its master is gazing.

No particular notice of merchants' Christian amorality appears in this rendering of the figure by an artist who shares Pope/Betterton's sociohistorical milieu. The stylish Urry-edition Merchant more resembles the typical literary "merchant as financial daredevil and exotic traveler [who] grew indistinguishable, in some eighteenth-century accounts, from the enterprising heroes who dominated the recently translated *Arabian Nights* (one of Pope's favorite books)."[19] Pope, who uses commercial images throughout his acknowledged works, would have known that a merchant's life is not always so exotic, nor is it ethically so simple.

In this case, as in that of the Prioress but not the Pardoner, it seems to be the Urry artist who is incorporating a standard interpretation and Pope/Betterton who is changing it, motivated by circumstances of Pope's life. After them William Blake will take from the Urry-edition Merchant primarily the worried look; he will aim it, however, not at ships but at Alysoun, the Whore of Babylon.

Between Urry and Blake intervenes another eighteenth-century visualization, also definitely known to Blake. For J. H. Mortimer, the Merchant's concerns have already veered from commerce toward the wiles of women.

In *Departure of the Canterbury Pilgrimes,* the Merchant has not yet mounted. (See figure 5.) He stands on a raised platform just behind the Friar, who is holding reins for the Wife of Bath and gazing deep into her eyes. Framing the Merchant's head are those of the Wife and Miller, the latter fingering his bagpipe and looking, puzzled, toward the Friar. Mortimer's Merchant looks that way too. His half-closed eyelids give him a look of lethargic surprise, as if just glancing up at the scene before him of open flirtation with such a haggard old crone as Alysoun, whose nose and chin almost meet.

Besides knowing Mortimer's work well, Blake certainly knew also the frontispiece to volume 14 of John Bell's *Poets of Great Britain,* designed by Stothard, in which an attractive Wife flirts simultaneously with all three men in the picture, Friar and Squire and Monk.[20] (See Frontispiece.) Casting especial scorn on Stothard's later portrayal of the Wife as a "young, beautiful, blooming damsel," Blake in his *Descriptive Catalogue* calls her briefly "a scourge and a blight."[21]

In his painting Blake, like Mortimer, juxtaposes the Merchant and the Wife of Bath, she who in any age radiates energy that can activate hell or heaven. (See figure 2.) She is flanked also by an apelike Cook, obliviously swigging ale, and by the Miller, absently playing his pipes while staring wonder-struck at the back of her thronelike headpiece. The Merchant rides ahead of her but turns to peer, heavy-lidded like Mortimer's, at the back of her headpiece also. She ignores all three to glance seductively toward the solidly turned back of the Parson.

In Blake's interlocking visual details, the brim of the Merchant's hat encircles his face as the Wife's headpiece frames hers; his neckline plunges as does her magnificently immodest one; his forked beard reflects images of her flamelike collar, of the Gothic spires of false religion above their heads, and of her pointed shoes beneath blatantly spread knees (this last detail taken from the Urry-edition artist). Like the Urry-edition Merchant, Blake's turns down his mouth and raises the inside corners of his eyebrows in a worried expression. But he seems instead smug, not as worried as he ought to be about his fascination with the female who has brought wide-eyed fear to the face of the Miller—the Miller being the Blakean "spectrous shadow" of "Hercules in his supreme eternal state . . . a terrible fellow, such as exists in all times and places for the trial of men, to astonish every neighbourhood with brutal strength and courage, to get rich and powerful to curb the pride of Man." [22]

If she can spark terror in the brawny Miller's bulging eyes, why does the Merchant remain so unafraid? Blake's *Descriptive Catalogue* offers no verbal interpretation. He mentions the Merchant only to exclude him from the company of the "Three Citizens, as his dress is different, and his character is more marked, whereas Chaucer says of his rich citizens: 'All were yclothed in o liverie.'" [23]

Three Citizens? Blake in passing proposes a way to reduce the thirty-one listed pilgrims to the twenty-nine of *GP* l. 24. He strains the text no more than does Tyrwhitt, who simply wipes out two of the priests from *GP* l. 164. [24] Well aware what punctuation does in his own poems, Blake suggests that

> The Webbe, or Weaver, and the Tapiser, or Tapestry Weaver, appear to me to be the same person; but this is only an opinion. . . . But I dare say that Chaucer wrote "A Webbe Dyer," that is, a Cloth Dyer:
> "A Webbe Dyer, and a Tapiser" [i.e., one man total]. [25]

In Blake's painting the Merchant differs visually and (as always for Blake) spiritually from a Merchant he portrayed only a few years earlier, during his "three years' Slumber on the banks of the Ocean," [26] to wit in

1800–1803 in Felpham, restless under the earthbound patronage of William Hayley. To portray Chaucer with *Heads of the Poets* for the library walls, Blake

> could have used the plate Vertue engraved for Urry's edition of Chaucer's works (1721) which appears in the sale catalogue of Hayley's library. . . . Blake must have consulted Urry's edition of Chaucer, for the two subsidiary figures of the Merchant and Wife of Bath are faithful copies of the engraved headpieces on pages 66 and 76.[27]

Perhaps Blake chose the two of them to flank Chaucer because he was most familiar with them from Pope's oft-reprinted modernizations, familiar with their themes of old and young wife and husband, juxtaposed early in Urry's edition. Even while copying their exact lineaments for the unspiritual Hayley, then, Blake's imagination was expanding to create the ever-moving binary oppositions, independent of time and space and number, by which he would portray and arrange Chaucer's "visions of these eternal principles or characters of human life."[28] By pairing Merchant with the openly dangerous Wife, as he pairs Pardoner with the Prioress's more dangerous repressiveness, while in other ways pairing all of them with other pilgrims too, Blake calls into question ordinary society's labels of good and evil.

Ordinary society, as represented by Thomas Stothard, saw in 1807 just what it had seen in the fifteenth century: that a Merchant would have most in common with the other wealthy middle-class pilgrims, Franklin and Host. In Stothard's painting the Miller leads the procession, both hands on his bagpipes while his lop-eared horse nonetheless plods onward. Next the Host turns to the crowd, waving aloft the lots. In a neat row behind him ride five professionals: Physician, Merchant, Man of Law, Franklin, and Knight. Of the five only Merchant and Franklin make eye contact with the Host, creating a triangle of well-to-do bourgeois.

Stothard's sober, heavy-lidded Merchant sports a top hat and a pointed (not forked) beard above high-collared coat. William Carey further describes this Merchant:

> His indented brow is confident, shrewd, and speculative; his eye fixed earnestly on the Host, with a look of self-sufficiency. [Carey quotes *GP* ll. 274–75] . . . [He is] robust and above the ordinary stature. He is in the vigor of life. His visage is manly, and sunburnt.[29]

His sun-tanned traveler's face might link the Merchant's profession to that of the Shipman (*GP* l. 394). Stothard's Shipman, however, turns a hunched back to the observer in order to examine that "female latitudinarian. . . . the Bath Beauty. . . . the gay Lady wife . . . . the *Queen* of *Pilgrims.*"[30]

Stothard and Carey leave Alysoun basking in the last rays of her unquestioned popularity, as the nineteenth century unfolds in the darkness and slouches toward her. But abide. We have yet to examine the most complete item of evidence for a pre-Kittredgian interpretation of the Merchant's character, the only item that involves his wife as well as his son.

Publishing five years before his death in 1746, George Ogle may have projected a complete *Canterbury Tales . . . Modernis'd by several Hands.* The three volumes end with Ogle's own *Clerk's Tale* plus an epilogue by Chaucer who "his musing Eyes up-rais'd, and look'd around."[31]

Ogle reprints major earlier modernizations except Dryden's *Nun's Priest's Tale* (because he is following Urry's tale order). Most of these previously published modernizations, like Pope's, excise passages not essential to an eighteenth-century story line. But the two modernizations that first appear in Ogle's 1741 collection are, instead, much expanded: Samuel Boyse tells Chaucer's 664-line *Squire's Tale* in about 1400 lines, and Henry Brooke balloons the *Man of Law's Tale* from 1064 to 1644 lines. Ogle himself more than doubles the length of the *Clerk's Tale,* also, to sell it separately as a 2426-line *Gualtherus and Griselda* for two years before republishing it in his collection—no longer with R. Dodsley but rather with the firm of J. and R. Tonson, who had been first to pay Pope. (See Appendix B.)

Why expand Chaucer so? Ogle provides a rationale in his *Letter to a Friend,* which he printed with both *Clerk's Tale* publications. While giving "the Preference to Chaucer's Manner of Treating this Story. . . . I could not forbear Consulting the other Two," Petrarch's and Boccaccio's, "and found Occasion rather to add than to diminish." Ogle need not defend, he says, "this Kind of Translation; Mr. Dryden has sufficiently established the Use and Advantage of it."[32]

Another, presumably more impelling, motivation for lengthening links and *Tales* is mentioned by Thomas Lounsbury.[33] Of the translators hired specifically for this project, at least Boyse received three pence per line. Petrarch and Boccaccio aside, then, Ogle gladly puts onto paper the entire background that he, as a better-informed-than-average reader of Chaucer, imagines for the Merchant's prodigal son and his shrewish second wife.

Ogle's links, reprinted only by Lipscomb in 1795,[34] offer other opportunities to anyone seeking an eighteenth-century interpretation of key passages. The expanded *Prologue To The Miller's Tale* fills six pages. "Turne over the leef and chese another tale" produces, for example,

> But if the Prohibition more intice,
> For Curiosity may want Advice,
> Convey the Ribaldry from Vulgar Sight,
> Peruse it in the Closet, and by Night;
> Or with a female Friend in private read,
> So may the *Miller,* if you chuse, proceed.[35]

Ogle reprints the *General Prologue* portraits from 1712, but replaces Pope/Betterton's *GP* ll. 1–42 with his own modernization. We may cringe equally at Pope/Betterton's "'Twas when the Fields imbibe the Vernal Show'rs" and Ogle's "When *April,* soft'ning, sheds refreshing Show'rs," each rhymed with "Flow'rs."[36] But a comparison suggests that the Pope/Betterton version struck Ogle as a bit too smart-alecky for his own projected audience. Ogle inserts non-Chaucerian abstractions in lieu of such non-Chaucerian jabs as Pope/Betterton's

> There at the* *Martyr's* Shrine a Cure they find,   *Thomas Becket
> For each sick Body, and each love-sick Mind.
>   It so befel, that Season, on a Day,
> In *Southwark* at the *Talbot-Inn* I lay,
> Resolv'd with Zeal my Journey to begin;
> With no small Offering to St. *Thomas'* shrine.
> For *Priests* with empty Thanks are never shamm'd;
> The Rich buy Heaven, and ragged Rogues are damn'd.[37]

After two volumes to which Ogle further contributes his own Clerk's portrait replacing Pope/Betterton's, the Cook's and five citizens' portraits left undone by Pope/Betterton, and all needed *Tale* links, Ogle's third volume opens with his own *Prologue To The Merchant's Tale:*

> Well clos'd! (The *Merchant* thus applauds the *Squire*)
> Your Tale is full of Fancy and of Fire.[38]

The *Squire's Tale* seemed no better closed then than now. Ogle's second volume ends not with *SqT* l. 672 but rather with Ogle's attributed mod-

ernization of Edmund Spenser's continuation of Chaucer's *Tale*. Ogle's
Squire ends sensibly,

> But hold—'tis Time to check the forward Steed!—
> Nor should our Tale too long delay the Rest;
>   What yet remains, in Order may succeed,
> When next our Turn; Intemperance of Tongue,
> Mine *Host* will well excuse, his Orator is young.[39]

It is a Squire polite to his elders and charmingly aware of youthful
impetuosity, then, not just any upper-class twit to whom the Merchant
addresses a ten-line version of *SqT* ll. 675–81. Ogle's Host seems less
impatient of respect for high birth than does Chaucer's, who utters
"Strawe for youre gentillesse!" after listening to only thirteen lines about
the Franklin's disappointing son (*SqT* ll. 682–95). Ogle's Host responds
businessman to businessman, after patiently hearing the entire story of
the Merchant's broken home:

> Now by the Holy Trinity I swear,
> Blest, cou'd I die this Hour, in such an Heir.
> More Blest, than if this Hour I cou'd command
> Ten Thousand Marks a-year, in solid Land.
> Not that I want—some Fortune I have made—
> And all the World esteems me rich in Trade.
> But 'tis a Pain to live at large Expence,
> For One, that Spirit wants as well as Sense.
> Such is my Son! Whom, heartily I hate!
> What, *is the Man*, (quoth I) not what, *is his Estate?*
>
>   It joy'd Me, when I turn'd Him Boy to School;
> It griev'd me sore, when He return'd a Fool.
> But Scholars flourish thro' a Lucky Sign;
> And rare to meet, as Layman or Divine!
> Well! Soldier He shall be. I bought Him Lace;
> The Rest He had, a Person, and a Face!
> And soon He learn'd the Military Art,
> And soon He lost his Post, for Want of Heart!
> This sham'd Me much, and robb'd Me of my Wife;
> Love of my Youth! And Comfort of my Life!
> I join'd Him then, my Commerce to attend;
> He join'd Me, but to dissipate, and spend.
> Now, that my Turn is Frugal, I admit;
> Yet I am something gen'rous, for a Cit[izen].
> Plain as I go, or when I walk, or ride;

The Lord, that owes Me Money, gives me Pride.
And had I such a Son, as cou'd but write,
As Authors wrote; as Soldiers fought, wou'd fight;
Cit as I am, that Son I wou'd support.—
But Mine, will drink with Footmen of the Court.
With Knaves, at Dice, All I cou'd save, wou'd waste,
Nor knows one Man of Sense, or Man of Taste.

    I doubt, not much is gain'd, (return'd our *Host*)
By that same Sense, and Taste, tho' much is lost.
But, *Merchant,* Let me mind You of your Tale;
My Bill is drawn on Sight! You will not fail?

    Not (quoth the *Merchant*) tho' You take Me hors'd,
Suppose it but accepted and indors'd.
The *Squire* will well excuse me what was said;
I only wish'd my Son, so turn'd, and bred!

    In that (rejoin'd our *Host*) the Man is right;
But Cits grow tedious, as they grow Polite:
The Twine will break, too nicely that You spin.
Begin! Enough of this! Enough! Begin!—

    The *Merchant,* then. Your Mandate I obey;
Sir Host! I hold you Sov'reign for the Day.
Gracious, receive, what humbly is addrest,
So pleasing One, I hope to please the Rest.

    Yet grant Me, first to wail, if not atone,
A greater Ill; a Folly of my own!
For Store of Rancor, Malice, Spleen, and Spite,
Have I, from ev'ry Morn, to ev'ry Night![40]

Having omitted the subtitles of Speght's and Urry's editions, Ogle sands smooth the last trace of a seam between *SqT* ll. 673–708 and *MctT* ll. 1213–14, fusing them for another third of a century until Tyrwhitt rends them asunder.

Next, Ogle lengthens *MctT* ll. 1215–32 but adds nothing new. It is in the tripling of *MctT* ll. 1233–34 and the final exchange with the Host that Ogle provides his full-length interpretation of the effect of the Merchant's own marriage on his choice of tale:

    Here, shou'd You ask me, my right honest *Host,*
How long since I was shipwreck'd on the Coast?

With this my Second Choice what Time has past?
(Peace to my First of Wives, for this my Last!)
How long? You scarce will take it on my Word,
Two Months are past, We enter on a Third.
For slightly here to touch, not fully paint,
This marry'd Fiend of an unmarry'd Saint,
Who caught me with the Farce of Love she play'd,
But singly priz'd me for my Stock in Trade;
This Scold of Mine, keeps one Eternal Round,
Sure, never Youth to Age in Wedlock bound,
In Course of Years indur'd such Noise and Strife!
Her Lesson of an Hour wou'd marr his Life!

    We will not doubt your Word, (our *Host* reply'd.)
Yet some their Talents in a Napkin hide.
Now you that are a Master of the Art,
Conceal not all your Knowledge, but impart.

    Sir, (says the *Merchant*) 'tis the Thing I mean!
The Thing You seek; a Matrimonial Scene!
Not that my proper Farce I will disclose,
But laugh, as Others laugh, at Other's Woes;
None but the Fool his own Concern reveals;
For Who feels Pain for what his Neighbour feels?[41]

So, just as Alysoun warns while denouncing her old husbands' proverbs (*WBP* ll. 290–92), this Merchant's second wife has hidden her vices
until after the ceremony in order to get at his money. Ogle's Merchant
does not tell the ages of himself and his bride, keeping the pronoun carefully third person in the comparison of their union to "Youth to Age in
Wedlock bound" as it mars "his Life." His self-identification with January is no more definite than is that of Chaucer's Merchant on that count,
nor is it so in his final refusal to tell his own autobiography (as Alysoun
is about to). But we do learn just why, in Ogle's understanding, the Merchant refrains from telling his own story: he does not want to be laughed
at. Instead, he will tell a funny story about somebody else's bad marriage.

    Bertrand Bronson, despite extensive publication in folklore and medie-
val and eighteenth-century literature, never encountered Ogle's interpretation. Yet it is Bronson who at last raises his hand in a 1961 *Studies in
Philology*, swallows hard, and says, "Professor Kittredge? Excuse me, sir,
but I think you and Professor Tatlock are both wrong about the Merchant's bitter tone of voice." Robert Jordan, seeing Bronson about to
stand accused of the Folklore Bypass, quickly finds four voices in the text

on paper. But by then hands are waving all over the auditorium—Donaldson, Elliott, Harrington, Hartung—and back and forth still today.[42] And Kittredge? Let us hope that Professor Kittredge is not pounding for order, trying to reimpose his own imagined performance, but instead is leaning benignly on that great cosmic podium, smiling with pride as he watches it happen.

The Merchant as Character on Tape

Bitterness is a taste, not a sound. How do readers-aloud of the *Merchant's Prologue* express bitterness, or self-consciously refrain from expressing it, in this passage for which interpretive issues have been so thoroughly sifted, rolled out, kneaded, let rise, and baked solid in heated debate? (See *Texts Read Aloud,* Chapter 8.)

A thesaurus provides shades of meaning for emotionally bitter: resentful, acrimonious, unpleasant, hostile, caustic, sour-tempered. When I originally listened to the readings-aloud of *MctT* ll. 1213–39, at intervals in 1979–83, I was avoiding the term "bitter" but had not consulted a thesaurus for alternatives. I jotted something about resentment for twenty-one of the twenty-seven performances.

Cut J, MctT ll. 1213–44

Ogle's 1741 Merchant resents that his second wife married him for money. Likewise, each modern Merchant snarls for some specific reason rather than from ill temper in general.

Only a few readers-aloud resent everything equally. Most waver between that attitude and one of sad resignation. A sex-determinate tendency is audible here, in that only male voices maintain consistent resentment through the Merchant's entire autobiography. In comparison, along with many other males, those women who read the passage sound primarily resigned throughout and resentful only in spots (which almost always include lines 1218, 1222, and 1225).

Perhaps female voices have trouble projecting such harshness, as they did for the riotours in the *Pardoner's Tale*. A sex-determinate lack of interest is also obvious, manifested this time not in bland performances, as it was in the *Pardoner's Tale,* but in women's choosing not to read the passage at all.

I had asked all readers-aloud to begin with the passages that interested them most, among the selections for five pilgrims, and to send me back fewer than five rather than delay returning the tape. Of the thirty-two Chaucerians, twenty-one are male and eleven female. After the readers omitted passages, the proportion of males to females remained the same for each selection, except in the case of the *Merchant's Tale*. Six men and three women chose not to read the *Nun's Priest's Tale* selections, for example. In contrast, six women and one man eliminated the *Merchant's Tale* excerpts. Left with only five female to twenty male readers, therefore, I asked two more women to read the *Merchant's Prologue* and the opening of his *Tale*.

Sex-determinate disinterest in rabid misogyny should cause no surprise. It could perhaps be predicted, too, that women who do read the passage keep anger repressed. Although male readers may know that men hide only those emotions that make one seem sissy, women have learned secondhand that men are taught to hide their emotions. Thus female voices create Merchants trying hard to sound nonchalant, whereas some men's Merchants burst with righteous indignation at such a shrew.

Cuts J1–4 illustrate this sex-determinate contrast. J1 and J2, males reading respectively *MctT* ll. 1213–22 and 1223–32, prove that the text can indeed support a consistent reading of open resentment. Only at J2's line 1228 does a milder, rather petulant tone of voice edge in.

As the most resentful moment in any of the twenty-seven readings, J1 explodes "shrewe at al." In contrast a woman J3, reading *MctT* ll. 1213–22, slows down and distinctly separates the words "shrewe at al." Because J3's Merchant has been hoping for sympathy, in a tone of resignation verging on self-pity, he uses the phrase to inform listeners of the precise problem he faces. Similarly, with a pause before "wedded" in line 1216, J3 hopes that others will share his distaste.

J3's oral sense of "wedded" can be compared to that same word in *MctT* l. 1228 read by another woman, J4. J3 and J4 project this married man's attitude toward other men and marriage in ways that differ from each other, as well as from J1 and J2.

Instead of asking for pity from his fellows, as does J3's Merchant, J4 uses lines 1223–32 to express pity for fellow sufferers. Although J4's Merchant tries to repress resentment through lines 1223–27, it bubbles out on "crueltee" and "nevere eft." At line 1228, then, his sympathy wells up for all "wedded men" who endure similar situations. Accepting his own sorrow and care, he uses lines 1229–32 to convey a kind warning to anybody still unwed.

Can the text be read aloud successfully with no resentment at all? Is anything that Chaucer wrote forcing so many resentful readings? Or is bitterness a critical issue not reinforced by verbal texture on the page?

Even readers who elsewhere sound resigned spit out some degree of resentment on "shrewe" in *MctT* l. 1222. Its *roo* sound verges on onomatopoeia: to say it aloud, one's upper lip curls and nostrils flare as if sneering. This is not to claim that one sneers at every passing kangaroo, nor that *roo*s occur particularly often in the *Merchant's Prologue*. Simply, the data indicate near-universal resentment, including explosive resentment like J1's, on "shrewe." How do the six readers-aloud who sound resentful nowhere manage to bypass a "shrewe" without sneering?

Four of the six sound consistently resigned, throughout the *Prologue*, to a sad lot in life which includes such a spouse. The fifth reader creates a self-consciously comical scene at *MctT* ll. 1219–22. A chuckle highlights his animated cartoon of wife and devil squaring off, rolling pin and pitchfork in hand. It is a boxing-ring announcer who introduces the contender, Shrewe-At-Al.

The sixth nonresentful reader, J5, is not just untroubled; he is quite proud of his wife's behavior. J5's line 1221 has an edge of bragging about one's prize pit bull, and his "shrewe at al" accepts her with all her shortcomings. She may be mean and ugly, but she sure can hold her own.

Because J5's is by far the most cheerful and chatty of all twenty-seven Merchants, slipping into only the slightest of complaints on "cursednesse" in line 1239, Cut J5 continues through the dialogue with the Host (thus containing lines 1213–44). Like those recreated in the *Prologue* to the *Tale of Beryn*, J5's Host and Merchant are buddies with much in common. Perhaps they have already discussed their respective shrewish wives. At line 1233, J5's Merchant turns to the Host with a familiar chattiness. The jolly Host's reply reminds him that we are playing a public game with three ladies present, not sharing locker-room anecdotes. J5's Merchant cheerfully brushes aside the Host's suggested topic, though, explaining in lines 1243–44 his alternate choice.

J5's performance sounds fine to me. To maintain that something in the text itself causes aesthetic shortcomings in J5's cheerful reading, Chaucerians should pinpoint for discussion the precise spots therein that sound inappropriate to the text of the *Merchant's Prologue*. Critics should also propose imagined performances of the analogous epilogue, *MctT* ll. 2419–40. There the Host terms his own wife a shrew and refrains from further details, for a reason more practical than the Merchant's in lines 1243–44: word of the Host's complaints might reach Goodelief.

What if commentary this century had focused not on the Merchant's wife's behavior, as compared to Grisilde's, but rather on the Merchant's relationship with the Host? In the *Tales* overall, what would be the thematic and dramatic implications of collaboration, or antipathy, between these two money-grubbing wife-scorners, be they jolly or evil? Should the pilgrim Merchant be condemned in comparison to the merchant husband of the *Shipman's Tale*? And so on.

There is nothing inherently wrong with debating the issue of the Merchant's bitterness, but nothing exclusively right either. We must simply be aware that such a twentieth-century issue, defined mostly by white male English professors, is not the only possible one, and that what we or our students see as a text's previously unnoticed problems and implications may well exist.

Friendship between Host and Merchant predominates in their characterization in *Prologue* to the *Tale of Beryn,* our most thorough near-contemporary evidence. Analysis now of their relationship in *Canterbury Tales* would surely include the interchange in which the Host urges further autobiography but elicits instead the *Merchant's Tale.*

Cut K, MctT ll. 1231–44

No one at all has proposed a mental sounding for *MctT* ll. 1231–44, embedded inconspicuously amongst much-discussed passages. Readers' virgin experiences produce an unusually wide range of fully characterized oral possibilities for this dialogue, as they did for the Knight's intervention at *PardT* l. 962. I will account for all twenty-seven readings, therefore, while including only samples of each on Cut K.

Except for J5's cheerful Merchant and a few who are still resentful, most Merchants calm down and turn to the Host at line 1233 in expectation of sympathy. In response they hear

six Hecklers: Host mocks or teases Merchant;
four Happy-Go-Lucky Numskulls: Host is insensitive to Merchant's inner torment;
four Shrinks: Host encourages Merchant to talk out inner torment for own good;
three Sympathizers: Merchant gets hoped-for response;
four Lords of the Revels: Host reminds Merchant of tale-telling contest;
six Nosy Neighbors: Host hopes to hear more details of Merchant's sex life.

The Merchant's response to the Host in lines 1243–44 adds even more permutations. To a Host who makes fun of him, for example, a Merchant may respond by turning resentment on the Host, by not even noticing he is being mocked, by realizing he was indeed overdoing the melodrama, or by despairing of attempted human contact.

Cut K of the dialogue, lines 1231–44, begins with two of the Hecklers. K1's Host teases gently, whereas K2's mocks openly, two quite different Merchants.

K1's Merchant has been alternating between resentment and hopeless resignation, but as he turns to address the Host his sense of humor emerges. Although he hopes for sympathy, especially at the end of line 1233, he is a bit amused at himself for having gotten so upset. At his final word "cursednesse," however, resentment reemerges. K1's Host, a wise judge of character, realizes that by playing to that sense of humor he can tease the Merchant back onto the track. And indeed, chuckling at himself on "gladly," K1's Merchant distances himself from his own gloomy emotions to start the *Tale*.

K2's Merchant, unlike K1's, is in no danger of succumbing to gloom. He even says "cursednesse" calmly. He clenches his teeth to remain calm in his final couplet, retaining dignity despite the rudeness of K2's Host, who emits "now" with a whinny, a horselaugh, and goes on to make open and rather cruel mockery of the Merchant's plight.

Some of the Hosts whom I call Happy-Go-Lucky Numskulls laugh like K2's Host. They laugh out of bursting good nature, though, not at someone's distress. Rather than cruel, they are oblivious to the Merchant's churning emotions. K3's Merchant turns to the Host with especial hope for an understanding ear, as suggested by the stretched-out "A!" that starts line 1233 and by his eager speeding up of lines 1237–39. The thick-skulled Host's chortling reply lands like a boulder on the Merchant's budding good spirits. K3's grim "gladly" expresses high expectations abruptly flattened.

Cut K4 exemplifies those seven fortunate Merchants who get what they want: sympathy, whether from a Shrink like K4's Host or from a straight Sympathizer whose voice does not suggest how the Merchant can improve his mood. K4's Merchant begs for pity so openly (especially with the sob behind "monthes two") and articulates so clearly just what makes him angry (his "wyves cursednesse") that even a novice Shrink like K4's Host knows just what to do. Sincere and sympathetic, he boosts the Merchant's ego with a louder "ye" in line 1241: "Look, I know you're feeling bad about yourself, but there *is* something worthwhile about *you*." Then, with a pause before a louder "telle," K4's Host goes on, "And say, why don't you talk about it? *I* want to listen." (Let us hope that K4's Host is not luring lost souls into some wealthy guru's incense-sales cult.) K4's Merchant replies that, as the text says, he is too sad to talk about himself.

Other Hosts whom I classify as Shrinks sound more professional than does K4's. With well-modulated concern in their voices, they use *MctT* lines 1240–42 to tell distraught Merchants, "OK, but she's not here now. I'm here. Keep on talking. Keep on telling me *how you feel.*"

Other professional-sounding Hosts limit their expertise to their actual profession, that of Lord of the Revels. These Hosts are by no means unkind or oblivious to marital suffering, but the Merchant is only one of approximately nine and twenty for whose happiness and welfare the Host has assumed responsibility.

K5's Merchant tries particularly hard to make his own case sound dramatic and worthy of attention. He turns from amused reticence in lines 1231–32 to a self-effacing chuckle: "Only two short months—would you believe it?" But within a few lines, especially on "koude" in line 1237, he shifts to dark foreboding of unspeakable horrors, then finally to disgust at "cursednesse."

K5's Host, unlike both J5's and the one in the *Prologue* to the *Tale of Beryn*, has held no conversation on any topic with the Merchant. In fact, when the pilgrim in the beaver hat suddenly speaks up, K5's Host needs a stretched-out "now" during which to place him. He then issues his standard request for a tale. K5's Merchant replies curtly. A bit disappointed that he is merely one of the crowd, he is ready to go on with a story but not with his personal problems, which he now realizes matter only to him.

Notice that K5 adds an "a" such that *MctT* l. 1242 ends "telle us a part" without disrupting oral meter. Another reader expands "in" such that line 1227 becomes "I wolde nevere eft comen into the snare," the "–en in–" merging into one syllable in performance. These and other examples again indicate that scribal errors in manuscripts, and typographical ones in early editions, would create few problems for our aurally-attuned ancestors. We can appreciate the benefits of modern editions, therefore, without casting aspersions on the understanding of readers who lacked them.

Very unlike K5, K1–3, and all the other Hosts too little concerned, the final large group of Nosy Neighbors display more interest in his love life than the Merchant ever intended. Instead of gentlemanly sympathy, these Hosts convey wide-eyed eagerness to learn all the lurid details.

While holding back details of his sex life, in *MctT* ll. 1231–32, K6 teases a bit: "Alysoun of Bath may tell all, but no way will you get me to." K6's stress on "alle" brings the Wife of Bath to the text; other Merchants invoke her by stressing instead "*I* sey nat alle." In addition some Hosts, even sympathetic ones, use line 1242 to urge the Merchant to "telle us *part*" of his life history, not the whole of it as Alysoun did. This mental sounding was less available to early readers, who usually encountered the tale order *SqT-MctT-WBP*.

Unfortunately, K6 finds, he has chosen precisely the wrong person in whom to confide: a backyard gossip. The eager "ooooo!" of that Host's "now" particularly urges K6's Merchant to spill all. Merchants react to the six nosy Hosts with surprising consistency. Each performs lines 1243–44 in a glum but not despairing tone: "Oh man, why do I even bother talking to these people?"

Cut L, MctT ll. 1245–55

Instead of sharing autobiography, for this and for other reasons implied in the twenty-seven performances of lines 1243–44, nearly all of the twenty-six readers who continue the passage say "whilom" in the culturally expected tone, "Once upon a time." Representing this majority, L1 uses a straightforward storytelling tone to set the scene and introduce the protagonist. The personality of L1's Merchant reemerges, however, in his attitude toward women. As it does for many other Merchants, L1's line 1250 expresses a mixture of disgust and slobbering lust, which imitates January's attitude but which may also make us wish to hear the Merchant's bride's side of the story. L1's disgust subsides a bit in reference to the secular fools left behind in Chaucer's workshop, but he holds a grudge against them as well as against all women.

The Merchant's negative feelings about his wife expand, in every reading but one, to encompass women in general. Some Merchants resent women, rather than finding them repulsive as does L1; others sound indignant or just plain lecherous at *MctT* ll. 1249–50.

Now, a Merchant troubled by his recent marriage would not necessarily speak negatively of all women. He might long for a carefree bachelorhood like January's. He might morally condemn January for premarital sex. He could even sympathize with the women wronged. Yet in twenty-five of the readings-aloud, all those nameless women got just what they deserved: rape and desertion. Bitterness toward one woman blocks alternative attitudes toward other women.

As could be predicted, a woman reader produces the only performance with any hint of disapproval for January's forty-odd years of wham–bam–thank-you-ma'am. L2's Merchant, one of those genuinely too sad to say more in lines 1243–44, with a sigh and sarcastic quotation marks begins to tell of a so-called "worthy" knight. To L2 the phrase "on wommen" seems an afterthought, almost parenthetical. He had to rape something, so why not women?

Female readers other than L2 never convey the lustful hatred that many male readers perform for the Merchant here, but neither do they sympathize with the victims. Some female voices shrug aside January's bodily delights, while others imply that all those women probably asked for it.

What sort of a man is this January, who has left in the lurch so many? He is a man determined to marry on account of dotage, not holiness, according to seventeen of the twenty-six readers of *MctT* ll. 1253–54. According to six others, holiness and dotage are equally absurd reasons to marry. Only three of the twenty-six pass without notable inflection this well-established critical point—the first of many unresolved word pairs in the *Merchant's Tale*, this one more a hendiadys than an opposition.

L3 exemplifies the six readers of lines 1252–55 who use sarcastic quotation marks to term both holiness and dotage ridiculous. L4 represents one of the many ways in which readers' inflections say that January married for dotage, not for holiness at all.

Some of this largest group of readers highlight "dotage" itself. Only L4 actually chuckles at that point; others say "dotage" louder, or with an anticipatory up-pitch, or with a distinct pause before or after it. Others make the same point with sarcastic quotation marks around "hoolynesse." You can call it "dotage" or anything else you want, but it sure is not holy. Notice that L4 also encloses "wedded man" in nonsarcastic quotation marks: "Were it for so-called 'hoolynesse' or for [chuckle] dotage, he decided to try out an unfamiliar concept, 'wedded man.'"

Cut M, MctT ll. 1261–68

So, most readers imagine a doting January. How is this mental image expressed in January's first speech, lines 1263–65, and in the Merchant's subsequent comment on his wisdom?

For *MctT* ll. 1263–65, six of the twenty-six readers shift to the high-pitched quavery voice of a senile fool. Most others stay at the narrator's pitch and mark the shift in speaker by inserting vocal parentheses around "seyde he." Early editors did the same in print. For example, Speght's line 1263 is "Non other life (said he) is worth a bean." [1]

Among the readers who insert parentheses for the narrator's comment and do not imitate an old man's voice, thirteen make January sound primarily determined, firm in his resolve. Among the various other Januarys, one sounds pompous. Another issues a proclamation. One eagerly confides his learning, while another (resembling Pope's January, to be discussed) has laboriously memorized a few key theological terms. Yet another, not at all resolute, says "esy" and "clene" longingly: at least one January wants the easy way out.

All twenty-six readers shift to sarcasm—sarcasm that ranges from perfunctory to vicious—on *MctT* l. 1266, a textbook example of Augustinian irony. Illustrating shades of irony in *MctT* ll. 1261–68, Cut M consists of two teacher-student pairs, M1–2 and M3–4. They illustrate the same point about classroom influence as did I3–4 for the *Pardoner's Tale*. Indeed, the same pair again performs an old man, this time as M3–4.

Oral influence is tenacious. It may even last "lenger than thee list, paraventure" (*MctT* l. 1318). Notice, for example, that for no particular interpretive reason one teacher and student stress the adjectives in *MctT* l. 1264, the other teacher and student the adverbs. That is, M1 and M2 both say "so *esy* and so *clene*," M3 and M4 both "*so* esy and *so* clene."

M2 took M1's Chaucer course about fifteen years before making this tape. Both M1 and M2 make "seyde he" parenthetical, rather than shifting from January's voice as M3 and M4 do. Other resemblances include a mock-oratorical quaver on "hooly" in line 1261, the sort of quaver the Pardoner might use to sell relics, and milder quavers on "esy" and "clene." Both M1 and M2 relish the idea of "paradys." But their attitudes differ toward worthless beans. M2 sounds amused by a "bene," whereas M1 firmly rejects worthlessness. Both then make "seyde" louder in line 1266, evoking an unstated concept as in Cut B4: "This is what he said but not what he meant."

After this irony brought to the text by "seyde," M2 delivers the final clause as a casual shrug, with no breaks. Instead, here M1 makes vocal irony more overt by means of a chuckle to start, a slight pause before "so," and after "so" a pause implying something left unsaid (cf. Cut B3): "Thus *seyde* this old knyght . . . that was . . . so . . . (never mind what he really was) wys." That is, M2 has softened or made subtle the irony in the second half of *MctT* l. 1266, which she came to understand in M1's classroom.

Through most of the passage, M4 likewise softens the audible cynicism of her former teacher M3. At line 1266, however, M4's irony sounds more explicit than M3's.

Compared to M1 and M2, who sound primarily amused at the old knight, M3 tends to reject foolishness and its byproducts. Rather than

M1–2's overblown rhetorical inflections on "hooly," for example, M3's narrator scorns both "hooly" bond itself and the married "womman" (*MctT* ll. 1261–62). M3's January sounds very old and quavery then, blindly groping for each word. Although "noon oother lyf" is not quite in the narrator's voice, M3's full-scale, high-pitched, sunken-cheeked performance does not begin in earnest until after "seyde he."

M4's reading of *MctT* ll. 1261–65 echoes M3's effects in less exaggerated form. M4 conveys only mild scorn for "hooly" and "womman," with hesitation concerning the latter. On "is worth a bene" M4 shifts to a voice that is foolish, certainly, but not senile like M3's. Both M3 and M4, a bit less emphatically than M1 and M2, use "seyde" in line 1266 to specify the discrepancy between January's stated and actual intentions.

Diverging from her former teacher, then, M4 makes absolutely certain that no one misses the irony of the last clause. A chuckle accompanies "that was," and a pause before "so wys" says definitely, "The phrase I am about to utter is the opposite of what I mean." Since M4's foolish January lacks M3's excuse of senile dementia, M4's narrator speaks of him with unrelenting scorn.

Analogously, M2's narrator is more casual than M1's, shrugging aside the Italian knight's silliness without bothering to condemn it. Attitudes projected by M1 and M3, whether spoken aloud to their students or implied by commentary, have since been adapted by M2 and M4, respectively, to their own images of the situation.

The Chaucer tapes provide evidence for the power of classroom teaching and the power of independent response; and let us hope that the former has led to the latter. In each generation, authorities—usually well-meaning, never malevolent, sometimes now just desperate to publish—impose textual interpretations. It is in the nature of Authority to do so. Each reader of a text brings Experience to it. An educator should strike a balance between the two, Experience and Authority—not strangling the one, not shirking the other.

An editor's authority reaches wider than does any one teacher's and is likewise never malevolent. Suppose that Wright and then Skeat had inserted quotation marks around *MctT* ll. 1267–1392, such that January rather than a steadily sarcastic Merchant would keep on foolishly overpraising marriage. Assigning the encomium to January would not eliminate the possibility of a resentful attitude, which Ogle in 1741 heard and re-created as a full-length family saga, but it would eliminate some of the narrator's knotty psychological problems.

Among twenty-six readers-aloud of the blissful praise of marriage that begins at line 1267, however, nobody at all reads it as if it were January's speech. One reader comes close. After his narrator's caustic comment at line 1266, that reader shifts to the eager voice of someone who fully and sincerely believes in the good of marriage. But the characterization collapses, for that voice sounds nothing like January's in lines 1263–65.

Originally I had not requested that readings-aloud include *MctT* lines 1392–93, where a shift could occur from January's foolish encomium back to the Merchant's narration. Hoping to trick four Chaucerians into inserting vocal quotation marks at the end of line 1392, I made special requests that they read the *Merchant's Tale* through line 1398. The trick failed. None shifts speakers there. However, I would maintain that editorial punctuation, not Chaucer's text itself, diverts the possibility in oral performance.

Cut N, MctT ll. 1316–20

One problematic couplet blocks an easy alternative reading of *MctT* ll. 1267–1392 as January's opinions: in lines 1317–18 he seems aware that some wives last too long. Other problems that might arise by assigning the stretch to January are no stickier than is assigning to the secular Merchant a slur on secular fools (l. 1251). Unlikely though it seems that January could quote Theophrastus verbatim, for example, a British merchant would have less opportunity for classical education than would a knight of Lombardy. And although line 1310, "Deffie Theofraste, and herke me," seems to address an immediate audience of pilgrims, the same audience addressed in lines 1263–65 could be hearing January's advice. But line 1318 does jar.

One reader volunteered alternative readings-aloud of *MctT* ll. 1311–41, the first intended to sound sarcastic (i.e., by the Merchant) and the second sincere (i.e., by January). That reader having proved that the alternatives are indeed possible, let us instead hear four ways of dealing with *MctT* l. 1318, by four readers all intending to include it in the Merchant's extended Augustinian irony. In none of the four does the irony, halfway through this 125-line stretch, still sound harsh or bitter.

Cuts N1 and N2 present the same teacher-student pair as M1 and M2. Their two performances again project the same basic idea—here, that *MctT* l. 1318 is a direct warning to unmarried males—but in slightly different ways.

N1 conveys a good-natured Merchant, even though his warning tone for "laste" and "endure" edges toward the sinister. He chuckles as he thinks about a wife who lasts too long—chuckles perhaps at a sudden realization that, for him, two months of marriage is already too long.

N1's rising pitch on "greet sacrement" then teases any reader who might think that these are words to be believed. N1's Merchant, fully aware of the incongruity in *MctT* l. 1318, is amused not embittered by it.

Neither is N2's Merchant embittered, although he does express mild sarcasm on "laste" and "endure" (rather than N1's warning on those two words). Slowing down to issue *MctT* ll. 1317–18 as a solemn warning, N2 remains solemn rather than amused like her former teacher N1. N2's lines 1319–20 could, in fact, pass as a proclamation by January or by someone else fully convinced of the statement's truth.

Reader N3 issues a solemn warning, like N2's, that some wives outlast their usefulness. But N3 goes on to say, in line 1319, "Marriage as an institution may not be perfect, but it's the best we've got." The defensive tone of N3's lines 1316–20 could imply a self-aware, classically educated, sincere Merchant—one who knows just what Theophrastus wrote against marriage and who knows that other authorities also have denigrated this basic social institution, which he nonetheless chooses to support fully. Why? Therein, of course, lies the problem of assigning the passage to the Merchant, even to a Merchant joking earlier about his own marriage.

Aware like N1–3 of the incongruity of *MctT* l. 1318, N4 takes an audible step backward. As cheerful as N1, N4 is merely passing on something he has heard about marriage (rather than, like N1, warning others to avoid it). N4 embeds line 1318 in orally-created parentheses, then makes *MctT* ll. 1319–20 a proclamation of truth like N2's. Thus N4 uses a vocal technique analogous to early editors' parentheses around phrases like "quod he" to insert his narrator into a speech otherwise appropriate to January. N4's shift in tone also resembles that implied by Robinson's editorial dashes at *FrkT* l. 1018, commonly read as Chaucer-the-author's interruption of the Franklin's encomium on sunset.

Long before quotation marks, Pope read Chaucer's lines thus in his 1598 Speght edition:

> But dred nat, if plainly speke I shall
> A wife woll last and in thin house endure
> Well lenger than thee list parauenture

Pope uses the incongruity of *MctT* l. 1318 to help create a January who is so stupid—so old and spoiled too, but mainly stupid—that he fails to notice logical contradictions even within his own thoughts, or especially within his own thoughts:

This Blessing lasts, (if those who try, say true)
As long as Heart can wish—and longer too.[2]

Pope's January strains his minimal brain briefly, trying to reconcile two variant reports concerning the length of time marriage can be expected to last. He abandons the attempt as quickly as do buyers of Cream of Wheat cereal now, for example, who confront the slogan, "It's As Good As You Remember . . . And More!" The illogicality of line 1318 is far from severe, and constitutes no barrier to assigning *MctT* ll. 1267–1392 to January.

On the other hand, seven decades of commentary prove that the alternative is equally possible. Chaucer's text allows either one. Assignment of the passage to the Merchant makes for a more difficult reading, however. It is difficult orally, on account of the 125 lines of unabated sarcasm, and it is difficult to reconcile with the text of *Canterbury Tales,* in which the Host's marital problems do not cause him to revile all womankind, for example, and in which January brings a well-deserved punishment on himself by marrying against the laws of nature and by gullibly trusting his servant Damyan.

Pope cheerfully holds January thus to blame in his modernization, which was read instead of the *Merchant's Tale* for at least the subsequent century. Before Pope, there survives precisely one item of evidence for a reader's direct response to the *Tale* itself. In his new 1598 edition, Gabriel Harvey wrote beside the Argument to the *Merchant's Tale* the word "Comical."[3]

Apart from this single clue, in order to set the stage for Pope's imagined and then thoroughly articulated performance of January and May's courtship and marriage and its aftermath, we must acquire a sense of the couple's reputation before Pope made it his business. For those first three centuries, their marital escapades were talked about, were passed on and altered in oral tradition, but were seldom entered in books.

CHAPTER 9

The *Merchant's Tale* on Paper, Before Pope

Still today, book production takes time and money. A publisher needs months to convert an author's typescript or floppy disk into, say, two thousand salable copies. Slave labor might speed this process, of course. The owner of an ancient Roman scriptorium could guarantee production of five hundred to a thousand copies, on parchment or papyrus rolls, within one day of receiving the author's completed manuscript.[1] Then monks replaced slaves as scribes. Production slowed for some centuries but later perked up as print technology spread. Books, however, long remained luxury items.

Reading printed books aloud remained a most common means of using them, well into the nineteenth century. After Henry VIII defied the pope by authorizing a Bible in English, for example, his parliament found no need to restrict sales or silent reading of it. Alarmed by public discussions of the Great Bibles chained to St. Paul's, however, authorities passed laws stipulating which social ranks were permitted to read the Bible out loud, at home, quietly. They thereby outlawed readers-aloud like John Porter, "a fresh young man of big stature . . . [to whom] great multitudes would resort . . . because he could read well and had an audible voice." After a week in Newgate prison, in irons for his crime, Porter died.[2]

Chaucer aloud was never a crime, fortunately, and to read him silently was a great deal of bother. As bulky as the Bible, folio editions of Chaucer remained in black-letter typeface after printers abandoned it for anything else but Bibles and legal proclamations. Furthermore, as discussed, Chaucer did not come cheap before the late eighteenth century.[3]

Such practicalities of book use, along with the evidence of this chapter, outline the extent to which Chaucer's *Tales* lived on primarily in the oral tradition whence they came. Only for the final appearance of *Merchant's Tale* allusions before Pope's then-definitive modernization, in a truly abysmal 1641 play, does an author consult Chaucer's text directly. Chauceriana would have been better served had January and May remained in oral transmission for sixty years more, until Pope took them in hand.

Besides *January and May* and *The Wife of Bath Her Prologue,* Pope's early publications include *The Temple of Fame,* by his own annotation "Written in the Year 1711"[4] and certainly from a visual, not aural, experience with Chaucer's text. No modern critic need analyze Pope's process of adapting the *House of Fame,* for his own authorial notes quote parallel passages along with precise comments that, for example, "the reader might compare these twenty eight lines following which contain the same matter with eighty four of *Chaucer* ... too prolix to be inserted."[5] In 1976, with newly possible access to the autographed 1598 edition, David Nokes adds only that Pope notes in his margin one change more than he footnotes.[6]

In Pope's adaptation, a narrator falls asleep and describes first a temple of genuine ancient fame, then briefly a temple of present-day problematic rumour. This narrator, no bumbling bird-borne bookworm he, strikingly resembles a young Alexander Pope:

> While thus I stood, intent to see and hear,
> One came, methought, and whisper'd in my Ear;
> What cou'd thus high thy rash Ambition raise?
> Art thou, fond Youth, a Candidate for Praise?
>   'Tis true, said I, not void of Hopes I came,
> For who so fond as youthful Bards of Fame?
> But few, alas! the casual Blessing boast,
> So hard to gain, so easy to be lost:
> ....
>
> Nor Fame I slight, nor for her Favours call;
> She comes unlook'd for, if she comes at all:
> ....
>
> Then teach me, Heaven! to scorn the guilty Bays;
> Drive from my Breast that wretched Lust of Praise;
> Unblemish'd let me live, or die unknown,
> Oh grant an honest Fame, or grant me none![7]

Earnest and no doubt genuine sentiments these, in 1715, but by 1720 Bernard Lintot was still trying to sell copies from the *Temple's* second printing. Meanwhile *Rape of the Lock,* "Written in the Year 1712," was selling out four editions of over six thousand copies in about a year, heading for imitations, mock-commentary, a readership from seamstresses to royalty, and translations into French and Italian acclaiming

Pope as the greatest living poet.[8] The road lay clear and open past the House of Fame. Beyond it loomed not another cliff, but the bank.

Pope's *Temple of Fame* is only one in a long line of Ovidian temples that look more like each other than like Chaucer's.[9] Yet it is with an even duller thud than usual that we land sprawling on John Lydgate's *Temple of Glas*. Gazing across the subdivision, the references through three centuries to January and May as names for old husband and young wife, we see that behind the superficially varied façades of apparent textual interpretation lies an atextual cause: no one is looking at the *Merchant's Tale*.

During these centuries before Pope's interpretation, Chaucer primarily provides memorable names for a few of the many instances of *senex amans* themes in written-down folklore. Probably most of the authors of works naming January and May had actually read or heard some of *Canterbury Tales,* sometime in the past. Those discussed here mention Chaucer or a merchant along with the couple's names, combined with other possibly Chaucerian images. One author—not Lydgate—even makes a joke about his attributing to Chaucer an unrelated tale. A quick tour past these pre-Popean allusions supplies not varying interpretations of the *Merchant's Tale* itself, but rather consideration of analogous tales in oral transmission. They give us some idea of what listeners retain in aural understanding, and some idea of how very much else can be said about a *senex amans* other than what Chaucer artistically chooses to say.

Lydgate has converted Chaucer's rococo temple of Venus (*HF* ll. 119–467) into a concrete-block *Temple of Glas* with plenty of parking space. Derek Pearsall explains the monk's apparent motives for listing everybody who has ever been in love, including Alceste and Griselda and other Good Women, and Emily and Palamon and his brother, and Canace and her brother, plus somewhat less garbled references to other pairs mentioned by Chaucer.[10]

After pointing out that some men win love with riches, Lydgate's list lurches around a corner toward examples of

> ladies [who] complain, with a specific bitterness which is rare in
> the genre, of having been forced into marriages for wealth, or
> as children, and of having been dedicated to the cloister when too
> young to know love. It is rather difficult to see what the last
> group are doing in the temple of Venus in the first place.[11]

Briefly visible there at Lydgate's turning point is a couple named January and May, both bickering but otherwise in binary opposition as to disposition:

> And some ther were, as maydens yung of age,
> That pleined sore with peping and with rage
> That thei were coupled, againes al nature,
> With croked elde that mai not long endure
> Forto perfourme the lust of loues plai:
> For it ne sit not vnto fressh[e] May
> Forto be coupled to oold Ianuari.
> Thei ben so diuers that thei most[e] varie,
> For eld is grucching and malencolious,
> Ay ful of ire and suspecious,
> And iouth entendeth to ioy and lustines,
> To myrth and plai and to al gladnes.[12]

Chaucer's January could be called "suspecious" and his May lusty and briefly glad. But it is January who bubbles with joy and mirth and "the lust of loues plai," not May, and it would be difficult indeed to read even his exclamations in the last scene as grouchy or melancholy. Even if Chaucer's May were to complain outright, furthermore, her complaint would be other than that January will not last long enough. The less love's play the better, before that inheritance.

Lydgate does remember Chaucer's epithet "fressh," which is coupled with May's name in all but two of its twenty-five occurrences in the *Tale*. In "croked elde" perhaps he is blending with vague memories of the Pardoner's old man and crooked way the *Merchant's Tale* phrase that Pope will preserve in a rare direct translation, "When tender Youth has wedded stooping Age."[13]

It is interesting, if only relatively so for Lydgate, to note that his catalogue clunks to a halt before the next possible turn in this topic of couples "againes al nature," that of older women and younger men. Despite Alysoun's eager waving and yoo-hooing, Lydgate stolidly starts to describe the sunnish-haired lady of unsurpassable beauty who kneels before Venus.

In contrast to Lydgate's bleary binary abstraction, a contemporary of his writes in Harleian ms. 372 (folio 45) a rhyme royal stanza that names all the characters and paraphrases the *Merchant's Tale* accurately. Spurgeon attributes it to Lydgate or Hoccleve, but it has dropped quietly from both their canons and seems not to have been printed or referred to since.[14]

Without context we must move on past a walled-off century and a half of print technology before arriving at the gates to the great Scottish manor house at Lethingtoun. Its lord, Sir Richard Maitland, wrote poetry echoing Chaucer's. He must have known Chaucer from the 1561 Stowe edition, in that his *Satire on the Toun Ladyes* features the refrain, "And all for newfangilnes of geir." It shares genre and key word with *Against Women Unconstant* ("Madame, for your newefangelnesse") which the 1561 edition prints with "certaine woorkes of Geffray Chaucer, whiche hath not here tofore been printed, and are gathered and added to this booke by Iohn Stowe."[15]

In 1561, Maitland was stricken blind at age sixty-five. He remained active in politics, though, while a daughter Mary transcribed his earlier writings. In 1570, border troubles began that ejected him from his home until nearly the time of his death at age ninety.[16]

Between 1561 and 1570, from this expanded edition of Chaucer (the third major one during the lifetime of a man almost old enough to re-member the first printed books in Britain, including Caxton's Chaucer), probably Mary read aloud to her blind father what he had always meant to read. January's folly would have struck a particular chord for the knight Maitland—the father of seven children, all well established in career or marriage, whose beloved wife is said to have died on his funeral day.

Maitland's clearest debts to Chaucer occur in five rhyme royal stanzas that name January, May, and a merchant, *On the Folye of ane Auld Manis Maryand ane Young Woman*. A paraphrase follows.

I. It is great folly for an old man, "past fyftie yeir of aige," to grow so blind in vain conceit that he marries a young lass whose blood is "yit in raige," thinking he may serve her appetite. If he fails, she will despise him.

II. Old men should rejoice in "morall taillis; / And nocht in taillis." It is folly to marry when both strength and nature fail. Fresh May and cold January do not agree on one song in tune; the treble is wanting that should be sung above.

III. Men should start a journey at the lark's song, not at evening. "Efter mid-age" the lover lies too long. "Ane auld gray beird" lying by a white mouth in one bed is a piteous sight. This stanza ends with a near-Popean play on two kinds of helplessness: "The ane cryes help! the uther hes no mycht."

IV. Many a merchant, having traded for years in Antwerp and Burges and Berrie, then washes "in to Deip" only to lose all his gear, plundered and impoverished with vain conceit. It is great peril to trust a leaking boat or to "beir the saill nocht havand ane steife mast."

V. Tenant-farming is hard work, especially without equipment. Someone who lacks seed tires of tilling. Then another comes, finds waste land, yokes his plow, and tills with his own hand. Better that the first had never undergone that shame. "And sa my tale is endit." [17]

Maitland borrows beginning and end as quoted, *MctT* ll. 1248 and 2417. The problems and attitudes of each party in the marriage, the metaphorical blindness, the singing: Maitland adapts to his own purpose much besides names from Chaucer's *Tale*. His metaphors and wordplay flow stanza to stanza: from the inharmonious love song to the lark's song, then by way of life's journey to the Flaunderish merchant's travels until he loses it all "in to Deip." Maitland's original puns share the spirit of Chaucer's, especially his added twist to the "taillynge" at the end of the *Shipman's Tale*. Unlike Chaucer's noncommittal narrator, Maitland's condemns the match openly and cheerfully, on physical grounds, fully blaming the male contestant.

Thus, both Lydgate and the imaginative, blind Maitland respond to their memories of Chaucer's *Merchant's Tale* itself. Both respond demonstrably to the same quality of text analyzed by twentieth-century critics: its sets of unresolved binary oppositions, to be discussed concerning Pope's adaptation. Lydgate offers a sort of rational justification for Chaucer's artistically unresolved text: youth and age are mutually exclusive. Maitland instead passes judgment, as will other interpreters to come. January is wrong to marry against nature. We will see that it took Tyrwhitt's revised tale order and then (after a century and the ascension of "courtly love") Kittredge's impassioned classroom performances, to cast any blame at all on May.

At the next bout between the ill-matched couple, after Maitland's, the legalistic outcome remains in good-natured dispute. Should a young wife be condemned for trying to cuckold her old husband? Someone with initials O. B. in 1594 considers this along with, as his title tells us, other

> QVESTIONS OF PROFITABLE AND PLEASANT CONCERN-
> INGS, TALked of by two olde Seniors, the one an ancient retired
> *Gentleman, the other a midling or new upstart frankeling,*
> *under an* Oake in Kenelworth Parke, where they were met by an
> accident to defend the partching heate of a hoate day, in grasse
> or Buck-hunting time called by the reporter the *Display of vaine*
> *life,* together with a *Panacea* or suppling plaister to cure if it were
> possible, the principall diseases wherewith this present time is
> especially vexed.

As if in a transcribed conversation, Huddle tells Dunstable London gossip, including some about an "old courser of *Naples*" who

decaied as it should seeme in memorie, mistooke the season of
the yeare, perswading himselfe he felt Aprill flowers springing
fresh in his withered body, thought it had bene May in Ianuary.
Wherevpon, he ventured like a fresh gallant to marry a yong
damosell, to whom he might well haue bene grandfather.[18]

Huddle then tells a story that shares with the *Merchant's Tale* only gardening images (displaying more practical knowledge than Chaucer's), the
relative ages of the couple, and the wife's resigned reticence: "nature had
sufficiently furnished her with skill to dissemble her want . . . whensoeuer
this old yonker list to rage and play with her." (28r)

Her husband, named Oswould like Chaucer's elderly Reeve (30v; *RvT*
l. 3860), plies her with "plenty of all rich delights . . . as Iewels, apparrell,
and diet of the choisest." She nonetheless or therefore catches the eye of a

yong reueler, fresh budded Aprill indeed, [who] came by the
dore, where this faire flower stood, in the custodie and looking
to of a withered impotent gardiner, whose strength appeared
scarse sufficient to raise the dry and light moulds that grew about
this Rose, much lesse able to water and gage to the roote it
soundnesse. (28r)

The young man, "not hauing spent all his time at cards and dice, as some
vnthrifts do" (28r)—including the Merchant's son in early Chaucer editions—knows just where to find a procuress. Here a passage pulls into
awkward alignment several half-remembered images of Chaucer's. The
reveler pays the pander

with his purse in his hand ready drawne, for loosing of time, and
that as *Chaucer* saith, tied with a Leeke, that it may not be long
in opening, for the houres that are spent in making many words,
in such a matter, cannot be recouered back againe. (28r)

In the *Reeve's Prologue* Osewold compares himself to a leek (white
head, green tail) while paraphrasing his proverbial uselessness. In his
"tappe of lyf" speech, he flamboyantly paraphrases a proverb still used
today, "Lost time is not found again" (*RvT* ll. 3867–95; *HF* ll. 1257–58;
Tr 4.1283). Because O. B. likes gardening imagery and recalls an author's
use of familiar proverbs, he transplants the Reeve's self-image—leek,
grass, fodder, rotten fruit—into this tale of an old man who, unlike the
Reeve but like January, marries a girl.

In the shade of O. B.'s Chaucerian hybrid, cuckolding jolts under way according to the plan of the go-between, named Mother Ducke, and the April-like young man. Were it not for the latter, notes Huddle,

> this flower had seeded away vntimely, oppressed with too much heate by day, and the want of nightly moisture. *Dunst.* Before God, I begin to pittie the poor wench. (29r)

Mother Ducke helps the wooer disguise himself as a poulterer. He haggles over prices, then demands to see the lady of the house, who is pretending to be sick in bed. Despite our expectations for a denouement involving chickens used as bludgeons, or at least flying feathers, when the husband returns he merely spots a "peece of a wrought wastcoat" under the poulterer disguise and chases the intruder away (30r).

O. B.'s story, like the *Merchant's Tale,* ends unresolved. Therefore, discussion continues:

> *Hud.* What man how is it with you? me thinketh your lookes pleade the yong wenches case: say truly, is she guilty or not guilty? and if you were her husband, what would you do in this case? *Dunst.* Surely sir, where nothing can be prooued, suspition should not part a man and his wife. . . . [One obstacle to proof is] the shortnesse of the time he had with his mistrisse in the chamber. But euery man that breaketh his neighbors fence, trespasseth not against his inclosures. (30r–31v)

The legalistic decision, applicable to *MctT* l. 2353, still does not end the story. Conversation shifts next to what ever became of Mother Ducke and the young man.

En route, O. B. jokes about readers' spotty knowledge of written literature, which occasionally echoes what they already know so well from their own proverbs, gossip, jokes, rumor, legend, and tales. Furthermore, Huddle here articulates how an individual folk performer with aesthetic intentions creates a variant during the transmission of oral traditional material:

> *Dunst.* I beseech you sir haue you not taken this report out of *Chaucer* his Ianuarie and his May. *Hud.* Indeed yes, though not in euery halfe agreeing with the same, the rather, because I knew nothing but maruailes would delight you. (31r)

A few years after O. B. tries to capture natural-sounding conversation on the page, an author otherwise inclined tries to render in English the style of Juvenal's satires, believed to be purposely obscure. Editors have not fully sorted out the intentionally tangled syntax and allusions in the *Virgidemiarvm, Six Bookes* of Joseph Hall, aged twenty-five, who would become bishop and enemy pamphleteer against "Smectymnuus" and then Milton.[19]

The fourth satire of Hall's fourth book attacks lovers who make fools of themselves in as many ways as "yelping Begles busy heeles persue."[20] Last among these idiotic lovers is old Virginius. Unlike January, he has spent his youth and middle age eating antiaphrodisiacs in order to avoid following his bodily delight on women, until he gets too old to chew. Unlike January, he is the target of open scorn from maidens and narrator alike:

> *Virginius* vow'd to keepe his Mayden-head,
> And eats chast Lettuce, and drinkes Poppy-seed,
> And smels on Camphyre fasting: and that done,
> Long hath he liu'd, chast as a vayled Nunne,
> Free as a new-absolued *Damosell*
> That Frier *Cornelius* shriued in his Cell,
> Till now he waxt a toothlesse Bacheler,
> He thaw's like *Chaucers* frostie *Ianiuere*
> And sets a months minde vpon smiling *May.*
> And dyes his beard that did his age bewray;
> Byting on Annis-seede, and Rose-marine,
> Which might the Fume of his rot lungs refine:
> Now he in *Charons* barge a Bride doth seeke,
> The maydens mocke, and call him withered Leeke,
> That with a greene tayle hath an hoary head,
> And now he would, and now he cannot wed.[21]

Because Hall intends obscurity of style in these early satires, he may intend also that the Chaucer allusions be pieced together toward an end opposite that of the *Merchant's Tale,* from an opposite beginning, the whole allowing no sympathy whatsoever for a *senex amans* even when so soundly rejected by the ladies. That is, unlike other authors surveyed here, Hall might possibly be flipping through a ponderous volume of Chaucer, seeking and then adapting appropriate images. But such a hypothesis is not necessary to account for Hall's result, to account for these images of foolish old lovers that clump together in aural memory as if magnetized, though far apart in pages.

Like O. B., Hall links the *Merchant's Tale* names with the Reeve's proverbial comparison of an old man to a leek. For readers of early editions, the link would be solidified by a scribal interpolation to be discussed, in which May tells Damyan that her husband "may nat swiue worth a leke" because the relevant apparatus "foldeth twifolde."

The *Virgidemiae* image of ineffective beard-dyeing comes almost certainly from oral tradition, as will be mentioned again—although Chaucer's January does ineffectively shave (*MctT* l. 1826). Hall might have directly adapted Absolon's breath-sweetening tactics (from that young fool's failure to cuckold an old man, *MlrT* ll. 3690–92) to describe Virginius's futile efforts to combat leek breath. But the idea need not come from Chaucer. Elsewhere in the popular imagination, images of worthless leeks and old men with bad breath readily intertwine.

Here at the beginning of the seventeenth century, what can be determined about the relative strength of oral tradition versus Chaucer's text, now available in print to ever-widening circles of readers and hearers? Proverbs about leeks can serve to illustrate the issue. Although proverb dictionaries record only what authors wrote down, not which proverbs were spoken aloud at any time (the Folklore Dilemma, again), they do indicate that the leek's proverbial nature shifted decisively during two centuries of oral tradition—but shifted, quite possibly, on account of Chaucer's text.

At Chaucer's time, leeks were overwhelmingly noted for their worthlessness. Variants of "not worth a leek," including the one in the scribal interpolation quoted above, occur frequently throughout Chaucer and other Middle English texts. In the introduction to the fourth day of the *Decameron,* perhaps, or elsewhere in Italian, Chaucer could have encountered a proverbial expression that remained current in Italy at least until 1666—one to the effect that an old man, like a leek, has a white head and green tail. Chaucer worked this Italian image into his *Reeve's Prologue;* one author used it in 1532; then, beginning about 1590, a bevy of leeklike, white-and-green old men came to populate British letters. It is conceivable that improved travel conditions enabled the Italian proverb to arrive independently on the doorsteps of various British dramatists. But it seems likelier that they—looking for guidance to the father of English poetry—seized on the more elaborate leek image for characterization and let slide the leek's proverbial worthlessness.[22]

O. B. and Hall, writing just before this distinct shift in the nature of leek imagery, seem to be in transition. Hall apparently expects that his audience will know the "green tayle . . . hoary head" line with which maidens mock Virginius, but he specifies that they call him "withered" leek because it is perhaps no longer obvious that a leek in any condition is worthless. And O. B., with no intention whatsoever of retelling

Chaucer's stories when he has so many of his own, primarily remembers that something about a leek occurs somewhere in the vicinity of the long-lived proverb "Lost time is not found again."

Thus, these two sixteenth-century respondents to Chaucer would be only a bit likelier than us to notice the subtlety with which Chaucer uses implied proverbs to help characterize the Italian knight, January. No leek ever appears amidst the green and white patterns that play through January's concern for his own fertility, in *MctT* ll. 1457–66. With this boast, though, he is trying to deny the wisdom of both the common Middle English proverb and the Italian one. I am not worthless, he claims; my "hoor . . . heed" is blossoming before bearing fruit, and my greenness is not of a leek's tail but rather of my own limbs and heart, evergreen like the laurel.

Another work, also from the beginning of the seventeenth century, shows the interplay of oral and written traditions in a different light. I have just implied the power of Chaucer's text. One Italian proverb, apparently translated by one man then disseminated in print, comes to replace the simpler Middle English proverb in oral tradition (insofar as can be determined, as always). Evidence from the still-unpublished *Newe Metamorphosis* (1600–15?) implies the opposite: that a writer who knows Chaucer's name and even that Canterbury Tales are told en route to "St. Beckets shryne" may be only too glad to ignore such written literature in favor of his own fifteen thousand and more couplets that tell story after story after story until, at the end of the twenty-fourth book and the third quarto volume,

> My leave I here of Poetrie doe take
> for I have writte untill my hande doe ake[23]

The author J. M., apparently a career soldier, refers directly to Chaucer a few times—once with disapproval along with other makers of "Lyes . . . to blynde the simple ignorant," and again with standard praise as "the first life giver to o^r poesie."[24] John H. H. Lyon, outlining what are now Additional mss. 14824–26 in the British Library, notes other oblique references to Chaucer. Being a Shakespeare scholar rather than a folklorist, though, Lyon names as analogues to Chaucer's *Tales* of Merchant, Shipman, and Miller three stories with very distant parallels. Because closer analogues to all three *Tales* still occur in folklore not traceable to Chaucer, these provide no evidence that J. M. actually read *Canterbury Tales*.[25] Lyon summarizes his supposed analogue to the *Merchant's Tale* thus:

Cupid, because Saturn favors Mars, makes the old god love a
child of eight. (Digression on age and youth.) Her mother, to be
relieved of birth pangs, had promised Minerva to keep her
daughter unmarried. The girl spurns Saturn's advances when he
seeks to ravish her whilst in bathing. Minerva changes her to
an olive tree. Eusham, the daughter of the river Avon, laughs at
Saturn's disappointment. He then rapes her. A child is born with
one eye.[26]

This much action takes up only three of the more than thousand pages
of *The Newe Metamorphosis,* a still untapped source for folklorists and
literary sleuths, remarkable if only in that J. M. tells no story analogous
to any in Shakespeare and that his only mention of British literary figures
lists twenty-nine excluding Shakespeare.[27]

Lyon publishes excerpts from the text, including part of Saturn's preparations to meet Lady May. Resembling Hall's Virginius who dyes his
beard and January who shaves, "his beard he shorter cut." Otherwise
Saturn's gestures faintly reflect Absolon's if anyone's in Chaucer:

> his hoped ioye nowe maketh him to skippe
> ....

> and then he wisheth for his monthe of Maye.
> he lookes that th' seame on's hose doth rightly stande
> he often stroakes his leggs up wth his hande
> ....

> his shooes he caused to be wyped blacke
> riche shooe-tye-roses, there he doth not lacke[28]

The *senex amans* characters of Hall and J. M. make Chaucer's portrayal of January seem charitable in comparison because it is nonvisual.
We are party to January's inner thoughts and his foolish songs and
speeches. But of his clothing we see only shirt and nightcap, of his body
only those so effective glimpses of new-shaven bristly beard unsoft and
of slack skin quivering on his lean neck (*MctT* ll. 1824–26, 1849–53).
For January, as for ideal medieval beauties (e.g., *BD* ll. 895–960), Chaucer provides close-up detail above the collarbone, leaving the rest to our
various imaginations.

As J. M. was writing his long manuscript, and as Hall was beginning
to publish his *Virgidemiae,* access to Chaucer's actual images and plots
became easier with the publication of Thomas Speght's first edition. Besides the first glossary ever, as editorial apparatus Speght supplies "Arguments to euery Tale and Booke," still grouped with introductory

material in 1598.[29] Readers later than J. M. and Hall, including Gabriel Harvey who immediately marked up his margins far more than Pope would mark his a century later, found a convenient synopsis of the *Merchant's Tale* that characterized it as one in which justice is done: "Old Ianuarie marrieth young May, and for his vnequall match, receiueth a foule reward." In the margin of his brand-new copy of Chaucer, Gabriel Harvey wrote next to this plot summary the single extant word that indicates how a reader before Pope regarded the *Merchant's Tale:* "Comical."[30]

Speght resolves the *Tale*'s inconclusive ending by blaming January, and his contemporary Harvey finds January's just deserts funny. Speght comments on clearly unresolved endings such as those of the Franklin ("The scope of this tale seemeth a contention in curtesie") and of course the Cook and Squire ("The most of this Tale is lost, or els neuer finished by the Authour"). But Speght saw no such problem for the Merchant.

A glance through these Arguments can leave one pondering just how far Chaucer criticism has come since 1598. Like Skeat and other nineteenth-century scholars, Speght considers historical context and attributions to other authors, *Floure of Courtesie* being "made by Iohn Lidgate, as some thinke, in the behalfe of some gentlewoman in the Court." Like turn-of-the-century Chaucerians he notes sources and analogues, the *Tale* of the Shipman as well as that of the Reeve being "taken out of Bochas in his Nouels."

Like Kittredge, Speght finds certain tales appropriate to their tellers: "A Tale fitting the person of a Knight, for that it discourseth of the deeds of Armes, and loue of Ladies." Like Dryden and many twentieth-century critics Speght finds a vast human drama; like New Critics he finds carefully wrought irony:

> Vnder the Pilgrimes, being . . . all of differing trades, he comprehendeth all the people of the land, and the nature and disposition of them in those daies; namely, giuen to deuotion rather of custome than of zeale. In the Tales is shewed the state of the Church, the Court, and Countrey, with such Arte and cunning, that although none could deny himselfe to be touched, yet none durst complaine that he was wronged.

Like D. W. Robertson, Jr., Speght puts extra emphasis on religious elements—on anti-Catholic satire rather than pro-Catholic devotion, though, the *Summoner's Tale* being "A requitall to the Fryar, shewing their cousenage, loytering, impudent begging, and hypocriticall praying."

Like Charles Muscatine he treats the French tradition, the Argument to *Romance of the Rose* being longest by far, and like E. Talbot Donaldson he distinguishes Chaucer-the-pilgrim from Chaucer-the-author:

> *The Rime of Sir Topas.* A Northren tale of an outlandish Knight purposely vttered by Chaucer, in a differing rime and stile from the other tales, as though he himselfe were not the authour, but only the reporter of the rest.

Like most men, Speght blames Criseyde. And like many readers who spend time around Chaucer, Speght maintains a wide-eyed innocence— "What, me pun?"

> *The Millars tale.* Nicholas a Scholler of Oxford, practiseth with Alison the Carpenters wife of Osney to deceiue her husband, but in the end is rewarded accordingly.

In the next nondramatic work to mention January and May, a guffaw-ing pun appears at the end of the title:

> A DISCOVRSE OF MARRIAGE AND WIVING: AND Of the greatest Mystery therein contained: how to chuse a good Wife from a bad. . . . By ALEX. NICCHOLES, Batchelour in the Art he neuer yet put in practise.

Niccholes suggests at length that one take a wife appropriate to one's trade. For example, someone often away from home should choose one with a lethargic disposition, nudge nudge wink wink:

> Art thou a Merchant, a Marriner, a Termer, choose thee a wife of some Phlegmeticke humour, that like a rich Creditor, with her large stocke of vertue, without breaking out, can forebeare thee [for long periods of time] . . . if otherwise though thou escape the perils of the Sea, thou art in danger of the Pirates of the Land.[31]

Niccholes's advice on relative age could have occurred anywhere in the treatise, but he drifts into it via the merchant imagery in the same para-graph:

> Whence proceed these . . . disiunctions . . . whose conioyning of hands may resemble the league betweene the Low Countries & Spain, where hearts can no more be brought to unity . . . then

those euer vowed enemies thus taken truce: These respects I say
. . . haue prostituted vnder one covering, many a frosty January,
and youthfull May . . . which could no more cohabite then these
different seasons.

Niccholes paddles with more energy toward the reciprocal unseasonable
conjunction, toward that one cove of the topic left unexplored by his
soul-mate Lydgate: Autumn and Summer, to wit,

Croanes, and many of my late remembrance, lip-bearded, as
witches, with their warty antiquity, and age, [who] haue angled
into their beds with this baited golden hooke, (for lucre of desire
and lust) on their parties, youth whose chinnes have neuer yet
fallen under the razor.

Niccholes directly mentions neither the Wife of Bath nor the old
woman in her *Tale*. His unskillful treatment of old/young marriages,
however, casts further light on Chaucer's artistry concerning the same
two social taboos. Chaucer, like May, leaves much unsaid.

Among many analogues to the "Loathly Lady" motif in the *Wife of
Bath's Tale*, the other medieval British versions resemble one another and
differ from Chaucer's in the amount of space devoted to physical description of the old woman.[32] Like Niccholes, authors other than Chaucer
eagerly share their personal visions of ultimate female ugliness. To Gower
or his source "Hire Necke is schort, hir schuldres courbe," whereas the
Dame Ragnell author sees quite the opposite:

Her nek long and therto greatt,
. . . .

In the sholders she was a yard brode,
Hangyng pappys to be an hors lode;
And lyke a barelle she was made.[33]

As he does for old January, Chaucer supplies for the old hag the merest
flash of a picture, through the knight's eyes (*WBT* ll. 999, 1082). Each
silent reader must envision her in a way that makes personal sense, as
well as give her words a tone of voice.

A listener to Chaucer aloud must still interact with the text to visualize
pilgrims and characters, even while a particular reader-aloud is partly
interpreting them by means of vocal inflections. Chaucer's text permits
no lazy listeners. One not only can, but must constantly rouse personal

experience and expectations in order to see and hear the Canterbury drama.

Chaucer takes no cheap shots. His most effective visual details about characters' appearances cause readers to wonder, not judge. The Wife of Bath certainly has a gap between her front teeth, which certainly symbolizes outgoing sexuality, just as it does in present-day folklore. But should she be condemned for this physically manifested trait? The reader must decide. Or again, not everybody with a bad case of acne or stringy blond hair is evil; seeing evil in the actions of Summoner and Pardoner, we step back to find warning thereof in their appearances.

Because of its treatment of universal human conditions, manifested in specific but nonjudgmental details and specific human interactions, Chaucer's text makes readers want to dramatize it. In this way it differs from Lydgate's, full of abstractions removed from human sight and sound, and differs in another way from the texts on paper of the seventeenth century's burgeoning new genre, drama.

Instead of hearing a text and mentally picturing its action, London theatergoers came to expect full visual as well as flamboyant aural interpretations of texts written especially for performance—with conventions transcending the visual, though, such as disguises that fool others on stage but not the audience. In one such "inferior comedy" by Thomas Dekker and John Day occurs a line, "Old January goes to lie with May." [34] No other potentially Chaucerian allusion appears, however, amongst the words of the old married man in love with a witty young woman, nor of her brother in love with that same old man's wife until he (disguised as a sister of his sister) sees their daughter, nor of that daughter's brother (i.e., the old man's son) also in love with the witty young woman—not to mention the subplot couple, she lovesick and he a banished noble disguised as a French doctor with an Irish accent.

Perhaps coincidentally, Alexander Niccholes had juxtaposed merchant imagery with January and May. Not even such a tenuous connection to Chaucer's *Tale* occurs in this play of Dekker's, nor is there any in a poem on the birth of Prince Henry, published the same year as Niccholes's inflated treatise and likewise using the two names of months for old man and young woman. [35] In the decades leading up to 1642, one well-written play with allusions to Chaucer does emerge from the ever more restricted presses. Then from the final seventeenth-century work, from Chaucer's text rewritten for a *senex amans* in another play, one rises to leave quietly, musing that it may be just as well they closed the theaters the next year.

In the Dekker play, the poem to Prince Henry, Hall's satire, and *The Newe Metamorphosis*, emphasis falls on the old man as foolish wooer of a youngster, instead of on the couple's postmarital problems as it does in Chaucer, Lydgate, O. B., and Maitland. John Fletcher works both these issues into a proto-feminist play first acted in 1611 and censored in 1633. The main plot of Fletcher's *Woman's Prize: or, The Tamer Tamed* features a bride who gets her own way, the subplot her sister Livia being peddled by their father to a rich old wife-seeker.

The female lead barricades from their wedding-night bedroom the groom she has chosen for love, until he signs a contract providing her with

> [the husband:] As I expected: Liberty and clothes,   *Reads.*
> When, and in what way she wil: continuall moneys,
> Company, and all the house at her dispose;
> ....
>
>   And at the latter end a clause put in,
> That *Livia* shal by no man be importun'd,
> This whole moneth yet, to marry.
> [the girls' father:] This is monstrous.[36]

Amidst the hubbub of townswomen rallying to the bride's cause, the father finds a moment to promise Livia to old Moroso, who remains hesitant lest he "be made a whim-wham . . . . I know, being old, tis fit I am abus'd" (4.1.6, 38). By far the humblest and least self-deluded of any *senex amans* surveyed here,

>   I am old and crasie,
> And subject to much fumbling, I confesse it;
> Yet something I would have that's warme, to hatch me.
>   (4.1.20–22)

The father, wanting Moroso's money, scoffs at his hesitancy:

> Hast thou forgot the Ballad, crabbed age,
> Can *May* and *January* match together,
> And nev'r a storm between 'em? say she abuse thee,
> ....
>
> Art thou a whit the worse?
>   (4.1.32–34, 37)

The ballad on *The Wanton Wife of Bath,* who enters heaven after specifying sins of Biblical figures who try to stop her, kept popping into print for more than two centuries despite stern orders as of 1600 that these "ballates shalbe brought in and burnt ✠ And that either of the printers for theire Disorders in printinge yt shall pay vˢ A pece for a fine." [37] Does Fletcher refer to a specific ballad on January and May, perhaps one entitled *Crabbed Age,* now lost or awaiting rediscovery? Or does he merely have in mind Chaucer's names plus some other *senex amans* song such as *The Old Fumbler* collected by Thomas D'Urfey several decades later or the one that Robert Burns would scrub shiny for publication?

> John Anderson, my jo, John,
> When first that ye began,
> Ye had as good a tail-tree,
> As ony ither man;
> But now its waxen wan, John,
> And wrinkles to and fro;
> [I've t]wa gae-ups for ae gae-down,
> [John] Anderson, my jo. [38]

The ballad recalled by Fletcher's father of the bride, however, involves a scolding young wife; these examples do not.

Peddling his second daughter even while his first protests, the father offers Moroso man-to-man advice on aphrodisiacs, facial hair, boudoir attire, and Absolonian tactics against leek-infected breath:

> get warm broths,
> And feed apace; think not of worldly businesse,
> It cools the blood;
> ....
>
> Contrive your beard o'th top cut like Verdugoes;
> It shows you would be wise, and burn your night-cap,
> It looks like halfe a winding-sheet, and urges
> From a young wench nothing but cold repentance:
> You may eate Onyons,
> ....
>
> They purge the blood, and quicken,
> But after 'em, conceive me, sweep your mouth,
> And where there wants a tooth, stick in a clove.
> (4.1.51–53, 55–62)

Disgusting as he may seem, this brideprice-seeking father is delicate and polite compared to his counterpart in the next play to be discussed. Fletcher's characterization again backlights Chaucer's effectiveness in telling only January's inner thoughts of wooing, not his external actions, and in saying nothing of May's parents except that by "every scrit and bond . . . she was feffed in his lond" in passive voice, thus leaving the rest to our diverse imaginations (*MctT* ll. 1577–1606, 1691–98).

Fletcher knew *Canterbury Tales* well. He refers to Chaucer in other plays more specifically, and the distinguished father of Fletcher's partner Beaumont had originally urged Speght to undertake the editing task.[39] In *The Woman's Prize* and elsewhere, Fletcher's debt to Chaucer is minimal, and very well invested, compared to that of Shakerley Marmion.

Born in 1602, as was Speght's second edition, Marmion failed to earn a living alternately as a soldier and a writer. In 1639, two years before his play *The Antiquary* was printed, he died in London of illness contracted during an unsuccessful border expedition against Scotland.[40] He should have stayed home with his copy of Chaucer, lines of which he reuses from the page, not from aural memory.

The writhing, tortured plots of *The Antiquary* involve much unmotivated disguising: a sister dresses as a pageboy whose presence elicits pointless oaths "by Ganymede," for example, and a father just happens to be disguised as a killer-for-hire on the very day that the *senex amans* tries to hire someone to murder his son. This *senex amans* Moccinigo— "an old Gentleman that would appear young" and thereby distinguishable from Lorenzo, "an old Gentleman," and the Antiquary who is named Veterano and collects antiquities[41]—changes his beard like other oldsters including January. The incident's punch line, combined with Marmion's lack of imagination, marks it as a joke taken from oral tradition:

> For, going to a courtezan this morning,
> In his own proper colour, his grey beard,
> He had th' ill luck to be refus'd; on which,
> He went and dy'd it, and came back again,
> And was again, with the same scorn, rejected,
> Telling him, that she had newly deny'd his father.[42]

I will simply reproduce the entire passage of definite *Merchant's Tale* allusions, since the plot cannot be said to matter much to characterization here:

> LOR.   Was that . . . [the courtezan's] answer?
> GAS.   It has so troubled him,
> That he intends to marry. What think you, sir,
> Of his resolution?

LOR.   By'r lady, it shows
Great haughtiness of courage: a man of his years
That dares to venture on a wife.
MOC.   A man of my years? I feel
My limbs as able as the best of them;
And in all places else, except my hair,
As green as a bay-tree: and for the whiteness
Upon my head, although it now lie hid,
What does it signify, but like a tree that blossoms
Before the fruit come forth? And, I hope a tree
That blossoms is neither dry nor wither'd.
LOR.   But pray, what piece of beauty's that you mean
To make the object of your love?
MOC.   Ay, there
You 'pose me: for I have a curious eye,
And am as choice in that point to be pleased,
As the most youthful. Here one's beauty takes me;
And there her parentage or good behaviour;
Another's wealth or wit; but I'd have one
Where all these graces meet, as in a centre.
GAS.   You are too ambitious. You'll hardly find
Woman or beast that trots sound of all four:
There will be some defect.
MOC.   Yet this I resolve on,
To have a maid tender of age and fair.
Old fish and young flesh, that's still my diet.
LOR.   What think you of a Widow?
MOC.   By no means:
They are too politic a generation:
Prov'd so by similes. Many voyages
Make an experienc'd seaman; many offices
A crafty knave; so, many marriages,
A subtile cunning widow. No, I'll have one
That I may mould, like wax, unto my humour.
LOR.   This doating ass is worth, at least, a million,
And, though he cannot propagate his stock,
Will be sure to multiply. I'll offer him my daughter.
By computation of age, he cannot
Live past ten years; by that time she'll get strength
To break this rotten hedge of matrimony,
And after have a fair green field to walk in,
And wanton where she please [*aside*]. Signior, a word!
And by this guess my love: I have a daughter,
Of beauty fresh, of her demeanour gentle,

And of a sober wisdom: you know my estate.
If you can fancy her seek no further.
Moc.   Thank you, signior: pray of what age
Is your daughter?
Lor.   But sixteen, at the most.
Moc.   But sixteen? is she no more? She is too young, then.
Gas.   You wish'd for a young one, did you not?
Moc.   Not that I would have her in years.
Gas.   I warrant you!
Moc.   Well, mark what I say: when I come to her,
She'll ne'er be able to endure me.
Lor.   I'll trust her.
Gas.   I think your choice, sir, cannot be amended,
She is so virtuous and so amiable.
Moc.   Is she so fair and amiable? I'll have her!
She may grow up to what she wants; and then
I shall enjoy such pleasure and delight,
Such infinite content in her embraces,
I may contend with Jove for happiness!
Yet one thing troubles me.
Gas.   What's that?
Moc.   I shall live so well on earth,
I ne'er shall think of any other joys.
Gas.   I wish all joy to you! but 'tis in th' power
Of fate to work a miracle upon you.
You may obtain the grace, with other men,
To repent your bargain before you have well seal'd it.
Lor.   Or she may prove his purgatory, and send him
To Heaven the sooner.[43]

Probably Marmion used the 1598 Speght edition, as did Pope, or the corrected and rearranged one of 1602. In Marmion's grapplings with Chaucer's text, he bashes headlong into some of the same problems that Pope will conquer suavely.[44]

The bride's tender age in Speght's edition—under fifteen, not twenty as now for *MctT* l. 1417—bothers both Marmion and Pope. To the crass old would-be husband, Marmion gives a qualm of conscience, one promptly quenched with an empty promise of the adolescent bride's amiability. Worrying then that his happiness will rival Jove's, the *senex amans* is reassured with talk of Christian grace and purgatory. We will see how Pope, facing Chaucer's entangled Christian/pagan images and Speght's teen-age May, carefully sets the story at a time and place with customs unlike Britain's in 1700—sets it in Italy, perhaps a millennium and a half earlier, when some characters worship the Roman gods while others have newly embraced Christianity.

Marmion, writing for the stage, flattens the *Tale*'s potential for dramatization into an unmotivated exchange of Chaucer's least pleasant sexual images. Pope, while retaining Chaucer's form of narrative couplets, unifies the drama, motivates the characters, and supplies stage directions that—more fully than any other evidence on paper discussed in this book—provide analyzable parallels to the Chaucer tapes. The modernization provides an accurate gauge as to how the voice of at least one person, one very bright and self-educated teen-ager, would have given meaning in performance to Chaucer's text, at a point midway in time between Chaucer and us.

CHAPTER 10

How Pope Found the *Merchant's Tale*

> He set to learning Latin and Greek by himself [at] about twelve, and when he was about fifteen would go up to London and learn French and Italian. We in the family looked upon it as a wildish sort of resolution, for as his ill health would not let him travel we could not see any reason for it. He stuck to it, went thither, and mastered both those languages with a surprising dispatch. Almost everything of this kind was of his own acquiring. He had had masters indeed, but they were very indifferent ones, and what he got was almost wholly owing to his own unassisted industry.[1]

With one hand tied behind his back, Pope could have learned Middle English by modernizing the *General Prologue* and *Reeve's Tale*, before venturing publication under his own name. At his time and later, one normally studied a language by undertaking a translation. Literary interests did not necessarily predominate. In 1797–1801, for example, while serving as minister to Prussia, U.S. president-to-be John Quincy Adams learned German by four times translating his favorite book, Christoph Wieland's *Oberon: A Poetical Romance*. Adams thereby re-Englished Pope's modernization, which Wieland had woven into his plot as a tale of Gangolfo and Rosetta, "As much alike, as *January* and *May*."[2]

Before watching the waves of influence spread outward from the modernized *Merchant's Tale*, however, let us investigate its process of formation. Pope's enquiring mind fused discrete strata: classical literature, English literature including works by Addison and Shakespeare, Dryden's modernizations and commentary on Chaucer, oral ballads, visual art, stagecraft, and personal contact with people and dogs. In addition, the 1598 Speght edition would have provided the student with "Annotations vpon some places," a glossary, and two spurious passages that transmit a fifteenth-century scribe's understanding of some now-problematic elements in the *Tale's* marital dynamics.

Perhaps Thomas Betterton began Chaucer modernizations, which also would have influenced Pope. Perhaps Pope, as he claimed, merely completed the two pieces. I leave that possibility open, because a Pope scholar must have final say on inclusion of the *General Prologue* and *Reeve's Tale* modernizations in the canon. I will nonetheless dissect *The Miller of Trompington* and Bernard Lintot's account book to find evidence of Pope's style and interests, and of his motivation to keep republishing the two works under Betterton's name rather than his own, in the miscellanies he secretly edited for fifteen years.

Two more modernizations would simply reinforce what is so obvious to a medievalist: that Pope's life is framed in Chaucer. The adolescent began early his modernizations and his racy poem imitating Chaucer's style. "This Translation was done at sixteen or seventeen Years of Age," he footnotes *January and May*.³ Just a few years later Pope—the first writer who would earn a living from book sales—pocketed his first pay: thirteen guineas from Jacob Tonson, for "ye Tale of Chaucer" plus his own pastorals, "amounting to abt one thousand and 2 hundred lines," and an *Iliad* excerpt.⁴

And as Pope lay dying, rich and famous, he parodied Chaucer in the last couplet he ever wrote. Throughout his life he had loved his dogs, each in turn named Bounce; dogs leap to the foreground in Pope's poetry as birds do in Chaucer's. A puppy of Bounce's adopted by the Prince of Wales, for example, was to bear on its collar that quintessentially Popean couplet:

> I am his Highness' Dog at *Kew;*
> Pray tell me Sir, whose Dog are you?⁵

The last Bounce, sent for care to Lord Orrery, died seven weeks before Pope did in 1744. Writing to learn more particulars of the death, Pope recalls the women's lament for Arcite and closes his poetic career:

> Ah Bounce! ah gentle Beast! why wouldst thou dye,
> When thou had'st Meat enough, and Orrery?⁶

Pope's Merchant and Wife of Bath have long dwelt in the dim crack between academic specialties, no doubt chortling and toasting their escape. There is a German comparison of Pope's two acknowledged modernizations to their originals, before 1900, plus editorial notes and bare mentions in biographies. In a well-known essay, for example, W. K. Wimsatt, Jr., extensively compares Pope's end-rhymes to Chaucer's without so much as mentioning the modernizations, much less comparing Pope's to Chaucer's rendering of the same couplet.[7]

Only since 1976, to be fair, have most Pope scholars known precisely that in 1701 the 1598 Speght edition was given to this boy determined to overcome stunting of his physical growth by disease and his intellectual growth by Protestants.[8] Dryden had died one year earlier, leaving as his final work *Fables Ancient and Modern.* Besides first publishing modernizations of Chaucer, Dryden articulates a theory of translation for writers who would follow him and analyzes Chaucer's artistic genius more thoroughly than had anyone before him:

> He is a perpetual Fountain of good Sense . . . As he knew what
> to say, so he knows also when to leave off; a Continence which is
> practis'd by few Writers . . . . *Chaucer* follow'd Nature every
> where; but was never so bold to go beyond her,

and so on, in his well-known encomium. Indeed, "here is God's Plenty."[9]

Starting fresh, Pope took the torch from Dryden. Both modernizers close, and tamp down neatly with morals, Chaucer's open endings. Dryden even inserts "The Moral" before the last twelve lines of *The Cock and the Fox.*[10] Pope's closing for *January and May* owes more to the end of Dryden's *Wife of Bath Her Tale,* certainly, than to the *Merchant's Tale* in Speght's edition:

> Thus endeth here my tale of January
> God blesse vs al, and his mother Mary.

> [Pope:] Thus ends our Tale, whose Moral next to make,
> Let all wise Husbands hence Example take;
> And pray, to crown the Pleasure of their Lives,
> To be so well deluded by their Wives.

> [Dryden:] And so may all our Lives like their's be led;
> Heav'n sent the Maids young Husbands, fresh in Bed:
> May Widows Wed as often as they can,
> And ever for the better change their Man.
> And some devouring Plague pursue their Lives,
> Who will not well be govern'd by their Wives.[11]

Dryden takes for granted that readers of *Fables Ancient and Modern* know Chaucer's pilgrimage frame. Although his four modernizations are interspersed among other translations and poems, and although by his own three principles of translation Dryden has "often omitted what I

judg'd unnecessary" (as well as adding "somewhat of my own" and cor-
recting "Errors of the Press"), he does not omit but indeed expands passages appropriate only to the pilgrimage.[12] Alysoun retains her teasing
slur on the Friar, besides her benediction just quoted; the Nun's Priest
disclaims Chaunticleer's misogynistic sentiments as dangerous to the ut-
terer because "the Wife of *Bath* would throw 'em to the Ground"; the
Knight forbears a full account of Theseus's battles so that "others may
have time to take their Turn; / As was at first enjoin'd us by mine Host." [13]

Pope, in contrast, eliminates such references. His poems stand alone,
independent of a reader's familiarity with Chaucer's frame story. As non-
pilgrim narrator for *January and May,* however, Pope does retain elements from Chaucer's Franklin and his status-conscious Merchant, both
of whom apologize for rude speech (*SqT* ll. 673–708 attributed to the
Merchant by Speght; *MctT* l. 2351; *FrkT* l. 718).

In his *Preface* Dryden points to Chaucer's useful technique of apology
by a self-conscious narrator, using terms that would appeal to a young
writer determined to see print and already considered not truly Christian.
Since my enemies, says Dryden,

> are so far from granting me to be a good Poet, that they will not
> allow me so much as to be a Christian, or a Moral Man . . . I
> have confin'd my Choice to such Tales of *Chaucer,* as savour
> nothing of Immodesty. If I had desir'd more to please than to
> instruct, the *Reve,* the *Miller,* the *Shipman,* the *Merchant,* the
> *Sumner,* and above all, the *Wife of Bathe,* in the Prologue to her
> Tale, would have procur'd me as many Friends and Readers, as
> there are *Beaux* and Ladies of Pleasure in the Town. But I will
> no more offend against Good Manners: I am sensible as I ought
> to be of the Scandal I have given by my loose Writings; and make
> what Reparation I am able, by this Publick Acknowledg-
> ment. . . . *Chaucer* makes another manner of Apologie for his
> broad-speaking . . . . [He] thus excuses the Ribaldry, which is
> very gross, in many of his Novels.[14]

In his *Preface*'s only Middle English, Dryden here quotes Chaucer-the-
pilgrim's entire apology for rude speaking (*GP* ll. 725–42). So that readers do not skim past it, he promptly discusses metrics with reference to
this passage.

Thanks to Dryden, the proud thirteen-year-old owner of a black-letter
folio could flip straight to Chaucer's least modest, most marketable tales.
He could also begin learning how to develop narrative voices, including
that of Chaucer's game but embarrassed Merchant/narrator, who is

flustered at such matters as the ritual test of May's virginity, her visit to the privy, and her brief moment of union with Damyan (*MctT* ll. 1888–96, 1950–51, 2350–53, 2361–63).

Pope's narrator, like the Merchant, apologizes for what he must or must not say. Furthermore, he is more careful than Chaucer's narrator to provide sources for his knowledge of characters' inner thoughts and private actions (a technique noted for the Pope/Betterton *General Prologue* portraits). For example, replacing twenty-four lines of January's nudgings and unsoft nothings whispered in his new bride's scraped ear, an apologetic *occupatio* notes where Pope's narrator obtained his information:

> The Room was sprinkled, and the Bed was blest.
> What next ensu'd beseems not me to say;
> 'Tis sung, he labour'd 'till the dawning Day.[15]

Thus Pope, adapting Chaucer's techniques, eliminates the wedding-night scene that would most surely have offended Dryden's critics. He bypasses the toilet scene without even an apology. Pope's May secretly reads Damian's love note, but without pretending to go where Speght's edition sends her:

> Ther as ye wote, that euery wight hath nede
> And whan she of this bill hath taken hede
> She rent it all to cloutes, and at last
> Into the priuy sothly she it cast.[16]

Most Chaucerians will notice the textual variant in lieu of the phrase "pryvee softely" to which E. Talbot Donaldson tunes his sensitive commentary on the clash of vulgar and courtly terminology in the *Tale*.[17] But most would be hard put to claim that the further, quite extensive variations change the sense much at all. W. W. Skeat and other Victorian scholars, having devoted their lives to tidy texts, left a legacy of scorn for corrupt texts and, by implication, for their users. Yet, like rumors of Mark Twain's death, difficulties of reading corrupt texts are much exaggerated. Pope was smart: even at age thirteen he like us could spot a typographical error, "Buth natheles, yet had he great pite" (Speght 29r, for *MctT* l. 1755). And anybody troubled by shifty spelling and engaging meter ought not to read Chaucer in any edition.

Also, Pope could read relatively untroubled by an editor's attempt to impose vocal inflections and assign speeches. Speght's punctuation, more plentiful than his predecessors', is sparse by present customs. Commas or colons or parentheses, not quotation marks, separate narrative from direct discourse and indicate pauses within lines. Even misplaced parentheses, presumably meant to enclose "he gan to crye," would not block a reader's understanding of January's mood when his sight returns. Adding two now-spurious lines, he shrieks couplets worthy of Pope's contemporaries:

> Out helpe, alas (harowe) he gan to crye
> For sorow almost he gan to dye
> That his wife was swiued in the pery
>   O stronge lady hore what dost thou?
>   (Speght 32r, for *MctT* ll. 2366–67)

Speght refrains from punctuating line ends except when question marks are needed, and except when he puts periods at the ends of some paragraphs to indicate a distinct shift in scene, mood, or speaker.[18] One emerges from Speght's edition with a growing feeling that any punctuation at line ends is downright superfluous, even oppressive.

Of all the differences between Robinson's edition and Speght's, three would have made Pope's experience of reading the text differ much from ours. The bride is even younger, Pope's own age: "She shall not passe fiftene yere certain" (Speght 28v, for *MctT* l. 1417). And two extra passages appear in Speght's pear-tree scene, as in other editions until Tyrwhitt's. Only as my scholarly duty, of course, do I quote in full the first of these passages, which Pope assumed Chaucer wrote about the act in the tree.

>   Ladies I pray you be not wroth
> I can nat glose, I am a rude man
> And sodainly anon this Damian
> Gan pullen up the smocke, & in the [*sic*] throng
> A great tent, a thrifty and a long
> She said it was the meriest fit
> That euer in her life she was at yet
> My lordes tent serueth me nothing thus
> It foldeth twifolde by swete Jesus
> He may nat swiue worth a leke
> And yet he is full gentil and ful meke
> This is leuer to me than an euensong[19]

For Pope, Chaucer's teen-age May speaks three times, all boldfaced lies, but in this extra speech she honestly articulates what she thinks in her heart about January's leeklike efforts, while giving him full credit for his good qualities. Although the folding image might seem less than delightful to some readers, to me her extra speech seems one of naive enthusiasm and her character thereby more appealing than without it. Where would a virgin bride learn delicacy in sexual reference, after all? Surely not from January's request, for example, that she strip herself naked so he can have some pleasure (*MctT* ll. 1958–60). To the scribe who added the passage, as to Speght in his plot summary and to authors surveyed in the previous chapter, May's antics justly repay January for his foolish attempt to divert the course of nature.

This scribal insertion gives Pope the opportunity to characterize his own narrator as one who, like many readers-aloud to be discussed, belies the content of his apology by the relish with which he refrains from describing what he knows he has forced the ladies to picture:

> Now prove your Patience, gentle Ladies all,
> Nor let on me your heavy Anger fall:
> 'Tis Truth I tell, tho' not in Phrase refin'd;
> Tho' blunt my Tale, yet honest is my Mind.
> What Feats the Lady in the Tree might do,
> I pass, as Gambols never known to you:
> But sure it was a merrier Fit, she swore,
> Than in her Life she ever felt before.
> (J&M ll. 740–47, for MctT ll. 2350–53)

In the other passage now considered spurious, January expresses doubt that May and Damyan were merely struggling overhead:

> Strogle (qd he) ye algate in it went
> Stiffe and rounde as any bell
> It is no wonder though thy bely swell
> The smocke on his brest lay so theche
> And euer me thought he pointed on ỹ breche
> God giue you both on shames deth to dien
> (Speght 32r, for MctT ll. 2376–77)

"Though thy bely swell"? For Pope the *Merchant's Tale* does not end with the unresolved issue "Is she or isn't she?" She is. Pope need not thrash quite so deep into the textual thicket of disputed paternity, nor peer past shadows cast onto May if she is using not just any pretense to set her foot upon his back but the very pretense that mocks January's desperate desire to prove his manhood by fertility. No modern critic has suggested, by the way, that May herself might not be sure yet whether she is pregnant.

Whence came that scribe's certainty, passed on by Speght, that May was already pregnant before Damyan throng? We must don anthropological and socioeconomic spectacles to examine two passages little discussed: the narrator's roundabout account of the custom whereby the bride stays in bed for four days "or thre dayes atte leeste," and January's abrupt decision to sign over his heritage a few months after the wedding (*MctT* ll. 1859–65, 1885–92, 2132–84). Chaucer uses the technique of the self-conscious narrator to create an atmosphere redolent with the mechanics and economics of heir production.

Around weddings still cluster rituals related both to explicit mechanics of sexual intercourse and to socioeconomic transactions—fingers penetrating rings, jointly-held knife cutting cake, and so on. In white Anglo-Saxon Protestant communities in late-twentieth-century Pennsylvania, for example, an older unmarried brother of the groom or sister of the bride must dance in a pig trough. The present-day ritual of the honeymoon preserves some of the implications that Chaucer's narrator, an outside observer to the customs of "thise nobles alle" (*MctT* l. 1889), notes euphemistically regarding the bride's four days in bed. Some cultures have bluntly displayed bloodstained sheets as proof of virginity. Chaucer's narrator instead, even more embarrassed than he is in regard to privies or pear-tree struggling, circles and recircles the point he is trying to get across. May, certified virgin by the post-wedding ritual, is fulfilling her end of the marriage contract.

In elaborately avoiding mention of one kind of female blood, the narrator uses imagery evoking the even less mentionable kind. He tells time by the moon (*MctT* l. 1885) and keeps repeating that this one-time seclusion of the bride lasts four days out of the month, or sometimes only three. The next definite length of time named is "that dayes eighte," which have not yet passed when January in the garden joyfully prepares to sign over his heritage to May (*MctT* ll. 2132–33).

At least "a month or tweye" has gone by since the wedding, conjecturally dated March 25.[20] January does not succeed on first try. But "er the moneth Jule befill," in Speght's edition, he learns that he has successfully impregnated his wife. That is why he burbles with happiness. That is why he makes her his legal heir.

The scribe who inserted the "bely swell" passage took the hint from the narrator's post-wedding euphemisms combined with *MctT* l. 2132, for which Speght and other early editors put "the" rather than "that" eight days:

> But now to purpose, er the daies eight
> Were passed, er the moneth Jule befill
> That January hath caught so great a will
> Through eggyng of his wife him for to play
> (Speght 31v, for MctT ll. 2132–35)

Here "er" simply means "before" in both lines 2132 and 2133. "The daies eight" specifies a length of time, not a date, and "that January" is a phrase like "this fresshe May" (*MctT* l. 2185). It was Tyrwhitt in 1775 who created a *locus obscurus* for modern editors by his choice of particles and punctuation and by his silently changing the second line's "er" to "of":

> But now to purpos; er that daies eighte
> Were passed of the month of Juil, befill,
> That January hath caught so gret a will
> Thurgh egging of his wif, him for to play.[21]

To readers before 1775 including Pope, however, the eight days have not even passed yet before May eggs her husband out to the garden to celebrate this blessed event-to-be with the promised economic transaction. The eight days: a practical and perhaps traditional length of time to wait before announcing. This narrator, of all narrators, would not say outright, "May's period was a week late. So, she told January she was pregnant."

May has satisfied the socioeconomic conditions of the marriage deal. The exclusive-sexual-rights clause is another story. But she knows enough to put off her tryst with Damyan until she can produce a legitimate heir. Someone might, after all, tell January that the baby doesn't have his eyes.

Pope did not have to figure out these explicit sexual mechanics. He used an edition in which scribes and editors had jumped to conclusions for him, thus providing Pope a narrator even more circumspect about female matters than is the narrator now in Robinson's text. Chaucer's own text, unpunctuated, contains the menstrual imagery. The now-spurious passage simply provides evidence that, before the nineteenth century, even male readers could see it there.

Besides adapting the apologies of Chaucer's Merchant for his own purpose, that of wide readership for his modernization, Pope borrows from elsewhere the Chaucerian technique of intrusion by an author less pompous than his narrative persona. The key line, echoed also on Cut N4, cuts short the Franklin's flowery sunset: "This is as muche to seye as it was nyght" (*FrkT* l. 1018).

Another rhetorical sundown occurs, with no such punch line, while "this hastif Januarie" is shooing out the wedding guests in anticipation of his night's labor (*MctT* ll. 1795–99, 1805). At this point in the modernization, Pope's narrator humbly credits the elaborate figure of speech: "The weary Sun, as Learned Poets write." Yet Pope's narrator himself has more book-learning than does Chaucer's; elsewhere, for example, he carefully attributes songs of Hester to the Hebrews and songs of Ovid to days of yore.[22]

A scholar thoroughly respectful of his betters might speak of "Learned Poets" without cynicism. Pope's own disrespectful voice, however, would here place sarcastic quotation marks around his phrase, which reverberates in two directions. One echoes Chaucer-the-author's voiceover at the Franklin's like image, just described.

The other reverberation travels from "Learned Poets" to, thirteen lines later, "Criticks learn'd." Biographical headphones can attune more precisely the two phrases. The sun laboriously having set, Pope's January ingests not the aphrodisiacs that Chaucer attributes to "the cursed monk," but instead aphrodisiacs listed in a translation of *Ovid's Art of Love* by Dryden and others, one to which Pope had access before its publication in 1709 and found "a thousand errors in the notes." His January eats satyrion, eringos, and cantharides,

> Whose Use old Bards describe in luscious Rhymes,
> And Criticks learn'd explain to Modern Times.[23]

We know numerous details about Pope's attitude toward elder scholars, especially toward those who published careless translations despite the advantages of their formal classical educations. Therefore, we can say with certainty that Pope-the-author intends irony regarding "Criticks learn'd" and, by implication, "Learned Poets."

Lacking any such biographical details for Chaucer, a modern reader can be far less sure about points at which his authorial voice would intend ironic reference. Silent readers must make careful distinctions between attitudes of other people who wrote at Chaucer's time or earlier, and attitudes provably Geoffrey Chaucer's. Only for the latter could intended irony be justified. At other apparently ironic points in the text, a reader might well be inserting and arguing the validity of his own sarcastic quotation marks.

At two other superficially respectful mentions of book-learning, likewise, biographical details amplify Pope-the-teen-age-author's sly voice breaking past the narrator's to mock pompous literary authorities.

One point has been noted by Norman Ault, who in tracing Pope's satiric jabs at Joseph Addison shows one of the few glimmers of interest by Pope scholars in *January and May*. Addison had ended his *Letter from Italy* with not a bang but a pretentious whimper:

> I bridle in my struggling Muse with Pain,
> That longs to launch into a bolder strain.
>   But I've already troubled you too long,
> Nor dare attempt a more advent'rous Song.
> My humble Verse demands a softer Theme,
> A painted Meadow or a purling Stream.

Born the year that Pope first published, Samuel Johnson would dominate letters in the next generation as fully as Addison did in the preeminent generation in Pope's youth. Pope would have joyed to hear Dr. Johnson explode:

> To *bridle* a *goddess* is no very delicate idea; but why must she be *bridled?* because she *longs to launch* . . . . She is in the first line a *horse,* in the second a *boat,* and the care of the poet is to keep his *horse* or his *boat* from *singing.*[24]

Pope mocks Addison more subtly than does Johnson, during his *occupatio* concerning January's pleasure garden:

> *Priapus* cou'd not half describe the Grace
> (Tho' God of Gardens) of this charming Place:
> A Place to tire the rambling Wits of *France*
> In long Descriptions, and exceed *Romance;*
> Enough to shame the gentlest Bard that sings
> Of painted Meadows, and of purling Springs.
>   (*J&M* ll. 450–55, for *MctT* ll. 2034–36)

The wide-eyed innocence that names Priapus's primary attribute is Chaucer's own. The ethnic slur sounds appropriate not so directly to the *January and May* narrator as to the poet in whose *Rape of the Lock* the baron, perhaps recalling Palamon's success, will build "to *Love* an Altar" of "twelve vast *French* Romances, neatly gilt."[25] And the final couplet mocks Addison's poem even more decisively in its first printing, as Ault shows, for there it credits not the "gentlest" but rather the "boldest Bard that sings."[26]

As grace note to this dissonant Addisonian chord, another phrase original to Pope's modernization likewise echoes the leaden finale of *A Letter from Italy*. Chaucer recounts the quarrel between Pluto and Proserpyne, then with a simple "lat us turne agayn to Januarie" begins the pear-tree scene. Having nudged out the classical deities, as will be shown, Pope amplifies tones by which the fairy queen resembles the Wife of Bath and the fairy king his counterpart in *Prologue* to the *Legend of Good Women*, then adds overtones from Shakespeare's pettily quarreling Titania and Oberon. The resultant cosmic/domestic bickering seems not at all a "Heroick Strain"—unless in the sarcastic quotation marks that would evoke Addison's bridled Muse stuck struggling on the shore:

> We leave them here in this Heroick Strain,
> And to the Knight our Story turns again,
> Who in the Garden, with his lovely *May*
> Sung merrier than the Cuckow or the Jay:
> This was his Song; Oh kind and constant be,
> Constant and kind I'll ever prove to thee.[27]

In the second and third couplets quoted, Pope's adaptations mock no one outside the poem. Instead, they exemplify his technique throughout of specifying for Chaucer's text sounds meaningful to an eighteenth-century audience. After the sarcastic "Heroick Strain" comes the sound of music. But both the bird and the song have changed in the course of three centuries.

Chaucer compares January's singing to that of a croak-voiced parrot. The neutral name of the bird at Chaucer's time, "papejay," by Pope's time referred to the color parrot-green (appropriate to January's vain attempts to claim natural fertility, such as *MctT* ll. 1461–66) or else to "a type of vanity or empty conceit, in allusion to the bird's gaudy plumage, or to its mechanical repetition of words and phrases, and thus applied contemptuously to a person" (*OED*, s.v. "popinjay"). To convey amusement but not contempt toward January, Pope instead compares him first to the bird that suggests cuckoldry in both name and nesting habits, then to a less exotic squawker than the parrot.

In other passages as well, Pope amplifies Chaucer's references to song. Like the blind Scottish knight Maitland, discussed in my previous chapter, Pope finds musical imagery appropriate for such a disharmonious couple. Twice, for what Pope will hear as feeble singing of a "lusty Roundelay," Chaucer tells of the groom's joyous, slack-skinned song after the wedding night. As Chaucer's January prepares to sign over his heritage a few months later, however, he just "seith" words that echo the

Song of Songs. Pope's January, instead, on that gleeful morning in the garden "thus his Morning Canticle . . . sung." [28]

After paraphrasing the Biblical imagery, Chaucer's January says to his wife, in essence, "I will be kind and constant to you, and here are three good reasons why you should be kind and constant to me" (for *MctT* ll. 2160–84). Pope is unfamiliar with the song January then sings, "You loue I best, and shall, and o ther non" (Speght 32v, for *MctT* l. 2323). Knowing a ballad refrain that neatly summarizes January's heritage-offer speech, however, Pope inserts it instead. A. B. Friedman and others have documented the interest in ballads of Pope's later circle. No one has noted, though, his incorporation here of a floating refrain still sung, nowadays usually as "I'll be true to my love if my love'll be true to me." [29]

Pope scholars do not claim that Pope invented single-handedly the heroic couplet. But they do analyze his process of perfecting it without sufficient reference to his knowledge of oral ballads and of Chaucer's text, both of which make extensive use of neatly closed antithetical couplets. Such couplets are one of many textural features that give the *Merchant's Tale* such a disconcerting effect of binary irresolution, be it termed ambiguity or irony or black comedy or bitterness. [30]

If internal evidence were needed to prove that Pope modernized *January and May*, however, one could not count on his presumed fondness for closed antithetical couplets. He eliminates some of Chaucer's best ones. Pope's January does not choose May of his own authority, for love is blind and may not see, nor does he kiss her oft with thick bristles of his beard unsoft. Pope's narrator like Chaucer's does fruitlessly warn January, though:

> 'Tis better sure, when Blind, deceiv'd to be,
> Than be deluded when a Man can see! [31]

Another characteristic of Pope's style, one less widely known than his barbed couplets, likewise has not yet emerged in these early modernizations. Ault delineates the extent to which Pope, especially in the years just before he took painting lessons, adds numerous color terms to his Greek translations and *The Temple of Fame*. Color imagery by itself would not prove Pope's authorship of these slightly earlier pieces, however, were proof needed. To the *Merchant's Tale* he adds just a few nonliteral shades of gray, carefully chosen: a silver sound, for example. Similarly, Pope's Wife of Bath specifies only a few more colors than does Chaucer's. She drinks wine from a brown bowl, and Jankyn beats her (yes, outright) black and blue. [32]

Pope/Betterton adds only the daughter's tawny skin to the *Reeve's Tale*. He actually removes colors from the modernized *General Prologue* portraits, already so brightly tinted that they may well have helped inspire the technique. The blue hood is gone, leaving the Pope/Betterton Miller merely gold, black, red, and white. And replacing the Clerk's longed-for red and black books is a row of what a young scholar might actually afford at Pope's time, "A score of Books, some stitch'd, the rest ill-bound." [33]

One indication of Pope's known interests does appear in images added to the Pope/Betterton pieces, however: dogs. In the *Merchant's Tale* both dog images denigrate their referent. Therefore, Pope omits the hounds that January hopes will eat him if he does not procreate and the dog that Damyan emulates after he gets good news from May.

Pope's Wife of Bath acquires a dog simile instead, one needed to make better sense of Speght's text wherein Alysoun keeps her old husbands under control, "For as an hors I coud both bite and whine." [34] Living when understanding of Chaucer's final *e* was at low ebb, Pope did not realize that "whine" could serve onomatopoetically for both a horse's whinny and a dog's whine. So even though horses do bite, as Pope knew since he rode almost every day for his health, he changed the image from equine to canine for artistic reasons: "I, like a Dog, cou'd bite as well as whine." [35]

Elsewhere throughout his life's work, though, Pope writes about dogs just because he likes them, not because of clear aesthetic needs. In his translations Pope stresses canine roles, notably for the scene wherein Ulysses's dog recognizes him, then dies. As discussed by Ault, Pope's own works abound with dogs and include *Bounce to Fop. An Heroick Epistle From a Dog at Twickenham to a Dog at Court.*[36] A lap dog like Lady Suffolk's Fop lies behind Belinda's in *Rape of the Lock,* and behind the ones hand-fed and bedded down by the Prioress in *Chaucer's Characters.* A country dog like Bounce would gladly follow Pope/Betterton's Monk, with the extra hounds who replace hare and expense:

> He lov'd the Chase, the Hounds melodious Cry,
> Hounds that ran swiftly as the Swallows fly.[37]

Similarly, the dog added to the Pope/Betterton *Miller of Trompington* seems appropriate but is not artistically essential. Modernized, the miller in the *Reeve's Tale*

> Could Pipe, and Fish, and Wrestle, throw a Net,
> Turn drinking Cups, and teach young Dogs to Set.[38]

In this and other features, the *Reeve's Tale* modernization seems less artistically polished than that of the *Merchant's Tale,* even though *January and May* saw print three years earlier than did *The Miller of Trompington.* In the latter, character motivations are muddied, and Chaucer's problematic scenes become even more so. Images are developed, but mechanistically. Allusions remain allusions, without reaching the smoother fusion that Pope would attain for his pair Proserpyne/Wife of Bath/Titania and Pluto/*PLGW* King of Love/Oberon. In particular, the farewell at dawn in *The Miller of Trompington* seems to respond to a young scholar's self-imposed assignment, "Compare the parting scene of Chaucer's Troilus and Criseyde to that of Shakespeare's Troilus and Cressida."

In its text, the *Merchant's Tale* has at least as much potential as does the *Reeve's Tale* for the problems that beset the Pope/Betterton modernization of the latter. In both originals, the characters' potential for sexual cruelty remains unresolved. But Pope set his hand to the *Merchant's Tale* with a plan in mind: he would develop character motivations and unify the action by adapting techniques from drama. In contrast, the modernizer of the *Reeve's Tale* is working into his conception a knowledge of Shakespeare's text, along with other printed books, but as yet he lacks familiarity with the stage.

Could these literary inadequacies conceivably be assigned to a famous tragic actor on his deathbed, rather than to a boy teaching himself Middle English with the help of Speght's glossary, Dryden's *Preface* and examples, other works of English literature and theology, and a self-propelled mastery of at least four foreign languages? I suppose so. Thomas Betterton did know the Shakespeare passages evoked. He might also have read theology and a translation of the *Decameron* analogue. Therefore I will simply outline some discrepancies hard to account for other than by Pope's authorship and then discuss the *Reeve's Tale* modernization as if it were practice for *January and May.* If the Betterton poems somehow remain fifty-one percent Betterton's, so be it. This discussion could apply to *The Miller of Trompington* as an exact and certain influence on Pope's work, rather than as his own trial run.

Betterton died in 1710 after a full life in the London theater. He wrote seven minor plays but nothing else, according to the *Dictionary of National Biography.* Tucked into a footnote on the next-to-last page of his most recent biography, however, is mention that Pope "published a modernization of some of Chaucer's poems in Betterton's name, though they were, no doubt, the poet's own productions."[39]

In the eighteenth century both Dr. Johnson (in *Lives of the Poets*) and Joseph Warton (editing Pope) report that Pope's friends say he wrote them.[40] Even while Pope was alive, in 1737, the "profound and laborious Scholar" Thomas Morell matter-of-factly gives to his edition plus modernizations of *General Prologue* and *Knight's Tale* the title *The Canterbury Tales of Chaucer, in the Original, From the Most Authentic Manuscripts; And as they are Turn'd into Modern Language by Mr. Dryden, Mr. Pope, and Other Eminent Hands.* In it, Morell's own eminent hands adapt and expand *Chaucer's Characters.*

Morell omits Pope's name from his 1740 second edition, however. Why? Arnold Henderson regards the omission as "acquiescence in hard facts" — that is, as Morell's realization that he would not live to publish his projected entire *Tales* including Pope's publicly acknowledged modernizations. Henderson took most of his information from unfinished work left by William Alderson, whose files have since passed into my possession. They contain notes from Alderson's unsuccessful efforts to find additional evidence of any sort that Betterton did the two modernizations.[41]

Thus, unless further evidence appears, Pope's pen provides our only word that Betterton composed *Chaucer's Characters* and *The Miller of Trompington*, which first appeared in the same 1712 Lintot's miscellany as did Pope's early *Rape of the Lock.* Norman Ault has proved that at least one unclaimed translation in this volume is Pope's and that Pope secretly edited this and the next four of six such miscellanies published by Lintot.[42] In them Pope continued to print the Betterton pieces while changing the other contents considerably. In the 1712 and 1714 editions Pope credits Betterton on the title page of each poem as well as in the index. Thereafter *Chaucer's Characters* has no attribution at all on its title page; following it is *The Miller of Trompington*, "By the same."

Pope set the trend in miscellanies as in so much else. His Lintot's miscellanies, with mixed genres and some anonymous poems, led to a mid-century outburst of miscellanies that contain only comic tales, most of them anonymous. With names like *The Muse in Good Humour* and *The Altar of Love*, these compilations are "enough to give a bibliographer the shakes," to quote Alderson's note to himself, for contents may vary widely under the exact same title page and date. Although Chaucer's name only occasionally occurs, his influence pervades the contents in various forms: overt imitations like Elijah Fenton's *Curious Wife*; Pope's modernizations and other "Popeana" (as a section is sometimes entitled); other modernizations such as Samuel Cobb's *Miller's Tale*, entitled *The*

Credulous Husband and credited to neither Cobb nor Chaucer; and *The Miller of Trompington,* likewise credited to nobody. (See Appendix B.)

Pope often delayed acknowledgment of his own poems. For example, he wrote his Chaucer imitation before 1709, first published it in a 1727 miscellany as if "Lately found in an old Manuscript," and in 1736 began to include it in his *Works.* Other poems that he never acknowledged are now considered certainly his, such as *The Capon's Tale.* "Recent discoveries," says Ault in 1949, "show that concealment of both editorship and authorship was practised by him on a far greater scale than has hitherto been suspected." [43]

Pope, in his well-indexed life and works, mentions the Betterton pieces once. In 1735 he published with his own correspondence (thoroughly edited, as always) a footnote explaining that "*Betterton*'s remains," mentioned in a letter from John Caryll as having been left to him, consisted of "A Translation of some Part of Chaucer's Canterbury Tales, the Prologues, &c. printed in a Miscellany with some works of Mr. Pope, in 2 Vol. 12° by B. Lintot." Besides directing prospective purchasers to Lintot's miscellany, this footnote has distracted Pope's biographers from noticing that in this letter Caryll is as yet unaware that Mrs. Betterton had died six weeks earlier:

> May 23, 1712.
> I am very glad for the sake of the Widow and for the credit of the deceas'd, that *Betterton*'s remains* are fallen into such hands as may render 'em reputable to the one and beneficial to the other.

Perhaps Pope could make any such remains reputable to the deceased Betterton, but they had been beneficial to his widow for less than a week. Her health declined rapidly after her husband's death on 28 April 1710. Her will shows her "by no means in prosperous circumstances" on 10 March 1712, her largest bequest being £20 to her sister. She was buried on 13 April 1712.[44]

On 7 April 1712, according to Lintot's account book, "Betterton" received a payment of £5 7s.6d. for "The Miller's Tale, with some Characters from Chaucer." I would like to think that Pope (who two weeks earlier received £7 for "First Edition of the Rape") was able to pass the cash before Mrs. Betterton's closing eyes and thereafter to, perhaps, her sister. But any surviving relatives would probably not even have heard about the innovative economic transaction first made possible by the 1709 Copyright Act: an author could now claim a percentage of sales instead of a one-time payment from the publisher. They would not have undertaken what Pope did in rewriting and selling "Additions to the Rape" to Lintot two years later for an additional £15.[45]

Thus Pope could do what he wanted with these Betterton pieces. He could convey at least token money to the poorly-off widow of his childhood friend and then keep alive Betterton's name on paper after the memory of him had begun to fade from the stage. I will let others suggest, if they will, what further facets of Pope's "peculiarly complex character" kept him from claiming authorship.[46]

I suspect that one facet will reflect Pope's gradual acceptance and exploitation of the moral role thrust upon a brilliantly satiric hunchback four and a half feet tall. He could hardly have acknowledged *Chaucer's Characters* while continuing to deny the *Miller of Trompington* with its harsh sexuality.

Pope's modernizations of Wife and Merchant tone down potentially prurient parts, but the Pope/Betterton *Reeve's Tale* is even more callous than Chaucer's. As soon as a Chaucer student in the 1980s notices *RvT* l. 4248, "she gan to wepe," a teacher must tense up for "Wait a minute, what about the daughter? I mean, she gets raped." As indeed she does, and gloated over. Pope/Betterton's version makes the sex act even seamier. Also, Chaucer's beguiler-beguiled ending is replaced by one related to *Decameron* 9.6, but with characters far more harsh and vengeful than in Boccaccio's analogue—available then in several seventeenth-century translations and noted in Speght's Arguments to the 1598 edition:

> Denyse Simkin, the Millar of Trompington, deceiuth two Clarkes
> of Schollers Hall in Cambridge, in stealing their corne: but they
> so vse the matter, that they reuenge the wrong to the full. The
> Argument of this Tale is taken out of Bochace in his Nouels.

In Speght's 1598 text (with only insubstantial variations from Robinson's), male characters variously seek revenge in a bedroom farce that reflects its other sexual imagery, including the wife's bastardy and the horse's lust for wild mares. Pope/Betterton's expansion of the latter image creaks its literary joints. In addition to *RvT* l. 4065 with "Mares and Fillies" both, the sexual connotation is driven home when the wife repeats the image instead of scolding the students for unknit reins:

> Which Way? they both demand—With wanton Bounds,
> I saw him scamp'ring tow'rd yon Fenny Grounds:
> Wild Mares and Colts in those low Marshes feed.[47]

Pope/Betterton adapts the other reflexive sexual imagery more subtly, in ways appropriate both to an eighteenth-century audience and to early circumstances of Pope's life. The miller's wife is still the "Parson's Daughter of the Town," educated "in that choice School, the *Nunnery*" (Lintot pp. 302–3, for *RvT* ll. 3943, 3968). Pope/Betterton considers inessential to the story the information that this incontinent parson, who in the eighteenth century could be Protestant, has not only procreated but also openly designated his granddaughter his heir.[48] Omitting *RvT* ll. 3977–86, Pope/Betterton makes satire—milder than Chaucer's against randy priests—fall instead upon hoity-toity nuns, quite like Madame Eglentyne, thanks to whose lessons the miller's wife

> Walk'd like a Duck, and chatter'd like a Pye:
> Proud of her breeding, froward, full of Scorn.
> (Lintot p. 303, for *RvT* ll. 3963–65)

Pope preserved no fondness for the Catholic schools, theoretically illegal, which he sometimes attended before age twelve. He later claimed to have been expelled from the first for "a satire on some faults of his master." Instead, from books, he taught himself. As a boy he owned three of his own: Speght's Chaucer, George Herbert's poems, and part of *Don Quixote*. From the latter two books, respectively, could have come the theological imagery and broad satire of *The Miller of Trompington*. In addition, in his teens Pope "ran through all the books in his father's library. Books of religious controversy . . . stating and restating with much deployment of learned texts the main points at issue between the Roman and English churches."[49]

Whatever its exact source, theological imagery does in the modernization what Symkyn challenges the clerks to do in his house: it expands its intellectual space (*RvT* ll. 4120–26). Pope/Betterton cuts past Aleyn's legal evasions to Allen's blunt

> Our Corn is stoln, and we like Fools are caught,
> The Daughter shall repay the Father's Fault.
> (Lintot p. 313, for *RvT* ll. 4183–86)

Grace repays the Father's Fault then, for the daughter is named Grace, not Malyne.

Elsewhere too, Pope/Betterton's theological terms accumulate in their effect. When Chaucer's Symkyn returns from loosing the horse, "no word he seyde" to the avid grain-watchers, whereas Pope/Betterton's miller comments,

> Now do me Justice Friends, he says, you can
> Convince your *Warden* I'm an honest Man.
> (Lintot p. 307, for *RvT* l. 4067)

Mercy follows close on Justice. As the scholars dash for the fen, "Their Sack does at the Miller's Mercy lie" (Lintot p. 308, for *RvT* l. 4092). And whereas Chaucer's Mrs. Symkyn "wente hire out to pisse," Pope/Betterton uses theological imagery for a euphemism reminiscent of that in the *Merchant's Tale* but more grandiloquent:

> The proper Utensil not plac'd at hand,
> She rose, by pure Necessity constrain'd.
> That grand Affair dispatch'd, and feeling round
> Her Husband's Bed; no Cradle could be found.
> (Lintot p. 315, for *RvT* ll. 4215–16; *MctT* ll. 1950–51)

In addition to theological imagery, this passage and others could reflect Pope's concurrent interest in the *Merchant's Tale*. Like May, Sim's wife always has a lie on hand. This trait is specified when the students cry out that their horse is gone, no longer with "Step on thy feet"—a regrettable loss along with the horse's "wehee" (*RvT* ll. 4074, 4066)—but with another theological image:

> Gone! whither? says he, —Nay Heav'n knows, not I—
> Out bolts *Sim*'s Wife, and (with a ready Lie)
> She cries, I saw him toss his Head and play,
> Then slip the loosen'd Reins, and Trot away.
> (Lintot p. 308, for *RvT* ll. 4078–83)

Sim's wife lies again after the scholars leave, with a prompt excuse quite as elaborate as May's cure for January:

> The Wife the Scholars curses, binds his Head,
> Then lifts him up, and lays him on the Bed.
> O Wife, says *Sim*, our Daughter is defil'd,
> ....
>
> O false abusive Knave! (the Wife reply'd)
> In ev'ry Word the Villain spake he ly'd.
> I wak'd, and heard our harmless Child complain;

And rose, to know the Cause, and ease her Pain.
I found her torn with Gripes, a Dram I brought,
And made her take a comfortable Draught.
Then lay down by her, chaff'd her swelling Breast,
And lull'd her in these very Arms to Rest.
All was Contrivance, Malice all and Spight,
I have not parted from her all this Night.
Then is she Innocent? Ay by my Life,
As pure and spotless—as thy Bosom Wife.
I'm satisfied, says *Sim.* O that damn'd *Hall!*
I'll do the best I can to starve 'em All.
   And thus the Miller of his Fear is eas'd,
   The Mother and the Daughter both well pleas'd.
   (Lintot pp. 319–20, for *RvT* ll. 4313–21; *MctT* l. 2368ff.)

This perfunctory closing couplet, like masking tape around a bale of hay, fails to hold down the loose ends in this version of the tale. Conclusions vary greatly in *Reeve's Tale* analogues. In several the wife turns on her husband with "if I'm a whore you're a thief so shut your damn mouth" or words to that effect. Of twelve accessible analogues,[50] none ends with the wife inventing a lie to cover both herself and her daughter, as do both Boccaccio's and Pope/Betterton's tales. Although substance and spirit differ markedly in the two versions, Boccaccio's lie covering both females' behavior could have merged with medical imagery from May's excuse to create Pope/Betterton's conclusion.

Compared to either Chaucer or Boccaccio, everyone in the modernization stays bitter and spiteful. Pope/Betterton's characters turn upon one another the gall that Chaucer's Reeve can direct at the Miller. Simkin—no Aeschylus he—vows that the cycle of revenge will continue. His wife curses the students even while protecting them. Has she already forgotten her enthusiasm when John in the dark (like Damyan in the now-spurious pear-tree passage) aroused theological imagery concerning so "myrie a fit"?

[John] kindly treats her with unusual Charms.
She thought (strange Fancies working in her Mind)
Some *Saint* had made her Husband over-kind.
   (Lintot p. 315, for *RvT* ll. 4229–31)

And the clerks get no satisfaction, uttering a curse after Chaucer's line 4307:

O I am Slain, the Miller loudly cry'd.
Live to be hang'd, thou Thief, *Allen* reply'd.

(Lintot p. 319)

They leave "pleas'd with the strange Adventures of the Night," but seem no more genuinely so than do the "well pleas'd" mother and daughter. Grace's role, much expanded from Malyne's, becomes even more problematic. Like the wild-mares image, it shows not adult Popean perfection but the attempts of an inexperienced writer to blot up an issue left sticky by an experienced one.

Pope/Betterton attempts to divert sympathy from Grace by giving her no female charms other than genitals. Besides Chaucer's details she is "course and bold. . . . short, and brawny . . . plump . . . . with Breasts up to her Chin" and tawny skin (Lintot pp. 303–4, for *RvT* ll. 3969–76). Sexual foreshadowing is added, too: while the goose cooks it is Grace, not her father, who makes the clerks' bed (Lintot p. 311, for *RvT* ll. 4136–41). The dinner scene expands, as in several analogues excluding *Decameron* 9.6:

The Supper does with sprightly Mirth abound,
Each has his Jest, the nappy Ale goes round.
Nor the Squab Daughter, nor the Wife were nice,
Each Health the Youths began, *Sim* pledg'd it twice.
The heady Liquor stupifies their Care,
But Midnight past, they all to Rest repair.

(Lintot p. 311, for *RvT* ll. 4146–48)

Pope/Betterton combines the horse and harmony imagery from the Symkyn family snores, then adds to Aleyn's complaint the last image from the Wife of Bath's portrait. Chaucer's gloriously onomatopoetic "fnorteth" was long since lost to printing history, by the way; both here and in Speght's 1598 edition the initial letter is certainly a long *s*.

The Miller's lusty Dose of potent Ale
Made him like any Stone-Horse snort and snore,
The Treble was behind, the Base before:
The Wife's Horse-Tenor vacant Parts did fill,
The Daughter bore her part with wondrous Skill,
They might be heard a Furlong from the Mill.

When this melodious Consort first began,
Young *Allen* tumbling, pushes his Friend *John*.

> It is impossible to sleep, he says,
> I'll up and Dance, while this choice Musick plays.
> (Lintot pp. 312–13, for *RvT* ll. 4162–70; *GP* l. 476)

Pope/Betterton's five-line rape scene is far harsher than Chaucer's, then, twisting even theological terms to do its will:

> The Daughter's Trumpet, led him to her Bed.
> Half stupified with Ale, she sprawling lay;
> He softly creeping in, soon hit his way;
> Soon put all knotty Questions out of doubt,
> Stopping her Mouth, prevented crying out.
> (Lintot pp. 313–14, for *RvT* ll. 4193–97)

Pope/Betterton has exacerbated in small the same dilemma that frustrates modern critics of the *Merchant's Tale*. A reader's sympathy rests with neither antagonist, one's "emotion sloshing back and forth between the weaker and the uglier vessel."[51] Sloshing reaches tidal-wave proportions during the much expanded aubade of Allen and Grace:

> Now *Allen* fancied Light would soon appear,
> He kiss'd the Wench, and said, My *Grace,* my Dear;
> Thou kindest of thy Sex, the Day comes on,
> And we must part—Alas, will you begon,
> She said, and leave poor harmless me alone?—
> If I stay longer, we are both undone;
> For should your Father wake and find me here,
> What will become of me, and you, my Dear?
> That dreadful Thought (she cries) distracts my Heart;
> Too soon you won me, and too soon we part.
> Then clinging round his Neck, with weeping Eyes,
> She says, Remember me! *Allen* replies,
> I'll quickly find occasion to return;
> You shall not long for *Allen*'s Absence mourn.
> Farewel she cries! But, Dearest, one Word more;
> ....
>
> [she tells where the stolen meal is hidden]
> Be careful, Love,—not a Word more, begone.
> (Lintot pp. 315–16, for *RvT* ll. 4234–48)

Promptly Pope/Betterton's midnight rambler, like Chaucer's, awakens his supposed buddy with "Wake Swineherd . . . I've joyful News" (Lintot p. 317, for *RvT* ll. 4262–63).

Other than with his more specific promise to return, Allen equals Aleyn in insensitivity. Grace differs vastly from Malyne. By moving her tears to the middle of the scene, and to the end the betrayal of her father followed by a professional-sounding caution, Pope/Betterton creates definite doubt about her innocence and honesty both. She has kept dad in the dark, though, for his just-wakened fury is not deflected onto the lost inheritance as in Chaucer:

> O thou false Traytor, Clerke! Thou hast defil'd
> Our honest Family, deflower'd our Child!
> > (Lintot p. 317, for *RvT* ll. 4269–72)

The difference in mood between Chaucer's and Pope's farewell scenes much resembles the difference between Chaucer's and Shakespeare's scenes of the parting of Troilus and Criseyde. To the tangle in the bedroom at the mill, Pope/Betterton adds Shakespeare's knotty Cressida. The couplet above that ends "too soon we part," for example, echoes:

> CRES.   Boldness comes to me now and brings me heart.
> Prince Troilus, I have loved you night and day
> For many weary months.
> TRO.   Why was my Cressid then so hard to win?
> CRES.   Hard to seem won; but I was won, my lord,
> With the first glance that ever—pardon me:
> If I confess much you will play the tyrant.[52]

Because Pope knew Shakespeare by the time he was using his copy of Chaucer, allusions might certainly creep between the sheets of his other authors, especially in a parallel scene. But then again, Thomas Betterton also knew Shakespeare, including the ghost's farewell to Hamlet, "Remember me," spoken by Grace as she clings and weeps.[53]

This modernized *Reeve's Tale* adapts imagery from theology and literature available to the young Pope, as well as from Chaucer's other works and in particular the *Merchant's Tale*. It is as if the bitterness purged from the latter, by Pope's aligning the binary imagery and concluding the conclusion, flowed not into gutters but onto the grave of Betterton.

Regardless of punctuation, *Prologue,* and tale order, that is, Chaucer's own text of the *Merchant's Tale* contains the potential for a narrative voice that could justifiably sound bitter. The text has such potential because Chaucer, as Dryden points out, knows when to leave off. Chaucer knows how to keep readers off balance and thereby still attentive six centuries later. If you refrain from resolving your binary oppositions, in text and texture both, your work might well outlive its context.[54]

Besides its frequent antithetical couplets noted, textural features of the *Merchant's Tale* include an unusually high number of puns, oxymorons, word pairs, words with implications in contradictory contexts, and couplets that span shifts in speaker and mood (especially in the closing dialogue). The structure of the text also remains unresolved, most obviously in its conclusion featuring deluded happiness and young lust with no future. So too, incidents within the plot remain off balance. The *Tale* splices, without reconciling, an academic treatise and a bawdy fabliau on the same topic. The marriage debate in the first half does not present arguments for and against marriage; instead Placebo argues that one ought not to argue, and Justinus argues that one ought to weigh pros and cons. The other debate, in the fabliau, ends with Proserpyne's "I wol no lenger yow contrarie" (*MctT* l. 2319), empty words since her gift to not just May but also all future women surely supersedes Pluto's single-occasion gift to January.

This battle of the sexes—during which the pagan goddess of rebirth cites scripture to the god of hell and winter—adds its implications to the extreme polarization of the *Tale*'s male and female protagonists. Besides that most unresolvable of all binary oppositions, sex, May and January differ as youth versus age, beauty versus ugliness, poverty versus wealth, potential fertility versus apparent sterility, leafy green versus hoary (not virginal) white, self-serving reticence versus self-deluded effusiveness, divinely-inspired wit versus subhuman stupidity, and so on.

Such extreme polarization leads readers down the garden path. We want one or the other protagonist to win, want to uncover good versus evil, right versus wrong, reward versus punishment somewhere within our horizon of expectations. But then it is our own responses, our own emotions, that are seduced, polarized, and abandoned spread-eagled at the end of the *Tale*. It is readers who are bitter, however the Merchant may feel.

As Pope does in his modernization, though, we readers can bring our own experiences and expectations to the black marks on white paper. We can twist mental knobs until we feel comfortable watching and listening to scenes that make living sense to each one of us, somehow.

God blesse vs al, and his mother Mary.

CHAPTER 11

How Pope Left the *Merchant's Tale*

Pope both learned from and adapted the *Merchant's Tale,* in preparation for its eighteenth-century screening. He learned how to use a narrator's voiceover, but sparingly, and how to end with a superficial resolution that leaves binary complexity intact. And he learned most thoroughly of all how to cultivate the potential for dramatization in Chaucer's text.

Thomas Betterton and others urged the young Pope to write stage plays.[1] He modernized Chaucer instead. Unlike *The Miller of Trompington,* which is not precisely relevant to my overall thesis, *January and May* provides essential data on the modernizer's imagined performance, complete with stage directions.

Pope's early interest in the classics has borne fruit, too, by the time he comes to *January and May,* again in contrast to *The Miller of Trompington* wherein most added images come from Shakespeare or theology. Freshly aware of an entire Graeco-Roman religion different from both Christian ones at his time, Pope found Chaucer insufficiently precise in his distinctions. For example, Chaucer's narrator vouches for Ovid by evoking the capitalized Christian deity: "O noble Ouid, soth sayeth thou God wote."[2]

Twentieth-century critics have seldom penetrated the entangled Christian-pagan references in the *Merchant's Tale.* In contrast, several have cut paths through the *Franklin's Tale.* Although Dorigen prays to God and Aurelius to Apollo, the rocks disappear because of human learning and the problems because of human understanding. But for the *Merchant's Tale* no one since Pope has sorted out the extent to which the stupid and devious characters cite scripture only, whereas the well-balanced Justinus, triumphant queen, and omniscient narrator make appropriate selections from both classical and Christian wisdom. Let us therefore first pass through Chaucer's text, sorting images as did Pope when he set out to present the *Tale*'s binary irresolution in yet another arena, Christian versus pagan.

Briefly, not counting references to heaven or astrology or priests or holiness that could conceivably be either Christian or pagan, Chaucer's narrator draws examples and oaths from both worlds about equally. As will Pope's narrator, he switches from a Christian wedding ceremony to a pagan celebration (pagan except for the reference to Joab, *MctT* l. 1719). Chaucer's Justinus cites both Seneca and God (*MctT* ll. 1523, 1660, 1665). Placebo cites only scripture, making reference to God, Solomon, and Christ (*MctT* ll. 1478–1518). Pluto also quotes Solomon, but he does so to make his own point, not refute Solomon's as Placebo has tried to do (*MctT* ll. 2242–48).

Here and elsewhere Solomon is a dubitable authority, being both wise and sexually active. In one version of *The Wanton Wife of Bath* that has survived censorship efforts, for example, Alysoun aims a four-stanza barb, her lengthiest, when Solomon steps to the pearly gates to block her entry:

> You had seven hundred wives, she said,
> For whom thou didst provide;
> Yet for all this three hundred whores
> Thou didst maintain beside.[3]

In Chaucer's *Merchant's Tale* the Wife of Bath, now one up on Jankyn's scholarship, dons a pagan-goddess outfit and calls herself Proserpyne. She gets her own way by reviewing good women both "in Cristes hous" and in "Romayn geestes," then by glossing her husband's Old-Testament verse with a New-Testament one and a "sentence" analogous to *ClT* ll. 1142–62, then by undercutting Solomon's authority altogether (*MctT* ll. 2264–2310). The other character who gets what he wants however briefly, Damyan, speaks only once, but Chaucer's narrator specifies his religious commitment to Venus (*MctT* ll. 1942–43, 1777, 1875, 1971).

In contrast, in Chaucer's text, Damyan's lord makes frequent reference to Christian ideas and institutions only, with the one exception of his slobbery thoughts during dinner,

> That he that nyght in armes wolde hire streyne
> Harder than evere Parys dide Eleyne.

Amidst his other tidying up, Pope bowdlerizes this reference to the Troy story, which he would translate also. He replaces Chaucer's effect of an old lech who has heard the phrase "rape of Helen" somewhere, and makes up the rest of the story, with the effect of an old lech who cannot remember women's names:

> The joyful Knight survey'd her by his Side,
> Nor envy'd *Paris* with the *Spartan* Bride.[4]

January's unblushing bride is a good Christian, too, throughout Chaucer's text. Besides swearing by God three times, she frames the closing dialogue with oaths by the queen and king of heaven (*MctT* ll. 2195, 2341, 2375, 2334, 2407). Christian in immediate context, these two oaths reverberate with the queen and king whose altercation has reached the human world. By "hevene queene" May pregnantly craves fruit, Proserpyne being goddess of fruitfulness not to mention rebirth. By "hevene kyng" May convinces January not to believe what he can now see thanks to Pluto, god of darkness. Then the narrator reenters to take a bow along with God and his mother (*MctT* l. 2418). But where is the director?

And from the back of the dim auditorium, down the aisle past three centuries in which lounge a few other interested souls, now briskly comes striding Alexander Pope, young friend of the famous actor Thomas Betterton. OK you guys—pagans stage left, Christians stage right. January, Justinus, Placebo, Damyan. Stay right where you are. May, you're a pagan pretending to believe in holy matrimony to fool your rich suitor. And practice that crying, girl—I want to see real tears next time. Narrator, you're a Christian who's read the classics. Pluto and Prosperpine. Look, there's just no way we can reconcile these lines with those togas. Tell the costume people I'm sorry. I'll call in some extras, some of those kids from last year's *Midsummer Night's Dream*. The next time the curtain goes up I want to see and hear

> The dapper Elves their Moonlight Sports pursue;
> Their Pigmy King, and little Fairy Queen,
> In circling Dances gambol'd on the Green,
> While tuneful Sprights a merry Consort made,
> And Airy Musick warbled thro' the Shade.
> (*J&M* ll. 460–64, for *MctT* ll. 2038–41)

Yes, yes, I know the wardrobe mistress will flip out. Look, show her Speght's 1598 text. It says "king of Fayry" twice. I'm simply removing the proper names and this reference to Claudian's story, briefer in Speght than in Robinson because of a line that the nineteenth century will declare spurious.[5]

Goodness, would she suggest I do that with my Speght folio? OK, try telling her that Pluto and Proserpine appear in none of the scores of known analogues to folktale motif K1518, "The enchanted pear tree," and that she should be glad I'm not changing the divine powers back to God and St. Peter or to Jesus and Mary as in the vast majority.[6]

Good point. I do not want one of her halos wrapped around my neck. Try—no, I'll go tell her myself that these fairies will flutter well into the next century. Cristoph Wieland will openly name them Oberon and Titania, as Pope only hints, and will not only retell *January and May* in German but also propel vast segments of his epic-length plot from the Shakespearian idea that Titania's winning this argument must have infuriated Oberon. As summarized by John Quincy Adams,

> Rosetta . . . assures Gangolfo that she was only struggling with
> an evil spirit in the shape of a man, for the sake of restoring him
> to sight. Gangolfo easily believes her and is immediately recon-
> ciled to her. Oberon, yet more exasperated at this issue, now
> declares to Titania, that from that instant he separates himself
> from her, and never must they come together again, until a couple
> of faithful lovers shall bid defiance to death, rather than be false
> to each other, for all the glory of a throne. —He then disappeared
> in spite of all Titania's entreaties; and . . . has dwelt in some
> mountain, wood or valley, and made it all his delight to torment
> lovers.[7]

Despite the apparent conclusion of *January and May*, weighted down with the moral absent from Chaucer, Wieland nonetheless finds and strings out at epic length a loose end. In Wieland's imagined performance of Pope's text, the fairy king cannot really mean it when he says, "Nay . . . dear Madam be not wroth; / I yield it up," and the queen must be lying or deluded herself when she says "thus an End of all Dispute I make" (*J&M* ll. 700–701, 707, for *MctT* ll. 2311–12, 2318–19).

Wieland well exemplifies the extent to which Pope's staging of the *Tale* held sway for the rest of the century, even—or especially—for readers abroad. Wieland is certainly developing traits of Pope's characters, not Chaucer's. Pope, borrowing from both *Prologue* to the *Legend of Good Women* and *Midsummer Night's Dream*, had expanded Chaucer's "Now wol I graunt of my maieste" to an angered, awe-inspiring king's rolling tones:

> Thus, with a Frown, the King bespoke his Queen.
> ....
>
> Now, by my own dread Majesty I swear,
> And by this awful Scepter which I bear,
> No impious Wretch shall 'scape unpunish'd long,
> That in my Presence offers such a Wrong.[8]

Yet Wieland credits Chaucer not Pope—albeit with equal inaccuracy, since Pope's Pluto substitute has no proper name. My tale is of Oberon, explains Wieland, "welcher in Chaucer's *Merchant's-Tale* und Shakespeare's *Midsummer-Night's-Dream* als ein Feen- oder Elfenkönig (*King of Fayries*) erscheint."[9]

A compatriot in 1793 is more straightforward, or less garbled, in recommending Pope's version over Chaucer's. He matter-of-factly includes it among Chaucer's comic tales: "In der komischen Gattung sind *The Tale of the Nonnes Priest* und *January and May*, durch Dryden's and Pope's Modernisirungen, die bekanntesten geworden."[10]

Furthermore, permutations of Pope's fairy couple do not stop with Wieland. As the nineteenth century emerged, *Oberon: A Poetical Romance* became a favorite not only of an American en route to the presidency but also of young British poets traversing the continent in search of new ways to live, love, and lyricize, particularly John Keats and Samuel Taylor Coleridge. From *Oberon* and opium, not necessarily in that order, come many of Coleridge's *Kubla Khan* images, including the "woman wailing for her demon lover."[11]

Were it not for Pope's addition of audiovisual details and subtraction of classical deities from Chaucer's poem, Wieland would have propelled his plot otherwise than by royal fairies respectively angry and forsaken. Coleridge might then have been having a dream not worth writing down, might still have been snoozing when the man from Porlock knocked. And were that the case, the Medieval Institute would not now host the annual meeting of the Porlock Society, featuring discussion of works besides *Kubla Khan* which ought to have been interrupted, of authors who ought to have been interrupted *in utero,* and of the next issue of the society's journal *Cogito Interruptus.* Our world would be far less rich had the sixteen-year-old Pope not set his hand to sort Chaucer's religious imagery.

In Pope's retelling he mainly adjusts references by the narrator and the two women. Placebo and the fairy king still cite only scripture. Damyan, serving "Pow'rs Divine," must pray to them in secret (*J&M* ll. 416–17, for after *MctT* l. 1943).

January is a new convert. He tries to think Christian thoughts only, with the exception as in Chaucer that, among pagan friends at his wedding reception, he has a passing vision of Paris and what's-her-name. From the optimistic musings on marriage that editors now assign to the narrator, for instance, Pope excises January's knowledge of Seneca and Cato along with the rest of *MctT* ll. 1375–92. Roman secular authors would never have penetrated the Italian knight's consciousness. Formerly, however, he has been "led astray by *Venus'* soft Delights." His laborious piecing together of bits he wants to believe from the new religion convinces him at length that it too supplies space for sexuality. He decides to "try that Christian Comfort, call'd a Wife." [12]

Justin carefully explains to his dull-witted brother his reference to a "Heathen Author . . . / (Who, tho' not *Faith*, had *Sense* as well as We)" (*J&M* ll. 178–79, for *MctT* l. 1523). For Justin's second speech, then, Pope edges into crisper focus Chaucer's picture of the old nobleman who has absorbed just enough odds and ends of Christian doctrine to justify his sin, and his well-read brother who realizes that a counterargument using contradictory Christian sources would just befuddle January, not budge him.

Chaucer's Justinus speaks intending to "non aucthorite allege" (Speght 29v, for *MctT* l. 1658). Chaucer does have him avoid authorities' proper names then, except for the Wife of Bath, but Justinus names God six times along with holy church, grace, repentance, sin and purgatory. Instead of promising not to cite Christian authorities, Pope's Justin refrains from doing so. He refers January directly to "Old Wives . . . of Judgment most acute," using no doctrinal term except a dismissive "do Penance" (*J&M* ll. 278–98, for *MctT* ll. 1659–88).

January ignores his heathen-citing brother, of course, in favor of Placebo's assurance that

> Your Will is mine; and is (I will maintain)
> Pleasing to God, and shou'd be so to Man.
>   (*J&M* ll. 168–69, for *MctT* ll. 1508–12)

Placidly certain to please the right God thereby, Pope's January chooses May. She professes Christianity to wed for the sake of economic arrangements, concerning which Pope expands Chaucer's one line to five, ending "When Fortune favours still the Fair are kind." May obediently accompanies her groom "at once with carnal and devout Intent" to a church, where a priest explicit about her wifely duties prays for their "fruitful Bed." [13]

Several months later in the garden, heir in progress as contracted, May weeps and sighs about soul and honor, pretending that she would never break those vows she took "in holy Church" with "Wedlock's sacred Band" (*J&M* ll. 581–82, for *MctT* ll. 2191–92). She has learned the lingo, for this calm moment.

But in the excitement of spotting "her Love / Full fairly perch'd among the Boughs above," and then hearing her own mouth utter a remarkable excuse, May begins to lose track of deities. Craving pears, May appeals to "good Gods" as well as to "Heav'ns' immortal Queen," then simpers further for "Charity's sweet sake" as if invoking a minor goddess. To prove her good intent she calls indiscriminately on the "Pow'r of Magick," "good Angels," "Fates," and "all those [immortal] Pow'rs," until from her final couplet we learn who her "hevene kyng" really is:

> *Jove* ne'er spoke Oracle more true than this,
> None judge so wrong as those who think amiss.[14]

The queen who supplies May's excuse likewise draws deities and ideas from both religions. While Pope's May is alert to her husband's proclivities but remains pagan at heart, Pope's fairy queen is Christian and even more scholarly than Justin. Carefully drawing attention to historical distinctions, she exemplifies "Romain iestes" so as to produce a couplet apiece, a file folder apiece for virtuous Christian and virtuous pre-Christian women. Chaucer just hints at analogy with Alysoun of Bath, especially in Proserpyne's scorn for "auctoritees."[15] Pope's queen instead, having soberly presented her data, whips off the glasses and tweed jacket, shakes out the bun: Superwyf!

> What tho' this sland'rous *Jew,* this *Solomon,*
> Call'd Women Fools, and knew full many a one?
> The wiser Wits of later Times declare
> How constant, chast, and virtuous, Women are.
> Witness the Martyrs, who resign'd their Breath,
> Serene in Torments, unconcern'd in Death;
> And witness next what *Roman* Authors tell,
> How *Arria, Portia,* and *Lucretia* fell.
> But since the Sacred Leaves to All are free,
> And men interpret *Texts,* why shou'd not We?
> (*J&M* ll. 669–78, for *MctT* ll. 2276–87; *WBP* ll. 1–162, 689–96)

Like the fairy queen, Pope's Christian narrator has an orderly grasp of history. He sets the opening scene at a time when Roman deities were still in the running. Its second couplet ends in that characteristically Popean

anticlimax, as for her who may "stain her Honour, or her new Brocade
... / Or lose her Heart, or Necklace, at a Ball," or for her who assures
the miller of Trompington that their daughter is still "as pure and spotless—as thy Bosom Wife." [16] Notice the pun on "Sense" and the tongue-
in-cheek last couplet—"Of *course* it's not true any*more*"—with which
Pope adjusts the still-problematic "foles that ben seculeres."

> There liv'd in *Lombardy,* as Authors write,
> In Days of old, a wise and worthy Knight;
> Of gentle Manners, as of gen'rous Race,
> Blest with much Sense, more Riches, and some Grace.
> Yet led astray by *Venus'* soft Delights,
> He scarce cou'd rule some Idle Appetites;
> For long ago, let Priests say what they cou'd,
> Weak, sinful Laymen were but Flesh and Blood. [17]

Pope's narrator reports what he has read about January's attitude toward marriage. Having transferred mention of the knight's wisdom to
the opening couplet of his story, before revealing anything of January's
actual thinking, this dignified narrator can avoid the overt sarcasm conveyed by many readers-aloud of Chaucer's line 1266, "Thus seyde this
olde knyght, that was so wys" (Cut M). Pope also eliminates Chaucer's
"seyde he" and "herke me" (*MctT* ll. 1263, 1310) so that his narrator
consistently reports January's thoughts rather than his speech.

Besides crediting the source of this information, the narrator inserts a
generalization to prove that authors' reports on January's private musings make sense in terms of mankind's known potential for self-delusion.
As a transition between January's particular decision to wed and his encomium on marriage, which quotation marks now assign to a snarling
Merchant, Pope's balanced couplet makes January's pigheadedness seem
an even more unassailable character trait:

> These Thoughts he fortify'd with Reasons still,
> (For none want Reasons to confirm their Will)
> (*J&M* ll. 19–20, for *MctT* ll. 1263–66)

January's fortifying reasons include the notion somewhat illogical, but
fully convincing to him, that the blessing of a wife may well last "as long
as Heart can wish—and longer too," perhaps even into the afterlife that
so interests him. [18]

As January finishes his blissful thoughts and summons his friends, Pope interjects two phrases in parentheses. With one, the narrator reiterates January's stubbornness, again generalizing to reinforce his report on the knight's inner feelings. The other parenthetical passage supplies Pope's imagined performance of this, the first scene fully suitable for staging:

> His Friends were summon'd, on a Point so nice,
> To pass their Judgment, and to give Advice;
> But fix'd before, and well resolv'd was he,
> (As Men that ask Advice are wont to be.)
>   My friends, he cry'd, (and cast a mournful Look
> Around the Room, and sigh'd before he spoke:)

Understanding Chaucer's "face sadde" in the sense that has survived, Pope adds the mournful sigh. Had he pictured a serious face he might have added a dignified throat-clearing. The shift in meaning of this one adjective demonstrates precisely how a reader adds sound effects appropriate to his own subjective experience of the text.[19]

Pope's January concludes his first public speech with slightly more pretense than Chaucer's, who asks outright that all assent to his will. The first line quoted below, however, as well as both generalizations discussed, all specify that January's mind is made up. We can thus assume that for the second line below, Pope intends the vocal inflection that would make "Friend" mean "friend, as opposed to anyone who might disagree," as on Cut B4. That inflection would recur when January observably turns away "with Scorn" from Justin's advice: "What does my Friend, my dear *Placebo* say?"

> Now Sirs you know to what I stand inclin'd,
> Let ev'ry Friend with Freedom speak his Mind.[20]

In the transition to the first debate between the brothers, Pope's balanced phrases and closed couplets create definite expectations that clear-cut arguments for and against marriage will follow, expectations thereby more decisively thwarted:

> He said; the rest in diff'rent Parts divide,
> The knotty Point was urg'd on either Side;
> Marriage, the Theme on which they all declaim'd,
> Some prais'd with Wit, and some with Reason blam'd.
> 'Till, what with Proofs, Objections, and Replies,
> Each wondrous positive, and wondrous wise;

> There fell between his Brothers a Debate,
> *Placebo* This was call'd, and *Justin* That.
> (*J&M* ll. 139–46, for *MctT* ll. 1469–77)

As the out-of-kilter debate begins, in Chaucer's text Placebo just "seyde." Pope adds a line: "(Mild were his Looks, and pleasing was his Tone)." Justinus replies after sitting through Placebo's speech "ay stille" in Robinson's edition, although in Speght the line is "Justinus that aie sat and herde." Pope imagines the scene as do most scribes, however, and so specifies Justin's silence. He adds a frown, described with the technique used for the Pope/Betterton Pardoner's "Patriarchal Face": an abstraction used as if it were a visual adjective.

> *Justin,* who silent sate, and heard the Man,
> Thus, with a Philosophick Frown, began.[21]

Chaucer's text provides a sad face but no sound for January seeking advice. It provides no audio or visual at all for Placebo, and a motivation for silence but no picture for Justinus. Pope works toward stereophonic full-screen action, mostly in shades of black and white, avoiding insofar as possible the need for a voice relating characters' thoughts.

To introduce Justin's speech in response to January's worries about his afterlife, therefore, Pope gives the wise brother observably churning emotions. In Speght Pope found, but did not understand, a contrast between Justinus's inner feelings and the joking tone of voice with which he addresses this fool:

> Justinus, which that hated his folie
> Answerd anon right in his iaperie

Pope could picture someone's hatred, all right, but had to skim past "iaperie." Speght's glossary includes no form of "jape," which in 1600 was just becoming obsolete. Thus the repressed disapproval of Chaucer's Justinus appears in Pope's Justin as clenched fists, glaring eyes, voice breaking with fury:

> This *Justin* heard, nor cou'd his Spleen controul,
> Touch'd to the Quick, and tickl'd at the Soul.[22]

For the queen's angry response to her husband's declaration that he will restore eyesight to January, in contrast, Pope found in Speght's text

sufficient indication of how she looked and sounded. "Ye shal (qd Proserpine) and woll ye so?" becomes simply "And will you so, reply'd the
Queen, indeed?" (*J&M* l. 656, for *MctT* l. 2264; Speght 32v). Syntax
and rhythm convey the clenched jaw, the narrowing eyes, the head nod-
ding slightly and lips pursing only to break into a small smile as she
thinks up just the right countergift.

Pope does not always add stage directions, then. The second speeches
by fairy king and queen and by Placebo have none, nor do two of January's many speeches after his image and sound have been established.[23]

The staging possibilities of Chaucer's text emerge fully, though, at the
pagan feast that follows the Christian wedding. Chaucer's enigmatic May
just smiles benignly all through dinner. Pope's adolescent bride is pleased
at the attention from all these rich people during this the biggest event of
a girl's life; she plays her role to the hilt in ways visible to the narrator:

> The beauteous Dame sate smiling at the Board,
> And darted am'rous Glances at her Lord.
> > (*J&M* ll. 341–42, for *MctT* ll. 1742–43)

She is asking for it then, as indeed she will finally get it along toward
dawn from her legal husband. Although her glances must be driving him
quite mad, Pope's January shares less than does Chaucer's of his inner
thoughts. His sexually explicit worries, *MctT* ll. 1755–63, Pope reduces
to one couplet. The geezer's wish "that all these people were ago" becomes a reversion to thoughts of the old gods, brought on by restlessness
seen by the company:

> Still as his Mind revolv'd with vast Delight
> Th'entrancing Raptures of th'approaching Night;
> Restless he sate, invoking ev'ry Pow'r
> To speed his Bliss, and haste the happy Hour.
> > (*J&M* ll. 349–52, for *MctT* ll. 1755–67; Speght 29r)

Besides switching off January's inner thoughts, Pope curtains the
twenty-line bedroom scene with just "What next ensu'd beseems not me
to say."[24] At dawn we with the narrator can see and hear a bit more, but
still not the all-too-vivid audiovisual effects of *MctT* ll. 1847–56. Wide-
screen action replaces Chaucer's close-up shot and his report on the
bride's opinion. Silhouettes on the shade show a more energetic January
than Chaucer's. He "briskly sprung from Bed" to get the drink himself,
sits back down for a snuggle and a quaff, then stands back up for the
serenade:

He kiss'd his balmy Spouse, with wanton Play,
And feebly sung a lusty Roundelay:
Then on the Couch his weary Limbs he cast;
For ev'ry Labour must have Rest at last.
　　　　(*J&M* ll. 385, 388–91, for *MctT* ll. 1844–57)

Pope found in Chaucer's text an analogy, one not fully developed, between this scene and the simultaneous one in Damyan's bedroom. Chaucer hints at weeping and complaining audible down the hall from January's dawn song. To retain Chaucer's sound effects and focus the split-screen picture, Pope adds the first phrase and specifies Damian's action toward his bed:

His Task perform'd, he sadly went his Way,
Fell on his Bed, and loath'd the Light of Day.
There let him lye, 'till his relenting Dame
Weep in her turn, and waste in equal Flame.
　　　　(*J&M* ll. 363–66, for *MctT* ll. 1779–82)

This flame of mutual attraction grows until the key to the now-blind January's garden becomes imprinted in warm wax and passed to his squire. The next fully dramatized scene opens, as the wedding-night scene had closed, with January's full-throated singing. Echoing less of the *Song of Songs* than does Chaucer's January, he then stops singing and enters the garden to offer his heritage, with just "he said" for Chaucer's "(qd. he)." Chaucer ends the offer, "Now kisse me wife," so that readers must visualize what follows. Challenged to try a subtler theatrical technique, by which the lines themselves create the kiss, Pope recalls the scene in which Cressida confesses her love for Troilus:

　　Sweet, bid me hold my tongue,
....

　　See, see! your silence,
Cunning in dumbness, from my weakness draws
My very soul of counsel. Stop my mouth.
Troilus.　And shall, albeit sweet music issues thence.
Pandarus.　Pretty, i'faith.

Moving the kiss to midscene, as in the modernized *Reeve's Tale* aubade, Pope has a January blinder than Chaucer's deny his jealousy rather than admit it:

> I seal the Contract with a holy Kiss,
> And will perform, by this—my Dear, and this.—
> Have Comfort, Spouse, nor think thy Lord unkind;
> 'Tis Love, not Jealousie, that fires my Mind.[25]

For May's benign reply, Pope adds precise aural details to the weeping that Chaucer specifies:

> He ceas'd, and *May* with modest Grace reply'd;
> Weak was her Voice, as while she spoke she cry'd.
> Heav'n knows, (with that a tender Sigh she drew)
> I have a Soul to save as well as You.
> (*J&M* ll. 575–78, for *MctT* ll. 2185–89)

May continues to weep and sigh throughout Pope's final dialogue. In this tactic she differs from the Mays of most readers-aloud to be discussed. Only six of twenty-six sound weepy anywhere at all in *MctT* ll. 2320–2418, usually during her request for pears, and only one reader-aloud makes May burst into full-scale bawling at the same point that Pope does, *MctT* l. 2389.

From the *Wife of Bath's Prologue,* which he would later modernize, Pope knew the three proverbial gifts of womankind: deceit, weeping, and spinning.[26] The last is Alysoun's business, and the first is the gist of the *Merchant's Tale.* But Pope wants to polish, for a display more prominent than Chaucer's, May's ultimate weapon of tears. He does so by changing Chaucer's neutral speaking verbs to specific ones throughout the closing dialogue.

The neutral speaking verbs in Chaucer's text allow leeway to readers-aloud as well as to Pope. Throughout Chaucer's pear-tree scene only "answerde," "seyde," and "quod" occur, with three exceptions: January sings *MctT* l. 2323, May "gan for to syke" when she spots Damyan, and January "gan to crye" when he spots the two of them.

Modernizing *MctT* ll. 2320–2418, Pope leaves seven verbs as neutral as Chaucer's—several forms each of "quoth," "reply'd," and "said"—though usually in company of some other audiovisual aid. Elsewhere, Pope's January answers May's sighed request with a sigh for his own inadequacy. His eyesight restored, "He cry'd, he roar'd, he storm'd, he tore his Hair." Finally, he cheers his spouse with a remorseful apology.

That cry uttered by Pope's January, upon looking up, echoes May's first one:

> She stopp'd, and sighing, Oh good Gods, she cry'd,
> What Pangs, what sudden Shoots distend my Side?

May thereby pleads in a voice louder and more anguished than that used by most readers-aloud. "Cry" has consistently had its alternate meanings of "weep" and "exclaim loudly," yet Pope's May does not weep for a while. Twice more, Pope replaces Chaucer's "quod" with "cry'd the gentle *May*" and "(she cry'd)."[27] Besides weeping, that is, Pope's May cries out three of her six speeches. The preparations for and results of her most successful ploy hang in the air like aural mist.

Just when it seems that January will not deny his conviction outright, May hears in his voice the same note of doubt as do most critics and readers-aloud. Pope uses italics to convey that "me thoughte," in *MctT* l. 2386, marks the point at which January turns to self-delusion. Seeing is not, after all, believing. When Pope's May hears his *"seem'd,"* she plays her ace:

> What I have said, quoth he, I must maintain;
> For, by th'Immortal Pow'rs, it *seem'd* too plain—
>   By all those Pow'rs, some Frenzy seiz'd your Mind,
> (Reply'd the Dame:) Are these the Thanks I find?
> Wretch that I am, that e'er I was so Kind!
> She said; a rising Sigh express'd her Woe,
> The ready Tears apace began to flow,
> And as they fell, she wip'd from either Eye
> The Drops, (for Women when they list, can cry.)
>   (*J&M* ll. 778–86, for *MctT* ll. 2384–89)

Except that Pope uses no quotation marks, his punctuation resembles that in modern editions. To help convey imagined performance, he has access also to a now-demoted print resource, italics, for significant vocal inflections including loudness. Printers of his time, with their limited fonts, eagerly italicized not only foreign phrases but also proper names and key nouns such as that in the queen's challenge, "And Men interpret *Texts,* why shou'd not We?" (*J&M* l. 678, for *MctT* l. 2286 approx.).

Verbs are seldom italicized, however. In this poem, Pope has the printers italicize two verbs only—the *"seem'd"* just quoted and "I *wende* han seyn" in *MctT* l. 2393—the second reiterating January's gullibility in the same way as do several readers-aloud. Pope's May, tears drying fast, replies with an italicized noun:

> The Knight was touch'd, and in his Looks appear'd
> Signs of Remorse, while thus his Spouse he chear'd:
> Madam, 'tis past, and my short Anger o'er;
> Come down, and vex your tender Heart no more:
> Excuse me, Dear, if ought amiss was said,
> For, on my Soul, amends shall soon be made:
> Let my Repentance your Forgiveness draw,
> By Heav'n, I swore but what I *thought* I saw.
>   Ah my lov'd Lord! 'twas much unkind (she cry'd)
> On bare *Suspicion* thus to treat your Bride.
>   (*J&M* ll. 787–96, for *MctT* ll. 2390–96)

Unfortunately, italics not only occur for purposes other than indication of significant vocal inflections, but also they do not discriminate among various kinds of significance. Context implies that Pope intends January to sound doubtful on "it *seem'd* too plain" but soothing on "I *thought* I saw." On "bare *Suspicion*" Pope's May would sound accusatory, perhaps pouting, like the readers-aloud who have her stress January's credulity as "ye may *wene* as yow lest."

As we have heard, the human ear can discriminate among inflections that a machine would measure as equally loud, or that a printer would render simply as italics—can distinguish, for example, toleration from accusation on "*nat* undergrowe" (Cuts D5, D7). Only italics and punctuation were available for two more centuries after Pope, though, until the earliest sound recordings were produced in Camden, New Jersey.

While taking into account Pope's artistic intentions for *January and May*, I can make educated guesses as to what inflections he silently heard in Chaucer's text. Pope aligned Christians and pagans not because he thought Chaucer had, but rather because he intended that his eighteenth-century audience experience yet another binary opposition. Yet I am assuming that Pope does not drastically change but instead reproduces the performance he imagined while reading Chaucer's pear-tree scene. I assume so because I see no artistic or economic motivation for major changes here, just for relatively minor ones such as a more genteel-speaking January.

Let me run through Pope's imagined performance of *MctT* ll. 2320–2418 as a preview to the readings-aloud thereof. (See *Texts Read Aloud*, Chapter 12.) As the scene opens, a soon-to-be-cuckolded January sings screechily a familiar ballad refrain. Pope's May, spying Damian above, abruptly sighs and exclaims *MctT* ll. 2329–37, with no out-and-out lie except calling Damian's metaphorical fruit green. On account of the spurious passage discussed, that is, Pope's May pleads openly that January "save at once the Life / Of thy poor Infant, and thy longing Wife."[28]

Pope's January replies to her plea with a sigh at *MctT* ll. 2338–40. Several readers-aloud sigh. Others deliver January's wish for a climbing knave in degrees of perturbation that range from soul-wrenching anguish through befuddlement to calm recognition of yet another inadequacy, this one relatively minor.

Because Pope preserves Chaucer's content and neutral speaking verbs for the couple's next exchange, *MctT* ll. 2340–47, his imagined performance is muffled. Perhaps his elimination of "For wel I wotte that ye mistrust me" lightens May's request in that Pope disallows accusation in her voice (*MctT* l. 2343; Speght 32v).

The apology by Pope's narrator, *MctT* ll. 2350–53, differs from the Merchant's apology in that he not only excuses blunt language but also refrains from using it. Instead of flashing the crude verb "throng," as discussed, Pope's narrator carefully circumvents the spurious passage of crude but enthusiastic terms with which May compares the two tents she has ever seen.

Sound returns full-blast to Pope's screen just when sight returns in full color to the "wondring Knight," who casts up "eager Eyes" to see Damian with his wife. The inexpressibility thereof is transferred from their doings to January's mood and voice: "His Rage was such, as cannot be exprest" (*J&M* ll. 748–53, for *MctT* ll. 2354–63). Thus Pope eliminates the narrator's second apology, *MctT* ll. 2362–63, and with it the opportunity most readers-aloud take to make him again express relish or distaste or fluster at talking dirty to ladies.

Pope's January cries, roars, and storms in rage. So do those of most readers-aloud, although several Januarys sound petulant and one just bewildered. The readings-aloud of May's reply vary greatly. In most she sounds utterly self-assured from the first, often surprised or irritated as well. Only two readers-aloud produce the effect that Pope does: at that first moment May herself is the empty vessel into which Proserpyne pours the promised "suffisant answere" (*MctT* l. 2266).

Does Pope both see and hear May trembling? If the latter, does her voice firm up as words come to her, as it does for those two readers-aloud who sound tentative on *MctT* l. 2368? Perhaps so, since she—unlike Chaucer's May—promptly converts the issue to the quality of January's alleged love for her:

> What ails my Lord? the trembling Dame reply'd;
> I thought your Patience had been better try'd:

Is this your Love, ungrateful and unkind,
This my Reward, for having cur'd the Blind?
Why was I taught to make my Husband see,
By Strugling with a Man upon a Tree?
Did I for this the Pow'r of Magick prove?
Unhappy Wife, whose Crime was too much Love!
                    (*J&M* ll. 758–65, for *MctT* ll. 2368–75)

That very Popean couplet, with rhyme twisted like January's emotions, has the desired effect. Sooner than in most readings-aloud, wherein January continues to accuse May even more indignantly in *MctT* ll. 2376–79, Pope's January begins to remember his station in life. He immediately shifts blame from his successfully impregnated wife to his perfidious servant. He avoids the blunt verb "swived," still current at Pope's time, in favor of one that condemns Damian's act in terms more societal than physical. Pope borrows this verb "whor'd" from January's first accusation, which in Speght reads "O stronge lady hore what dost thou?"[29] Far less explicit than the January in Speght's edition, who yells all he saw of May's swelling belly and Damyan's bell-like member, Pope's January just repeats the accusation against Damian.

If this be Strugling, by this holy Light,
'Tis Strugling with a Vengeance, (quoth the Knight:)
So Heav'n preserve the Sight it has restor'd,
As with these Eyes I plainly saw thee whor'd;
Whor'd by my Slave—Perfidious Wretch! may Hell
As surely seize thee, as I saw too well.
                    (*J&M* ll. 766–71, for *MctT* ll. 2376–79)

Chaucer's own text most assuredly provides evidence for blaming not May but Damyan. Damyan has against his name "servant traytour, false hoomly hewe," and other oxymoronic aspersions in a passage of foreshadowing omitted by Pope (*MctT* ll. 1783–94). But twentieth-century critics, to a man, shift blame to May.

Notice that in this passage just quoted, as is the case throughout Pope's final dialogue, each speech's closing couplet supplies a sense of finality. Pope's May convinces January firmly, step by step, and he stolidly lets himself be convinced. In Chaucer's text, instead, urgency and irresolution emit from dialogue during which each new speech begins midcouplet. The last line of each speech by January rhymes with the first line of each by May or the narrator, that is, and vice versa.

In the one exception, Chaucer's January completes both a couplet and his turning-point speech with a thereby more emphatic "me thoughte he dide thee so." Chaucer's May starts off the entire exchange with a couplet, though, and ends it very conclusively with a couplet in which the last line contains the midline rhyme characteristic of oral proverbs.[30]

This rhyme exchange helps keep readers-aloud lively. When January swears that he saw her swived, "elles be I hanged by the hals," the attitudes of Mays toward the ineffectiveness of "medicyne fals" range from that of a little girl holding up a broken dolly to that of a very practical nurse mildly disappointed to learn that despite experiments her subject is no longer viable.

Pope excises the medical imagery (for transplant, perhaps, to *The Miller of Trompington*). A practical Christian wife instead exclaims:

> Guard me, good Angels! cry'd the gentle *May*
> Pray Heav'n, this Magick work the proper Way.
> (*J&M* ll. 772–73, for *MctT* l. 2380)

She knows that religious vows will penetrate his skull and knows just how to twist the knife of guilt. Pope's January has just called her or Damian "Perfidious Wretch" but with his next couplet expresses doubt. Just before her tears, as quoted, May converts his accusatory term to a self-pitying one that ends not just a couplet but a triplet, thus doing him one better in verse and word use both: "Wretch that I am, that e'er I was so Kind!" (*J&M* ll. 770, 778–79, 782, for *MctT* ll. 2378, 2384–86, 2389).

After specifying the volitional nature of her tears, Pope's narrator devotes a couplet to January's inner feelings, made known by facial expression and tone of voice:

> The Knight was touch'd, and in his Looks appear'd
> Signs of Remorse, while thus his Spouse he chear'd.
> (*J&M* ll. 787–88, for *MctT* before l. 2390)

January ends this speech by reiterating "it *seem'd* too plain" with "I swore but what I *thought* I saw." He has again refrained, as a gentleman ought, from explicit description of the supposed scene (*J&M* ll. 779, 794, for *MctT* ll. 2386, 2393–95).

Pope's January, ready from the start to blame Damian rather than his heir-producing wife, at the end is easily convinced of her virtue by her words, facial expression, and hugs. Despite the notorious ambiguity of pagan oracles, he fails to note the double meaning of what she cites in place of "He that misconceiueth oft misdemeth."

> *Jove* ne'er spoke Oracle more true than this,
> None judge so wrong as those who think amiss.
>   (*J&M* ll. 809–10, for *MctT* ll. 2407–10; Speght 32r)

Sound fades first, after May has the last word. Visual action continues for a few lines, as in Chaucer's text. But instead of an abrupt benediction, which switches off the picture to leave observers scratching their heads in puzzlement for six hundred years, Pope fades the picture gradually while telling what has happened to these characters since.

As before, Pope's narrator reports observable embraces. Then he steps toward omniscience by reporting, without citing his source, January's inner peace of mind and the couple's future bliss. This narrative voice-over, misty with romantic abstractions, lets Pope-the-author glide past the ambiguous antecedents and implications of "pleas'd and blest," to proffer the eighteenth century the neat moral it wants.

> With that, she leap'd into her Lord's Embrace,
> With well-dissembl'd Virtue in her Face:
> He hugg'd her close, and kiss'd her o'er and o'er,
> Disturb'd with Doubts and Jealousies no more:
> Both, pleas'd and blest, renew'd their mutual Vows,
> A fruitful Wife, and a believing Spouse.
>   Thus ends our Tale, whose Moral . . .

Wait a minute. Run those closing credits by again. Who is pleased, who blessed, and how? and why? What kind of fruitfulness and what kind of belief? In the wake of shipshape deities and motivations for his projected performance, Pope has left intact the basic binary irresolution of Chaucer's text.

To what extent can readers-aloud do the same? Investigators in the field of oral interpretation use analytic methods such as the Trager-Smith system to show how ambiguity may be preserved—albeit not always easily—in oral performance.[31] Without such technical transcription, we will nonetheless hear how some readers-aloud conclude the *Merchant's Tale* with a moral, while others' voices remain as neutral, as unresolved, as is the text on paper.

In the meantime, as well, two eighteenth-century artists have left evidence that Pope's superficially balanced conclusion could inspire

Old as he was, and void of Eye-sight too,
What coud alaſs!a helpleſs Husband do.

Jan. & May.

FIGURE 10: Scene from Alexander Pope's *January and May* (captioned with Pope's lines 728–29), by S. Wale, facing p. 209 of vol. 1 of *The Works of Alexander Pope, Esq.*, ed. William Warburton (London: Bathurst et al., 1776). Reproduced by permission of the Van Pelt Library, University of Pennsylvania. Actual size, 4″ × 2¾″.

FIGURE 11: *January and May,* drawn by J. H. Mortimer and engraved by J. Hogg. Leaf of unknown origin bound into a copy of John Urry's edition of *The Works of Geoffrey Chaucer* (London: B. Lintot, 1721), fEC. C3932.C/ 721W. Reproduced by permission of the Houghton Library, Harvard University. Actual size, 7¼″ × 9½″.

divergent visualizations. Both artists choose the pear-tree scene to illustrate the tale—Pope's tale rather than Chaucer's, certainly in one case and possibly in the other.

S. Wale certainly worked from Pope's version, for he illustrates the 1776 printing of *The Works of Alexander Pope, Esq.*, edited by William Warburton. (See figure 10.) In the engraving, active little figures carved on the garden wall point at and gossip about Damian perched in the pear tree. The adultery's impact thus seems more social than moral. January, in cape and plumed hat of an Elizabethan courtier, gropes with outstretched hands. May, leading him on, tugs her husband's elbow with her right hand. With her left she reaches to stroke the bark. Pears dangle.

Before his death, John Mortimer could have had access to Tyrwhitt's new tale order and other features of that editor's presentation of Chaucer's own text. Might it, as well as Pope's retelling, have affected Mortimer's visual interpretation of the pear-tree scene as one in which May is to be blamed, indeed loathed or feared?

Mortimer's India-ink drawing with touches of blue and sepia, its original now in the Victoria and Albert Museum, shares Pope's title *January and May*. (See figure 11.) Unlike his *Three Gamblers and Time*, its title offers no allegorical interpretation. Mortimer's pear tree stands front and center. May, in the act of stepping from January's back to the lowest branch of the tree, is boosted by Damyan's eager embrace and by her catching a twist above: this is the precise moment of *MctT* l. 2349. May spreads her legs to make the step. Her scarf billows almost as suggestively. And, even more clearly in the original than in engravings, Mortimer has designed her shoe as the devil's cloven hoof.

For reasons far more amorphous than any influence Mortimer could have had, then, the entire nineteenth century turns its back on even the shadowy action that Pope's narrator lets show through bedroom shades. The *Merchant's Tale* does not appear in early school editions or modernizations. When the lights return they play on the podium, where Kittredge is telling his classes of a furious outburst from a disillusioned Merchant "half-mad with rage and shame." Tatlock chimes in with "unrelieved acidity" and "unlovely virtuosity."[32] New Critics whistle, stomp, shout "irony." And the battle is on as to whether and if so what and how we can learn from the *Tale* about the Merchant's personal problems—about the personal problems, that is, of the voice each reader thinks is telling the *Tale*.

CHAPTER 12

The Pear-Tree Scene on Tape

> A potentially fertile young woman tells an old man, who claims exclusive
> sexual rights because he wants a child to outlive him, that she will die
> unless he provides a certain food.

Not an anthropologist's paraphrase of a tale opening from, say, back-woods New Guinea, this sentence summarizes *MctT* ll. 2329–37. Besides male/female roles, every society so far discovered (always an anthropological *caveat*) takes some significant notice of birth, death, food, and sexual intercourse. These few universally shared human experiences constitute the primary human condition on which culture-variant images are based. As Alan Dundes says succinctly, many cultures call spring a kind of rebirth, but no one tries to understand a baby's birth by contemplating spring.

Critical commentary on the *Merchant's Tale* often aims to resolve what Chaucer left unresolved in the conflict of that most primary of all binary oppositions, male versus female, adorned by layer after layer of second-ary images likewise in unresolved opposition: fertility/sterility, age/youth, seeing/believing, winter/spring, and so on. The closing dialogue pulls to-gether the strands of imagery interwoven throughout the *Merchant's Tale* itself, imagery meaningful to speakers of English in the fourteenth and twentieth centuries both. The closing moreover brings to the foreground these few universal conditions of human existence.

Any professor is lying who claims to harbor no personal attitudes to-ward birth, death, food, and sex—lying less justifiably than is any May to be heard in this chapter. An authority figure has the responsibility, not the option, to sort out private, idiosyncratic responses toward old men, pregnant women, and sexual intercourse out-of-doors, while analyzing for students and colleagues how the text comes to mean all that it can legitimately mean.

By the time the pear-tree scene opens at *MctT* l. 2320, the stage is set for complex vocal relationships among the three characters: January, May, and a Merchant/narrator who nowadays is usually resigned or resentful. Pope dramatized the scene with narrator and January both quite calm and dignified, especially in view of the now-spurious passages. Both Pope's male characters blame Damian for tempting May, rather than May for succumbing, despite the pregnant teen-ager's controllable tear valves and her service as surrogate mouthpiece for the fairy queen's lie.

Alternative performances of the interaction vary vastly among twenty-six readers-aloud. (See *Texts Read Aloud,* Chapter 12.) Is January a senile fool, deaf as well as blind to May's machinations, or an overly romantic, utterly sincere aged gentleman? Is May a young girl being exploited, a cold calculating bitch, or a new Eve feeding an old Adam yet another fruit? Does a pilgrim Merchant in some mood, or another narrator, disapprove of these goings-on, or resent or relish or just report them? Furthermore, do any necessary or even probable relationships occur among the multitude of characterizations of the three? Is a misogynistic narrator more likely to malign a May who whines like a spoiled child at her indulgent husband, for instance, or to scorn a January who whines in protest at his nursemaid's lapse of attention to him and his needs?

The possibility of sex-determinate interpretations provides a peekhole into the kaleidoscope of interactions in the *Tale,* though by no means a control over its patternings. For the Chaucer-tapes project, seven women and eighteen men read *MctT* ll. 2320–2418; I add to the count Francis Lee Utley's reading of *MctT* ll. 2348–96, which he provided for his students in the language lab at Ohio State. In contrast to the readings from the *Pardoner's Tale* and *Merchant's Prologue,* the seven women produce lively and fully dramatized dialogues in which May outwits her mate. Thus, enthusiasm and involvement do seem gender-related. These women's dramatizations are definitely among the most colorful. Most male readers shift among three different voices, but quite a few do not thereby create motivated interaction among characters.

As distinguished from involvement and enthusiasm, however, interpretation of the pear-tree scene seems not at all sex-determinate. The seven female readers are distributed evenly among four audible types of confrontations. Strength and weakness define these categories, as they do for the old man and riotours in the *Pardoner's Tale.* Readers project sovereignty and mastery in the couple's relationship, as Alysoun might well have predicted (*WBT* ll. 818, 1038–40, 1236).

May, who wins the match, cannot remain the weak one throughout. But in the opening exchange, *MctT* ll. 2329–40, all four possibilities can be heard: a weak, sniveling May begs fruit from a weak, whimpering husband; a strong woman, sometimes frighteningly nasty, demands fruit from a weak, pathetic old fool; a strong May requests pears from her stupid but strong-willed husband; and a clever May fools a relatively intelligent January by pretending that she is weak and helpless.

This last-described staging, my personal favorite and the one that most resembles Pope's, occurs the least frequently among the twenty-six performances. Only one male reader and one female (to be heard as Cut O5) imagine May sobbing and otherwise playing Daddy's little girl to get her own way.

In the next smallest group of initial confrontations, attempted by one woman and three men, effective performance is difficult. The text permits a weak, pathetic May and a weak, pathetic January only as far as *MctT* l. 2340. For May to win, she must somehow attain strength. Such an opening, therefore, encourages inconsistent characterization.

The one woman reader in this weak/weak category performs *MctT* ll. 2320–2418 in a way not defensible aesthetically. She does dramatize the scene far more fully than do the three analogous male readers, however. Judged by Monroe C. Beardsley's aesthetic criteria for performance, the reader excels at regional intensity and projects some complexity, but she lacks unity.[1] At first her couple both weep in unashamed self-pity, May about pearlessness and January about blindness. Midpoint in *MctT* l. 2340, however, a dry-eyed and efficient May bobs briskly above their flood of tears to propose and execute a fully-engineered plan of action. Oblivious to her instant capability, January continues near tears at her plight, desperately glad to do what little he can to help.

January whines throughout this version of the dialogue—whines even where most Januarys sound indignant (*MctT* ll. 2366) or conciliatory (line 2390). With line 2391 he begs May to come down and beat him with chains if she wants. His audible terror of Head Nurse May would create in listeners a sympathy presumably unintended by the reader-aloud and difficult to justify from the text. Clearly, should this January dare to speak other than with abject humility, his legal heir would begin introducing daily doses of quinine into his porridge.

A May who begins by weeping in self-pity, that is, overcompensates by metamorphosing at line 2340 into a monstrous wife beside whom Grendel's mother would pale. This May thereupon joins the largest category of couples, represented by Cut O1, in which a strong woman consistently manipulates a male made helpless by old age or stupidity or both. Nearly

half the readers-aloud, three women and eight men, project such an un-
even match from the start. Because the outcome is never in doubt, this
most popular dramatization usually sounds less artistically complex than
that in the nine readings wherein strong-willed Mays manipulate strong-
willed Januarys with tactics including honey-dripping sensuality (projected by seven men and two women, represented by Cuts O2–4).

Before hearing the variety of goings-on in the garden, as Cut O, let us
survey the lookers-on. The narrator's attitude is not sex-determinate:
again, women readers are evenly distributed among the audible categories.

The narrator's personality emerges in the opening and closing lines of
the scene, at his two apologies (*MctT* ll. 2350–51, 2362–63), and most
clearly of all on "throng" in line 2353, for there we learn whether or not
he sincerely wishes to spare ladies the explicit details. The largest group
of apologizers do not: five male readers and one female mouth "throng"
with the slobbery relish of a Merchant only too eager to shock so-called
ladies with the foulest language possible. Including one to be heard as
Cut O5, they resemble the bitter Merchants like L1, who begin their tales
with negative concern for ladies' feelings.

The next largest category of narrators, including two male and two
female readers, project a less offensive Merchant who is nonetheless determined to defy social propriety for the sake of narrative honesty at
"throng." Remaining characterizations include two men and one woman
reader who express distaste for the act of thronging in public, another
two men and one woman who sound indignant at it, two men who disapprove, two men who shrug aside the act, and one man and one woman
who continue to plead for the ladies' indulgence through line 2353.

Members of another group, even more polite than this last pair, explain
with kind regret what unfortunately seems to have happened in the pear
tree. This configuration hints at another of those vast areas of reader
response left unexplored in this pioneering study, like religious upbringing, for these three extremely polite apologizers are three of the four
British males in the sample. The cultural training of Americans, it may
seem, provides no aural model for a polite apology. On the other hand,
the fourth British male mouths "throng" with lustful relish.

In short, I merely claim a multitude of Merchant narrators. Using the
Chaucer tapes as evidence, I cannot honestly tabulate any predictable
relationship of a given Merchant's personality to the attitudes of that
particular reader's ill-matched couple, as Cut O will demonstrate, or to
that reader's life situation. As is the case for diachronic evidence, in which
exact contemporaries such as Pope and the Urry-edition artist produce

widely differing interpretations, here too subjectivity overcomes sociology. To predict readers' varying interpretations based on little or no evidence, as many theorists pretend to do, is a self-indulgent game suitable for theorists.

Cut O, MctT ll. 2320–2418

Cut O begins with the most studiously neutral narrator I have on tape and ends with one of the most bitter. In between, though, the performances are arranged not according to narrator's attitude but rather according to relative strength of the two combatants, January and May, and also according to the appeal of each scenario to me, Betsy Bowden. Again, I thus wish to confront rather than ignore issues of subjective response. I hasten to add, however, that this chapter will include no delving into my personal experiences with old men, pregnant women, birth, death, food, or outdoor sports.

In this case my preferences are governed by factors besides the aesthetics of performance. On Cut O all five readings are fully dramatized and fully appropriate to the text, and all five are funny. Only those readers-aloud who recite rather than act, indeed, make the pear-tree scene sound at all serious.

In Cuts O1–4 each narrator helps convey the humor of the situation. But Cut O5 features an explosively bitter Merchant who temporarily escapes his own problems by relating a funny story about somebody else's bad marriage. In this attitude O5's narrator resembles Ogle's in 1741. In other ways, besides, O5's January and May project attitudes parallel to their counterparts in Pope's modernization.

O5 assures me by mail that she has never heard of Ogle and had no idea that Pope modernized the *Merchant's Tale*. Before going on to a doctorate in folklore, O5 studied Middle English at Harvard with B. J. Whiting, William Alfred, and E. Talbot Donaldson. While retaining the Merchant's overwhelming bitterness, passed directly from Kittredge to Whiting to her, O5 in other interpretive matters seems to let the text speak for itself. She does so, at any rate, compared to the other readers-aloud, all of whom are Chaucer professors for whom the text speaks through thick blankets of twentieth-century criticism and classroom practices.

I do not mean to imply that O5 has come full circle to an interpretation somehow more correct than all those of Chaucer scholars, just because hers parallels eighteenth-century interpretations. I primarily wish to end Cut O and this book with emphatic notice of the remarkable versatility of Chaucer's text and the remarkable impact of oral performance by professors. In direct aural line from Kittredge, but comparatively innocent of subsequent critical controversies in print, O5 retains her grandteacher's vocal tones for the narrator. But O5's *Tale* itself speaks in the tone that it always did before Tyrwhitt and Kittredge, according to extant evidence, and always has wanted to since: comical. This weak or strong May's cuckolding of a weak or strong January can sound comical in a variety of ways, all of them at least potentially appropriate to the text.

Among the eleven readings-aloud in which a strong young woman effortlessly manipulates her weak old husband, most lack dramatic tension. A few readers shift dynamics from the January/May nonconflict to teller/listener interaction, conveying a bitter narrator who wants to teach us and the pilgrims not to trust women.

Although it is difficult to create dramatic conflict if May sounds unassailable, O1 proves the possibility of doing so successfully. This dramatization implies the relationship's history before the present moment. O1's May is still testing just how far she can go, in light of January's recent senility.

O1's reading also demonstrates that a competent May can manipulate her senile husband without necessarily serving as exemplum for a misogynistic narrator. To project the most inconclusive conclusion among my data, O1 inserts a vocal question mark into *MctT* l. 2417: "Thus endeth heere? my tale of Januarie." I myself would not be treated thus, says O1's narrator. But January is genuinely glad, and it is not for us to question the quality of his gladness.

Simply opening a story, with neither sympathy nor scorn for its hero, O1 lets January himself trumpet what a fool here strolls amidst fruited trees. O1 sings *MctT* l. 2323 in a simplistic up-and-down melodic profile, the "tra la tra la" of someone oblivious to subtleties in himself or others, someone blind and tone-deaf to boot.

O1's reading differs in many ways from O3's, which will feature a narrator who archly disapproves while a femme fatale manipulates her kindly old husband. Yet among twenty-four performances of *MctT* l. 2323, including several by readers who approach the much-discussed boundary between speech and song, only O1 and O3 actually sing January's song.[2]

How much of readers' reluctance to sing *MctT* l. 2323 comes from imagined performance and how much from stage fright? Pope imagined it sung but might not have sung it himself were he reading Chaucer aloud, especially at age sixteen when he did the modernization. Or was Pope unhampered by the particular shyness that affects my generation and some previous, due to a now roundly denounced pedagogical technique by which children were in first grade labeled Lark, Robin, or Bluebird and treated accordingly ever after? We Bluebirds were asked just to move our mouths in certain situations, for example. Were O1 and O3 perhaps the only Larks among these twenty-four readers-aloud?

I ask this question lightly because to stomp on it would make us leap back as edges crumble away and a vast, bottomless chasm opens. What, after all, about that gap between a reader's imagined performance and his innate or acquired ability to produce it aloud? What about the issue I have very decisively ignored: interpretive gaps between the performances of these readers-aloud and their published criticism? More ice ledges break loose, more avalanches roar. What about reader's intention versus reader's execution? What about legitimate versus illegitimate oral, and silent, interpretations? Is there a gap, or a hairline crack, or nothing at all in between?

Having raised these questions with a book-length flourish, and feeling chilled already, I will let others haul up and dissect more evidence. For now, I will meet you back at the climate-controlled pleasure garden, which O1's singing *senex amans* and carefully neutral narrator are entering. In *MctT* l. 2328 the latter names May with calm, fully justified disapproval—no call to sneer.

O1's May has heard her husband's burbling as so much elevator music while planning exactly what words and tone of voice to use for her request. She sounds elegant throughout. Both times she speaks the word "peres" (ll. 2331, 2333), vocal stress signals her pregnancy, which is unmentionable in polite company including that of her high-born husband. Similar stress, indistinguishable by any objective means, will make "peres" signal instead "sex with Damyan" in readings O2 and O3, and in O4 signal both "item requested" to January and "sex with Damyan" to us other listeners.

Unusual phrasing by O1's May helps convey her reluctance to ask of her lord a favor that normally a servant would perform. In line 2334, her stated "help" expresses propriety, not insincerity like O2's to come, and her pause after "for" conveys regret for troubling him with female problems. She hurries past the taboo term "in my plit" to pause after both occurrences of the word "may" (ll. 2336, 2337). Midverb hesitation each time tells him that she absolutely would not be asking were she not utterly, but in a ladylike way, desperate.

Her careful appeal to knightly values may be necessary, if somone so very old as January has ever acquired any wisdom. He quavers sadly

MctT ll. 2338–40. Perhaps in her eager planning she forgot just how senile he has recently become, for O1's May promptly becomes more brisk, less elegant, less apologetic. She sounds matter-of-fact about his mistrust (l. 2343) and rather glad to place her foot upon his back, which is surely no polite position for a great lord's wife great with child (l. 2345).

"Certes," replies O1's January, in a momentarily sinister tone that becomes the high-pitched happy quavers of lines 2346–47, including satisfaction at his generous offer of "herte blood." To illustrate that full characterization may conflict with the demands of meter, this reader elsewhere provides an alternative performance of *MctT* ll. 2338–47 in which January, upon offering his heart's blood, collapses in a fit of tubercular coughing.

With a pause before "stoupeth" in line 2348, O1's narrator keeps under control his own distaste concerning the actions. Refraining from moral judgment, he projects elaborate oral onomatopoeia with *MctT* ll. 2348–49. His vocal pitches first imitate the "doun" that January stoops, then May's careful balancing on his level back, then her cautious reaching for (on "caughte hire") and grabbing upward at the "twiste," and in the last half line her easy climb up. Reminded by May's tomboy antics of the ladies present who know no such gambols themselves (as is Pope's narrator, *J&M* ll. 744–45), O1's narrator tries very hard during lines 2350–51 to think how to tell the story while avoiding its topic. He decides on brevity. The two pauses in line 2353 mark his continued grappling with its graphic nature: "Gan . . . pullen up the smok, and . . . in he throng."

O1's tone says "As well he might!" concerning Pluto's gift, especially after "se" in the pause and last half line of 2356. On "thyng so fayn" (l. 2358) he lightly teases January for his initial viewing direction. Rapt in contemplation of January's foolishness, he does not notice until almost too late that his story has led him straight back to the same X-rated scene that he so carefully skirted earlier. He must disrupt meter—but to no detriment of characterization, certainly—to stammer "uh um uh" before line 2362. He hurries past his apology to describe the safer topic of January's feelings (ll. 2364–65).

O1's January howls the *oo* sounds in *MctT* l. 2366, then shifts to a very different *oh* followed by a long pause in line 2367. May was right in her initial approach: January's lifelong sense of propriety, not to mention proprietorship, is strong enough to survive senility. He stretches his shocked "O" for so long that line 2367 divides into three segments, each projecting "Shame on you!" in a slightly different shade. A remarkable number of readers-aloud either howl like dogs or scold dogs at lines 2366–67, especially on the four interjections. And any dog still on the sofa after O1's line 2367 would be deaf or defiant indeed.

May is neither. She is simply brisk. As do other Mays, O1 uses the low-content lines 2369–73 to stall for time while she thinks up an excuse—she, not Proserpyne, in this and all but two of the twenty-six readings. Only O5's May, and one other, resemble Pope's by sounding tentative until supplied with a reply.

Syntax helps all Mays hold off answering. The three sentences before the long one of *MctT* ll. 2371–74 convey little information, just filler to keep January from butting in; the six half-line segments that follow convey even less. O1's May delays further by means of pauses after "pacience" in line 2369 and "yow" in line 2370, an extra "and" in line 2369, and a particularly thoughtful last half of line 2372. All help her stall until—"So there!"—just the right verb "strugle" occurs to her. "Oh well, I did my best," says her line 2375, which follows no line-end break at all, certainly not Robinson's period.

With a whimper, O1's January begins line 2376 with a sobbed "strugle" and then a "ye" with its vowel stretched to quavery meaninglessness. Stammering what he saw, he takes a deep breath to bolster his failing strength before line 2377. O1 sacrifices metrical regularity to comic drama, as his January gasps "He . . . he . . . he *swyved* thee." He gasps also oaths by bodily parts "yen" and "hals" (ll. 2378–79), all with creaky incredulity.

Knowing just how to counter creaky incredulity, O1's May begins line 2380 elegantly and ends it with hurt feelings, reminding him of his chivalrous duties as knight and gentleman. Speeding up through lines 2381–83 in her pretended efforts to hold back improperly public tears, May pouts a bit on her decisive "glymsyng." Her last phrase, "parfit sighte," however, oozes toward threat.

Changing her noun to the verb, January's defenses rise with the pitch of "I se" (l. 2384). But with a pause before "wel" he begins to doubt. He hurries rhythmically past God and eyes (l. 2385) to the problematic issue of his own "trouthe." The long pauses before and after "me" in line 2386 mark his distinct shift from partial to complete self-doubt, as he succumbs totally to May's argument.

In line 2387, the first "maze" of O1's May trumpets triumph. Swallowing in her attempt to control vocal inflections, she delivers the second "maze" with high-pitched concern. By lines 2388–89 she has her voice where she wants it: weepy, with a hint of hurt defiance.

Her ploy works even better than she expected, her husband's senility being recent. O1's January not only forgives her but with his calm level tone in lines 2390–92 seems already to have forgotten what the issue was. Very unlike O2's to come, O1's January goes on to remind himself what he now fully realizes he did not see. He addresses wondering tones to himself, not to May, with stutters full of self-doubt on "how," "and," and "his" (ll. 2394–95).

Though unaddressed, O1's May replies to his self-musings with fast, high-pitched tones of victory on line 2396. With a firm "but, sire" and pauses, however, she again regains control of her inflections. Happy to explain his acquisition of eyesight, a scientific phenomenon which she has had opportunity to study whereas he apparently has not, her voice occasionally edges back toward triumph, especially on line 2405 preceding the eager "ther may . . . ful . . . many a sighte yow begile" with which she anticipates future beguilements with Damyan. Wagging her finger already on "beth war" (l. 2407), O1's May firmly delivers line 2410 as unassailable proverbial wisdom, "So there!" booming in its background.

"Would you believe it?!" concludes O1's narrator on line 2411, with a wry smile and eyes rolling upward. To make up for his hint of personal disapproval toward womb-stroking, O1 slows down to inject into line 2415 the formulaic tones of "and so they lived happily ever after." His speeding up for the next-to-last half line, then, makes it nonformulaic in contrast—makes it a genuine wish for God's blessing in this and in all other such situations, which God, not narrators, ought to judge.

O1 is rare in his restraint. Excluding O4–5, most other readers perform *MctT* ll. 2412–18 as a moral of some sort. Many narrators sound self-satisfied, sure that they are not as stupid as January—perhaps, indeed, too sure. Some sound sad that so many men will fail to take heed. Some, like O3, fully disapprove of January's actions but do not imply that we listeners are apt to follow his path. Others, like O2, make absolutely certain that listeners comprehend the danger to us. Among all twenty-five readers who close the *Tale*, though, only O5 (a woman) returns in lines 2412–18 to the full-scale resentment against women with which so many narrators open the *Merchant's Prologue*.

In oral or imagined performance, tone of voice can create a moral even in a passage that, like *MctT* ll. 2412–18, contains no overt one. This fact has wide implications; it applies most obviously to the several overt, interlocking, contradictory, proverbial morals that end the *Nun's Priest's Tale*, which I also have on tape. Some critics believe only one of the *Nun's Priest's Tale* morals; some believe all, or try to believe all by positing a jocular tone of voice where others would hear dead earnestness.

In O1's reading-aloud, the unarticulated question answered in per-

formance is, "What sort of weakling would let his wife push him around
so?" Each of the next three ask, instead, "What is the source of May's
strength in the confrontation?" Each answer is straightforward, albeit
projected variously: SEX. The three Januarys' minds are fine, but each
lets bodily impulses distract him. None notices, however, that similar
impulses are affecting his wife. The Mays of O2–4, in looking up and
twice requesting "peres," have on their minds Damyan's dangling fruit,
not the tree's.

In the many folktale and literary analogues to the "enchanted pear
tree" story, the tree, unless unspecified, bears pears—there is nary a plum
tree in the lot.[3] Why such consistency? Critics differ, sometimes vehemently, on the issue of "Freudian" imagery. The Parson's staff is not phallic, presumably, but what about Absolon's hot poker? (*GP* l. 495; *MlrT*
l. 3776).

I have shown that the fifteenth-century author of the *Prologue* to the
Tale of Beryn keeps the Absolon-like Pardoner's gratuitous staff present
in scenes of potential and frustrated sexuality, but that this author remains unmoved by the homosexual potential which twentieth-century
commentators hear in "burdoun." Potential for sexuality may reside am-
biguously in a given text, that is, along with so much else. Its actualiza-
tion depends on the mental ear of the beholder. To O2–3 and several
other readers-aloud, "peres" overtly symbolize genitals; to most readers-
aloud and to nearly any teller of an "enchanted pear tree" analogue, they
do not.[4]

In this first of three representative confrontations between strong, virile
men and strong, sexy women, O2 stages a sort of caricatured wrestling
match. Its fixed outcome conveys its moral: Beware of dangerous female
sexuality. In this corner, ladies and gentlemen, the black-caped evil queen
who threatens Snow White, or who attempts to foil the hero's search for
her secret headquarters from which she will orchestrate galactic takeover.
In the other corner, ladies and gentlemen, a big, dumb ox like Shakespeare's Ajax in *Troilus and Cressida,* recently blinded.

At first O2's narrator carefully withholds judgment. Decide for your-
selves after hearing the story, he tells listeners in *MctT* ll. 2320–23. The
pauses around "than" pinpoint the one satiric image in the text itself, in
that papejays do not sing merrily. O2 casts no aspersions on human song,
however. With line 2323, O2's January confidently announces his love to
the world at large.

As the combatants bound from their corners, O2's sarcasm on
"fresshe" (l. 2328) prepares us to expect other than springlike innocence
in May's voice. Indeed, her words emerge not as pleas but as sinister

threats, especially "allas, my syde!" and "moste han." Both her mouthings of "peres" clearly name Damyan's tempting fruit. If she dies, her line 2337 says, January will certainly be condemned to a torturous death for her foul and unnatural murder. O2's May puts no pretense whatsoever into her voice, particularly not into the "help" that she states with exasperation in line 2334. She stresses *"my . . . plit,"* and pauses afterward, as a reminder that he will murder both wife and fetal heir (l. 2335).

O2's January is deaf indeed to insincere vocal inflections—who could believe she asks help of any sort with line 2334?—and dense in other ways. He pauses before line 2340 in wonderment, as if just realizing or remembering his blindness. His disability is recent, as senility is for O1's January. But with his voice, still loud and strong, O2's January gives May a match for our money.

May's next words, nurselike, soothe January's agitation at his unaccustomed handicap. Immediately after *MctT* l. 2340 though, her voice slides back toward cunning. O2's January, being not of a suspicious nature, believes her. Placid like an ox, he agrees to help in lines 2346–47.

With strong caesuras in lines 2348–49, plus a louder "up she gooth" that imitates May's action with rising vocal pitch, O2's narrator predicts exciting times ahead. Rushing on, at line 2350 he interrupts himself with a sudden realization, finger upraised, of responsibility toward the fairer sex. He switches his tone from "stay-tuned-for-further-adventures" to stern disapproval. He certainly would not want Madame Eglentyne to question his position on sin. Yet, as he slows down for the juicy lines 2352–53, long pauses force the ladies to picture the scene that his overt vocal tone condemns: "this Damyan . . . / Gan pullen up . . . the smok . . . and *in* . . . he *throng*." He does not splatter the ladies' faces with filth, as do six narrators including O5's, but he does rather enjoy making them tacitly acknowledge that large domestic animals have to relieve themselves someplace.

Back to adventures then, O2's more and more excited narrator imitates January's moods even when not quoting him directly. This oral onomatopoeia occurs most decisively in the shift from January's feelings when he sees his wife dressed by Damyan, back to the narrator's second apology. The sharp break between "been" and "expressed," in line 2362, is followed by a slyly parenthetical line 2363 that reminds the ladies how much fun we all had picturing the upraised smock and thringing ten lines earlier. Imitating January's feelings again for lines 2364–65, O2 roars "roryng."

January's scolding exclamations sound firm, indeed demanding, especially on "stronge lady stoore" (l. 2367). Likewise firm and demanding,

O2's May calls out from higher in the tree than are most Mays. Even before she thinks up a precise excuse, she notes that leaves and branches might have blocked his view. After line 2371 she shifts from long-distance down-calling to a more thoughtful tone, using each half line of 2372–73 as another stalling tactic. Then she shouts downward again, with her solution. Perhaps Proserpyne provides the final phrase, in between "man" and "upon a tree" (l. 2374). But the pause seems instead to express May's own satisfaction at her apt choice of verb.

Verb or no verb, O2's January is 100 percent certain that he saw not struggling but swiving: "in it *wente*." He accuses her in lines 2376–79, angrily demands answers now for lying as well as for infidelity. O2's May accuses him in return of unappreciativeness. Her irritation flames into open anger in line 2382. But, like an elementary-school teacher in a very tough neighborhood, she then controls herself to state in line 2383 an excruciatingly clear contrast between what he supposes is the case and what is in fact the case.

On "I se" (l. 2384) an angry chuckle erupts from O2's January, so sure of himself that already he is planning her punishment. Owing to doubt about his own "trouthe," apparently, not to anything May has said, January suddenly wonders in a pause before "me thoughte" what it was he did see. Catching himself, he finishes line 2386 in tones again loud and demanding. But his softer "me thoughte" pokes a hole through the dyke at last.

Too smart to change tactics that have produced the desired effect, O2's May performs lines 2387–89 in irritated tones precisely echoing those in lines 2380–83. She does not scold but calmly states his inadequacy in each first line (2380, 2387), then in the rest of each speech points out the further inadequacy of his failure to appreciate her recent efforts on his behalf.

Sounding unhappy but somewhat more subdued, O2's January asks her to come down. Are his lines 2390–92 a ploy to get her within wife-battering range? Certainly his anger seems barely under control as he repictures the scene, with resentful pauses after "hadde" in line 2394 and before "hadde" in line 2395, followed by a half line again agitated.

O2's May is one good worker with streetwise, potentially violent children. She appreciates January's viewpoint with line 2396, which her didactic tone makes proverbial. Then she launches into a very firm and ultimately calming explanation of what she knows, which he would be better off knowing. She ends her lecture with a second proverb, line 2410, though with only a hint of the finger-wagging tone that here will emit from O3's sex-symbol-turned-grandmother. Although O2's January would not stand for such condescension, he does respond well to pretended respect for his opinion.

By now May's dangerous sexuality seems rather in abeyance, certainly left outside the graffiti-scarred classroom door. She leaps down, accompanied by oral onomatopoeia. The carefully neutral narrator of O2's line 2411, however, then reevokes the sinister female sexuality that lurks behind May's control of such a formidably muscled opponent. During *MctT* ll. 2412–18, O2 performs both words "glad" with up-pitches echoing each other, exuding irony and caution. Beware, good men, says O2, for your own gladness may be as self-deluded as January's. O2's calmly sarcastic sexual words "kisseth," "clippeth," "wombe," and "stroketh" specify the exact moral. Beware of the sexual evil that Eve brought to man in another garden, under another fruit tree—Eve, as opposed to God's mother, St. Mary. All women are not alike.

Nor are all Mays alike, by a long shot, not even the two Mays performed by O2 and O3 as near-allegorical models of manipulative female sexuality. O3's narrator sympathizes with January. He himself expresses disapproval only of the situation, however, and lets listeners form their own opinions of its victim, who at *MctT* l. 2323 sings the pathetic song of a very, very old man. Having outlived his allotted time on earth but still chipper, O3's January sings kindly and shakily. The long pauses suggest both hopeful tentativeness—will she like my song this time?—and aged shortness of breath.

It is no wonder that O3's narrator disapproves of May from the start, for his well-meaning oldster must cope with the likes of Marilyn Monroe, Mae West, Cleopatra. Whomever she echoes in lines 2329–37, O3's sexpot May speaks firmly, without threatening like O2's. No need for threats when the outcome is certain. She speaks of the dangling pears and her imminent death in tones that would make a request to take out the garbage sound like an ad for nude rap sessions. January must already know she is pregnant, for both "my syde" and "plit" (ll. 2329, 2335) are matter-of-fact reminders. A blonde bombshell needs no aid from motherhood to get her own way.

O3's May conveys sensuality with breathy eagerness, especially on lines 2332 and 2334. In between she slows down and develops fully the sexual possibilities of "smale peres grene," with tones already hinted in the "peres" of line 2331. We sighted listeners hear the dramatic irony, for we see Damyan crouched overhead. But to O3's January, her hungry sensuality on "peres" blends right into his wife's standard tone of request.

O3's May ends her first speech with a note of warning in her voice, a reminder that January will never understand the mysterious ways of the

fairer sex. Sedate and sad in *MctT* ll. 2338–40, January accepts his mas-
culine shortcomings in hopes she will do likewise. She does. Then, as she
eagerly shares with her sugar daddy a plan she thought up all by her lil
ol self, her red satin voice ripples toward a pout. But such is not her style:
the "mystruste me" of O3's May charmingly protests his attitude without
risk of cracking her makeup (l. 2343).

As a very sincere January agrees to help her, the narrator's warning
glows dimly through his "herte blood" (l. 2347). O3's narrator, however
stern his personal stance, respects the intelligence of his listening audience
(whether us or the pilgrims or both). He knows that a gloomy lecture has
far less effect than does a tale that forces us to decide right and wrong
for ourselves. So he clenches his jaw and describes the action in lines
2348–49 with long pauses, pretending it does not bother him, sighing
midway through line 2350 at the difficulty of holding back disapproval.
His effort to arrive at a nonjudgmental way of saying "*in* . . . he throng"
lets him pass almost without notice his automatic polite apology.

By speeding up throughout *MctT* ll. 2354–65, O3's narrator converts
the reluctance he felt about creative adultery into eagerness to share January's all-too-brief moment of joy (ll. 2355–60). The narrator's second
apology is again polite, but more pointed, like a curse word spoken from
a pulpit to direct the congregation's attention toward tortures that could
await them there (ll. 2362–63). Verbal propriety must sometimes bow to
greater causes.

O3's January exclaims in near-physical pain. No dogs are about, unfortunately: his torment at line 2366 consists of a switchblade thrust to
his heart on "ooo-ooout!" followed by shouts to passers-by, "Stop that
man!" By the next line (2367) his pain has become emotional, even a bit
accusatory. A pause after "stronge" calls into question the appropriateness of the term "lady."

A blonde bombshell conducts herself becomingly at all times, even in
unforeseen circumstances. At first scolding January with the self-
assurance of a hostess crooking her finger to the butler, as she confronts
a supposed friend of delayed guests stuffing his threadbare tuxedo with
the more protein-rich hors d'oeuvres, by line 2371 May's voice shifts to
clear irritation. Speeding up until the last half of line 2375, she pointedly
uses "*ful* . . . *good* . . . entente" to let him know who will have to bear
the consequences should he fail to appreciate her good intentions.

The gloriously, rapturously indignant "strugle!" of O3's January
makes for a moment of laugh-out-loud comedy in O3's conception of the
dialogue. January hollers indignation that is almost as forceful on the

verbs "swyved" and "hanged," gasping disbelief at her denial, especially on the word "yen" (ll. 2376–79).

Very quietly and elegantly, in contrast to her husband, O3's May expresses a ladylike indignation that he would address her so at all, much less in front of one of the servants (ll. 2380–83). January's phrase "I se" already conveys self-doubt: loud, low, and almost mean on "I," his voice decreases in volume and rises in pitch to a falsetto on "se" that projects both old age and a question mark. His voice goes on to waver uncontrollably between loud and soft volume and high and low pitches, a transmitter on the blink throughout *MctT* ll. 2384–86.

No break to indicate doubt occurs at O3's "me thoughte," just a gradual slowdown and decrease in volume after the phrase, accompanied by markedly more regular shifts from too-high to too-low pitches in the last half line of 2386. May responds in a voice louder than before. Perhaps Damyan, who so loyally helped cure his lord's blindness, has discreetly moved out of earshot since her last speech. With line 2387 May scolds her lord, more in disappointment than in anger, and with line 2388 she lets him know that she too can suffer from hurt feelings. If O3's January were a fully acute listener, he with us could detect the insincerity of her "allas!" on up-leaping pitches, which slip of the tongue she covers by pounding extra sincerity into "was . . . so . . . kynde" (*MctT* l. 2389).

After a long pause before "now" to think matters through, O3's January decides, "Oh dearie me, mustn't have a fuss," and so speaks kindly in lines 2390–92. He repictures the scene's details with long pauses, particularly before and after "by thee leyn." Like O1's duller-witted January, he is talking to himself rather than to May.

Slowly, still bearing the burden of hurt feelings during *MctT* l. 2396, O3's May inserts vocal quotation marks around "wene" to specify that the flaw in his assumption was "I wende han seyn" (l. 2393). Her sad voice slides sometimes toward cunning, especially on "sleep," "ybe," "yse," and "yseyn" (ll. 2397, 2401–4). The long *e* sound shared by these line-ending words helps create the cunning here in O3's reading, though not necessarily at O3's long *es* elsewhere nor at these lines in other readings. An extended expulsion of breath after each long-*e* syllable suggests May's shifty-eyed stall for time while she checks the effect on January of each step of her argument. O3's May pauses before "ful" in line 2406 to cheer herself with the realization that more trysts are sure to follow this too-brief one (cf. O1).

With her louder words "many," "weneth," and "seen" in line 2408, O3's May again points out January's flawed assumption of line 2393.

Wagging her finger then, scarlet lady playing rosy-cheeked grandma, May aims these traditional words of wisdom straight at her husband. She pauses after each pronoun such that "he" means "you."

Folklorists seeking the elusive definition of a proverb might consider these various readings-aloud of *MctT* l. 2410 (and O2's l. 2396). One instantly recognizes the proverbs of one's own culture but not of another. Attempts to define even just Western proverbs in terms of their usual binary structure still do not distinguish a proverb from any made-up balanced sentence.[5] How do we know that a given sentence, often containing binary opposition, conveys the wisdom of the ages rather than just that of the speaker? Performance, again: Mays O1–4 are passing on traditional words of advice by applying them to the immediate situation, whereas O5's May will exclaim line 2410 as a well-turned phrase without the advisory tone of voice that would signal a proverb.

Perhaps discouraged at May's use of folk wisdom in addition to female sexuality, O3's narrator sounds rather glum as he reports her leap with an oral onomatopoetic drop in pitch from "leep" to "doun" in line 2411. Throughout *MctT* ll. 2412–18, he represses disapproval by means of long pauses and a clenched jaw. The effect resembles that with which C9 opens the Prioress's portrait, except that O3 carefully continues to refrain from open scorn toward the characters being described. If the content alone of the story does not warn listeners, they themselves are as foolish as January.

O3's January is not all that foolish, though, compared to O1's and many others not heard here. O3's May must watch her tongue to deliver in convincing tones of voice a story that he will believe. Sensuality works on him, she knows, as do proverbial wisdom and appeal to his noble station in life and proper behavior therein. She quickly makes up for her few inflectional slips. While we listeners know that she is contemplating Damyan's "smale peres grene," for example, O3's January assumes that as usual she is hungry for his own lovin', and she follows her momentarily insincere "allas!" with an extra-sincere claim of kindness (ll. 2333, 2389). O3's May addresses a real challenge.

O4's May likewise faces a challenge. So does O4's January. Moreover, each character respects and appreciates the other's strength, and O4's narrator appreciates the roles of both in a good story—in a *Merchant's Tale* told for its own sake, in the contest en route to Canterbury, rather than for the sake of a moral or misogyny.

From line 2323, O4's January sounds fatherly and sincere in his love. O4's May projects adult female sexuality but without the exaggerated sensuality of O3's or the evil threat of O2's. Sounding more like a very classy mistress than a wife, she makes her latest request for a gift in exchange for sexual favors sound reasonable indeed. After a sad "allas, my syde!" a long pause gives her lover time to wonder. Her elegantly agitated lines 2330–34 would leave January relieved to hear "peres" in lieu of the "minke cote" he might well expect her to claim to die without. To O4's January, that is, vocal quotation marks around "peres" specify it as the item being requested, whereas we overhearers can understand these as euphemistic quotation marks around what besides pears may dangle in a tree. May as courtly mistress stresses the verbs "dye" and "dyen" (ll. 2332, 2337) in the exaggerated metaphorical sense familiar from "courtly love" conventions: "Oh, please do. I'll just die if you don't." "How sad that would be! But first you must prove yourself worthy."

O4's May knows perfectly well that January will not believe that failure to provide green fruit can actually kill her and January Junior. But she does know how to use vocal tones that wrap him around her little finger without his even feeling bent. Note the contrast between line 2334 read by O4 and O2. Each reader-aloud states "help" rather than asking for help. But O2's May invokes heaven's queen almost as a curse, lip curled in scorn at her husband's thick head, whereas O4's May speaks gently of the Virgin. Her pause after "love" radiates that tender heavenly emotion, suffusing it into January's brain as if meant for him.

O4's May, like O3's, must use every vocal trick in the book to persuade the brisk, kindly soul who regretfully points out some logistical problems in *MctT* ll. 2338–40. In her calm presentation of a plan, May's voice tilts briefly toward a sinister tone on "take" (l. 2342). But she recovers, using the entire next line as cover-up for that one inflectional slip of her tongue. With "mystruste *me*" rather than the usual "mys*truste* me," her stress pattern makes his jealousy sound particularly unfair, as if he gives free rein to his other women.

After January agrees, still kindly, O4's discreet narrator begins to tell what happened. The strong caesuras in *MctT* ll. 2348–49 indicate hesitation to describe—hesitation caused primarily by his awareness from the start that such actions are not properly told in mixed company and only secondarily by the narrator's distaste for the actions themselves. Having apologized sincerely, O4's narrator eliminates even the tone "Imagine that!" that he had interjected into lines 2348–49. He hurries past lines 2352–53 to get on with the less problematic parts of the story, satisfied to have done just what Miss Manners would advise.

The narrator's "Imagine that!" recurs during O4's lines 2354–65, notably on "evere he myghte," "wyf," and "Damyan" (ll. 2356, 2359,

2361). Lowered pitch for the second apology makes it sound both regretful about Damyan's treachery and parenthetical (l. 2363).

With four exclamations, O4's January angrily scolds his four dogs for jumping on the postman, among them Out actually nipping. His line 2367 then conveys surprised accusation by a kind, dignified provider who has never before had reason for shock.

Just as surprised as January, O4's May explains what she had assumed he already knew. Her pause after "holpe" particularly projects, "How could you think otherwise?" (l. 2370). She realizes then that she may be being a bit rough on him: a man could watch women quilting all day and remain quite unable to form the stitches himself. So she patiently and kindly explains just what she has done, how, and why.

She has not reckoned with the potential for outburst in O4's January. Perhaps he has never before lost his temper in her presence. In his line 2376 indignation prevails, then accusation of shameful behavior in line 2377, then righteous anger in lines 2378–79. A bit peeved, O4's May narrows her eyes during line 2380. She considers her next move with an edge of cunning in her voice. She decides to act just a bit hurt, indicated by separated words in line 2382, and very, very sure of herself. She states *MctT* l. 2383 as if to conclude the argument.

No such luck. Her tactic almost backfires, bringing a mean sneer to January's line 2384. He is calm, certain, loud—then very slightly softer just for "me thoughte" in line 2386 before boosting his volume again. But the dyke has been penetrated. As does O2's, O4's May aims straight for the crumbling edges.

"Ah, he can be made to believe he's mad," says May's line 2387—mad/crazy, that is, not the mad/angry that he sounds. She tells him so in brisk exasperated tones, shrugging off his attitude as if she would be only too glad to shrug off the entire relationship and go find someone who appreciates her medical as well as sexual skills.

It takes O4's January only two long pauses, before "now" and after "passe" in line 2390, to decide with a sad sigh, "Why bother?" In the long run, he tells himself, this incident of infidelity will fade and our relationship be all the stronger for it. He sounds kind and forgiving throughout *MctT* ll. 2390–95, adding a note of puzzlement as he reportrays the scene. He is not puzzled by what he saw; he knows perfectly well what he saw and intends never to let it happen again. Instead, he delivers lines 2394–95 as a challenge to May, curious what she will come up with next.

She does him proud. The next time January gets stopped for speeding in his Mercedes, even if she hasn't time to slide a pillow up her dress and fake labor pains, O4's May will come up with some excuse as plausible and elaborate as this one. Alternating between the well-bred voice of a prep-school student repeating yesterday's science lesson to the class as requested and the wise advisory tones that culminate in the proverbial line 2410, O4's May shows him that she's Big Daddy's girl after all—no, Big Daddy's lady, and a worthy opponent in the battle of the sexes. Leading into his cheerful, amoral conclusion, O4's narrator takes two pitch leaps to bring May down out of the tree, creating oral onomatopoeia with "that word" as well as on "leep doun" (l. 2411).

Suppose that the speech synthesizer, so useful now to technical linguists, could someday be programmed to compensate for differences in individual voices, such that cuts O2, O3, and O4 each would display a comparable pitch drop from "leep" to "doun." From the voiceprints, could we then predict that O3's "leep doun" helps characterize a glum narrator about to repress disapproval, O2's an adventure-show host about to draw a misogynistic moral, and O4's a cheerful storyteller ending a story? In a word, no. Human language must describe human texts.

Each of us reads the same text. To describe its meaning, we use critical terminology developed since the time of Aristotle. With the advancing technology of that time, men had begun using the craft of writing for epic, drama, and song as well as for business transactions, to the dismay of many who feared that loss of human memory and improvisational skill would result.[6] These detractors were quite right.

Twenty-five centuries later, literary critics are hauling around an immense critical vocabulary and spewing reams of interpretation, just to try to analyze literature as it ought to be understood—as human interaction, as words by and about and for humans, all of whom respond as individual men or women to birth, death, food, sexual intercourse, and sometimes dogs and horses. Humans do not change, but they do invent things and they do tell stories, whether or not they write them down. This recent development in technology, sound recording, at last provides material for close comparisons that show how fully versatile some written texts can be.

Close comparison will eventually allow examination of the process by which one passes aesthetic judgments on possible interpretations of a text, that huge issue I have studiously evaded here. Chaucer's text itself is aesthetically good, I maintain, and has lasted through the centuries as great literature precisely because it does allow such a variety of aesthetically possible interpretations. We all have our favorites, though, and mine is O5's.

Why do I like this performance best? I preferred it before I came to realize how remarkable were its parallels to Pope's modernization—the dignified January, the sweet-talking May who trembles at line 2368 and bawls at line 2389—parallels seen from the opposite moods, though, of O5's bitter narrator and Pope's genial one. I like O5, I suppose, primarily because it makes me laugh the hardest. It brings out Chaucer's sense of humor, which is why I like Chaucer. In addition, it proves untrue critics' assumption that the *Tale* must either be funny or else be told by a misogynist, for O5's *Tale* is both.

Initially reluctant to describe the scene, O5's narrator overlays January's song with tones conveying that the blind knight expects to command love with *MctT* l. 2323. Although O5's January assumes that he is in total control of the situation, listeners can soon hear that he is not quite as smart as he thinks.

Listeners begin to feel amused disdain for January's acuity as the voice of Daddy's little girl heaps pink, ruffled flounces to smother his mind. Then we can hear, as O5's January cannot, that in line 2331 May's pause stops her from naming what she really craves other than "peres." O5's May brushes past the first "dye" (l. 2332) in an adorably brave attempt to pretend she is not scared to death, but then gets weepier and weepier at the thought of it. Her pauses in *MctT* l. 2335, "in . . . my . . . plit," differ from the pause before "peres" in that both January and we listeners-in hear the phrase's pregnant significance. As soon as she announces the news to her husband, her weepiness slackens. When she speaks again of her death (l. 2337) it is with wonderment: "Wouldn't dying be just too awful?"

Other than giving rather a quack on his first "allas!" O5's January responds quite sedately for someone who has just learned that his child-wife is about to expire and take his heir with her. He states the problem. She suggests the solution, still little-girl weak (especially for "sauf" in line 2341) but no longer weepy. With just the teensiest cute pout on "mystruste me" (l. 2343) she clinches her request. O5's narrator snarls his disapproval of her, particularly on "quod she" (l. 2344).

A slow, respectable January agrees to her request in lines 2346–47. Expressing sympathy for January by continuing to disapprove of May's actions, in lines 2348–49, O5's narrator then shifts to address the pilgrim audience. He turns resentment about his wife into hatred for all women, as do many Merchants both here and at *MctT* l. 1250 (Cut L1). O5 explodes "throng" in the vocal equivalent of a flasher exposing himself. For lines 2354–62 he shifts back to disapproval of May and Damyan, gloating at the shock he has caused the two nuns if not Alysoun, pretending that by labeling adultery "wrong" (l. 2354) he can deny responsibility for the insult. The long pauses before and after line 2363, with its smirking, dare-ya-to-stop-me tone, reassert his misogyny. Even the image of mothers mourning babies rouses in him no softer emotions toward womankind, just sarcasm.

January's dignity remains, albeit altered, in *MctT* ll. 2366–67. He gasps in shock, in near-physical pain like O3's. His separate, gasping words sound as if he is being jabbed time after time with a cattle prod supplied by the C.I.A., and is holding back the shrieks that a weaker man might utter.

A long pause before "sire" leaves May's reply far less ready to hand than are those of other twentieth-century Mays. She sounds surprised, as do many, but a bit frightened besides. As the answer comes to her, that fright in retrospect might seem to be concern that January has flipped out. But in *MctT* l. 2368, especially in contrast to the fake, little-girl timidity with which she earlier contemplated dying, her voice momentarily projects genuine fear that after so much planning she has been caught *in flagrante* after all.

Surprise and fear continue for one and one-third lines more. By no means commanding him with line 2369, she gasps the first words that pop into her head, just in order to block whatever he might say next. But during the pause in *MctT* l. 2370, precisely between "yow" and "holpe," Proserpyne's radio signals reach May's brain and take control of her tongue. The surprise and fear in her voice become surprise and relief as line 2370 ends.

Clear transmission of Proserpyne's gift is a skill not acquired smoothly. Maintaining her tone of wonder at the phenomenon, O5's May pauses twice more to await clearer reception: in line 2372 at "was . . . taught" and in line 2374 at "than . . . struggle." By "ful . . . good . . . entente" (l. 2375) her voice has become openly defiant, a far cry indeed from pink, ruffled pouts.

If O5's January gasped in pain at the sight, how much harder must he gasp at the sound of his child-wife's defense and defiance. His snorting, sputtering indignation is so extreme as to disrupt meter for *MctT* l. 2376, the same as it does in several lines by O1 and others.

Such metrical disruption is an issue but not really a problem. Reading silently, one can imagine a character speaking and coughing or sputtering simultaneously. Writing, one can describe the implications of any imagined sound effects. Reading aloud, in one's own classroom or in the occasional public situation that some Chaucerians encounter, each individual must decide whether attempted metrical regularity (not to call it monotony) should take precedence over imaginative, living oral perform-ance. Far be it from me to express any subjective prejudice on the matter.

A related problem applies more specifically to the classroom, since no one would publicly mispronounce as many vowels as does O5. Her fre-quent Modern English vowels do grate on my ears as they would not grate on the ears of one of O5's students, for whom these oddly-spelled words in a small-print text would be leaping off the page to form full-color comic characters in spite of the bitter pilgrim who describes them.

As noted, however, O5 is the only reader-aloud for this project who is not a Chaucer professor. If she were, she would practice pronunciation, as we all did before we began teaching. Like most Americans, she could take as model Helge Kökeritz's phonetic transcriptions of Middle En-glish. Apparently, in fact, some professors have termed Kökeritz's tran-scriptions so authoritative that their former students, now heading classrooms of their own, hesitate to read Chaucer aloud for fear of mak-ing a mistake. Anyone thus intimidated should listen to the recording that Kökeritz made to accompany his pamphlet, on which he occasion-ally deviates from his own transcriptions. He also cannot act, not at all, but that is another issue.[7]

Criseyde forgave Pandarus, and I forgive O5 for incorrect vowels. Oth-ers may make their peace otherwise. Nearly every reader-aloud taped, including top-rank Chaucerians, occasionally in the press of oral delivery let slip an "aye" for an "I."

Neither pronunciation nor performance is there on the page. Out loud, the offended amazement in the voice of O5's January quite overshadows the Modern English pronouns in "he swyved thee" (l. 2378). And one barely notices the metrical irregularity due to O5's ending *MctT* l. 2382 with "wordes to me," for O5's May begins to cry during line 2381, sinks to weep weakly while accusing him of meanness in line 2382, and then summons her pretense of courage to sound slightly defiant again for line 2383.

January's tone of defiance on line 2384, echoing hers, is mixed with worry not weeping. Brow furrowing, he rushes through automatic vows to God and trouthe only to pause, confused, before a quick "me thoughte he dide thee so" made doubtful by up-pitches (l. 2386). The moment has come for May's full-scale tears, as in Pope. Two whimpers lead off, one displacing "ye" such that only one syllable disrupts the meter. Then she bursts into bawling so severe that she can barely choke out the words and ends line 2389 trailing off in a blubber.

January is aghast. Oh my goodness gracious, whatever have I done?

He stutters in amazement without marring the meter of line 2391, "Com
. . . com doun," and on "my lief" shifts from amazement to the soothing,
stroking voice of an adult who takes responsibility for a child's hurt. In
the aural effect of Pope's "I *thought* I saw," O5's January hesitates for a
moment to abandon his vision: "I . . . I *wende* han seyn" (l. 2393).
Slightly defying her again, but more gently than before, he pauses to
recall the exact details twice, once before "by thee" in line 2394 (this
pause also expressing reluctance to name such an unthinkable action)
and again before the clause in line 2395.

May emerges only gradually from her crying fit, dabbing her mascara
lest Damyan see while addressing January in the triumphant tone of
someone who has just been assured that that nasty old table corner did
indeed reach out and hit her. The tears are gone by *MctT* l. 2400, replaced
by May's earlier tone of wonder as Proserpyne's full-length scientific explanation emits from her mouth with only a few pauses to articulate
details. May's more frequent pauses in line 2406, however, "Ther may
ful . . . many a . . . sighte . . . yow . . . begile," suggest not a delay in
rebroadcasting but instead May's own interaction with Proserpyne's
words, her own hopeful realization that if this trick worked once it might
work again (cf. O1, O3).

May's air of wonder continues through the elsewhere-proverbial line
2410, which she exclaims as if it were a new revelation. O5's narrator,
sounding more resigned than resentful on line 2411, promptly reverts to
the bitter autobiographer. Although he stresses "kisseth" and "clippeth"
in line 2413, as does O2, he creates an inner- rather than outer-directed
effect. O2 makes the sexual verbs sarcastic so that listeners will hear and
heed the moral, that is, whereas O5 draws no moral at all beyond scath-
ing indignation at his own situation. Indignation flares too in the long
pause and intake of breath before line 2415. The address to "goode men"
assures them that they, unlike O5's Merchant, would never act so foolishly as to trust any woman.

Alexander Pope's good-natured narrator, in contrast, tacks a still-
ambiguous moral onto a similarly staged comic story. As mentioned, only
one reader-aloud other than O5 projects a dignified January's manipulation by Daddy's little girl. That reader's similar May is fully in control
at line 2368, however, sounds weepy only at the end of line 2388, and in
other ways differs slightly from the conceptions of both Pope and O5.
This other narrator ends the *Merchant's Tale* with the sad resignation
which began it, futhermore, not with Pope's amusement or O5's bitterness.

Though told by three such different narrators, these three stagings eerily resemble one another otherwise and differ from all the rest. They are done by a British male educated at Oxford in the 1940s, an American female educated at Harvard in the 1960s, and a British male educated at home in the 1690s. Would Chaucer's own dramatization have been the same as theirs, or different? Or ambiguous?

Bringing It All Back Home

For tyme ylost may nought recovered be.   (*Tr* 4.1283)

For tyme ylost, this knowen ye,
Be no way may recovered be.   (*HF* ll. 1257–58)

Odds and ends, odds and ends,
Lost time is not found again.   (Bob Dylan, © 1970, Dwarf Music)

He that mysconceyveth, he mysdemeth.   (*MctT* l. 2410)

Come mothers and fathers, throughout the land,
And don't criticize what you can't understand.
(Bob Dylan, © 1963, M. Witmark)

Bob Dylan, writing couplets intended for oral delivery, uses proverbs and proverblike lines just as Chaucer did. As does other folklore, a proverb represents the expression of whatever in human nature stays the same across time and space, even while each individual member of each specific culture uses and understands differently that item of folklore. Individual authors live and die, reach and do not reach intended audiences. Oral proverbs endure. On the page, January claims the potential of green-and-white laurel rather than the worthlessness of a leek. Yet for three centuries nearly everybody, including the scribe whose May evaluates her husband's swiving, remembers January as a worthless old man with green tail and white head.

Early editors printed little hands in margins to point out Chaucer's proverbs and sententiae. Early college teachers of Chaucer did the same orally by citing analogous proverbs from nineteenth-century folklore collections. A century ago, they and their successors taught equally the value of folklore studies for English and that of English for folklore studies, as well as the relevance of both for the accepted academic disciplines of classical literature and rhetoric/oratory/elocution. In the beginning, one individual—Francis James Child, George Lyman Kittredge, F. N. Robinson, B. J. Whiting, Stith Thompson—would both analyze English literature and collect or organize ballads, proverbs, folktales, customs. The Modern Language Association was founded in 1883, the American Folklore Society in 1888; the same individuals were active in the leadership of both organizations.

The history has yet to be written of the process by which folklore so abruptly became regarded as a ragged stepsister of the legitimate, indeed indubitable, academic discipline of English. I have noted that, because of the Folklore Dilemma, a modern folktale cannot justifiably represent the probable form in which Chaucer heard a story. Yet this dilemma slides away knotless in modern times, for which we do know the folklore current in an author's milieu. Probability even becomes certainty in a case like that of William Butler Yeats, who collected and published Irish folktales. Yet literary scholars shy from the wide-open field of folklore, preferring to plod back to the barn in the ever-deepening ruts of New Criticism, authorial biography, and (lately) demonstrations that every text is really about the act of reading texts.

As the history of the discipline is studied, the elevation of English and degradation of folklore will be shown to involve, at least in part, the prompt establishment of a canon of great English authors decreed worthy of study. Folklorists, instead, limited their material from neither a practical nor a theoretical viewpoint. Every performance of a text constitutes another valid variant, meaningful to that particular performer and audience in that particular context and just as worthy of study for its own sake as any other variant. Had the House Unamerican Activities Committee noticed the field's theoretical basis, in the early 1950s, it would have included folklorists in the Red Menace right along with singers of folk songs (such as Pete Seeger), would have made accusations and destroyed careers. For a time folklorists had to lie low, tabulate texts, sound nonsubversive. English professors, teaching Great Works, would presumably have no such problems unless they were to actually do or say something.

The essence of folklore scholarship is and has been the study of variation—of how different individuals, in different social contexts, variously interpret the same song or tale or other item. The methodology of folklore scholarship is changing, of course, changing as rapidly as is the recording technology it uses; the old historic-geographic method (i.e., mapping variants according to time and place collected) has given way to performance analysis and ethnographic research. But the study of folklore remains the study of different interpretations of the same artistic construct.

No wonder literary theorists often dissolve into jargon when they attempt to discuss the issue. Their former professors against whom they are rebelling, those professors who under the aegis of New Criticism had implied one correct interpretation per text, also neglected to teach them folklore. Subjectivist literary theory is groping to create its own methodology from the mud at the bottom of the celestial sea of English studies. Yet it need only turn its white, male, magnificently bearded head slightly to observe a fully operational world of folk and folklorists already busy doing just what theory has decreed is henceforth important to do.

Folklorists already know how interpretations vary. To some extent they even know why, know that each performer is able to express his or her own concerns and creativity within a traditional form. Similarly, a silent reader of an author's fixed text experiences and thereby recreates it anew.

Even bigger questions loom ahead, though, questions best approached by the two disciplines hand in hand. Folklorists cannot consider aesthetic development across time, because badly told stories that appeal to no one die instantaneously. Plots analogous to the *Shipman's Tale* and *Wife of Bath's Tale* circulate now as jokes, whereas no one still tells the *Man of Law's Tale*. Did anyone ever? Presumably, but we can never prove so and cannot even guess the form of oral constancy romances.

In English studies, however, we do have as basis for aesthetic comparison written texts that survive because they are written, not because they are good. Why would *Five Hundred Years of Lydgate Criticism and Allusion* fill no more than a pamphlet? Why do twentieth-century Lydgate scholars differ primarily in their tones of justification for reading him at all? Chaucer has something that Lydgate lacks, something that involves the continuity of humans as beings who share inexpressible feelings as well as articulable thoughts.

Because people invent technology, society's external appearances do change across time. Technology, in turn, translated into tape recorders and computers and photocopiers and telecommunications and travel and interlibrary loan, can help us understand more fully how very different each person is from another and how very much alike people always have been.

Blake says so too—Blake, who invented a new engraving technique, proposed public frescoes, and in other ways hoped to use new technologies of visual and verbal art to let the general public experience the nonrational force of creative genius that unites all humanity. In his *Descriptive Catalogue*, echoing Dryden, Blake says that

> Chaucer's characters . . . are the physiognomies or lineaments of universal human life, beyond which Nature never steps. Names alter, things never alter. I have known multitudes of those who would have been monks in the age of monkery, who in this deistical age are deists. As Newton numbered the stars, and as Linneus numbered the plants, so Chaucer numbered the classes of men.
>
> The Painter has consequently varied the heads and forms of his personages into all Nature's varieties; the Horses he has also varied to accord to their Riders.

APPENDIX A

Identities of Readers-Aloud Who Wish To Be Identified

Marie Borroff: F6, G22, J3, K6, L3
Erika Brady: A4, C5, D8, F7, G8, O5
Derek Brewer: E1, E4, L1
Emerson Brown, Jr.: G17, K2, O3
John Burrow: C2, D4, E6, G7, J5
Michael D. Cherniss: C7, G13
Howell D. Chickering, Jr.: A2, G3
Susan Crane: G14, G25, J4, M2, N2
Alfred David: F1–3, G18, K4
E. Talbot Donaldson: C3, G21
Peter Elbow: G11
Hardy Long Frank: A3, A5, G16, H2
Robert Worth Frank, Jr.: B2, C4, G6, H1, J1
Elizabeth Hatcher: B4, G24, I4, M4

Donald R. Howard: D5, E2, G9, I3, K3, M3, O1
Priscilla Martin: A1, E3, L2, O4
Miriam Youngerman Miller: B3, D3
Alice Miskimin, Esq.: G26, N3
Charles A. Owen: G23, L4
Derek Pearsall: G4, I1, N4
Florence Ridley: C6, F4, G19
Bruce Rosenberg: G12
Paul Ruggiers: G15
Wayne Shumaker: G2
Daniel Silvia: B1, C9, D1, G1, K1
Anthony C. Spearing: C8, D2, F5, G5, I2
Martin Stevens: D7, O2

Canterbury Tales Modernizations, 1700–1775

Introduction

The first modernizations of Chaucer's tales were John Dryden's in 1700. In 1775 Thomas Tyrwhitt's manuscript-collated edition (with glossary added in 1778), the first edition published smaller than folio size, began to make *Canterbury Tales* itself available to a wide reading audience. In between these two dates, the eighteenth century's understanding of Chaucer was governed in large part by the Chaucer accessible: modernizations published in periodicals, miscellanies, editions of Dryden and Pope, and Ogle's 1741 collection.

In this appendix, the modernizations are accounted for following the *Tale* order of Robinson's second edition (i.e., *KnT, MlrT, RvT, CkT, MLT, WBP, WBT, FrT, SumT, ClT, MctT, SqT, ShipT, NPT, MancT*), then for each *Tale* according to the date of its original publication. For each modernization I provide the following information:

1. Name of tale; name of author, with attributions whenever possible for anonymous and pseudonymous poems; number of lines in the poem. I do not guarantee exact line counts, especially for the longest poems.
2. Bibliographic entry for first printing of the poem; in brackets, library where I examined it. I do not indicate varying typefaces in titles.
3. First four lines and last two lines (or triplet) of the poem. The capitalization, punctuation, and italics are not necessarily those of the first printing; I may copy from Ogle's reprint or a modern edition, for example.

4. Bibliographic entries for reprintings, arranged by title (if it
    varies) and then by date of publication; in brackets, library
    where I examined each.

I include only full-length modernizations, those that follow Chaucer's
entire *Tale,* the only borderline case being the 1769 *Nun's Priest's Tale* in
which the cock makes no attempt to escape from the fox's jaws. I exclude
the many cases of definite Chaucerian influence. They deserve at least a
monograph; the most recent discussion of them is Alfred Tobler's *Geoffrey Chaucer's Influence on English Literature* (1905; reprint, New York:
AMS Press, 1973). In the plan for his never-completed book, William
Alderson intended a bibliographical account of pre-1800 modernizations
of all Chaucer's works, apocryphal and not, as well as (to quote from a
handwritten draft) "some rather free improvisions on Chaucerian matter
and a few works whose titles have the interest of claiming a stricter relationship with Chaucer's poetry than their contents warrant"—his fill-
ing-out, that is, of Eleanor P. Hammond's list in her *Chaucer: A
Bibliographic Manual* (1908; reprint, New York: Peter Smith, 1933),
220–33.

I hope that someone undertakes this bulky but finite accounting, a vital
preliminary step toward understanding another century's attitudes toward Chaucer. Meanwhile, I here provide full information for pre-1775
modernizations of those *Tales* now considered Chaucer's. I exclude the
General Prologue because of complexities tangential to my immediate
inquiries: reusers of the Pope/Betterton modernization like to substitute
portraits of their own creation for one or more pilgrims.

Although I have followed all leads, I cannot guarantee that I have
found every reprinting of every modernization. Still, the present assem-
blage shows the undeniable trend: to make public Chaucer's bawdy. The
Shipman's Tale and *Reeve's Tale* attracted three modernizers apiece,
the *Miller's Tale* and *Wife of Bath's Prologue* two apiece. In contrast, the
never-reprinted *Man of Law's Tale* and *Squire's Tale* were modernized
only under contract for Ogle's collection, by hack writers apparently
being paid three pence per line. The poems most frequently reprinted
were those by Pope and Dryden, of course. But among poems by lesser-
known writers, the only ones reprinted more often than twice were the
racy ones: three reprintings for the *Summoner's Tale* (plus, as documented there, at least one apparently quashed attempt at publication),
nine reprintings for the Cobb *Miller's Tale,* and eleven reprintings for the
Pope/Betterton *Reeve's Tale.*

Abbreviations

For Chaucer's works, as usual, I have followed the abbreviations in F. N. Robinson's second edition, p. 647, with exceptions noted in abbreviations table of this book.

Because Ogle's collection (George Ogle. *The Canterbury Tales of Chaucer, Modernis'd by several Hands*. 3 vols. London: J. & R. Tonson, 1741. [NYPL; Princeton]) is cited so frequently here, I refer to it simply as Ogle. Everything included in Ogle was reprinted a year later in a Dublin edition (1742, two volumes paginated as four parts), which I do not cite.

Contents may vary widely in eighteenth-century miscellanies, even ones that share the same title, publisher, and date of publication. Therefore, for the original and each reprint of a poem, I supply the name of the library at which I examined a physically existing copy of the book or from which a specialist librarian or trusted colleague sent me precise information. I use the following abbreviations for libraries:

Folger	Folger Shakespeare Library, Washington, D.C.
Harvard	Houghton Library, Harvard University
NYPL	New York Public Library
Penn	Rare Book Collection, Van Pelt Library, University of Pennsylvania
Princeton	Firestone Library, Princeton University
Yale	Beinecke Library, Yale University

Knight's Tale, *John Dryden (2431 lines)*

"Palamon and Arcite: Or, The Knight's Tale, from Chaucer. In Three Books." In Dryden's *Fables Ancient and Modern; Translated into Verse*, 1–90. London: J. Tonson, 1700. [Penn]

> In Days of old, there liv'd, of mighty Fame
> A valiant Prince; and *Theseus* was his Name:
> A Chief, who more in Feats of Arms excell'd
> The Rising nor the Setting Sun beheld.
> ···
>
> So may the Queen of Love long Duty bless,
> And all true Lovers find the same Success.

In anticipation of the relevant volume of the new Dryden edition from the University of California Press, I have not sought reprint information.

Besides in Ogle, 1:60–183, "Palamon and Arcite" must recur in every edition of the *Fables,* at least: London printings in 1713, 1721, 1734, 1745, 1755, 1773, and 1774; Edinburgh in 1773; Glasgow in 1771. In addition, Dryden's *Knight's Tale* (and the Pope/Betterton *General Prologue* with substitutions) is the modernization provided by Thomas Morell along with his edition, *The Canterbury Tales of Chaucer, in the Original, From the Most Authentic Manuscripts; And as they are Turn'd into Modern Language by Mr. Dryden, Mr. Pope, and Other Eminent Hands* (London: For the Editor, 1737), 247–348, and in the work's second edition for J. Osborn in 1740. Concerning the Chaucer texts based on Speght's 1598 edition that were printed in the 1700 *Fables* (only), see William L. Alderson and Arnold C. Henderson, *Chaucer and Augustan Scholarship* (Berkeley and Los Angeles: Univ. of California Press, 1970), 53–68.

Miller's Tale, *Samuel Cobb (632 lines)*

"The Miller's Tale, From Chaucer. To N. Rowe Esq." In *The Carpenter of Oxford, Or, The Miller's Tale, From Chaucer. Attempted in Modern English . . . To which are added, Two Imitations of Chaucer . . . By Matthew Prior,* 1–46. London: E. Curll, R. Gosling, and J. Pemberton, 1712. [Harvard; Library of Congress; British Library]

> Whilom in *Oxford,* an old *Chuff* did dwell,
> A Carpenter by Trade, as Stories tell.
> Who by his Craft had heap'd up many a hoard,
> And furnish'd Strangers both with Bed and Board.
> ....
>
> While Nicholas is scalded in the Breech,
> My Tale is done, God save us all, and each!

Reprints under that title:
> In *A Collection of Original Poems, Translations, and Imitations, By Mr. Prior, Mr. Rowe, Dr. Swift, And Other Eminent Hands,* 2–46. London: E. Curll, 1714. [British Library]
> By itself, 3–23. London: E. Curll, 1725. [Folger]
> In *A Collection of Merry Poems: Consisting of Facetious Tales, Epigrams, &c. From Oldham, Brown, Prior, Swift, and other Eminent Poets; With some from the Weekly Papers and Miscellanies. Proposed as a pleasant Cure for the Hyp and Spleen. The Second Edition,* 7–26. London: T. Cooper, 1736. [Harvard]

Reprint as "The Carpenter of Oxford: Or, The Miller's Tale." In Ogle, 1:191–228.

Reprints as "The Credulous Husband. A Tale":

> In *The Muse in Good Humour: Or, A Collection of Comic Tales &c. from Chaucer, Prior, Swift, La Fontaine, Dr. King, and other eminent Poets. Together with some Originals. Part Second and Last,* 63–90. London: J. Noble, 1744. [Yale]
>
> In *The Muse in Good Humour: Or* [same subtitle] *Originals. Part II . . . The Second Edition,* 59–86. London: J. Noble, 1745. [Yale]
>
> In *The Muse in Good Humour: Or* [same subtitle] *Originals. Part II,* 209–36. London: F. & J. Noble, 1746. [Harvard]
>
> In *The Muse in Good Humour: or, a Collection of Comic Tales. By the most Eminent Poets. The Sixth Edition,* 234–61. London: F. & J. Noble, 1751. [Yale]
>
> In *The Muse in Good Humour: A Collection of Comic Tales. By the most Eminent Poets. The Seventh Edition,* 2 vols., 1:234–61. London: F. Noble, W. Bathoe, & J. Noble, 1766. [Indiana University]

Miller's Tale, *John Smith (827 lines)*

"The Miller's Tale. From Geoffrey Chaucer." In Smith's *Poems Upon Several Occasions,* 307–57. London: H. Clements, 1713. [Yale]

> In Days of Old, if Story does not err,
> In *Oxford* dwelt an aged *Carpenter;*
> But tho' with Riches he was amply stor'd,
> Greedy of Pelf, he *Scholars* kept at Board;
> ···
> As for the *Clerk* I leave him to resent,
> The injur'd *Husband* to his Discontent,
> The *Philomath* and Wife for ever to repent.

No reprints found.

Reeve's Tale, *Thomas Betterton [and/or Alexander Pope, according to me] (327 lines)*

"The Miller of Trompington, Or, The Reve's Tale from Chaucer." In *Miscellaneous Poems and Translations. By Several Hands,* 301–20. London: B. Lintott [*sic*], 1712. [Princeton; Folger]

At *Trompington*, not far from *Cambridge*, stood;
Across a pleasant Stream, a Bridge of Wood.
Near it, a *Mill*, in low and plashy Ground,
Where Corn for all the neighb'ring Parts was grown'd.
....

And thus the Miller of his Fear is eas'd,
The Mother and the Daughter both well pleas'd.

Reprints as "The Miller of Trompington, Or, The Reve's Tale from Chaucer," in all further editions of Lintot's miscellany, all with same title as above, all but the sixth secretly edited by Alexander Pope. The dates and page references follow:

 1714. 301–20. [Folger]
 1720. 2:261–77. [Folger; British Library]
 1722. 1:269–85. [Rice University]
 1727. 2:87–103. [Dickinson College]
 1732. 2:87–103. [University of Minnesota]

Reprints under that title also:

 In Ogle, 1:234–50.
 In *The Poetical Tell-Tale; or, Muses in Merry Story*, 80–90. London: J. Fletcher, 1764. [Yale]

Reprint as "The Miller of Trompington, From Chaucer." In *The Muse in Good Humour: Or, A Collection of Comic Tales, &c. from Chaucer, Prior, Swift, La Fontaine, Dr. King, and other eminent Poets. Together with some Originals. Part I. . . . The Fourth Edition*, 121–33. London: J. Noble, 1745. [Yale]

Reprints as "The Miller of Trompington. A Tale":

 In *The Muse in Good Humour: Or* [same subtitle] *Originals. Part I . . . The Fifth Edition*, 119–31. London: F. & J. Noble, 1746. [Harvard]
 In *The Muse in Good Humour: or, a Collection of Comic Tales. By the most Eminent Poets. The Sixth Edition*, 147–59. London: F. & J. Noble, 1751. [Yale]
 In *The Muse in Good Humour: A Collection of Comic Tales. By the most Eminent Poets. The Seventh Edition*, 2 vols., 1:147–59. London: F. Noble, W. Bathoe, & J. Noble, 1766. [Indiana University]

Reeve's Tale, *anon. (approx. 2400 lines)*

The Miller of Trompington: Being an Exercise upon Chaucer's Reeve's Tale, 9–117. London: Jonas Brown, 1715. [Harvard; Folger]

Canto I
The Argument
Of Symkin's self, and Spouse, and Daughter,
How th'Manciple fell into the Water;
How the Miller did, in Tolling, take up,
And how he set the Warden's Back up.
....

And Justice counts it nothing hard,
If Rogues receive a Rogue's reward.

No reprints found.

Reeve's Tale, *Henry Travers (378 lines)*

"The Miller of Trompington; Or, The Reeve's Tale From Chaucer." In Travers's *Miscellaneous Poems and Translations,* 2d ed., 138–60. York: C. Ward & R. Chandler, 1740. [Harvard; poem cut out of NYPL copy]

There stands at *Trompington* a Bridge of Wood,
Not far from *Cambridge* o'er the gliding Flood,
Where long had liv'd within a noted Mill
A Miller fam'd for Works of various Skill;
....

Now Purple Morn disclos'd her orient Ray,
Swift they mov'd on, and pleas'd pursu'd the Way.

No reprints found.

Cook's Tale, *George Ogle (72 lines)*

Inserted without break within his *Prologue To The Cook's Tale,* in Ogle, 2:4–8. Ingeniously, Ogle incorporates the *Cook's Tale* fragment into the teasing exchange between Host and Cook. The Cook outlines the tale he will refrain from telling, leaving it for the Host, then goes on to tell the *Tale of Gamelyn.* The transitions into and out of the *Cook's Tale* fragment are:

"But lest it shou'd be thought, I mean to rail,
"Or fret, like *Oswalde;* I defer the Tale.
"Nay, to mine *Host,* who seems full well inclin'd,
"Will sketch a Story to his Hand and Mind.
"The Flow'r of *Cooks,* young *Perkin,* let Him take,

"Whose *Christian* Name was lost in That of *Rake.*
....

"Who kept a Shop, for Fear what Folks might say,
"But kept Herself a much genteeler Way!
    "I leave it to mine Host, what Quarrel wrought
"Their high Dislike, and How, and Where they fought;

No reprints found.

Man of Law's Tale, *Henry Brooke (1644 lines)*

"Constantia: Or, The Man of Law's Tale." In Ogle, 2:104–95.

Hence, *Want,* ungrateful Visitant, adieu,
Pale Empress hence, with all thy meager Crew,
Sour Discontent, and mortify'd Chagrin;
Lean hollow Care, and self-corroding Spleen,
....

In Shouts to Heav'n their Exultations fly,
And universal Joy torments the Sky.

No reprints found.

Wife of Bath's Prologue, *Alexander Pope (439 lines)*

"The Wife of Bath Her Prologue, From Chaucer." In *Poetical Miscellanies, Consisting of Original Poems and Translations. By the best Hands. Publish'd by Mr. Steele,* 1–27. London: J. Tonson, 1714. [Penn]

Behold the Woes of Matrimonial Life,
And hear with Rev'rence an experienc'd Wife!
To dear-bought Wisdom give the Credit due,
And think, for once, a Woman tells you true.
....

That Rest they wish'd for, grant them in the Grave,
And bless those Souls my Conduct help'd to save!

I leave to Pope scholars a full accounting of reprints. Besides in Ogle, 3:51–73, the poem appears at least in the editions of Pope's *Works* of 1717, 1736, and 1751, full citations for which may be found in *Alexander Pope: A Bibliography,* by Reginald H. Griffith (1922–27; reprint, New York: AMS Press, 1975), 79, 418, 644. I have serendipitously found a reprint in *The Muse in Good Humour: Or, A Collection of the Best Poems, Comic Tales, Choice Fables, Enigmas, &c. From the most Eminent Poets. With some Originals. Volume II, Part I* (London: M. Cooper, 1745), 60–76. [Villanova University]

Wife of Bath's Prologue, *[Andrew Jackson*]* (634 lines)

"The Tale of the Wife of Bath, and her five Husbands, recounted by herself." In *Matrimonial Scenes: Consisting of The Seaman's Tale, The Manciple's Tale, The Character of the Wife of Bath, The Tale of the Wife of Bath, and her Five Husbands. All modernized from Chaucer,* 34–64. London: A. Jackson, T. Payne, & W. Shropshire, 1750. [Harvard]

> Of Marriage, Love, Contention, Joys and Woes,
> I tell what from a long Experience flows.
> My Knowledge bought with Grief, in many a Year,
> You purchase, for one Hour's Audience, Here.
> ....
>
> And ev'ry nuptial Plague their Lives devour,
> Who dare refuse their Wives the sov'reign Pow'r!

No reprints found.

Wife of Bath's Tale, *John Dryden* (546 lines)

"The Wife of Bath Her Tale." In Dryden's *Fables Ancient and Modern; Translated into Verse,* 477–99. London: J. Tonson, 1700. [Penn]

> In Days of Old when *Arthur* fill'd the Throne,
> Whose Acts and Fame to Foreign Lands were blown;
> The King of Elfs and little Fairy Queen
> Gamboll'd on Heaths, and danc'd on ev'ry Green.
> ....
>
> And some devouring Plague pursue their Lives,
> Who will not well be govern'd by their Wives.

'* Andrew Jackson (1695–1778), a publisher who issued book catalogues in rhymed couplets, is credited as author by David F. Foxon, *English Verse, 1701–1750,* 2 vols. (Cambridge: Cambridge Univ. Press, 1975), 1:382–83, item J9. See also Chester Linn Shaver, "Two Eighteenth-Century Modernizations of Chaucer," *Harvard Studies and Notes in Philology and Literature* 16 (1934): 199–201; and Richard Gough, "Progress of Selling Books by Catalogues," 1788, reprint in *Literary Anecdotes of the Eighteenth Century,* by John Nichols, 9 vols. (1812–16; reprint, New York: AMS Press, 1966), 3:625–26.

See reprint information above under Dryden's *Knight's Tale*. In addition
to Ogle, 3:76–104, an early school anthology includes excerpts from
Dryden's poem and Chaucer's text: James Greenwood, ed. *The Virgin
Muse. Being a Collection of Poems from our most Celebrated Poets. Designed for the Use of Young Gentlemen and Ladies, at Schools* (London:
T. Varnam, J. Osborne, R. Halsey, J. Brotherton, & Jonas Brown, 1717),
147–48 for "The Story of Midas. Dryden from Chaucer" (i.e., "Wife of
Bath Her Tale" ll. 157–200), and 172–73 for "The Story of Midas, as
told by Geffrey Chaucer" (i.e., *WBT* ll. 952–82). [Penn]

Friar's Tale, *John Markland* (353 lines)*

"The Apparitor's Match: or, A Bargain with the Devil. Being the
Fryar's Tale, from Chaucer." In *Cythereia: or, New Poems upon Love and
Intrigue,* 1–22. London: E. Curll & T. Payne, 1723. [Yale; Harvard]

> A Rigorous Arch-Deacon *whilom* liv'd,
> From whom severest Justice *Guilt* receiv'd;
> Him no evasions ever could elude;
> Offending sinners strictly he pursu'd.
>
> ....
>
> Her pow'rful Wishes critically fell,
> So, 'faith, Sir *Sumner,* you must go—to Hell.

Reprint under the same title in some but not all copies of *The Altar of
Love. Consisting of Poems, And other Miscellanies. By the most eminent Hands. Now first collected into a Volume,* 1–22 of seventh
separately numbered page grouping. London: H. Curll, 1727. [Har-
vard; not in copy at Yale]
Reprint as "The Sumner and the Devil: Or, The Fryar's Tale." In Ogle,
3:108–26.

---

* Under item M104 in his *English Verse, 1701–1750,* 2 vols. (Cambridge: Cambridge
Univ. Press, 1975), 1:448, David F. Foxon notes that "*Nichols* . . . wrongly identifies [the
credited Mr.] Markland as Jeremiah; a Curll receipt to John is recorded above under *Cythereia.*" John Markland, an attorney from near Williamsburg, Virginia, was the first
American resident to modernize Chaucer, although he did so before emigrating.

Summoner's Tale, *"Mr. Grosvenor" [Eustace Budgell?*] (202 lines)

"The Whimsical Legacy. A Tale." In *The Bee,* ed. Eustace Budgell. Vol. 2, no. 23 (28 July to 4 August 1733): 1020–25. [NYPL on microfilm]

> Where *Humber's* Streams divide the fruitful Plain,
> There liv'd a Fryar of the *begging Train;*
> Who, as *Dan Chaucer's* merry Tales have told,†
> Wou'd give his *Prayers,* his *Mass,* or *Heav'n* for Gold.
> ....
>
> With a new Coat that *Jenkin* should be clad,
> And that the Churl was neither *Fool* nor *Mad.*

Reprint as "The Farmer and the Fryar: Or, The Sumner's Tale." In Ogle 3:132–42.

Reprint as "The Comic Gift: or, The Sumner's Tale, Imitated from Chaucer." In *The Universal Spectator,* ed. Henry "Stonecastle" [pseudonym for Baker], 3d ed. Vol. 2 (1756): 197–202. [NYPL]

Reprint as "The Whimsical Legacy. In Imitation of the Summer's [*sic*] Tale in Chaucer." In *The Merry Droll, or Pleasing Companion,* 84–90. London: C. Parker, 1769. [Bodleian Library, Oxford]
**

Clerk's Tale, *George Ogle (2426 lines)*

Gualtherus and Griselda: or, The Clerk of Oxford's Tale From Boccace, Petrarch, and Chaucer. To Which Are Added A Letter to a Friend, with the Clerk of Oxford's Character, &c, 5–102. London: R. Dodsley, 1739. [Harvard]

> Down at the Foot of *Vesulus* the Cold,
> (Thus ancient Bards the moral Tale unfold)

* Caroline Spurgeon attributes the work to Budgell in her *Five Hundred Years of Chaucer Criticism and Allusion, 1357–1900,* 3 vols. paginated as 6 parts (1925; reprint, New York: Russell & Russell, 1960), 3:4.86. The *DNB* account of Eustace Budgell (1686–1737) leaves unclear the degree of likelihood that he composed this piece in *The Bee,* which periodical he started in February 1733 and produced weekly until June 1735, two years before he jumped into the Thames to commit suicide.

† I quote here from the *Universal Spectator* version. In Ogle's collection the third line is, "Who, licens'd, hypocritically bold."

** David F. Foxon, *English Verse, 1701–1750,* 2 vols. (Cambridge: Cambridge Univ. Press, 1975), 1:117, item C140, accounts for a 1746 advertisement for "Chaucer's Farmer and fryar modernized" to be published by Cooper, Jones, and G. Woodfall, of which I have found no further record.

Where first, thro' subterraneous Caverns led,
The Springs of *Po* expand their silver Bed;
....

Each wrapt in Each, the Concord They improve;
Their Life, was one long Day, of Harmony and Love.

Reprint as "Gualtherus and Griselda: Or, The Clerk of Oxford's Tale."
    In Ogle 3:148–263.

Merchant's Tale, *Alexander Pope (820 lines)*

"January and May; or, The Merchant's Tale: From Chaucer." In *Poetical Miscellanies: The Sixth Part*, 177–224. London: J. Tonson, 1709.
[Penn]

There liv'd in *Lombardy*, as Authors write,
In Days of old, a wise and worthy Knight;
Of gentle Manners, as of gen'rous Race,
Blest with much Sense, more Riches, and some Grace.
....

And pray, to crown the Pleasure of their Lives,
To be so well deluded by their Wives.

I leave to Pope scholars a full accounting of reprints. Besides in Ogle, 3:9–50, the poem appears at least in the editions of Pope's *Works* of 1717, 1736, 1741, 1745, and 1751, full citations for which may be found in *Alexander Pope: A Bibliography*, by Reginald H. Griffith (1922–27; reprint New York: AMS Press, 1975), 79, 418, 521, 611, 644. I have serendipitously found three reprints. Notice that although all three miscellanies share the same main title, the publishers differ and the contents of the first differs almost completely from the other two.

In *The Muse in Good Humour: Or, A Collection of the Best Poems,*
Comic Tales, Choice Fables, Enigmas, &c. From the most Eminent Poets. With some Originals. Volume II, Part I, 15–46.
London: M. Cooper, 1745. [Villanova University]

In *The Muse in Good Humour: or, a Collection of Comic Tales. By*
the most Eminent Poets. The Sixth Edition, 8–38. London: F.
& J. Noble, 1751. [Yale]

In *The Muse in Good Humour: A Collection of Comic Tales. By the*
most Eminent Poets. The Seventh Edition, 2 vols, 1:8–38. London: F. Noble, W. Bathoe, & J. Noble, 1766. [Indiana University]

Squire's Tale, *Samuel Boyse (approx. 1400 lines)*

"Cambuscan: Or, The Squire's Tale." In Ogle, 2:199–277.

> Where peopled *Scythia*'s verdant Plain extend,
> East in that Sea, in whose unfathom'd Flood,
> Long-winding *Volga*'s rapid Streams descend,
> On *Oxus'* Bank an ancient City stood;
> ....
>
> She modest was, in all her Deeds and Words;
> And wondrous chaste of Life, tho' lov'd of Knights and Lords.
> *What follows is continued by Mr. Ogle, from the Fourth Book of*
> Spenser's Fairy Queen.

No reprints found.

Shipman's Tale, *[John Markland*] (413 lines)*

"Family Duty: Or, the Monk and the Merchant's Wife. Being the Shipman's Tale from Chaucer. Moderniz'd." In *Three New Poems*, 1–26 of second separately numbered page grouping. London: E. Curll, 1721. [Folger]

> Whilome a Merchant at St. *Dennis** liv'd,   *In *France*.
> Who in all trafficking Adventures thriv'd.
> A Wife he had, whose Beauty far excell'd
> All that in Competition might be held;
> ....
>
>   Then Husband, *Sign the Peace*, since we're agreed,
> I'll *hold the Parchment,* you shall *Seal the Deed.*

Reprint as "The Shipman's Tale" in some but not all copies of *The Altar of Love. Consisting of Poems, And other Miscellanies. By the most eminent Hands. Now first collected into a Volume,* 1–26 of tenth separately numbered page grouping. London: H. Curll, 1727. [Harvard; Princeton; not in copy at Yale]

* For the attribution, see item M104 in David F. Foxon, *English Verse, 1701–1750,* 2 vols. (Cambridge: Cambridge Univ. Press, 1975), 1:448.

Shipman's Tale, *Henry Travers (394 lines)*

"The Shipman's Tale from Chaucer." In Travers's *Miscellaneous Poems and Translations,* 104–30. London: B. Motte, 1731. [Harvard]

> There liv'd in *France,* as ancient Stories tell,
> A wealthy Merchant skill'd in trading well;
> Wise he was deem'd by all whose Maxims hold
> That he's no Ideot who abounds in Gold.
> ....
>
> Thus ends my Tale; may Fortune crown our Lives
> With Wealth enough for us, and something for our Wives.

Reprint in the second edition of Travers's work: *Miscellaneous Poems and Translations,* 161–84. York: C. Ward & R. Chandler, 1740. [NYPL; Harvard]

Shipman's Tale, *[Andrew Jackson; see note on his* WBP *above] (444 lines)*

"The Seaman's Tale." In *Matrimonial Scenes* [full title given above under Jackson's *WBP*], 1–20. London: A. Jackson, T. Payne, & W. Shropshire, 1750. [Harvard]

> Long since, a Merchant, where St. *Dennis* lies,
> Reputed, for his Riches, wond'rous wise,
> Possess'd a Wife, young charming, brisk and gay,
> Who lov'd to feast and revel Life away;
> ....
>
> Expert in all the *Shifts,* which Devils teach 'em,
> But *more* than Devils have Monks that over-reach 'em.

No reprints found.

Nun's Priest's Tale, *John Dryden (821 lines)*

"The Cock and the Fox: or, The Tale of the Nun's Priest, from Chaucer." In Dryden's *Fables Ancient and Modern; Translated into Verse,* 223–53. London: J. Tonson, 1700. [Penn]

> There liv'd, as Authors tell, in Days of Yore,
> A Widow somewhat old, and very poor:

Deep in a Dell her Cottage lonely stood,
Well thatch'd, and under covert of a Wood.
....

And in a Heathen Author we may find,
That Pleasure with Instruction should be join'd:
So take the Corn, and leave the Chaff behind.

See above under Dryden's *Knight's Tale* for reprint information. In addition, see under Dryden's *Wife of Bath's Tale* for full citation of *The Virgin Muse*, 1717, which includes excerpts from Dryden's poem and Chaucer's text: 23–25 for "The Poor Old Widow" and "The Cock. Dryden from Chaucer's Cock and the Fox" (i.e., "The Cock and the Fox" ll. 1–54), and 173–74 for "The Poor Old Widow, as it was written by Geffrey Chaucer" (i.e., *NPT* ll. 2821–64).

Nun's Priest's Tale, *anon. (68 lines)*

"The Cock and the Fox: or, Flattery is the Food of Fools. An Original Fable." In *The London Chronicle*. Vol. 26 (23–25 November 1769): 508. [Yale]

Once, as sage Chaucer let us know,
(No matter for how long ago)
A certain widow held a farm;
The land was fat, the house was warm;
....

He seiz'd, he choak'd, bounc'd back again,
And bore the victim to his den.

Reprint with same title in *The Universal Magazine of Knowledge and Pleasure*. Vol. 45 (December 1769): 321–22. [NYPL]

Manciple's Tale, *[Andrew Jackson; see note on his* WBP *above]* (254 lines)

"The Manciple's Tale." In *Matrimonial Scenes* [full title given above under Jackson's *WBP*], 21–31. London: A. Jackson, T. Payne, & W. Shropshire, 1750. [Harvard]

When bright *Apollo*, exil'd from the Sky,
Dwelt here on Earth, depriv'd of Deity,

He far exceeded all the Youth below,
In Vigour, Beauty, Wit, and Arch'ry too:
. . . .

Associate where you will, with high or low,
Restrain your Tongue, and recollect the Crow.

No reprints found.

NOTES

Introduction

1. Caroline Spurgeon, *Five Hundred Years of Chaucer Criticism and Allusion, 1357–1900*, 3 vols. paginated as 6 parts (1925; reprint, New York: Russell & Russell, 1960), 1:cxxv–cxxvi; originally published by The Chaucer Society in 1908–17.

2. Concerning Thomas Tyrwhitt's 1775 paragraph indentation and Thomas Wright's 1847 quotation marks, see respectively my chapters 4 and 8, "The Eighteenth-Century Pardoner(s)" and "The Merchant as Character on Tape." G. L. Kittredge was first to articulate both issues—the Pardoner's sincerity and the Merchant's bitterness—even though he was fully aware of the recency of editorial punctuation; in his personal copy of W. W. Skeat's 1894 edition of Chaucer's *Complete Works*, now in Houghton Library, Harvard University, Kittredge has replaced Skeat's punctuation with his own for the first forty-five stanzas of *Troilus and Criseyde*. Howell D. Chickering, Jr., has experimented with the issue by giving his students unpunctuated passages of *Troilus:* "Unpunctuating Chaucer" (paper delivered at the Nineteenth International Congress on Medieval Studies, Kalamazoo, Mich., 12 May 1984).

   Surprisingly little attention has been paid to manuscript punctuation, and even less to the effect of later editors' punctuation on readers' understandings. Concerning the former, see Paul G. Arakelian, "Punctuation in a Late Middle English Manuscript," *Neuphilologische Mitteilungen* 76 (1975): 614–24; Norman Blake, *The English Language in Medieval Literature* (London: J. M. Dent; Totowa, N. J.: Rowman & Littlefield, 1977), 66–74; George B. Killough, "Punctuation and Caesura in Chaucer," *Studies in the Age of Chaucer* 4 (1982): 87–107; Walter J. Ong, "Historical Backgrounds of Elizabethan and Jacobean Punctuation Theory," *PMLA* 59 (1944): 349–60; M. B. Parkes, "Punctuation, or Pause and Effect," in *Medieval Eloquence: Studies in the Theory and Practice of Medieval Rhetoric*, ed. James J. Murphy (Berkeley and Los Angeles: Univ. of California Press, 1978), 127–42; Alan T. Gaylord, "Scanning the Prosodists: An Essay in Metacriticism," *Chaucer Review* 11 (1976–77): 22–82; and David Burnley, *A Guide to Chaucer's Language* (Norman: Univ. of Oklahoma Press, 1983), 85–97.

3. Presentations of evidence include David Bleich, *Subjective Criticism* (Baltimore: Johns Hopkins Univ. Press, 1978); Norman Holland, *5 Readers*

Reading (New Haven: Yale Univ. Press, 1975); and Eugene R. Kintgen, *The Perception of Poetry* (Bloomington: Indiana Univ. Press, 1983).

4. Wolfgang Iser, *The Act of Reading: A Theory of Aesthetic Response* (Baltimore: Johns Hopkins Univ. Press, 1978), 149. Overviews of two theoretical perspectives, synchronic and diachronic, can be found respectively in *Reader-Response Criticism, from Formalism to Post-Structuralism,* ed. Jane P. Tompkins (Baltimore: Johns Hopkins Univ. Press, 1980); and Robert C. Holub, *Reception Theory: A Critical Introduction* (New York: Methuen, 1984). Holub notes (xiii) that only Iser has received much attention from both schools of theorists. That is, only Iser so far has combined diachronic and synchronic approaches, thereby ignoring at the same time both flaws that I discuss here.

5. Paula Johnson, *Form and Transformation in Music and Poetry of the English Renaissance* (New Haven: Yale Univ. Press, 1972), 59; Leonard B. Meyer, *Emotion and Meaning in Music* (Chicago: Univ. of Chicago Press, 1956).

6. Iser, *Act of Reading,* 100.

7. For accounts of the incident, see Mona Wilson, *The Life of William Blake,* ed. Geoffrey Keynes, 3d ed. (Oxford: Oxford Univ. Press, 1971), 232–41; and Alexander Gilchrist, *Life of William Blake,* 2d ed., 2 vols. (London: Macmillan, 1880), 1:250–55. For economic backgrounds to the controversy, see Alice Miskimin, "The Illustrated Eighteenth-Century Chaucer," *Modern Philology* 77 (1979): 26–55. Concerning Blake's painting and his intentionally contradictory verbal description of it, see Betsy Bowden, "The Artistic and Interpretive Context of Blake's 'Canterbury Pilgrims,'" *Blake: An Illustrated Quarterly* 13 (1980): 164–90. Blake's painting is now in Pollock House, Glasgow; Stothard's is in the Tate Gallery, London, grouped with nineteenth-century scenery just outside the entire refurbished gallery now devoted to Blake's work.

8. Two previous scholars have worked extensively with intervening centuries' interpretations of Chaucer: Alice Miskimin, *The Renaissance Chaucer* (New Haven: Yale Univ. Press, 1975); and William L. Alderson (and Arnold C. Henderson), *Chaucer and Augustan Scholarship* (Berkeley and Los Angeles: Univ. of California Press, 1970). Both their books stagger under the weight of detail. Professor Alderson, in fact, was able to complete only five chapters in his lifetime, concerning the Chaucer editions of 1687, 1700, and 1721; his student Henderson added the chapter on Morell's 1737 edition. Thanks to Charles Muscatine, Alderson's files are now in my possession. I would be glad to share them with researchers, who would, however, have to be already well versed in eighteenth-century Chauceriana to interpret Alderson's cryptic notes and references. Realizing the immensity of the task, thanks to Alderson, I have limited (in ways described therein) my Appendix B: Canterbury Tales Modernizations, 1700–1775.

9. Terry Jones, *Chaucer's Knight: The Portrait of a Medieval Mercenary* (Baton Rouge: Louisiana State Univ. Press, 1980).

10. Augustine of Hippo, *De Doctrina Christiana,* PL 34, col. 81, as translated by Beryl Rowland in her "*Pronuntiatio* and its Effect on Chaucer's Audience," *Studies in the Age of Chaucer* 4 (1982): 34.

11. Unless specified otherwise, all quotations from Chaucer come from *The Works of Geoffrey Chaucer,* ed. F. N. Robinson, 2d ed. (Boston: Houghton Mifflin, 1957).

12. Monroe C. Beardsley, "Right Readings and Good Readings," *Literature in Performance* 1 (1980): 16.

13. In addition to Beardsley, "Right Readings and Good Readings," 10–22, studies include Wallace A. Bacon, "An Aesthetics of Performance," *Literature in Performance* 1 (1980): 1–9; Arnold Berleant, "The Verbal Presence: An Aesthetics of Literary Performance," *Journal of Aesthetics and Art Criticism* 31 (1973): 339–46; Seymour Chatman and Katharine T. Loesch, "The Forum: On 'The Intentional Fallacy,'" *Quarterly Journal of Speech* 52 (1966): 283–89; Samuel R. Levin, "Suprasegmentals and the Performance of Poetry," *Quarterly Journal of Speech* 48 (1962): 366–72; Katharine T. Loesch, "Literary Ambiguity and Oral Performance," *Quarterly Journal of Speech* 51 (1965): 258–67; and William Craig Forrest, "Literature as Aesthetic Object: The Kinesthetic Stratum," *Journal of Aesthetics and Art Criticism* 27 (1969): 455–59.

14. Beardsley, "Right Readings and Good Readings," 20–22.

15. For a survey, see David Crystal, *The English Tone of Voice: Essays in Intonation, Prosody and Paralanguage* (New York: St. Martin's Press, 1975). Grant Fairbanks published his results in "Recent Experimental Investigations of Vocal Pitch in Speech," *Journal of the Acoustical Society of America* 11 (1940): 457–66.

16. William Thoms coined "folklore" in a letter to *The Athenaeum,* no. 982 (22 August 1846): 862; reproduced in *The Study of Folklore,* ed. Alan Dundes (Englewood Cliffs, N.J.: Prentice-Hall, 1965), 4–6. A facsimile is now available of Thomas Wright, *Essays on Subjects Connected with the Literature, Popular Superstitions and History of England in the Middle Ages,* 2 vols. (1846; reprint, New York: Burt Franklin, 1969). For more on Wright's work, see Thomas W. Ross, "Thomas Wright (1810–1877)," in *Editing Chaucer: The Great Tradition,* ed. Paul G. Ruggiers (Norman, Okla.: Pilgrim Books, 1984), 145–56.

17. Frederick J. Furnivall, Edmund Brock, and William A. Clouston, *Originals and Analogues of Some of Chaucer's Canterbury Tales* (London: N. Trübner for The Chaucer Society, 1872–87). The scope of investigation of folklore analogues to Chaucer's works can be estimated from the folktale section under each work in Lynn King Morris, *Chaucer Source and Analogue Criticism: A Cross-Referenced Guide* (New York: Garland, 1985). Nine of the major books, thanking Kittredge in their prefaces, are listed in my n. 63, Chapter 1, "The Prioress on Paper."

18. W. F. Bryan and Germaine Dempster, eds., *Sources and Analogues of Chaucer's Canterbury Tales* (1941; reprint, Atlantic Highlands, N.J.: Humanities Press, 1958). For access to Professor Utley's MLA address and his other unpublished papers, I thank the medievalists, folklorists, and librarians at Ohio State University for arranging my 1980 visit there, and Dean Thomas Magner of Penn State for financing it. Annotations to some of Utley's unfinished works are included in Mark E. Amsler, "A Bibliography of the Writings of Francis Lee Utley," *Names* 23 (1975): 130–46. The rare books

librarian at Ohio State has copies of "An Index to the Papers of Professor Francis Lee Utley," prepared by his last graduate assistant, William J. Host, in 1975.

19. Key articles include two by Alan Dundes: "Who Are the Folk?" in *Frontiers of Folklore,* ed. William Bascom, American Association for the Advancement of Science Selected Symposium no. 5 (Boulder, Colo.: Westview Press, 1977): 17–35; and "Texture, Text, and Context," *Southern Folklore Quarterly* 28 (1964): 251–65. See also Richard A. Reuss, "'That Can't Be Alan Dundes! Alan Dundes Is Taller Than That!' The Folklore of Folklorists," *Journal of American Folklore* 87 (1974): 303–17. The best introduction to the current field is Barre Toelken, *The Dynamics of Folklore* (Boston: Houghton Mifflin, 1979).

20. Bleich, *Subjective Criticism,* 16–18. For discussion and bibliography, see Elizabeth Fine, *The Folklore Text: From Performance to Print* (Bloomington: Indiana Univ. Press, 1984).

21. Rowland, "*Pronuntiatio* and its Effect on Chaucer's Audience," 33–51.

22. Two examples of methodological justification, from Tompkins's anthology *Reader-Response Criticism,* are those by Stanley Fish in "Literature in the Reader: Affective Stylistics," 89, and Jonathan Culler, "Literary Competence," 105. W. K. Wimsatt, Jr., and Monroe C. Beardsley dismiss "The Intentional Fallacy," *Sewanee Review* 54 (1946): 468–88. F. R. Leavis comments in his *Living Principle: "English" as a Discipline of Thought* (New York: Oxford Univ. Press, 1975), 58.

23. Steven Knapp and Walter Benn Michaels question the issue's validity in "Against Theory," *Critical Inquiry* 8 (1982): 723–42; reprinted along with articles in response to it as *Against Theory: Literary Studies and the New Pragmatism,* ed. W. J. T. Mitchell (Chicago: Univ. of Chicago Press, 1985). That authors want to make money is my simplification of the analyses of critics who use phrases like "the dialectic of production and consumption," for example, Peter Uwe Hohendahl, "Introduction to Reception Aesthetics," trans. Marc Silberman, *New German Critique* 4 (1977): 62. See also Hohendahl, *The Institution of Criticism* (Ithaca: Cornell Univ. Press, 1982); Manfred Naumann, "Literary Production and Reception," trans. Peter Heath, *New Literary History* 8 (1976): 107–26; and others surveyed in Holub, *Reception Theory,* cited in n. 4.

24. *Chaucer Life-Records,* ed. Martin M. Crow and Clair C. Olson from materials compiled by John M. Manly and Edith Rickert, with the assistance of Lilian J. Redstone and others (Austin: Univ. of Texas Press, 1966). As distinguished from Chaucer's personal life, his social context is being energetically researched and illuminated in such studies as Janet Coleman, *Medieval Readers and Writers, 1350–1400* (New York: Columbia Univ. Press, 1981); Carl Lindahl, "The Festive Form of the *Canterbury Tales,*" *English Literary History* 43 (1985): 531–74; idem, *Earnest Games: Folkloric Patterns in The Canterbury Tales* (Bloomington: Indiana Univ. Press, forthcoming); Jill Mann, *Chaucer and Medieval Estates Satire: The Literature of Social Classes and the General Prologue to the Canterbury Tales* (Cambridge: Cambridge Univ. Press, 1973); Glending Olson, *Literature as Recreation in the Later Middle Ages* (Ithaca: Cornell Univ. Press, 1982);

Paul Strohm, "Chaucer's Audience," *Literature and History* 5 (1977): 26–41; idem, "Chaucer's Fifteenth-Century Audience and the Narrowing of the 'Chaucer Tradition,'" *Studies in the Age of Chaucer* 4 (1982): 3–32; and B. A. Windeatt, "The Scribes as Chaucer's Early Critics," *Studies in the Age of Chaucer* 1 (1979): 119–41.

25. Ruth C. Crosby, "Oral Delivery in the Middle Ages," *Speculum* 11 (1936): 88–110; and idem, "Chaucer and the Custom of Oral Delivery," *Speculum* 13 (1938): 413–32. More recent studies include Gerald A. Bond, "The Last Unpublished Troubadour Songs," *Speculum* 60 (1985): 827–49; Alan T. Gaylord, "Scanning the Prosodists," cited in n. 2; Martin Irvine, "Medieval Grammatical Theory and Chaucer's *House of Fame*," *Speculum* 60 (1985): 850–76; Lindahl, "Festive Form of the *Canterbury Tales*"; William A. Quinn and Audley S. Hall, *Jongleur: A Modified Theory of Oral Improvisation and Its Effects on the Performance and Transmission of Middle English Romance* (Washington, D. C.: University Press of America, 1982); Beryl Rowland, "Chaucer's Speaking Voice and Its Effect on His Listeners' Perception of Criseyde," *English Studies in Canada* 7 (1981): 129–40; and two special issues of *New Literary History,* 10 (1979): 181–416, and 16 (1984): 1–206.

26. *HF* ll. 1079–80, discussed in fuller context by Irvine, "Medieval Grammatical Theory and Chaucer's *House of Fame*."

27. Phillips Barry offered this phrase as an eventually effective compromise in the Ballad War; see D. K. Wilgus, *Anglo-American Folksong Scholarship since 1898* (New Brunswick, N.J.: Rutgers Univ. Press, 1959), 68–73.

28. Crosby, "Chaucer and the Custom of Oral Delivery," 415n. But see also Manfred Günter Scholz, "On Presentation and Reception Guidelines in the German Strophic Epic of the Late Middle Ages," trans. Rebecca Williams Duplantier and Crozet Duplantier, Jr., *New Literary History* 16 (1984): 137–51, concerning the widespread secular use of the equivalent formulae "lire et chanter" and (primarily) "lesen oder singen."

29. David C. Fowler accounts for the two songs, and quotes from the Ashmole ms., in his *Literary History of the Popular Ballad* (Durham, N.C.: Duke Univ. Press, 1968), 101–2, 153.

1: The Prioress on Paper

1. George Lyman Kittredge, *Chaucer and His Poetry* (Cambridge: Harvard Univ. Press, 1915), 178; John Livingston Lowes, *Convention and Revolt in Poetry,* 2d ed. (New York: Barnes & Noble, 1930), 41; Eileen Power, *Medieval People,* 10th ed. (New York: Barnes & Noble, 1963), 73–95, originally published in 1924; Mary Madeleva, "Chaucer's Nuns," in her *Lost Language and Other Essays on Chaucer* (1951; reprint, New York: Russell & Russell, 1967), 47, originally published in 1925.

2. Isaac D'Israeli, *Amenities of Literature,* 1841, quoted in Caroline Spurgeon, *Five Hundred Years of Chaucer Criticism and Allusion, 1357–1900,* 3 vols. paginated as 6 parts (1925; reprint, New York: Russell & Russell, 1960), 2:2.231; Arthur Hoffman, "Chaucer's Prologue to Pilgrimage: The Two Voices," *English Literary History* 21 (1954): 7; Jill Mann, *Chaucer*

and Medieval Estates Satire: The Literature of Social Classes and the General Prologue to the Canterbury Tales (Cambridge: Cambridge Univ. Press, 1973), 128–37. An even earlier notice of Chaucer's ambiguity is by John Payne Collier, *The Poetical Decameron,* 1820, quoted in Spurgeon, *Five Hundred Years of Chaucer Criticism,* 2:2.122. In "Is Chaucer's Irony a Modern Discovery?" *Journal of English and Germanic Philology* 41 (1942): 303–19, Earle Birney traces recognitions of Chaucer's sense of humor through the five centuries of Spurgeon's allusions.

3. Leigh Hunt, "Specimens of a Dictionary of Love and Beauty," *The New Monthly Magazine and Literary Journal,* n.s., 17 (1826): 50; Charles Muscatine, "*The Canterbury Tales:* Style of the Man and Style of the Work," in *Chaucer and Chaucerians,* ed. Derek S. Brewer (University, Ala.: Univ. of Alabama Press, 1966), 96; D. W. Robertson, Jr., *A Preface to Chaucer: Studies in Medieval Perspectives* (Princeton: Princeton Univ. Press, 1962), 246; Robert M. Lumiansky, *Of Sondry Folk: The Dramatic Principle in the Canterbury Tales* (Austin: Univ. of Texas Press, 1955), 79; E. Talbot Donaldson, *Speaking of Chaucer* (New York: Norton, 1970), 61; G. H. Russell, "Chaucer: The Prioress's Tale," in *Medieval Literature and Civilization: Studies in Memory of G. N. Garmonsway,* ed. Derek Pearsall and R. A. Waldron (London: Athlone, 1969), 212.

4. For a discussion of Chaucer's prosody, with further references, see Alan T. Gaylord, "Scanning the Prosodists: An Essay in Metacriticism," *Chaucer Review* 11 (1976–77): 22–82. The standard reference for pronunciation is Helge Kökeritz, *A Guide to Chaucer's Pronunciation* (1961; reprint, Toronto: Univ. of Toronto Press for the Mediaeval Academy of America, 1978). Authenticity of reconstructed Middle English pronunciation has lately been called into question, however, most pointedly by Michael Murphy in a panel discussion, "On Not Reading Chaucer Aloud: Problems in Pronunciation," at the Fifth International Congress of the New Chaucer Society, Philadelphia, Pa., 21 March 1986.

5. John Ferne, *The Blazon of Gentrie,* 1586, quoted in Spurgeon, *Five Hundred Years of Chaucer Criticism,* 1:129. I discuss Dryden below, as cited in n. 7.

6. Spurgeon, *Five Hundred Years of Chaucer Criticism,* 3:Index.29–30, 69, 84; *Richard Brathwait's Comments, in 1665, upon Chaucer's Tales of the Miller and the Wife of Bath,* ed. Caroline Spurgeon, The Chaucer Society, 2d ser., no. 33 (London: Kegan Paul, Trench, Trübner & Co., 1901); John Dryden, *The Wife of Bath Her Tale,* in his *Fables Ancient and Modern; Translated into Verse,* 1700, now in *The Poems of John Dryden,* ed. James Kinsley, 4 vols. (Oxford: Clarendon, 1958), 4:1703–17; Alexander Pope, *The Wife of Bath Her Prologue, From Chaucer,* 1714, now in *The Rape of the Lock and Other Poems,* ed. Geoffrey Tillotson, 3d ed. (London: Methuen; New Haven: Yale Univ. Press, 1962), vol. 2 of *The Twickenham Edition of the Poems of Alexander Pope,* ed. John Butt, 11 vols. in 12 (1939–69), 2:57–78; John Gay, *The Wife of Bath. A Comedy,* 1713, and also *The Wife of Bath. A Comedy. Revised and Altered by the Author* [to exclude the Chaucer character], 1730, both now in *John Gay: Dramatic Works,* ed. John Fuller, 2 vols. (Oxford: Clarendon, 1983), 1:101–71,

2:147–219. Concerning what promises to be the complicated life of the ballad usually entitled *The Wanton Wife of Bath,* see Spurgeon, *Five Hundred Years of Chaucer Criticism,* 1:288, 480, 3:4.54; David F. Foxon, *English Verse, 1701–1750,* 2 vols. (Cambridge: Cambridge Univ. Press, 1975), 1:511; and Albert B. Friedman, *The Ballad Revival: Studies in the Influence of Popular on Sophisticated Poetry* (Chicago: Univ. of Chicago Press, 1961), 113, 197, 201.

7. For the fifteenth-century characters, see ll. 281–94 of *The Tale of Beryn, with A Prologue of the merry Adventure of the Pardoner with a Tapster at Canterbury,* ed. Frederick J. Furnivall and W. G. Stone, Early English Text Society, extra ser., no. 105 (1887, 1909; reprint Millwood, N.Y.: Kraus Reprints, 1975), 10. See also Dryden, *Preface* to *Fables Ancient and Modern,* 1700, now in *Poems of John Dryden,* 4:1455; Walter Scott, review of William Godwin's *Life of Chaucer,* 1804, quoted in Spurgeon, *Five Hundred Years of Chaucer Criticism,* 2:2.18; Blake as analyzed by Betsy Bowden, "The Artistic and Interpretive Context of Blake's 'Canterbury Pilgrims,'" *Blake: An Illustrated Quarterly* 13 (1980): 164–90.

8. Hunt, "Specimens of a Dictionary of Love and Beauty," 50; Lowes, *Convention and Revolt,* 45.

9. Information on Child is taken from Eleanor P. Hammond, *Chaucer: A Bibliographical Manual* (1908; reprint, New York: Peter Smith, 1933), 521. According to Jonathan Z. Smith, post-secondary English literature was first taught at Lafayette College in 1857–60 by Francis March; in his inaugural address of 1869, Harvard president Charles Eliot proposed inclusion of English literature in the Harvard curriculum. See Smith's "Re-forming the Undergraduate Curriculum: A Retrospective," in *Re-forming the Undergraduate Curriculum: Invitation to Dialogue,* ed. James W. Reed for The Academic Forum of Rutgers University, 7 April 1986, p. 5. A slightly different genesis for "English" as a university subject, beginning at Princeton as early as 1846–47, is provided by Lionel Grossman, "Literature and Education," *New Literary History* 13 (1982): 341–71. Longer studies include D. J. Palmer, *The Rise of English Studies: An Account of the Study of English Language and Literature from its Origins to the Making of the Oxford English School* (New York: Oxford Univ. Press for Univ. of Hull Publications, 1965); and Jo McMurty, *English Language, English Literature: The Creation of an Academic Discipline* (Hamden, Conn.: Archon, 1985).

10. Charles D. Deshler, introducing *Selections from the Poetical Works of Geoffry Chaucer* (New York: Wiley & Putnam, 1847), 32–35. Most medievalists will forgive me for dealing with interpretations of Chaucer exhaustively through the eighteenth century, but only spottily thereafter. It is of course proliferation of material, not nausea alone, that stops me.

11. Kittredge, *Chaucer and His Poetry,* 176–79.

12. Ferne, cited in n. 5; N. H. Nicolas, "The French of Stratford atte Bowe," *Gentleman's Magazine,* Aug. 1841, quoted in Spurgeon, *Five Hundred Years of Chaucer Criticism,* 2:2.239.

13. Thomas Betterton, *Chaucer's Characters, Or The Introduction to the Canterbury Tales;* Betterton, *The Miller of Trompington, Or, The Reve's Tale*

from Chaucer; Alexander Pope, *The Rape of the Locke. An Heroi-Comical Poem;* all three in *Miscellaneous Poems and Translations. By Several Hands* (London: Bernard Lintott [*sic*], 1712), 247–82, 301–20, [353]–376. As I will mention in Chapter 10, "How Pope Found the Merchant's Tale," Norman Ault has shown that Pope secretly edited this and other of Lintot's miscellanies; see his *New Light on Pope, with Some Additions to His Poetry Hitherto Unknown* (1949; reprint, Hamden, Conn.: Archon, 1967), 27–38.

14. If indeed by Pope, the modernization was made from his copy of Thomas Speght's 1598 edition of Chaucer's *Workes,* now in the library at Hartlebury Castle, Worcestershire. Because we lack information as to edition owned by most commentators, illustrators, and modernizers, I will quote throughout this book from F. N. Robinson's second edition, except concerning Pope's particular details in modernizing his acknowledged work. The 1598 text of the Prioress's *General Prologue* portrait, at any rate, varies only slightly from Robinson's text.

15. Full citations to the controversy concerning the existence of "courtly love" are supplied in Joan Ferrante's defense of the concept, albeit not the term: "*Cortes' Amor* in Medieval Texts," *Speculum* 55 (1980): 686–95. The idea was introduced by Gaston Paris, "Études sur les romans de la Table Ronde. Lancelot du Lac," *Romania* 12 (1883): 519, and developed by C. S. Lewis in *Allegory of Love: A Study in Medieval Tradition* (1936; reprint, New York: Oxford Univ. Press, 1958), 1–43. Lewis's formulation has been attacked on various grounds by, for example, Robertson, *Preface to Chaucer,* 391ff.; John F. Benton, "Clio and Venus: An Historical View of Medieval Love," in *The Meaning of Courtly Love,* ed. F. X. Newman (Albany: State Univ. of New York Press, 1968), 19–42; E. Talbot Donaldson, "The Myth of Courtly Love," *Ventures* 5 (Fall 1965): 16–23; and Betsy Bowden, "The Art of Courtly Copulation," *Medievalia et Humanistica,* n.s., 9 (1979): 67–85.

16. Betterton, *Chaucer's Characters,* in *Miscellaneous Poems and Translations,* 253, for *GP* ll. 118–20. All further quotations from this modernization occur on pages 253–55.

17. *The Compact Edition of the Oxford English Dictionary* (New York: Oxford Univ. Press, 1971), s.vv. "coy," "address." Hereafter I cite this work in my text as *OED.*

18. Charles Cowden Clarke, ed., *The Riches of Chaucer,* 2 vols. (London: Effingham Wilson, 1835), 1:63.

19. Richard H. Horne, *Prologue to the Canterbury Tales,* in *The Poems of Geoffrey Chaucer modernised,* ed. Horne (London: Whittaker, 1841), 9.

20. Muscatine, "*The Canterbury Tales,*" 96; Robertson, *Preface to Chaucer,* 245.

21. Donaldson, *Speaking of Chaucer,* 61; Bernard F. Huppé, *A Reading of the Canterbury Tales* (Albany: State Univ. of New York Press, 1967), 33–34; quotation from Judith Grossman, "The Correction of a Descriptive Schema: Some 'Buts' in Barbour and Chaucer," *Studies in the Age of Chaucer* 1 (1979): 52.

22. Edgar Hill Duncan, "Narrator's Points of View in the Portrait Sketches,

Prologue to the *Canterbury Tales*," in *Essays in Honor of Walter Clyde Curry,* Vanderbilt Studies in the Humanities, vol. 2 (Nashville: Vanderbilt Univ. Press, 1955): 81; Gordon H. Harper, "Chaucer's Big Prioress," *Philological Quarterly* 12 (1933): 308; Charles Moorman, "The Prioress as Pearly Queen," *Chaucer Review* 13 (1978–79): 27; John Gardner, *The Poetry of Chaucer* (Carbondale: Southern Illinois Univ. Press, 1977), 234.

23. Charles Muscatine, *The Book of Geoffrey Chaucer* (San Francisco: Book Club of California, 1963). This limited-edition folio is usually confined to rare-book rooms. A more accessible source for a variety of woodcut pilgrims, identified according to edition, is the *Chaucer Coloring Book,* available as of 1986 from Bellerophon Books, 36 Anacapa Street, Santa Barbara, Ca 93101. It also includes a floppy record of Professor Muscatine reading *General Prologue* selections.

24. Besides Muscatine, *Book of Geoffrey Chaucer,* see Beverly Boyd, *Chaucer and the Medieval Book* (San Marino, Calif.: Huntington Library, 1973), 52–54; and Colin Clair, *A History of Printing in Britain* (New York: Oxford Univ. Press, 1966), 51–53.

25. In "The Illustrated Eighteenth-Century Chaucer," *Modern Philology* 77 (1979): 30, Alice Miskimin provides background and attributes the pilgrim portraits to Vertue. They do closely resemble his style and are copied in the departure scene (fig. 1), which he lists among his works in *A Catalogue of Engravers,* ed. Horace Walpole from papers of George Vertue (London: Shakespeare Press, 1828), vol. 5 of Walpole's *Anecdotes of the Arts in General in Great Britain, 5* vols. (1828), 5:304, 311. (In other editions since its first in 1762, this work is usually entitled *Anecdotes of Painting in England.*)

Using apparently the same evidence as Miskimin, however, I remain unconvinced. I do not see why Vertue would not claim credit for the pilgrim portraits as well as for the departure scene; also, his students' work might closely resemble his. Moreover, if only Vertue is involved, I do not understand the use of the plural in the "Proposals of Subscriptions for Urry's Chaucer," *Daily Courant,* 27 January 1715, advertising "30 Copper Plates by the best Gravers . . . before each Tale"; quoted in Richmond P. Bond, "Some Eighteenth Century Chaucer Allusions," *Studies in Philology* 25 (1928): 336. Although several engravers might render pictures by the same designer, the identity of the artist(s) seems unclear to me.

The pilgrim portraits are not mentioned in descriptions of this art academy (the first in England) by Sidney C. Hutchison, *The History of the Royal Academy, 1768–1968* (London: Chapman & Hall, 1968); nor by William T. Whitley, *Artists and Their Friends in England, 1700–1799,* 2 vols. (1928; reprint, New York: Benjamin Blom, 1968), 1:3–16; nor are they mentioned in George L. Lam and Warren H. Smith, "George Vertue's Contributions to Chaucerian Iconography," *Modern Language Quarterly* 5 (1944): 303–22; nor in the chapter on Urry's edition in William L. Alderson and Arnold C. Henderson, *Chaucer and Augustan Scholarship* (Berkeley and Los Angeles: Univ. of California Press, 1970), 69–140. However, Alderson's unpublished papers, now in my possession, show evidence of his unsuccessful pursuance of the issue; they include the note "probably *not* by Vertue, since he doesn't show any interest in his notebooks," i.e. in *A Catalogue of Engravers,* cited above.

For purposes of this book I consider that John Urry's idiosyncratically adapted text, as distinguished from its illustrations known by Blake and probably other artists, had little impact on eighteenth-century interpretations of Chaucer. As I discuss in Chapter 4, "The Eighteenth-Century Pardoner(s)," scholars knew to use Speght, and everybody else read modernizations. (See Appendix B.) Urry remained unsold and unread. See Spurgeon, *Five Hundred Years of Chaucer Criticism,* 1:cxix–cxxi; and Alderson's cited chapter, part of which is reprinted as "John Urry (1666–1715)" in *Editing Chaucer: The Great Tradition,* ed. Paul G. Ruggiers (Norman, Okla.: Pilgrim Books, 1984), 93–115.

26. Biographical information is compiled from Ault, *New Light on Pope,* 68–75, 325–27, 357–58; and from the *Dictionary of National Biography,* ed. Leslie Stephen and Sidney Lee, 22 vols. (1885–1901; reprint, London: Oxford Univ. Press, 1937–38), s. vv. "Jervas, Charles," "Kneller, Godfrey," "Vertue, George." Hereafter I cite this latter work in my text as *DNB.*

The association of Pope and Kneller did not end with the death of the latter, who had been churchwarden where Pope's father was buried. Kneller had suggested to the poet, and then his widow insisted, that the monument to Pope's father (which now includes Pope's and his mother's names as well) be torn out to make room for a large Kneller monument. After negotiations, Pope composed an epitaph for such a monument, to be placed in Westminster Abbey instead, and privately a satiric epitaph on Mrs. Kneller: *Epitaph On Sir Godfrey Kneller, In Westminster-Abby, 1723,* and *Epitaph On Lady Kneller,* both now in Pope's *Minor Poems,* ed. Norman Ault and John Butt (London: Methuen; New Haven: Yale Univ. Press, 1954), vol. 6 of *Poems of Alexander Pope,* 6:312–13, 249.

27. William Blake, *A Descriptive Catalogue of Pictures, Poetical and Historical Inventions,* 1809, now in *Blake: Complete Writings,* ed. Geoffrey Keynes (London: Oxford Univ. Press, 1966), 567. Although Keynes's edition is no longer considered scholarly, because he replaces Blake's eccentric punctuation and other features with his own, I cite it throughout this book rather than appear to take sides in what promises to become a long-term controversy concerning David Erdman's second edition of *The Complete Poetry and Prose of William Blake* (Berkeley and Los Angeles: Univ. of California Press, 1982), which was meant to be definitive. For a strong negative response to it, see the review by the Santa Cruz Blake Study Group, *Blake: An Illustrated Quarterly* 18 (1984): 4–31.

28. Plutarch, in his *Lives,* describes the training of Bucephalus by Alexander the Great. Xenophon's treatise on horsemanship provides even more specific evidence that for over two millennia horses have been refusing the bit, trying to head back to the barn, trying to follow groups of other horses going elsewhere than the rider wants, and balking in panic at the horse-eating monsters that still populate the imaginative worlds of high-strung horses. John K. Anderson translates Xenophon's treatise in his *Ancient Greek Horsemanship* (Berkeley and Los Angeles: Univ. California Press, 1961), 155–80.

Such eternally equine behavior is controlled by the bit and bridle, which have changed hardly at all since the millennium before Xenophon, according to an Iranian bridle preserved at the University of Pennsylvania Museum. Tack remained the same in intervening centuries—according to any collection of medieval horse armor (e.g., that in the Philadelphia Museum of Art) and illustrations and other evidence—except the introduction of the stirrup, from China to Western Europe in about the eighth century A.D., resulting eventually in chivalry, which had far more to do with horsemanship than with love.

On Chaucer's references to horses, see A. A. Dent, "Chaucer and the Horse," *Proceedings of the Leeds Philosophical and Literary Society* 9 (1959): 1–12; John H. Fisher, "Chaucer's Horses," *South Atlantic Quarterly* 60 (1961): 71–79; and Rodney Delasanta (considering them allegory), "The Horsemen of the *Canterbury Tales*," *Chaucer Review* 3 (1968–69): 29–36. I am working on an article entitled "Horse Source: Blake's Use of the Urry-Edition Canterbury Pilgrims."

29. Sometime before his death in 1779, John H. Mortimer made drawings of the *Departure* and eight scenes from within *Tales* for a projected Chaucer edition about which nothing else is known, according to F. J. Furnivall in *Notes and Queries*, 6th ser., 2 (1880): 325–26. On 12 February 1787, J. R. Smith published the drawings, engraved by J. K. Sherwin, E. Williams, William Sharp, and Jacob Hogg, according to Hammond, *Chaucer: A Bibliographical Manual*, 324. They were reproduced in a few extra-fancy copies of Thomas Tyrwhitt's 1798 second edition of *Canterbury Tales*, including one now at the British Library, and then in *Mortimer's Works: A Collection of Fifty Historical Designs* (London: T. Palser, 1816).

Plates from *Mortimer's Works* are now at the Victoria and Albert Museum, along with Mortimer's original drawings for four of the nine: *January and May; Three Gamblers and Time* (both to be discussed in coming chapters); *The Sompnour, the Devil, and the Widow;* and *The Coke and Perkin.* The museum's photographic services can no longer (as of 1984) supply photographs, unless you hire a private photographer, but do have on file at Photo Sales negatives for the *Departure* and *The Coke and Perkin.*

In the United States, the only copies of the engravings I have been able to locate have been interbound into a copy of Urry's 1721 edition at Houghton Library, Harvard: fEC.C3932.C 721w. Another elegant Chaucer edition there has what appears to be Stothard's pilgrimage reproduced in gilt along the page edges (i.e., when closed), almost rubbed off: Tyrwhitt's second edition, fEC. 3932C.1798.

30. Blake, *Descriptive Catalogue,* now in his *Complete Writings,* 567; Walter Scott, quoted in J. L. Adolphus, *Memoranda,* 1827, quoted in Spurgeon, *Five Hundred Years of Chaucer Criticism,* 2:2.165. George Stubbs, probably the best-known painter of horses ever, lavishly praised those by Stothard, according to Stothard's daughter Anna E. Bray who published her father's biography in 1851 (quoted in Miskimin, "Illustrated Eighteenth-Century Chaucer," 53–54). See also, for example, the continuous comments on the pilgrims' horses, including comparison to those of Rubens and Vandyke, by William P. Carey, *Critical Description of the Procession*

of Chaucer's Pilgrims to Canterbury, painted by Thomas Stothard, Esq. R.A., 2d ed. (London: Glindon, 1818), esp. 26, 58, 62.

31. Concerning this controversy, see n. 7 of my Introduction.

32. Carey, *Critical Description of the Procession*, 48–49. I have not been able to include a reproduction of Stothard's painting in this book. It can be found in the readily available *English Literature: An Illustrated Record*, by Richard Garnett and Edmund Gosse, 4 vols. (New York: Macmillan, 1905), 1:156/7, a still remarkably useful source also for too-seldom-reproduced pictures such as those in the *Pearl* manuscript and Cambridge ms. Gg.4.27; and in Spurgeon, *Five Hundred Years of Chaucer Criticism*, 2:2.36/7.

33. Bertrand Bronson, *Printing as an Index of Taste in Eighteenth Century England* (New York: New York Public Library, 1958), 38.

34. Blake, *Descriptive Catalogue*, now in his *Complete Writings*, 568–72. In my Blake article, cited in n. 7, I do not trace the Prioress's resemblance to repressive female figures elsewhere in Blake's work because Karl Kiralis has already done so in his "William Blake as an Intellectual and Spiritual Guide to Chaucer's *Canterbury Pilgrims*," *Blake Studies* 1 (Spring 1969): 148, 151–59. He thereby supports S. Foster Damon's suggestions in *A Blake Dictionary* (1965; reprint, New York: Dutton, 1971), 79.

35. Blake's genius did not go wholly unappreciated. John Linnell, a civil servant, bought Blake's artwork throughout his later years without attempting to dictate subject or style. A convenient summary of Blake's life and art is Morton Paley, *William Blake* (Oxford: Phaidon; New York: Dutton, 1978).

Concerning Blake's *Canterbury Pilgrims* itself, Charles Lamb admired it and called the *Descriptive Catalogue* "the finest criticism he had ever read of Chaucer's poem," according to Henry Crabb Robinson, *Diary*, 1810, quoted in Spurgeon, *Five Hundred Years of Chaucer Criticism*, 2:2.49. Robinson notes that "Stothard's work is well known; Blake's is known by very few." A more ordinary reaction is that of one Thomas Frognall Dibdin, *Reminiscences of a Literary Life*, 1836, quoted in Spurgeon, *Five Hundred Years of Chaucer Criticism*, 2:2.203–4: "When Blake entered the arena with Stothard, as a rival in depicting the *Dramatis Personae* of Chaucer's Canterbury Tales he seems to have absolutely lost his wits."

36. For Ellesmere history, see Muscatine, *Book of Geoffrey Chaucer*, cited in n. 23, 2; John M. Manly and Edith Rickert, eds., *The Text of The Canterbury Tales, Studied on the Basis of All Known Manuscripts*, 8 vols. (Chicago: Univ. of Chicago Press, 1940), 1:149; and Alix Egerton, *Preface* to *The Ellesmere Manuscript, Reproduced in Facsimile*, 2 vols. (Manchester: University Press, 1911), 1:7.

37. In "The Ellesmere Miniatures as Illustrations of Chaucer's *Canterbury Tales*," *Studies in Iconography* 7–8 (1981–82): 113–34, Martin Stevens argues that the manuscript artists illustrate exact details of Chaucer's text. Blake and Stothard diverge markedly from Chaucer's text as well as from each other.

38. Miskimin, "Illustrated Eighteenth-Century Chaucer," 36–40.

39. P. M. Handover, *Printing in London from 1476 to Modern Times* (London: Allen & Unwin, 1960), 148.

40. Thomas Tyrwhitt, "Letter to a Friend," *Gentleman's Magazine*, June 1783, quoted in Spurgeon, *Five Hundred Years of Chaucer Criticism*, 1:474. See further B. A. Windeatt, "Thomas Tyrwhitt (1730–1786)," in *Editing Chaucer*, ed. Ruggiers, 117–43.

41. William Lipscomb, *The Canterbury Tales of Chaucer, completed in a Modern Version*, 3 vols. (London: J. Cooke & G. G. & J. Robinson, 1795), 1:173, for *GP* l. 542. Volume and page references in my text are to this edition.

42. Dryden, *Preface* to *Fables Ancient and Modern*, 1700, now in *Poems of John Dryden*, 4:1457. Concerning Dryden's immense influence as a translator, see William Frost, *Dryden and the Art of Translation* (New Haven: Yale Univ. Press, 1955). Dryden's modernizations were the first ones published; but a modernized *Troilus* has been edited from manuscript as *A Seventeenth-Century Modernisation of the First Three Books of Chaucer's "Troilus and Criseyde,"* ed. Herbert G. Wright, Cooper Monographs on English and American Language and Literature, no. 5 (Bern: A. Francke, 1960). The author of British Museum Additional ms. 29494, probably Jonathan Sidnam, purposely stops there because "I am loath to doe true loue that wrong. / To make her fall, the subject of my song" (238).

43. Dorothy Wordsworth, *Journal*, 1801, quoted in Spurgeon, *Five Hundred Years of Chaucer Criticism*, 2:2.2. They used Robert Anderson's edition of *The Works of the British Poets*, 13 vols. (London: J. & A. Arch, 1795)— the text of which is accounted for in Hammond, *Chaucer: A Bibliographical Manual*, 134–35—according to E. de Selincourt and Helen Darbishire, eds., *The Poetical Works of William Wordsworth*, 5 vols. (Oxford: Clarendon, 1940–49), 4:443.

44. William Wordsworth, *Selections from Chaucer, modernised*, 1820, now in *Poetical Works of William Wordsworth*, 4:209; W. Wordsworth, letter to John Wilson, 1841, quoted in *The Critical Opinions of William Wordsworth*, ed. Markham L. Peacock, Jr. (1950; reprint, New York: Octagon, 1969), 213.

45. W. Wordsworth, *The Prioress' Tale*, l. 122, for *PriT* l. 573, in his *Selections from Chaucer, modernised*, 1820, now in *Poetical Works of William Wordsworth*, 4:213.

46. W. Wordsworth, *Prioress' Tale*, ll. 233–39, for *PriT* ll. 684–90, now in *Poetical Works of William Wordsworth*, 4:217; editorial note on the lines, ibid., 4:444.

47. W. Wordsworth, *Prioress' Tale*, ll. 60–62, for *PriT* ll. 512–13, now in *Poetical Works of William Wordsworth*, 4:211.

48. W. Wordsworth, *Ecclesiastical Sonnets, Part II*, "XXXI: Edward VI," 1822, now in *Poetical Works of William Wordsworth*, 3:376.

49. Donald R. Howard, *The Idea of the Canterbury Tales* (Berkeley and Los Angeles: Univ. of California Press, 1976), 276; Duncan, "Narrator's Points of View," cited in n. 22, 80–81.

50. W. Wordsworth, letters to Moxon and to E. Q., both 1840, both now in

Peacock, *Critical Opinions,* 212. Concerning the near universal condemnation of the 1841 modernizations, see Spurgeon, *Five Hundred Years of Chaucer Criticism,* 1:lviii–lix; Alfred Tobler, *Geoffrey Chaucer's Influence on English Literature* (1905; reprint, New York: AMS Press, 1973), 106–11; and Thomas R. Lounsbury, *Studies in Chaucer, His Life and Writings,* 3 vols. (1892; reprint, New York: Russell & Russell, 1962), 3:213–29.

51. Horne, *Poems of Geoffrey Chaucer modernised,* xviii, explicating *MlrT* ll. 3383–84.

52. Ibid., xxxiii.

53. W. Wordsworth, letter to Henry Reed, 1841, quoted in Spurgeon, *Five Hundred Years of Chaucer Criticism,* 2:2.242.

54. W. Wordsworth, letter to Dora, 1840, now in Peacock, *Critical Opinions,* 214.

55. W. Wordsworth, *Selections from Chaucer, modernised,* 2d ed., 1827, now in *Poetical Works of William Wordsworth,* 4:209.

56. A quarter century after Wordsworth's comment, historian Henry H. Milman takes for granted that the *Prioress's Tale* shows Chaucer's "touch of bigotry" in his *History of Latin Christianity,* 1855, quoted in Spurgeon, *Five Hundred Years of Chaucer Criticism,* 2:3.24. Florence Ridley summarizes the twentieth-century debate in *The Prioress and the Critics* (Berkeley and Los Angeles: Univ. of California Press, 1965), 1–14. Of works published since 1965 see, among many examples, Howard, *Idea of the Canterbury Tales,* 277–79; Russell, "Chaucer: The Prioress's Tale," 217, 220–21; Derek S. Brewer, *Chaucer,* 3d ed. (London: Longman, 1973), 127–28; Christopher Brookhouse, "In Search of Chaucer: The Needed Narrative," in *The Learned and the Lewd,* ed. Larry D. Benson (Cambridge: Harvard Univ. Press, 1974), 79; Albert B. Friedman, "The *Prioress's Tale* and Chaucer's Anti-Semitism," *Chaucer Review* 9 (1974–75): 118–29; John C. Hirsh, "Reopening the *Prioress's Tale,*" *Chaucer Review* 10 (1975–76): 30–45; and Paul Strohm, "Chaucer's Fifteenth-Century Audience and the Narrowing of the 'Chaucer Tradition,'" *Studies in the Age of Chaucer* 4 (1982): 27–28.

57. For both motifs, see Stith Thompson, *Motif-Index of Folk Literature,* rev. and enl. ed., 6 vols. (Bloomington: Indiana Univ. Press, 1955–58), 5:471, 465.

58. Carleton Brown, *A Study of the Miracle of Our Lady Told by Chaucer's Prioress,* The Chaucer Society, 2d ser., no. 45 (London: Kegan Paul, Trench, Trübner, & Co., 1910); Bill Ellis, "De Legendis Urbis: Modern Legends in Ancient Rome," *Journal of American Folklore* 96 (1983): 200–208; Gavin I. Langmuir, "Thomas of Monmouth: Detector of Ritual Murder," *Speculum* 59 (1984): 820–46; Cecil Roth, ed., *The Ritual Murder Libel and the Jew: The Report by Cardinal Lorenzo Ganganelli* (London: Woburn Press, n.d. [after 1934]).

59. Barre Toelken, *The Dynamics of Folklore* (Boston: Houghton Mifflin, 1979), 176–79; J. L. Langlois, "The Belle Isle Bridge Incident: Legend Dialectic and Semiotic System in the 1943 Detroit Race Riots," *Journal of American Folklore* 96 (1983): 183–99. On this tale in particular, see also

Florence Ridley, "A Tale Told Too Often," *Western Folklore* 26 (1967): 153–56. On urban legends in general, see Jan H. Brunvand, *The Vanishing Hitchhiker: American Urban Legends and Their Meanings* (New York: Norton, 1981).

60. Toelken, *Dynamics of Folklore*, 178–79.

61. Subjectivist literary critics seem unaware of Tom Burns's pioneering, albeit inconclusive, study of the entire psychological backgrounds of a dozen students who all claimed the same joke as their favorite: *Doing the Wash: An Expressive Culture and Personality Study of a Joke and Its Tellers* (Norwood, Pa.: Norwood Editions, 1975).

62. Richard L. Levin, *New Readings vs. Old Plays: Recent Trends in the Reinterpretation of English Renaissance Drama* (Chicago: Univ. of Chicago Press, 1979), 194–207; Karl Kroeber, "The Evolution of Literary Study, 1883–1983," *PMLA* 99 (1984): 331.

63. Frederick J. Furnivall, Edmund Brock, and William A. Clouston, *Originals and Analogues of Some of Chaucer's Canterbury Tales* (London: N. Trübner for The Chaucer Society, 1872–87); W. F. Bryan and Germaine Dempster, eds., *Sources and Analogues of Chaucer's Canterbury Tales* (1941; reprint, Atlantic Highlands, N.J.: Humanities Press, 1958); Kate O. Petersen, *On the Sources of the Nonne Prestes Tale* (1898; reprint, New York: Haskell House, 1966); idem, *The Sources of the Parson's Tale* (1901; reprint, New York: AMS Press, 1973); Gustavus H. Maynadier, *The Wife of Bath's Tale: Its Sources and Analogues* (1901; reprint, New York: AMS Press, 1972); Karl I. Young, *The Origin and Development of the Story of Troilus and Criseyde* (1908; reprint, New York: Gordian Press, 1968); Brown, *Miracle of Our Lady*, cited in n. 58; Margaret Schlauch, *Chaucer's Constance and Accused Queens* (1927; reprint, New York: AMS Press, 1973); John Webster Spargo, *Chaucer's Shipman's Tale: The Lover's Gift Regained* (1930; reprint, Folcroft, Pa.: Folcroft Library Editions, 1971); Dudley D. Griffith, *The Origin of the Griselda Story*, Univ. of Washington Publications in Language and Literature, vol. 8 (Seattle: Univ. of Washington Press, 1931); and Bartlett Jere Whiting, *Chaucer's Use of Proverbs* (1934; reprint, New York: AMS Press, 1973).

64. Dryden, *Preface to Fables Ancient and Modern*, 1700, now in *Poems of John Dryden*, 4:1452, 1455. Dryden's pairing of pilgrim types (vicious/virtuous, learned/lewd) set precedent for Blake, as I show in my "Artistic and Interpretive Context," cited in n. 7. Warren Ginsberg takes similar notice of binary oppositions in Chaucer's characterization in his *Cast of Character: The Representation of Personality in Ancient and Medieval Literature* (Toronto: Univ. of Toronto Press, 1983), as does Peter Elbow in his *Oppositions in Chaucer* (Middletown, Conn.: Wesleyan Univ. Press, 1975).

2: The Prioress on Tape

1. See, for example, the letter of George Gordon, Lord Byron, to Douglas Kinnaird, 1821, now in *Byron's Letters and Journals*, ed. Leslie A. Marchand, 11 vols. (London: J. Murray; Cambridge: Harvard Univ. Press, 1973–80), 8:95–97.

2. In Chapter 1, "The Prioress on Paper," I discuss *The Poems of Geoffrey Chaucer modernised,* ed. Richard H. Horne (London: Whittaker, 1841); and (as an example) Charles D. Deshler, ed., *Selections from the Poetical Works of Geoffry Chaucer* (New York: Wiley & Putnam, 1847).

3. Thomas DeQuincey, "Homer and the Homeridae," *Blackwood's Edinburgh Magazine,* December 1841, quoted in Caroline Spurgeon, *Five Hundred Years of Chaucer Criticism and Allusion, 1357–1900,* 3 vols. paginated as 6 parts (1925; reprint, New York: Russell & Russell, 1960), 2:2.230. The italics are DeQuincey's.

4. For a survey, see David Crystal, *The English Tone of Voice: Essays in Intonation, Prosody and Paralanguage* (New York: St. Martin's Press, 1975).

5. Jacques Barzun, "Music into Words," 1951, now in *Lectures on the History and Art of Music: The Louis Charles Elson Lectures at the Library of Congress, 1946–1963* (New York: Da Capo, 1968), 92.

6. Charles Muscatine, "*The Canterbury Tales:* Style of the Man and Style of the Work," in *Chaucer and Chaucerians,* ed. Derek S. Brewer (University, Ala.: Univ. of Alabama Press, 1966), 96; D. W. Robertson, Jr., *A Preface to Chaucer: Studies in Medieval Perspectives* (Princeton: Princeton Univ. Press, 1962), 246; Robert M. Lumiansky, *Of Sondry Folk: The Dramatic Principle in the Canterbury Tales* (Austin: Univ. of Texas Press, 1955), 79; E. Talbot Donaldson, *Speaking of Chaucer* (New York: Norton, 1970), 61.

7. Raymond Macdonald Alden, "The Mental Side of Metrical Form," *Modern Language Review* 9 (1914): 297–98.

8. Leigh Hunt, "Specimens of a Dictionary of Love and Beauty," *The New Monthly Magazine and Literary Journal,* n.s., 17 (1826): 49.

9. For two opposing views on the relationship of punctuation to prescribed oral performance of a manuscript, each with further references, see Alan T. Gaylord, "Scanning the Prosodists: An Essay in Metacriticism," *Chaucer Review* 11 (1976–77): 22–82; and Norman Blake, *The English Language in Medieval Literature* (London: J. M. Dent; Totowa, N.J.: Rowman & Littlefield, 1977) esp. 67.

10. In the field of oral interpretation, scholars considering this issue include Katharine T. Loesch, "Literary Ambiguity and Oral Performance," *Quarterly Journal of Speech* 51 (1965): 258–67, and others cited in n. 13 of my Introduction.

11. Florence Ridley, "Readings from Chaucer" (paper and performance delivered at the Seventeenth International Congress on Medieval Studies, Kalamazoo, Mich., 8 May 1982); *NPT* ll. 2835, 2837, 2842.

12. For references, see n. 22 of Chapter 1, "The Prioress on Paper."

13. Mary Madeleva, "Chaucer's Nuns," in her *Lost Language and Other Essays on Chaucer* (1951; reprint, New York: Russell & Russell, 1967), 39.

14. Desmond Morris, Peter Collett, Peter Marsh, and Marie O'Shaughnessy, *Gestures: Their Origins and Distribution* (New York: Stein & Day, 1979); Desmond Morris, *Body Watching: A Field Guide to the Human Species* (New York: Crown, 1985). Other studies include Edward T. Hall, *The Silent Language* (Garden City, N.Y.: Doubleday, 1959); idem, *The Hidden Dimension* (Garden City, N.Y.: Doubleday, 1966): and Ray L. Birdwhistell,

Kinesics and Context: Essays on Body Motion Communication (Philadelphia: Univ. of Pennsylvania Press, 1970).

15. Referring to his *Twilight of the Gods: The Music of the Beatles* (New York: Viking, 1974), for example, Wilfrid Mellers says, "I have not . . . resorted to musical notation, as I did in my book on the Beatles, because I now accept that in relation to such music it is more misleading than illuminating," in his *Darker Shade of Pale: A Backdrop to Bob Dylan* (London: Faber & Faber, 1984), 232. Other approaches include Steven Feld, "Linguistic Models in Ethnomusicology," *Ethnomusicology* 18 (1974): 197–217; Mark W. Booth, *The Experience of Songs* (New Haven: Yale Univ. Press, 1981); Emil A. Guntheil et al., *Music and Your Emotions: A Practical Guide to Music Selections Associated with Desired Emotional Responses* (New York: Liveright, 1952); Charles Keil, "Motion and Feeling through Music," *Journal of Aesthetics and Art Criticism* 24 (1966): 337–49; Leonard B. Meyer, *Emotion and Meaning in Music* (Chicago: Univ. of Chicago Press, 1956), esp. 256–72; Richard Middleton, *Pop Music and the Blues: A Study of the Relationship and Its Significance* (London: Victor Gollancz, 1972); and Charles Seeger, "Music as a Tradition of Communication Discipline and Play," *Ethnomusicology* 6 (1962): 156–63.

16. I make this point concerning several songs in my *Performed Literature: Words and Music by Bob Dylan* (Bloomington: Indiana Univ. Press, 1982).

17. Donaldson articulated the issue in "Chaucer the Pilgrim," *PMLA* 69 (1954): 928–36. More recent studies, each with further references, include Donald Howard, "Chaucer the Man," *PMLA* 80 (1965): 337–43; Marshall Leicester, "A General Prologue to the *Canterbury Tales*," *PMLA* 95 (1980): 213–24; and Barbara Nolan, "'A Poet Ther Was': Chaucer's Voices in the General Prologue to *The Canterbury Tales*," *PMLA* 101 (1986): 154–69.

18. In *Interpretation: An Essay in the Philosophy of Literary Criticism* (Princeton: Princeton Univ. Press, 1980), 133–35, Juhl suggests that theorists distinguish between author's plan and author's intention. The latter, probably subconscious, is manifested when the author is satisfied enough to permit publication. Satisfaction is less certain among the Chaucer scholars kind and daring enough to provide me with data; well over half returned their tapes with *apologias* for interpretive imperfections. D4 and D5, as it happens, are among the minority of readers at least apparently satisfied with their performances.

19. Augustine of Hippo, *De Doctrina Christiana*, PL 34, col. 81, as translated by Beryl Rowland in her "*Pronuntiatio* and its Effect on Chaucer's Audience," *Studies in the Age of Chaucer* 4 (1982): 34; *Princeton Encyclopedia of Poetry and Poetics*, ed. Alex Preminger, enl. ed. (Princeton: Princeton Univ. Press, 1974), s.v. "irony"; William Empson, *Seven Types of Ambiguity: A Study of Its Effects in English Verse*, 3d ed. (1953; reprint, New York: Meridian, 1955). Concerning the mystical power of the number three, see Alan Dundes, "The Number Three in American Culture," in *Every Man His Way: Readings in Cultural Anthropology*, ed. Dundes (Englewood Cliffs, N.J.: Prentice-Hall, 1968), 401–24.

20. The term is Leicester's in his "General Prologue to the *Canterbury Tales*," 221.

21. A typical use of the term "horizon of expectations" is by Hans Robert Jauss, "Literary History as a Challenge to Literary Theory," trans. Elizabeth Benzinger, *New Literary History* 2 (1970): 7–37. For discussion and bibliography on worldview, see Barre Toelken, *The Dynamics of Folklore* (Boston: Houghton Mifflin, 1979), 225–61.

22. Spurgeon, *Five Hundred Years of Chaucer Criticism*, 3: Index.18–20. Arundell Esdaile prepared this index, according to William L. Alderson (and Arnold C. Henderson), *Chaucer and Augustan Scholarship* (Berkeley and Los Angeles: Univ. of California Press, 1970), 246 n. 16. In his unpublished papers, now in my possession, Alderson notes that Esdaile's "*expertise* in bibliography is here finally dependent on the judgments of Miss Spurgeon."

23. DeQuincey, "Homer and the Homeridae," quoted in Spurgeon, *Five Hundred Years of Chaucer Criticism*, 2:2.229–30. All italics are DeQuincey's.

3:   *The Pardoner on Paper, After and Before the Eighteenth Century*

1. G. G. Sedgewick, "The Progress of Chaucer's Pardoner, 1880–1940," *Modern Language Quarterly* 1 (1940): 442.

2. Ibid., 456.

3. Ibid., 453, 457. For Kittredge's interpretation of the Pardoner, see his *Chaucer and His Poetry* (Cambridge: Harvard Univ. Press, 1915), 211–18; for Curry's, see his *Chaucer and the Mediaeval Sciences*, 2d ed. (New York: Barnes & Noble, 1960), 54–70, originally published in 1926.

4. John Speirs, *Chaucer the Maker*, rev. ed. (London: Faber & Faber, 1960), 177; Dewey R. Faulkner, introducing his anthology *Twentieth Century Interpretations of The Pardoner's Tale: A Collection of Critical Essays* (Englewood Cliffs, N.J.: Prentice-Hall, 1973), 11; Edmund Reiss, "The Final Irony of the Pardoner's Tale," *College English* 25 (1964): 266.

5. James L. Calderwood, "Parody in The Pardoner's Tale," *English Studies* 45 (1964): 309; Robert M. Lumiansky, *Of Sondry Folk: The Dramatic Principle in the Canterbury Tales* (Austin: Univ. of Texas Press, 1955), 219.

6. Malcolm Pittock, "*The Pardoner's Tale* and the Quest for Death," *Essays in Criticism* (Oxford) 24 (1974): 121; Curry, *Chaucer and the Mediaeval Sciences*, 67; Charles Mitchell, "The Moral Superiority of Chaucer's Pardoner," *College English* 27 (1966): 443.

7. Donald R. Howard, *The Idea of the Canterbury Tales* (Berkeley and Los Angeles: Univ. of California Press, 1976), 363–64.

8. Eric W. Stockton, "The Deadliest Sin in *The Pardoner's Tale*," *Tennessee Studies in Literature* 6 (1961): 56; Ralph W. V. Elliott, *The Nun's Priest's Tale and the Pardoner's Tale (Geoffrey Chaucer)* (Oxford: Blackwell, 1965), 58; Paul E. Beichner, "Chaucer's Pardoner as Entertainer," *Mediaeval Studies* (Toronto) 25 (1963): 164–65.

9. Felicity Currie, "Chaucer's Pardoner Again," *Leeds Studies in English* 4 (1970): 19, 11.

10. Gordon Hall Gerould, *Chaucerian Essays* (Princeton: Princeton Univ. Press, 1952), 61.

11. Malcolm Pittock, *The Prioress's Tale, The Wife of Bath's Tale (Chaucer)* (Oxford: Blackwell, 1973), 44–45.

12. For the three possibilities, see Curry, *Chaucer and the Mediaeval Sciences,* 57–64; Monica E. McAlpine, "The Pardoner's Homosexuality and How It Matters," *PMLA* 95 (1980): 8–22; and Beryl Rowland, "Animal Imagery and the Pardoner's Abnormality," *Neophilologus* 48 (1964): 56–60. C. David Benson surveys the issue in "Chaucer's Pardoner: His Sexuality and Modern Critics," *Mediaevalia: A Journal of Medieval Studies* 8 (1985, for 1982): 337–49. See also John M. Bowers, "*The Tale of Beryn* and *The Siege of Thebes:* Alternative Ideas of *The Canterbury Tales,*" *Studies in the Age of Chaucer* 7 (1985): 29–30.

13. Reiss, "Final Irony of the Pardoner's Tale," 265; Winthrop Wetherbee, "Some Intellectual Themes in Chaucer's Poetry," in *Geoffrey Chaucer: A Collection of Original Articles,* ed. George D. Economou (New York: McGraw-Hill, 1975), 89; Robert P. Miller, "Chaucer's Pardoner, the Scriptural Eunuch, and the *Pardoner's Tale,*" *Speculum* 30 (1955): 198.

14. Charles Cowden Clarke, ed., *The Riches of Chaucer,* 2 vols. (London: E. Wilson, 1835), 1:x, 80, 267; Richard H. Horne, *Prologue to the Canterbury Tales,* in *The Poems of Geoffrey Chaucer modernised,* ed. Horne (London: Whittaker, 1841), 32.

15. For the MLA session, see *PMLA* 99 (1984): 1119. From consideration as "clear evidence" I mean to exclude the Ellesmere ms. illustrations, some details of which are as skillfully ambiguous as Chaucer's text (e.g., the Pardoner's vernicle), and John Lydgate's garbled recollection of a composite pilgrim in lines 32–35 of his *Siege of Thebes.*

16. William P. Carey, *Critical Description of the Procession of Chaucer's Pilgrims to Canterbury, painted by Thomas Stothard, Esq. R.A.,* 2d ed. (London: Glindon, 1818), 60.

17. Charles Dickens, letter to James Emerson Tennent, 1866, quoted in Caroline Spurgeon, *Five Hundred Years of Chaucer Criticism and Allusion, 1357–1900,* 3 vols. paginated as 6 parts (1925; reprint, New York: Russell & Russell, 1960), 2:3.82; Kittredge, *Chaucer and His Poetry,* 180.

18. William Blake, *The Marriage of Heaven and Hell,* ca. 1790–93, now in *Blake: Complete Writings,* ed. Geoffrey Keynes (London: Oxford Univ. Press, 1966), 149. Concerning my quoting from this outdated edition, see my n. 27, Chapter 1, "The Prioress on Paper."

19. L. B. Wright, "William Painter and the Vogue of Chaucer as a Moral Teacher," *Modern Philology* 31 (1933): 165–74. See also, for example, writers quoted in Spurgeon, *Five Hundred Years of Chaucer Criticism,* 1:85–86 (Ascham), 88 (Becke), 115 (Northbrooke).

20. In my text, *PTB* line references are to *The Tale of Beryn, with A Prologue of the merry Adventure of the Pardoner with a Tapster at Canterbury,* ed. Frederick J. Furnivall and W. G. Stone, Early English Text Society, extra ser., no. 105 (1887, 1909; reprint, Millwood, N.Y.: Kraus Reprints, 1975). Furnivall urges that a reader of his edition ignore the "needless little words in square brackets" with which he "for a time" attempted to regularize the

meter, or even "gratify his resentment at such impertinences by drawing a pen through them" (xi). I have done so. In addition, since the text cries out anyhow for a thorough reediting, I have here made it easier for nonmedievalists and typesetters by modernizing thorn, yogh, and u/v/w, and by sometimes fitting capitalization and punctuation into my own sentences. A manuscript virgule is indicated by +.

Besides its publication by Furnivall, by Urry in the 1721 edition, and by reusers of Urry's text for the next century and a half, the tale has been made public by F. J. Harvey Darton in his clean-scrubbed novel for young people, *The Story of the Canterbury Pilgrims Retold from Chaucer and Others* (New York: F. Stokes, 1914), 228–39. He entitles it "At Canterbury: The Chequer of the Hoope," presumably missing the pun in the inn's name.

21. *PTB* ll. 476, 480, 471; Furnivall, *Tale of Beryn*, 181; *Middle English Dictionary*, ed. Hans Kurath, 10 vols. to date (Ann Arbor: Univ. of Michigan Press, 1952–), s.v. "dischauce." Hereafter I cite this work as *MED*.

22. E. J. Bashe, "The Prologue of *The Tale of Beryn*," *Philological Quarterly* 12 (1933): 1–16.

23. Thomas W. Ross, *Chaucer's Bawdy* (New York: Dutton, 1972), 50.

24. Munro S. Edmonson, *Lore: An Introduction to the Science of Folklore and Literature* (New York: Holt, Rinehart & Winston, 1971), 88. For a variety of other approaches to puns, see Betsy Bowden, "The Art of Courtly Copulation," *Medievalia et Humanistica*, n.s., 9 (1979): 67–85; William Empson, *Seven Types of Ambiguity: A Study of Its Effects in English Verse*, 3d ed. (1953; reprint, New York: Meridian, 1955), esp. 117–74; Peter Farb, *Word Play: What Happens When People Talk* (1974; reprint, New York: Bantam, 1975), esp. 99–101; Joan Ferrante, "'Ab joi mou lo vers e'l comens,'" in *The Interpretation of Medieval Lyric Poetry*, ed. W. T. H. Jackson (New York: Columbia Univ. Press, 1980), 113–41; L. G. Heller, "Toward a General Typology of the Pun," *Language and Style* 7 (1974): 271–82; Joel Sherzer, "'Oh! That's a Pun and I Didn't Mean It,'" *Semiotica* 22 (1978): 335–50; Susan Slyomovics, "The Death-Song of 'Amer Khafaji: Puns in an Oral and Printed Episode of *Sirat Bani Hilal*," forthcoming in *Journal of Arabic Literature;* and Susan Stewart, *Nonsense: Aspects of Intertextuality in Folklore and Literature* (Baltimore: Johns Hopkins Univ. Press, 1979), esp. 161–63.

25. Larry D. Benson, "The 'Queynte' Punnings of Chaucer's Critics," in *Studies in the Age of Chaucer. Proceedings, No. 1, 1984: Reconstructing Chaucer*, ed. Paul Strohm and Thomas J. Heffernan (Knoxville: Univ. of Tennessee for the New Chaucer Society, 1985), 23–47.

26. John Gay, *The Shepherd's Week*, "Monday; or, The Squabble," 1714, now in *John Gay: Poetry and Prose*, ed. Vinton A. Dearing and Charles E. Beckwith, 2 vols. (Oxford: Clarendon, 1974), 1:99, l. 79; J. T., *To His Most ingenuous Friend, The Authour of the Exaltation of Hornes*, 1661, quoted in Spurgeon, *Five Hundred Years of Chaucer Criticism*, 3:4.74.

27. Letter from a Parliament-Officer at Grantham to John Cleveland, 1645–46; and A[lexander] B[rome], *A Canterbury Tale, Translated out of Chaucers old English Into our now vsuall Langvage. Whereunto is added the Scots Pedler*, 1641; both cited in Spurgeon, *Five Hundred Years of Chaucer*

Criticism, 1:224, 219. Alfred Tobler provides the entire text of the *Scots Pedler* in his *Geoffrey Chaucer's Influence on English Literature* (1905; reprint, New York: AMS Press, 1973), 4–6.

28. Elizabeth Cooper, *The Muses Library; Or, A Series of English Poetry* (London: James Hodges, 1741), xi, originally published in 1737.

29. Mikhail Bakhtin implies but does not address directly this economic issue in his discussions of medieval and Renaissance festival traditions in literature—e.g., *Rabelais and His World*, trans. Hélène Iswolsky (Bloomington: Indiana Univ. Press, 1984), originally completed in 1940 and published in 1965 in Moscow.

30. George Sampson, *The Concise Cambridge History of English Literature*, 3d ed. (Cambridge: Cambridge Univ. Press, 1972), 204.

31. For both plays by John Heywood named in my text, parenthetical page references are to *The Dramatic Writings of John Heywood*, ed. John S. Farmer (1905; reprint, New York: Barnes & Noble, 1966). In this quotation, from page 6, "holy Jew's hip" is the editor's misreading of "shepe" in the original.

32. For analogues to his "gaude," see W. F. Bryan and Germaine Dempster, *Sources and Analogues of Chaucer's Canterbury Tales* (1941; reprint, Atlantic Highlands, N.J.: Humanities Press, 1958), 411–14.

33. *Scots Pedler*, quoted in Tobler, *Geoffrey Chaucer's Influence*, 5–6.

4: The Eighteenth-Century Pardoner(s)

1. Concerning Pope's education and early book ownership, see Maynard Mack, *Alexander Pope: A Life* (New Haven: Yale Univ. Press in association with W. W. Norton, 1985), 3–12, 28–52, 76–87. As far as I have been able to determine, Mack knew by 1938 that Pope owned a copy of the 1598 Speght edition (now in Hartlebury Castle, Worcestershire) but did not publish that information until his "Pope's Books: A Biographical Survey with a Finding List," in *English Literature in the Age of Disguise*, ed. Maximillian E. Novak (Berkeley and Los Angeles: Univ. of California Press, 1977), 212, 242–43.

   In this paragraph I refer to *The Tale of Beryn, with A Prologue of the merry Adventure of the Pardoner with a Tapster at Canterbury*, ed. Frederick J. Furnivall and W. G. Stone, Early English Text Society, extra ser., no. 105 (1887, 1909; reprint, Millwood, N.Y.: Kraus Reprints, 1975); John Heywood, *A mery Play betwene the Pardoner and the frere, the curate and neybour Pratt*, 1533, and *The Playe called the foure PP*, 1544(?), both now in *The Dramatic Writings of John Heywood*, ed. John S. Farmer (1905; reprint, New York: Barnes & Noble, 1966), 1–25, 26–64; *Richard Brathwait's Comments, in 1665, upon Chaucer's Tales of the Miller and the Wife of Bath*, ed. Caroline Spurgeon, The Chaucer Society, 2d ser., no. 33 (London: Kegan Paul, Trench, Trübner & Co., 1901); the Great Fire of 1666 as described by Marjorie Plant, *The English Book Trade: An Economic History of the Making and Sale of Books*, 3d ed. (London: Allen & Unwin, 1974), 245; and Chaucer's seventeenth-century print reputation as accounted for in my n. 19, Chapter 3, "The Pardoner on Paper, After and

Before the Eighteenth Century." Before modern times Heywood's plays were published only in editions of 1533 and 1552–69, according to R. de la Bère, *John Heywood, Entertainer* (London: Allen & Unwin, 1937), 131, 184.

2. Thomas Speght, ed., *The Workes of our Antient and Learned English Poet, Geffrey Chaucer, newly Printed* (London: Adam Islip, 1598). In this first edition, the Arguments are grouped at the beginning of the *Tales,* on un-numbered pages. In Speght's 1602 and 1687 editions, they head each *Tale,* thereby perhaps serving a mnemonic or indexing function like that of pilgrim portraits in these positions in editions earlier than Speght's.

3. Caroline Spurgeon, *Five Hundred Years of Chaucer Criticism and Allusion, 1357–1900,* 3 vols. paginated as 6 parts (1925; reprint, New York: Russell & Russell, 1960), 1:xcvi.

4. Thomas Betterton, *Chaucer's Characters, Or The Introduction to the Canterbury Tales,* in *Miscellaneous Poems and Translations. By Several Hands* (London: Bernard Lintott [*sic*], 1712), 277, for *GP* l. 622.

5. Ibid., 279–80, for *GP* ll. 663–78. All further quotations from the Pope/Betterton modernization, in my chapter, occur on pp. 279–82, for *GP* ll. 669–714 (unless otherwise noted).

6. Ibid., 273, for *GP* ll. 549, 546, 551, 554.

7. A recent consideration of the same issue is Edgar Hill Duncan, "Narrator's Points of View in the Portrait Sketches, Prologue to the *Canterbury Tales,*" in *Essays in Honor of Walter Clyde Curry,* Vanderbilt Studies in the Humanities, vol. 2 (Nashville: Vanderbilt Univ. Press, 1955), 77–101.

8. William Blake, *A Descriptive Catalogue of Pictures, Poetical and Historical Inventions,* 1809, now in *Blake: Complete Writings,* ed. Geoffrey Keynes (London: Oxford Univ. Press, 1966), 570. Concerning my quoting from this outdated edition, see n. 27, Chapter 1, "The Prioress on Paper."

9. Betterton, *Chaucer's Characters,* in *Miscellaneous Poems and Translations,* 256, for *GP* ll. 170–71.

10. The comparative image is William Blake's in his *Marriage of Heaven and Hell,* ca. 1790–93, now in his *Complete Writings,* 152: "Sooner murder an infant in its cradle than nurse unacted desires."

11. Urizen is Blake's personification of the rational facility that limits or stifles artistic creativity. I mention the external evidence for Blake's use of the Urry edition in Chapter 7, "The Merchant as Character on Paper."

12. Not until a *Clerk's Tale* in 1813 was a direct translation again done from Middle English into French. See Spurgeon, *Five Hundred Years of Chaucer Criticism,* 3:5.6, 10, 32–34, 41–43.

13. [Antoine François Prévost d'Exiles], "Philologie. Vies des Poètes Anglois, par M. Colley Cibber . . . Geofroy Chaucer," *Journal Étranger,* May 1755, now in facsimile *Journal Étranger,* 45 vols. in 8 (Geneva: Slatkine Reprints, 1968), 2:300. Accents and spelling are those of the original.

14. Ibid.

15. Ibid., 2:301.

16. Blake, *Descriptive Catalogue,* now in his *Complete Writings,* 574–75.

17. William P. Carey, *Critical Description of the Procession of Chaucer's Pil-*

grims to Canterbury, painted by Thomas Stothard, Esq. R.A., 2d ed. (London: Glindon, 1818), 60.

18. Ibid., 61.

19. Blake, *Descriptive Catalogue*, now in his *Complete Writings*, 570.

20. I thank members of Prof. Robert Ryan's Blake course at Rutgers/Camden, spring 1984, including Joseph Perozzi and Carole Breakstone, for pointing out this resemblance. Blake had me fooled into thinking that the Parson represented goodness in both Blake's sense and that of the rest of the world, in my article, "The Artistic and Interpretive Context of Blake's 'Canterbury Pilgrims,'" *Blake: An Illustrated Quarterly* 13 (1980): 186. Much remains to be said about the picture's symbolism.

21. Blake, *Descriptive Catalogue*, now in his *Complete Writings*, 570.

22. Information on Lipscomb's life is taken from the *DNB*. Parenthetical volume and page references in my text are to his *Canterbury Tales of Chaucer, completed in a Modern Version*, 3 vols. (London: J. Cooke & G. G. & J. Robinson, 1795). All *Tales* modernized by Lipscomb are in vol. 3: Franklin's, 106–40; Physician's, 141–51; Pardoner's, 152–78; Shipman's, 179–93; Prioress's, 194–203; Thopas, 204–13; Melibeus, 214–81; Monk's, 282–313; Nun's Priest's, 314–36; Second Nun's, 337–52; Canon's Yeoman's, 353–78; Manciple's, 379–89. Lipscomb was unaware of Dryden's *Nun's Priest's Tale* modernization, as he apologizes in a postscript to his *Preface*, 1:xi, because it does not appear in George Ogle, ed., *The Canterbury Tales of Chaucer, Modernis'd by several Hands*, 3 vols. (London: J. & R. Tonson, 1741). I am at work on a comparison of the two *Nun's Priest's Tale* modernizations.

23. In his edition *The Canterbury Tales of Chaucer*, 5 vols. (1775–78; reprint, New York: AMS Press, 1972), Thomas Tyrwhitt numbers lines consecutively throughout the volumes, skipping over *Melibeus*, such that the last verse line before the *Parson's Tale* (3:140) is no. 17385 (for *ParsT* l. 74).

24. Tyrwhitt, *Canterbury Tales*, 2:197, for *PardT* l. 897.

25. George Lyman Kittredge, *Chaucer and His Poetry* (Cambridge: Harvard Univ. Press, 1915), 214.

26. Tyrwhitt, *Canterbury Tales*, 2:200.

27. "He set a stiff thing to my wame," in *There Cam a Soger*, in Robert Burns, *The Merry Muses of Caledonia*, ca. 1800, now in *The Merry Muses of Caledonia: A Collection of Bawdy Folksongs, Ancient and Modern*, ed. James Barke and Sydney Goodsir Smith (New York: Gramercy, 1959), 84.

28. Among larger slang dictionaries showing no entry for "coillon," "coin," or "cullion," see Francis Grose, *A Classical Dictionary of the Vulgar Tongue*, orig. 1785, 3d ed. 1796, reprint ed. Eric Partridge, 3d ed. of reprint (New York: Barnes & Noble, 1963); and John S. Farmer and William E. Henley, *Slang and Its Analogues, Past and Present*, 7 vols. (1890–1904; reprint in 1 vol., New York: Arno Press, 1970). The *OED*'s latest entry for "cullion" meaning "testicle" is in 1737; by Lipscomb's time it was primarily "a term of contempt: A base, despicable, or vile fellow; a rascal." But he would find the genital meaning in the glossary of Tyrwhitt's *Canterbury Tales*, 5:40. In the glossary to his 1598 edition of Chaucer's *Workes*, by the way, Thomas

Speght defines "coilons" as "stones," presumably the standard neutral term then.

29. The last account published of Cooper's work seems to have been that by Thomas R. Lounsbury, *Studies in Chaucer, His Life and Writings,* 3 vols. (1892; reprint, New York: Russell & Russell, 1962), 3:242–43. She is mentioned also by Spurgeon, *Five Hundred Years of Chaucer Criticism,* 1:li.

30. Concerning annotations by editors Thomas Speght, John Urry, and especially Thomas Morell, see William L. Alderson and Arnold C. Henderson, *Chaucer and Augustan Scholarship* (Berkeley and Los Angeles: Univ. of California Press, 1970). Cooper was probably influenced directly by Pope's citation of his own sources in, for example, his reworking of Chaucer's *House of Fame,* which I will discuss in Chapter 9, "The *Merchant's Tale* on Paper, Before Pope."

31. Elizabeth Cooper, *The Muses Library; Or, A Series of English Poetry* (London: James Hodges, 1741), 8, originally published in 1737. Page references in my text are to this edition.

32. Merritt Y. Hughes, ed., note to *Paradise Lost,* bk. 11, ll. 477–95, in *John Milton, Complete Poems and Major Prose* (New York: Odyssey Press, 1957), 444; Cooper, *Muses Library,* 17–18.

33. William Godwin, *Life of Geoffrey Chaucer, The Early English Poet,* 2d ed., 4 vols. (1804; reprint, New York: AMS Press, 1974), 3:361.

34. Giles Jacob, *Poetical Register: or, the Lives and Characters of the English [Dramatick] Poets* (1719–20); William Winstanley, a.k.a. "Poor Robin," *The Muses Cabinet, stored with Variety of Poems* (1655); idem, *England's Worthies: select lives of most eminent persons* (1660); idem, *Lives of the Most Famous English Poets* (1687); Edward Phillips, *Theatrum Poetarum* (1675); Anthony à Wood, *Athenae Oxonienses* (1691–92); Thomas Pope Blount, *De Re Poetica. or Remarks upon Poetry, with Characters and Censures of the Most considerable Poets, whether Ancient or Modern, extracted out of the best and choicest cricks* (1694).

35. After forty fifteenth-century manuscripts, *De Regimine Principum* lost popularity and was not printed until 1860 by Thomas Wright, according to M. C. Seymour, ed., *Selections from Hoccleve* (Oxford: Clarendon, 1981), xxxii–xxxiii. Cooper quotes Hoccleve from the Life of Chaucer section in Speght's edition of Chaucer's *Workes,* "But weylaway! is mine Heart wo . . . ," with spelling, punctuation, and capitalization modernized as in other passages she quotes.

36. *Of the Old English Poets and Poetry: An Essay,* 1707, quoted in Spurgeon, *Five Hundred Years of Chaucer Criticism,* 1:295. See the index to Spurgeon's work, 3:16–17, for an outline in regard to Chaucer's verse "thought irregular . . . . thought rhythmical . . . . thought only apparently irregular . . . . final *e* discovered [six times] . . . . decried."

37. For the plagiarism, compare William Winstanley, *Lives of the Most Famous English Poets* (1687; reprint, Gainesville, Fla.: Scholars' Facsimiles & Reprints, 1963), 33–34, and Thomas Fuller, *History of the Worthies of England,* ed. P. Austin Nuttall, 3 vols. (London: T. Tegg, 1840), 3:183, originally published in 1662. I quote Winstanley.

The Life and Death of Hector . . . . Written by Iohn Lidgate, Monke of

Berry (London: T. Purfoot, 1614) led directly to the prevalent notion that Lydgate wrote smoother verse than Chaucer's. Presumably better distributed than Lydgate's actual works, *The Life and Death of Hector* is in fact the only published modernization of Middle English before Dryden's. The passage quoted by Winstanley and Fuller is on page 316. The long title provides the total body count for the Trojan War: "Fourteene Hundred, and Six Thousand, Fourscore, and sixe men." The author may be Thomas Heywood, according to Herbert G. Wright's introduction to his edition (from manuscript) of *A Seventeenth-Century Modernisation of the First Three Books of Chaucer's "Troilus and Criseyde,"* Cooper Monographs on English and American Language and Literature, no. 5 (Bern: A. Francke, 1960), 14.

38. Edward Phillips, *Theatrum Poetarum, or a Compleat Collection of the Poets . . . The Ancients distinguish't from the Moderns in their several Alphabets* (London: C. Smith, 1675), 113–14 of second separately numbered page grouping.

39. Winstanley, *Lives of the Most Famous English Poets,* 195.

40. Cooper, *Muses Library,* 30. As a line inversion makes clear, the large folio that she purchased was Lydgate's *Fall of Princes,* printed by Richard Tottell in 1554. The lines from Lydgate that she quotes are actually ll. 665–72 of his *Daunce of Machabree,* which follows *Fall of Princes* in this edition. A convenient text of *Daunce of Machabree* is in *English Verse between Chaucer and Surrey,* ed. Eleanor P. Hammond (1927; reprint, New York: Octagon, 1965), 142 for lines quoted.

41. Cooper would have read *Piers Plowman* in one of the editions printed by Robert Crowley—three in 1550 and another in 1561. The first impression is available in facsimile: William Langland, *The Vision of Pierce Plowman,* ed. J. A. W. Bennett (London: David Paradine, 1976).

5: *The Pardoner on Tape*

1. As mentioned, the term "virgin experience" is Paula Johnson's, in her *Form and Transformation in Music and Poetry of the English Renaissance* (New Haven: Yale Univ. Press, 1972), 59. In this work she criticizes the theories on experiencing music of Leonard B. Meyer, *Emotion and Meaning in Music* (Chicago: Univ. of Chicago Press, 1956). Elizabeth Cooper wrote *The Muses Library; Or, A Series of English Poetry* (London: James Hodges, 1741), originally published in 1737, as just discussed.

2. Leo F. McNamara, "The Astonishing Performance of Chaucer's Pardoner," *Papers of the Michigan Academy of Sciences, Arts, and Letters* (Ann Arbor) 46 (1961): 597–604.

3. Penelope Curtis, "The Pardoner's 'Jape,'" *Critical Review* 11 (1968): 23, describing *PardT* ll. 472–85.

4. George Lyman Kittredge, *Chaucer and His Poetry* (Cambridge: Harvard Univ. Press, 1915), 155, 158.

5. Paul E. Beichner, "Chaucer's Pardoner as Entertainer," *Mediaeval Studies* (Toronto) 25 (1963): 161–62.

6. The reassurance is Steven Swann Jones's, in his review of *Breaking the*

Magic Spell by Jack Zipes, *Western Folklore* 41 (1982): 242. The phrase "global village" is used by Marshall McLuhan in several books; see, for example, his *Understanding Media: The Extensions of Man* (New York: McGraw-Hill, 1964).

7. Meyer, *Emotion and Meaning in Music*, 257.

8. Robert Ross can be heard on *Chaucer. The Canterbury Tales. The Nun's Priest's Tale. The Pardoner's Prologue and Tale*, Caedmon SWC 1008 (1953). Any reader who recalls Ross's pronunciation as faulty should listen again to the record. Its cover notes offer a gratuitous apology for Ross's pronunciation, which is no more imperfect than that on most commercial recordings. His acting is outstanding. In a simple but extremely effective move, for example, he reads Chaunticleer's words to the fox (*NPT* ll. 3407–13) while clutching his own throat. Concerning this and other recordings, see my forthcoming *Teachers' Guide to Chaucer Read Aloud: An Annotated Discography*.

9. Kittredge, *Chaucer and His Poetry*, 216.

10. Walter Clyde Curry, *Chaucer and the Mediaeval Sciences*, 2d ed. (New York: Barnes & Noble, 1960), 67.

11. Curtis, "The Pardoner's 'Jape,'" 30; Elise K. Parsigian, "A Note on the Conclusion of *The Pardoner's Tale*," *Rackham Literary Studies* (Univ. of Michigan) 6 (1975): 53; John Gardner, *The Poetry of Chaucer* (Carbondale: Southern Illinois Univ. Press, 1977), 303.

12. Alice R. Kaminsky, *Chaucer's Troilus and Criseyde and the Critics* (Athens: Ohio Univ. Press, 1980), 163.

13. For a summary of my views now, see my entry "courtly love" in the *Women's Studies Encyclopedia* (Westport, Conn.: Greenwood Press, forthcoming). By "bolstered" I mean that specialists in twelfth-century French literature and history have been citing my "Art of Courtly Copulation," *Medievalia et Humanistica*, n.s., 9 (1979): 67–85, using the obscene puns I point out to help prove that Andreas Capellanus's *De Amore* must be analyzed in terms of its own genre and audience, not as if intimately related to Provençal songs or some amorphous pan-European code of "courtly love." Studies include Hubert Silvestre, "Du nouveau sur André le Chapelain," *Revue du Moyen Age Latin* 36 (1980): 99–106; Bruno Roy, "À la recherche des lecteurs médiévaux du *De amore* d'André le Chapelain," *Revue de l'Université d'Ottawa/University of Ottawa Quarterly* 55 (1985): 45–73; and Georges Duby, "Love and Society in the Paris of Philip Augustus: The Perspective of Andrew the Chaplain," address at Rutgers Univ., New Brunswick, N.J., 4 November 1985. For opposing views, see Charles Muscatine, from whom I beg indulgence, review of *The Meaning of Courtly Love*, ed. F. X. Newman, *Speculum* 46 (1971): 747–50; and Joan Ferrante, "*Cortes' Amor* in Medieval Texts," *Speculum* 55 (1980): 686–95.

14. Thomas Burton, letter to author, 8 April 1985.

6: *The Old Man in the* Pardoner's Tale

1. See K1685 in Stith Thompson, *Motif-Index of Folk Literature*, rev. and enl. ed., 6 vols. (Bloomington: Indiana Univ. Press, 1955–58), 4:420; and

Lynn King Morris, *Chaucer Source and Analogue Criticism: A Cross-Referenced Guide* (New York: Garland, 1985), 156–59. *The Treasure of the Sierra Madre* was written and directed by John Huston, from the novel by B. Traven, and released in 1948 by Warner Brothers.

2. W. F. Bryan and Germaine Dempster, eds., *Sources and Analogues of Chaucer's Canterbury Tales* (1941; reprint, Atlantic Highlands, N.J.: Humanities Press, 1958), 436.

3. W. J. B. Owen, "The Old Man in *The Pardoner's Tale*," *Review of English Studies*, n.s., 2 (1951): 50; John M. Steadman, "Old Age and *Contemptus Mundi* in *The Pardoner's Tale*," *Medium Aevum* 33 (1964): 123. A convenient summary of old-man interpretations is provided by Christopher Dean, "Salvation, Damnation and the Role of the Old Man in the *Pardoner's Tale*," *Chaucer Review* 3 (1968–69): 44–49, wherein he argues unconvincingly that God's mercy as well as justice is dispensed.

4. George Lyman Kittredge, *Chaucer and His Poetry* (Cambridge: Harvard Univ. Press, 1915), 215; Richard H. Horne, ed., *The Poems of Geoffrey Chaucer modernised* (London: Whittaker, 1841), xciv.

5. Hunt provides Thomas Tyrwhitt's text and his own modernization of *PardT* ll. 329–406, 426, as "The Pardoner's Way of Preaching," in his *Wit and Humour, Selected from the English Poets* (London: Smith, Elder, & Co., 1846), 114–16.

6. Leigh Hunt, *Stories in Verse* (London: George Routledge & Co., 1855), 264.

7. Hunt, *Stories in Verse*, 262; Kittredge, *Chaucer and His Poetry*, 214.

8. In these two paragraphs I refer to the following lines: *GP* l. 123; *MlrT* ll. 3257–58, 3218, 3360; *GP* ll. 688, 264, 306; *SumT* ll. 1666–67 (not specifically voice); *GP* l. 468; *Tr* 5.813.

9. Information on Robinson is from *Directory of American Scholars: A Biographical Directory,* ed. The Jaques Cattell Press, 4th ed., 4 vols. (New York: R. R. Bowker, 1964), 2:259; that on Kittredge is from his obituary in the *New York Times,* 24 July 1941, 17.

10. William Lipscomb, *The Canterbury Tales of Chaucer, completed in a Modern Version,* 3 vols. (London: J. Cooke & G. G. & J. Robinson, 1795), 3:171. Lipscomb first published his *Pardoner's Tale* modernization separately in 1793.

11. Hunt, *Stories in Verse*, 269. I account for his remark on the motto at n. 8, Chapter 1, "The Prioress on Paper."

12. Hunt, *Stories in Verse*, 265, for *PardT* ll. 666–69.

13. Ibid., 266, for *PardT* ll. 692–701.

14. Ibid., 269, for *PardT* ll. 760–67.

15. Lipscomb, *Canterbury Tales,* 3:170, for *PardT* ll. 760–67.

16. Ibid., 3:170, 168, for *PardT* ll. 750–51, 692–704.

17. Victor Kaplan can be heard on *Chaucer. Readings from "Canterbury Tales,"* Folkways 9859 (1962); and Robert Ross on *Chaucer. The Canterbury Tales. The Nun's Priest's Tale. The Pardoner's Prologue and Tale,* Caedmon SWC 1008 (1953). For more on commercially produced recordings of Chaucer, see my forthcoming *Teachers' Guide to Chaucer Read Aloud: An Annotated Discography.*

18. Hunt, *Stories in Verse*, 267–69.
19. John S. Farmer and William E. Henley, *Slang and Its Analogues, Past and Present*, 7 vols. (1890–1904; reprint in 1 vol., New York: Arno, 1970), s.vv. "crawl," "crawler" 2, "nipper" 1–2.
20. Hunt, *Stories in Verse*, 267, for *PardT* ll. 714–20.
21. Lipscomb, *Canterbury Tales*, 3:168–69, for *PardT* ll. 714–20.
22. Concerning the origin and present whereabouts of Mortimer's drawings, see my n. 29, Chapter 1, "The Prioress on Paper."
23. Felicity Currie, "Chaucer's Pardoner Again," *Leeds Studies in English* 4 (1970): 18.

7: The Merchant as Character on Paper

1. Some contributions to this continuing debate include, in chronological or-der, George Lyman Kittredge, *Chaucer and His Poetry* (Cambridge: Har-vard Univ. Press, 1915), 201–2; Germaine Dempster, *Dramatic Irony in Chaucer* (1932; reprint, New York: Humanities Press, 1959), 46–58; J. S. P. Tatlock, "Chaucer's Merchant's Tale," *Modern Philology* 33 (1936): 367–81; Robert M. Lumiansky, *Of Sondry Folk: The Dramatic Principle in the Canterbury Tales* (Austin: Univ. of Texas Press, 1955), 152–75; Bert-rand H. Bronson, "Afterthoughts on the Merchant's Tale," *Studies in Phil-ology* 58 (1961): 583–96; John R. Elliott, Jr., "The Two Tellers of *The Merchant's Tale*," *Tennessee Studies in Language and Literature* 9 (1964): 11–17; Robert M. Jordan, *Chaucer and the Shape of Creation: The Aes-thetic Possibilities of Inorganic Structure* (Cambridge: Harvard Univ. Press, 1966), 132–51; A. E. Hartung, "The Non-Comic *Merchant's Tale*, Maxi-mianus, and the Sources," *Mediaeval Studies* (Toronto) 29 (1967): 1–25; E. Talbot Donaldson, "The Effect of the Merchant's Tale," in his *Speaking of Chaucer* (New York: Norton, 1970), 30–45; Mary C. Schroeder, "Fan-tasy in the Merchant's Tale," *Criticism* 12 (1970): 167–79; Norman T. Har-rington, "Chaucer's Merchant's Tale: Another Swing of the Pendulum," *PMLA* 86 (1971): 25–31; Peter G. Beidler, "Chaucer's Merchant and the Tale of January," *Costerus* 5 (1972): 1–25; Martin Stevens, "'And Venus Laugheth': An Interpretation of the *Merchant's Tale*," *Chaucer Review* 7 (1972–73): 118–31; Donald R. Howard, *The Idea of the Canterbury Tales* (Berkeley and Los Angeles: Univ. of California Press, 1976), 257–64; Rob-ert B. Burlin, *Chaucerian Fiction* (Princeton: Princeton Univ. Press, 1977), 207–16; Emerson Brown, Jr., "Chaucer, the Merchant, and Their Tale: Getting beyond Old Controversies," *Chaucer Review* 13 (1978–79): 141–56, 247–62; and Martin Stevens, "The Ellesmere Miniatures as Illustra-tions of Chaucer's *Canterbury Tales*," *Studies in Iconography* 7–8 (1981–82): 129 n. 40.
2. Alexander Pope, *January and May*, 1709, and *The Wife of Bath Her Pro-logue*, 1714, both quoted here as reprinted in George Ogle, ed., *The Can-terbury Tales of Chaucer, Modernis'd by several Hands*, 3 vols. (London: J. & R. Tonson, 1741), 3:50–51.
3. Thomas Tyrwhitt, ed., *The Canterbury Tales of Chaucer*, 5 vols. (1775–78;

reprint, New York: AMS Press, 1972), 4:151. Justinus refers to the Wife of
Bath at *MctT* l. 1685.

4. Tyrwhitt, *Canterbury Tales*, 4:158–59.

5. The tale-order fray is gathering force lately, as scholars lose faith in the
authoritativeness of John M. Manly and Edith Rickert, eds., *The Text of
The Canterbury Tales*, 8 vols. (Chicago: Univ. of Chicago Press, 1940). One
recent statement is Larry D. Benson, "The Order of *The Canterbury Tales*,"
Studies in the Age of Chaucer 3 (1981): 77–120, which includes bibliography of earlier proposals. See also Judson B. Allen and Theresa A. Moritz,
*A Distinction of Stories: The Medieval Unity of Chaucer's Fair Chain of
Narratives for Canterbury* (Columbus: Ohio State Univ. Press, 1981); and
George Kane, "John M. Manly (1865–1940) and Edith Rickert (1871–
1938)," in *Editing Chaucer: The Great Tradition*, ed. Paul G. Ruggiers
(Norman, Okla.: Pilgrim Books, 1984), 207–29. Kane analyzes the assumptions and procedures of Manly and Rickert to show the "a priori
unlikelihood of their results being sound. . . . [In addition, those] results
are untestable . . . because of the virtually impenetrable system of symbols
they employed in presenting their evidence" (229).

6. Kittredge, *Chaucer and His Poetry*, 201–2.

7. John Urry, unfinished draft of a preface, before 1714, quoted by Timothy
Thomas on the last page (unnumbered) of his own *Preface* to the Urry
edition of *The Works of Geoffrey Chaucer* (London: Bernard Lintot, 1721).
The subtitles quoted are from the articles by Harrington and Brown, cited
in n. 1.

8. Concerning the two riders' raised hands in the Ellesmere, I suggest this
more practical motivation than Martin Stevens's "hailing their viewers," in
his "Ellesmere Miniatures as Illustrations," 125–26. Concerning Stothard's
horses, see comments referred to in my n. 30, Chapter 1, "The Prioress on
Paper."

9. *The Tale of Beryn, with A Prologue of the merry Adventure of the Pardoner
with a Tapster at Canterbury,* ed. Frederick J. Furnivall and W. G. Stone,
Early English Text Society, extra ser., no. 105 (1887, 1909; reprint, Millwood, N.Y.: Kraus Reprints, 1975), 14, ll. 419–22. Line references in my
text are to this edition, with *PTB* for the *Prologue* and *TB* for the contin-
uously-numbered *Tale of Beryn* itself. Concerning my elimination of Furnivall's emendations, following his own suggestion, see my n. 20, Chapter
3, "The Pardoner on Paper, After and Before the Eighteenth Century."

10. Thomas Speght, ed., *The Workes of our Antient and Learned English Poet,
Geffrey Chavcer, newly Printed* (London: Adam Islip, 1598). In this edition
the *General Prologue* portraits are numbered, but the pages on which they
occur are not. Other Speght references in my text give folio numbers.

11. John K. Crane, "An Honest Debtor?: A Note on Chaucer's Merchant, Line
A276," *English Language Notes* 4 (1966): 84.

12. Thomas Betterton, *Chaucer's Characters, Or The Introduction to the Canterbury Tales*, in *Miscellaneous Poems and Translations. By Several Hands*
(London: Bernard Lintott [*sic*], 1712), 261, for *GP* ll. 270–73. All further
quotations from the Pope/Betterton modernization of the Merchant's *General Prologue* portrait occur on pp. 261–62.

13. Betterton, *Chaucer's Characters*, in *Miscellaneous Poems and Translations*, 279, for *GP* l. 670; Alexander Pope, *January and May; or, The Merchant's Tale: From Chaucer*, 1709, now in *The Rape of the Lock and Other Poems*, ed. Geoffrey Tillotson, 3d ed. (London: Methuen; New Haven: Yale Univ. Press, 1962), vol. 2 of *The Twickenham Edition of the Poems of Alexander Pope*, ed. John Butt, 11 vols. in 12 (1939–69), 2:23, l. 177, for *MctT* l. 1520, to be discussed.

14. Quotations and information both from George Sherburn, *The Early Career of Alexander Pope* (1934; reprint, Oxford: Clarendon, 1968), 32–33. See also Maynard Mack, *Alexander Pope: A Life* (New Haven: Yale Univ. Press in association with W. W. Norton, 1985), 28–52, 76–87.

15. Thomas A. Knott, "Chaucer's Anonymous Merchant," *Philological Quarterly* 1 (1922): 1.

16. Richard H. Horne, *Prologue to the Canterbury Tales*, in *The Poems of Geoffrey Chaucer modernised*, ed. Horne (London: Whittaker, 1841), 15; Arthur Hugh Clough, "Lecture on the Development of English Literature from Chaucer to Wordsworth," 1852, now in *Selected Prose Works of Arthur Hugh Clough*, ed. Buckner B. Trawick (University, Ala.: Univ. of Alabama Press, 1964), 126; Kittredge, *Chaucer and His Poetry*, 173.

17. Oscar E. Johnson, "Was Chaucer's Merchant in Debt? A Study in Chaucerian Syntax and Rhetoric," *Journal of English and Germanic Philology* 52 (1953): 51; Gardiner Stillwell, "Chaucer's Merchant: No Debts?" *JEGP* 57 (1958): 192; B. A. Park, "The Character of Chaucer's Merchant," *English Language Notes* 1 (1964): 173.

18. Johnson, "Was Chaucer's Merchant in Debt?" 52, 55.

19. David B. Morris, *Alexander Pope: The Genius of Sense* (Cambridge: Harvard Univ. Press, 1984), 7.

20. Regarding Blake's certain familiarity with the Bell frontispiece see Betsy Bowden, "The Artistic and Interpretive Context of Blake's 'Canterbury Pilgrims,'" *Blake: An Illustrated Quarterly* 13 (1980): 168, 170.

21. William Blake, *A Descriptive Catalogue of Pictures, Poetical and Historical Inventions*, 1809, now in *Blake: Complete Writings*, ed. Geoffrey Keynes (London: Oxford Univ. Press, 1966), 574, 572. Concerning my quoting from this outdated edition, see n. 27, Chapter 1, "The Prioress on Paper."

22. Blake, *Descriptive Catalogue*, now in his *Complete Writings*, 571.

23. Ibid., 572.

24. Tyrwhitt, *Canterbury Tales*, 4:125–29.

25. Blake, *Descriptive Catalogue*, now in his *Complete Writings*, 572.

26. Blake, letter to Thomas Butts, 1803, now in his *Complete Writings*, 823.

27. [William Wells], *William Blake's "Heads of the Poets"* (Manchester: City of Manchester Art Gallery, 1969), 18–19 (exhibition pamphlet).

28. Blake, *Descriptive Catalogue*, now in his *Complete Writings*, 571.

29. William P. Carey, *Critical Description of the Procession of Chaucer's Pilgrims to Canterbury, painted by Thomas Stothard, Esq. R.A.*, 2d ed. (London: Glindon, 1818), 21.

30. Ibid., 58, 63–64, 66.

31. Ogle, *Canterbury Tales*, 3:265, developing *Thop* ll. 696–98.

32. Ibid., 3:xiv–xv.

33. Thomas R. Lounsbury, *Studies in Chaucer, His Life and Writings*, 3 vols. (1892; reprint, New York: Russell & Russell, 1962), 3:193. For more on the archetypal Grub Samuel Boyse, who "wrote verse with great facility, as fast as most men write prose," and who "was found dead in his bed, with a pen in his hand" protruding "through holes in a blanket," see Edward L. Hart, ed., *Minor Lives: A Collection of Biographies by John Nichols* (Cambridge: Harvard Univ. Press, 1971), 341–52 (343 for quotations). Nichols originally published this section of his writings in 1780.

34. See Eleanor P. Hammond, *Chaucer: A Bibliographical Manual* (1908; reprint, New York: Peter Smith, 1933), 225.

35. Ogle, *Canterbury Tales*, 1:190, for after *MlrT* l. 3186.

36. Betterton, *Chaucer's Characters*, in *Miscellaneous Poems and Translations*, 247; Ogle, *Canterbury Tales*, 1:1; both for *GP* l. 1.

37. Betterton, *Chaucer's Characters*, in *Miscellaneous Poems and Translations*, 247–48, for *GP* ll. 17–22.

38. Ogle, *Canterbury Tales*, 3:1, for *SqT* ll. 673–74.

39. Ibid., 2:324, for before *SqT* l. 673, and after Spenser's tale as adapted from bk. 4 (from canto 2, st. 32, to canto 3, st. 52) of *The Faerie Queene*, 1596, now in *The Faerie Queene, Book Four*, ed. Ray Heffner (Baltimore: Johns Hopkins Press, 1935), vol. 4 of *The Works of Edmund Spenser: A Variorum Edition*, ed. Edwin Greenlaw, Charles Grosvenor Osgood, and Frederick Morgan Padelford, 11 vols. (1932–45), 4:25–44.

40. Ogle, *Canterbury Tales*, 3:2–4, for *SqT* ll. 682–708 and *MctT* ll. 1213–14.

41. Ibid., 3:6–7, for *MctT* ll. 1233–44.

42. See the works cited in n. 1 of this chapter by Bronson, Jordan, Donaldson, Elliott, Harrington, Hartung, Kittredge, and Tatlock. Just before his death, Professor Bronson acknowledged the fictional validity of my scenario and requested a full reference for Ogle's work (letter to author, 14 January 1986).

8: *The Merchant as Character on Tape*

1. Thomas Speght, ed., *The Workes of our Antient and Learned English Poet, Geffrey Chaucer, newly Printed* (London: Adam Islip, 1598), fol. 27r.

2. Speght, *Workes*, fol. 27r; and Alexander Pope, *January and May; or, The Merchant's Tale: From Chaucer*, 1709, now in *The Rape of the Lock and Other Poems*, ed. Geoffrey Tillotson, 3d ed. (London: Methuen; New Haven: Yale Univ. Press, 1962), vol. 2 of *The Twickenham Edition of the Poems of Alexander Pope*, ed. John Butt, 11 vols. in 12 (1939–69), 2:17, ll. 57–58.

3. *Gabriel Harvey's Marginalia*, ed. G. C. Moore Smith (Stratford-upon-Avon: Shakespeare Head Press, 1913), 227. For background see Virginia F. Stern, *Gabriel Harvey: His Life, Marginalia and Library* (Oxford: Clarendon, 1979).

9: *The* Merchant's Tale *on Paper, Before Pope*

1. Marjorie Plant, *The English Book Trade: An Economic History of the Making and Sale of Books*, 3d ed. (London: Allen & Unwin, 1974), 17.

2. John Foxe, *Actes and Monuments,* 1563, quoted in Barbara W. Tuchman, *Bible and Sword: England and Palestine from the Bronze Age to Balfour* (1956; reprint, New York: Ballantine, 1984), 98.

3. Colin Clair, *A History of Printing in Britain* (New York: Oxford Univ. Press, 1966), 5, 97. Seeing a market for a Chaucer folio in modern type, early in the eighteenth century, entrepreneurs at Oxford chose the artist(s) wisely, as discussed throughout this book, but the editor unwisely. Though unused, as mentioned in my n. 25, Chapter 1, "The Prioress on Paper," John Urry's 1721 edition had such elegant typography and illustrations that it would have remained costly even purchased second-hand. Furthermore, original owners of this edition, rather than selling their copies, seem to have passed them on from generation to generation with the result that numerous Urry editions have ended up in American university libraries. The proceeds of the edition were to be divided three ways among its publisher, the executor, and the college of Christ Church, Oxford. "College authorities had adopted a simple and effective method of disposing of theirs, which was to oblige all scholars upon entrance to buy a copy. The picture of the young fox-hunting squires of Christ Church being forced willy-nilly to carry off their Chaucer folios is a delightful one; and it may perhaps account for the number of copies of Urry's Chaucer to be found in the old country houses of England," remarks Caroline Spurgeon in her *Five Hundred Years of Chaucer Criticism and Allusion, 1357–1900,* 3 vols. paginated as 6 parts (1925; reprint, New York: Russell & Russell, 1960), 1:cxx–cxxi.

Thus, as I discussed in Chapter 1, "The Prioress on Paper," the first inexpensive edition was Thomas Tyrwhitt's of 1775–78, which he forgot to copyright. On Tyrwhitt and his background, see Alice Miskimin, "The Illustrated Eighteenth-Century Chaucer," *Modern Philology* 77 (1979): 26–55; and B. A. Windeatt, "Thomas Tyrwhitt (1730–1786)," in *Editing Chaucer: The Great Tradition,* ed. Paul G. Ruggiers (Norman, Okla.: Pilgrim Books, 1984), 117–43.

4. Alexander Pope, 1717, quoted by Geoffrey Tillotson, ed.,*The Rape of the Lock and Other Poems,* 3d ed. (London: Methuen; New Haven: Yale Univ. Press, 1962), vol. 2 of *The Twickenham Edition of the Poems of Alexander Pope,* ed. John Butt, 11 vols. in 12 (1939–69), 2:242.

5. Pope, notes to the 1736 edition of his *Temple of Fame,* now in *Poems of Alexander Pope,* 2:408. A. C. Cawley mentions both works in his "Chaucer, Pope, and Fame," *Review of English Literature* 3, no. 2 (1962): 9–19.

6. David Nokes, "Pope's Chaucer," *Review of English Studies* 27 (1976): 180–82.

7. Pope, *The Temple of Fame,* 1715, in *Poems of Alexander Pope,* 2:287–89. It repudiates Joseph Addison in ways discussed by Norman Ault, *New Light on Pope, with Some Additions to His Poetry Hitherto Unknown* (1949; reprint, Hamden, Conn.: Archon, 1967), 109–10.

8. Geoffrey Tillotson, introducing *Temple of Fame* and *Rape of the Lock,* in *Poems of Alexander Pope,* 2:244, 102–5.

9. Tillotson, introducing *Temple of Fame,* in *Poems of Alexander Pope,*

2:216–20. Most of the analogues listed by Tillotson are presumably trace-able to Ovid's *Metamorphoses*, bk. 12, more directly than he specifies.

10. Derek Pearsall, *John Lydgate* (Charlottesville: University Press of Virginia, 1970), 104–15, referring to ll. 43–246 of *The Temple of Glas*, before ca. 1412, now in *John Lydgate: Poems*, ed. John Norton-Smith (Oxford: Clarendon, 1966), 68–73.

11. Pearsall, *John Lydgate*, 104.

12. Lydgate, *Temple of Glas*, in *John Lydgate: Poems*, 72, ll. 179–90. I have modernized thorn and yogh, again for the sake of nonmedievalists and typesetters.

13. Pope, *January and May; or, The Merchant's Tale: From Chaucer*, 1709, now in *Poems of Alexander Pope*, 2:30, l. 340, for *MctT* l. 1738.

14. *The Prohemy of a marriage betwix an olde man and a yonge wife*, ca. 1430, quoted in Spurgeon, *Five Hundred Years of Chaucer Criticism*, 1:36.

15. Richard Maitland, *Satire on the Toun Ladyes*, before 1570, now in *The Poems of Sir Richard Maitland, of Lethingtoun, Knight*, ed. Joseph Bain for the Maitland Club (1830; reprint, New York: AMS Press, 1973), 27–31. In his second edition of *The Works of Geoffrey Chaucer*, F. N. Robinson includes *Against Women Unconstant* with "Short Poems of Doubtful Authorship," 540. John Stowe's 1561 heading is quoted by Eleanor P. Hammond, *Chaucer: A Bibliographical Manual* (1908; reprint, New York: Peter Smith, 1933), 120.

16. Bain, *Introductory Notice* to *Poems of Sir Richard Maitland*, xx–lx.

17. *Poems of Sir Richard Maitland*, 40–41.

18. O. B., *Display of Vaine Life* (London: Richard Field, 1594), fol. 28v. Subsequent folio references are given in parentheses in my text.

19. Arnold Davenport, *Introduction* to *The Collected Poems of Joseph Hall, Bishop of Exeter and Norwich*, ed. Davenport (1949; reprint, St. Clair Shores, Mich.: Scholarly Press, 1971), xxiii, xxv.

20. Joseph Hall, *Virgidemiarvm, The three last Bookes. Of byting Satyres*, 1599, now in his *Collected Poems*, 64, l. 89.

21. Hall, *Virgidemiarvm*, in his *Collected Poems*, 65, ll. 108–23.

22. Bartlett Jere Whiting does not mention the green tail/white head image in his account of the *Reeve's Prologue* in *Chaucer's Use of Proverbs* (1934; reprint, New York: AMS Press, 1973), 86; see page 187 for his list of worthless leeks in Chaucer's works. In Whiting's much more extensive *Proverbs, Sentences, and Proverbial Phrases from English Writings Mainly before 1500* (Cambridge: Harvard Univ. Press, 1958), he does however include *RvT* ll. 3878–79 in the entry H240, "To have a hoar *Head* and a green tail," along with an instance from 1532. Whiting's series of proverbs concerning leeks, entries L180–87, includes nearly fifty references to a leek's worthlessness, along with a few each to its greenness and pliability.

In the time period covered by both Morris Palmer Tilley in his *Dictionary of the Proverb in England in the Sixteenth and Seventeenth Centuries* (Ann Arbor: Univ. of Michigan Press, 1950) and Robert William Dent in his *Proverbial Language in English Drama Exclusive of Shakespeare, 1495–1616: An Index* (Berkeley and Los Angeles: Univ. of California Press,

1984), the weight of evidence shifts decisively. "Not worth a leek" has disappeared in any variant. L176, "As green as a leek," holds steady with a handful of entries. L177, "Like a leek, he has a white head and a green tail," has fourteen entries plus such apparent spinoffs as "Gray and green make the worst medley."

I have not attempted to trace the Italian proverb. It lasted at least the three centuries from Boccaccio's *Decameron* to Giovanni Torriano, *Piazza universale di proverbi italiani, or A Common Place of Italian Proverbs, and Proverbial Phrases* (London: F. & T. W., 1666). The image apparently did not survive the eighteenth century in either England or Italy. At any rate, it does not appear in collections such as *The Oxford Dictionary of English Proverbs*, ed. William George Smith and Paul Harvey, 2d ed. (Oxford: Clarendon, 1948), or *Proverbs, Proverbes, Sprichwörter, Proverbi, Proverbios . . . A Comparative Book of English, French, German, Italian, Spanish and Russian Proverbs with a Latin Appendix*, ed. Jerzy Gluski (New York: Elsevier, 1971).

I thank Wolfgang Mieder for help on this issue.

23. All quotations from *The Newe Metamorphosis* are taken not from the unpublished manuscripts themselves (B.M. Additional mss. 14824–26) but rather from what is included in John H. H. Lyon, *A Study of The Newe Metamorphosis* (New York: Columbia Univ. Press, 1919); this first couplet is from Lyon's page 7. In his unpublished papers, now in my possession, William L. Alderson credits the work to Jervase Markham, as does Lyon.

24. Lyon, *Newe Metamorphosis*, 62–63.

25. Ibid., 36–39. For scholarship concerning analogues of the three *Tales*, see Lynn King Morris, *Chaucer Source and Analogue Criticism: A Cross-Referenced Guide* (New York: Garland, 1985), 141–48, 176–77. Analogues (plus stories that share motifs but are not full analogues) are collected in W. F. Bryan and Germaine Dempster, eds., *Sources and Analogues of Chaucer's Canterbury Tales* (1941; reprint, Atlantic Highlands, N.J.: Humanities Press, 1958), 106–23, 341–56, 439–46; Larry D. Benson and Theodore M. Andersson, eds., *The Literary Context of Chaucer's Fabliaux: Texts and Translations* (Indianapolis: Bobbs-Merrill, 1971), 3–77, 203–337; John Webster Fargo, *Chaucer's Shipman's Tale: The Lover's Gift Regained* (1930; reprint, Folcroft, Pa.: Folcroft Library Editions, 1971); and William Edwin Bettridge, "The Folklore Background of Chaucer's *Miller's Tale*," M.A. thesis, Ohio State University, 1960.

26. Lyon, *Newe Metamorphosis*, xx.

27. Ibid., 62–63.

28. Ibid., 168–69. For Absolon's vague similarity, see *MlrT* ll. 3314–19, 3689–93.

29. Thomas Speght, ed., *The Workes of our Antient and Learned English Poet, Geffray Chavcer, newly Printed* (London: Adam Islip, 1598). The Arguments are not paginated in the 1598 edition. See also Hammond, *Chaucer: A Bibliographical Manual*, 125–28 (concerning changes in Speght's later editions) and 504–7 (concerning glossaries); and Johan Kerling, *Chaucer in Early English Dictionaries: The Old-Word Tradition in English Lexicography down to 1721 and Speght's Chaucer Glossaries* (The Hague: Mar-

tinus Nijhoff, for Leiden Univ. Press; distributed in the U.S. by Kluwer Boston, 1979), esp. 1–6, 28–42.

30. *Gabriel Harvey's Marginalia,* ed. G. C. Moore Smith (Stratford-upon-Avon: Shakespeare Head Press, 1913), 227. We know that he made the marginal comments before 1599 because he refers to Edmund Spenser as still living. For more background see Virginia F. Stern, *Gabriel Harvey: His Life, Marginalia and Library* (Oxford: Clarendon, 1979).

31. Alexander Niccholes, *A Discovrse of Marriage and Wiving* (London: G. Eld, for Leonard Becket, 1620), 16. The two other passages I quote also occur on pp. 16–17.

32. "Loathly Lady. Man disenchants loathsome woman by embracing her" is motif no. D732 in Stith Thompson, *Motif-Index of Folk Literature,* rev. and enl. ed., 6 vols. (Bloomington: Indiana Univ. Press, 1955–58), 2:84. Besides the ones provided by Bryan and Dempster, *Sources and Analogues,* 223–64, analogues (plus stories that share the motif but are not full analogues) are collected in Gustavus H. Maynadier, *The Wife of Bath's Tale: Its Sources and Analogues* (1901; reprint, New York: AMS Press, 1972), and Sigmund Eisner, *A Tale of Wonder: A Source Study of The Wife of Bath's Tale* (Wexford, Ireland: John English & Co., 1957). For additional scholarship see Morris, *Chaucer Source and Analogue Criticism,* 196–99. I know of no studies on the American jokes with parallels to this motif, still in lively oral circulation.

33. John Gower, *The Tale of Florent,* ca. 1390; and *The Weddynge of Sir Gawen and Dame Ragnell,* ca. 1450; both quoted in Bryan and Dempster, *Sources and Analogues,* 231 (l. 1687), 248 (ll. 238, 240–42). Thomas Hoccleve did not learn artistic reticence from his master: see, for example, his vision of female ugliness beginning "Of my lady well me rejoise I may," available in *Medieval English Lyrics: A Critical Anthology,* ed. Reginald T. Davies (Evanston, Ill.: Northwestern Univ. Press, 1964), 165.

34. The description is by George R. Price, *Thomas Dekker* (New York: Twayne, 1969), 144. The January/May reference occurs in 2.3.53 of *The Wonder of a Kingdom,* ca. 1623, now in *The Dramatic Works of Thomas Dekker,* ed. Fredson Bowers, 4 vols. (Cambridge: Cambridge Univ. Press, 1953–61), 3:600.

35. Henry Peacham, *Prince Henrie Revived* (London: W. Stansby, for I. Helme, 1615). Spurgeon quotes the January/May reference in *Five Hundred Years of Chaucer Criticism,* 1:190.

36. John Fletcher, *The Woman's Prize: or, The Tamer Tamed,* 1611, now in *The Dramatic Works in the Beaumont and Fletcher Canon,* ed. Fredson Bowers, 6 vols. to date (Cambridge: Cambridge Univ. Press, 1966–   ), 4:58 for lines cited (2.6.136–38, 145–47). Subsequent quotations in my text will be identified by act, scene, and line numbers from this edition.

37. Entry in Stationers' *Registers,* 1600, quoted in Spurgeon, *Five Hundred Years of Chaucer Criticism,* 3:4.54. For more on *The Wanton Wife of Bath,* see my n. 6, Chapter 1, "The Prioress on Paper."

38. *The Old Fumbler,* in Thomas D'Urfey, *Wit and Mirth, Or, Pills to purge Melancholy,* 1719–20, now in *Sixty Ribald Songs from Pills to Purge Melancholy,* ed. S. A. J. Bradley (New York: Praeger, 1968), 95–96; *John An-*

derson, My Jo, in Robert Burns, *The Merry Muses of Caledonia,* ca. 1800, now in *The Merry Muses of Caledonia: A Collection of Bawdy Folksongs, Ancient and Modern,* ed. James Barke and Sydney Goodsir Smith (New York: Gramercy, 1959), 147–48.

39. Concerning Speght and the elder Beaumont, see Spurgeon, *Five Hundred Years of Chaucer Criticism,* 1:145; for other Chaucer references by Fletcher, see her 1:183–84, 187, 206.

40. James Maidment and W. H. Logan, Prefatory Notice to *The Dramatic Works of Shackerley Marmion,* ed. Maidment and Logan (Edinburgh: William Paterson; London: H. Sotheran, 1875), xvi–xviii.

41. Shackerley Marmion, *The Antiquary,* 1641, now in his *Dramatic Works* just cited, 200.

42. Ibid., 211.

43. Ibid., 211–14.

44. That Pope knew Marmion's work is argued by Jackson I. Cope, "Shakerly [*sic*] Marmion and Pope's *Rape of the Lock,*" *Modern Language Notes* 72 (1957): 265–67.

10:   *How Pope Found the* Merchant's Tale

1. William Mannock, 1730, quoted in Joseph Spence, *Observations, Anecdotes, and Characters of Books and Men, Collected from Conversation,* ed. James M. Osborn, 2 vols. (Oxford: Clarendon, 1966), 1:12–13. Spence collected the observations and anecdotes from ca. 1726 until his death in 1768; they were first published in 1820. For more on Pope's self-education and the onset of the tubercular infection that resulted in curvature of the spine, see Spence, *Observations, Anecdotes, and Characters,* 1:6–14, 29–30, summarized in context in George Sherburn, *The Early Career of Alexander Pope* (1934; reprint, Oxford: Clarendon, 1968), 38–44; and Maynard Mack, *Alexander Pope: A Life* (New Haven: Yale Univ. Press in association with W. W. Norton, 1985), 35–52, 76–87, 153–58.

2. Albert B. Faust, ed., *Oberon: A Poetical Romance,* by Christoph Martin Wieland, trans. John Quincy Adams (New York: Crofts, 1940), xiii–xv passim, 135; originally translated in 1800.

3. Alexander Pope, note to 1736–51 editions of his *January and May; or, The Merchant's Tale: From Chaucer,* 1709, now in *The Rape of the Lock and Other Poems,* ed. Geoffrey Tillotson, 3d ed. (London: Methuen; New Haven: Yale Univ. Press, 1962), vol. 2 of *The Twickenham Edition of the Poems of Alexander Pope,* ed. John Butt, 11 vols. in 12 (1939–69), 2:15. For the bawdy imitation *Chaucer,* which in 1736 Pope acknowledged by note as "Done by the Author in his Youth," i.e., before 1709, see *Minor Poems,* ed. Norman Ault and John Butt (London: Methuen; New Haven: Yale Univ. Press, 1954), vol. 6 of *Poems of Alexander Pope,* 6:41–42.

4. Sherburn reproduces the receipt in *Early Career of Alexander Pope,* facing page 85. Only a few decades earlier, translation had been the "worst-paid work of all . . . the recompense was commonly a few copies of the work," according to Marjorie Plant, *The English Book Trade: An Economic His-*

tory of the Making and Sale of Books, 3d ed. (London: Allen & Unwin, 1974), 75.

5. Pope, *Epigram. Engraved on the Collar of a Dog which I gave to his Royal Highness,* 1738, now in *Poems of Alexander Pope,* 6:372.

6. Pope, letter to John Boyle, Earl of Orrery, 1744, now in *The Correspondance of Alexander Pope,* ed. George Sherburn, 5 vols. (Oxford: Clarendon, 1956), 4:517, adapting *KnT* ll. 2835–36. For more on Pope's love of dogs, see Norman Ault, *New Light on Pope, with Some Additions to His Poetry Hitherto Unknown* (1949; reprint, Hamden, Conn.: Archon, 1967), 337–50; and James M. Osborn, Appendix to item no. 265 in his edition of Spence, *Observations, Anecdotes, and Characters,* 2:629–30.

7. W. K. Wimsatt, "One Relation of Rhyme to Reason: Alexander Pope," *Modern Language Quarterly* 5 (1944): 323–38. The modernizations are discussed in A. Schade, "Ueber das Verhältniss von Pope's 'January and May' und 'The Wife of Bath. Her Prologue' zu den entsprechenden Abschnitten von Chaucer's Canterbury Tales," *Englische Studien* 25 (1898): 1–130, and 26 (1899): 161–228; Geoffrey Tillotson, introducing the two works in *Poems of Alexander Pope,* 2:3–12; Sherburn, *Early Career of Alexander Pope,* 85; Ault, *New Light on Pope,* 107–8; John M. Aden, *Pope's Once and Future Kings: Satire and Politics in the Early Career* (Knoxville: Univ. of Tennessee, 1978), 64–70; and Mack, *Alexander Pope: A Life,* 125–29.

8. Concerning this book now at Hartlebury Castle, Worcestershire, see David Nokes, "Pope's Chaucer," *Review of English Studies* 27 (1976): 180–82; Maynard Mack, "Pope's Books: A Biographical Survey with a Finding List," in *English Literature in the Age of Disguise,* ed. Maximillian E. Novak (Berkeley and Los Angeles: Univ. of California Press, 1977), 209–305; and idem, "Pope's Copy of Chaucer," in *Evidence in Literary Scholarship: Essays in Memory of James Marshall Osborn,* ed. René Wellek and Alvaro Ribeiro (Oxford: Clarendon, 1979), 105–21. Michael Hunter reports a 1602 Speght edition with Pope's signature, as well, in "Alexander Pope and Geoffrey Chaucer," in *The Warden's Meeting: A Tribute to John Sparrow,* ed. Oxford Univ. Society of Bibliophiles (Oxford: O.U.S.B., 1977), 29–32.

   According to Mack, "Pope's Books," 212, he had known since 1938 that Pope owned the 1598 edition. He apparently did not pass the word to Geoffrey Tillotson, who prepared the modernizations through the third edition of *The Rape of the Lock and Other Poems* while citing Speght's 1687 edition in his comparative notes (*Poems of Alexander Pope,* 2:12–78). My own examination of Pope's marginalia, made possible by the librarians at Hartlebury Castle and University of Birmingham, verifies the descriptions by Nokes and Mack. Pope was indeed disappointingly neat.

9. John Dryden, *Preface* to *Fables Ancient and Modern,* 1700, now in *The Poems of John Dryden,* ed. James Kinsley, 4 vols. (Oxford: Clarendon, 1958), 4:1452, 1455. Concerning Dryden's precedents and influence, see my n. 42, Chapter 1, "The Prioress on Paper," and n. 37, Chapter 4, "The Eighteenth-Century Pardoner(s)." The modernizations are in *Poems of John Dryden* as follows: *Palamon and Arcite,* 4:1468–1529; *The Cock and the Fox,* 4:1605–26; *The Wife of Bath Her Tale,* 4:1703–17; *The Character of*

   A Good Parson (expanded from *GP* ll. 477–528), 4:1736–40. Concerning the Middle English text included with the first printing of *Fables Ancient and Modern,* taken mostly but not wholly from Speght's 1598 edition, see William L. Alderson and Arnold C. Henderson, *Chaucer and Augustan Scholarship* (Berkeley and Los Angeles: Univ. of California Press, 1970), 53–68.

10. Dryden, *The Cock and the Fox,* ll. 810–21, for *NPT* ll. 3436–46, in *Poems of John Dryden,* 4:1625–26. Concerning possible face-to-face influence, as distinguished from certain literary influence, Pope told Joseph Spence that he "looked upon" Dryden, presumably by being taken to Will's coffeehouse before age twelve; related in Spence, *Observations, Anecdotes, and Characters,* 1:25. Pope is believed to be lying about the encounter in Sherburn, *Early Career of Alexander Pope,* 51, and to be telling the truth about it in David B. Morris, *Alexander Pope: The Genius of Sense* (Cambridge: Harvard Univ. Press, 1984), 3.

11. *The Workes of our Antient and Learned English Poet, Geffrey Chaucer, newly Printed,* ed. Thomas Speght (London: Adam Islip, 1598), fol. 32r, for *MctT* ll. 2417–18; Pope, *January and May,* ll. 817–20, for *MctT* ll. 2417–18, in *Poems of Alexander Pope,* 2:54; Dryden, *Wife of Bath Her Tale,* ll. 541–46, for *WBT* ll. 1257–64, in *Poems of John Dryden,* 4:1717.

12. Dryden, *Preface* to *Fables Ancient and Modern,* in *Poems of John Dryden,* 4:1457.

13. Dryden, *Wife of Bath Her Tale,* ll. 16–45, for *WBT* ll. 863–81; *Cock and the Fox,* ll. 570–71, for *NPT* l. 3265; *Palamon and Arcite,* ll. 30–31, for *KnT* l. 890; all three in *Poems of John Dryden,* 4:1704, 1619, 1468.

14. Dryden, *Preface* to *Fables Ancient and Modern,* in *Poems of John Dryden,* 4:1455–56.

15. Pope, *January and May,* ll. 382–84, for *MctT* ll. 1819–42, in *Poems of Alexander Pope,* 2:33. Hereafter I cite this work with line numbers, as *J&M,* in parentheses after passages quoted in my text.

16. Chaucer, *Workes,* ed. Speght, fol. 30r, for *MctT* ll. 1951–54. Hereafter I cite this work with folio numbers, as "Speght," in parentheses after passages quoted in my text.

17. E. Talbot Donaldson, "The Effect of the Merchant's Tale," in his *Speaking of Chaucer* (New York: Norton, 1970), 36–37.

18. In the next chapter I discuss the "hore" in Speght's equivalent of *MctT* l. 2367. As examples of Speght's use of periods, from fol. 30r, each of his equivalents of *MctT* ll. 1954, 1966, 1976, 1985, and 1994 concludes a paragraph and ends in a period. But he divides the continuous narrative that follows into three paragraphs (ending respectively at *MctT* ll. 2000, 2008, and 2018) plus a closing couplet, inserting no end punctuation until the narrator decisively shifts the scene with a period after *MctT* l. 2020.

19. Speght 32v-r, for *MctT* ll. 2350–53. The interpolation is mentioned in Alfred David, *The Strumpet Muse: Art and Morals in Chaucer's Poetry* (Bloomington: Indiana Univ. Press, 1976), 257 n. 2; and in Martin Stevens, "'And Venus Laugheth': An Interpretation of the *Merchant's Tale,*" *Chaucer Review* 7 (1972–73): 128.

How might Pope have regarded the typographical error "the throng" for "he throng"? In his text "throng" seems an inappropriate noun rather than the verb that Pope could understand as past tense of "thring, thrust" from Speght's unpaginated glossary, "The old and obscure words of Chaucer, explained." Speght lists misprints, not including this one, in his sections "Corrections of some faults, and Annotations vpon some places" and "Faults escaped, and some things omitted in the newe Additions."

I suspect that Pope could have spotted the typo. If not, "throng" as a noun seems part of a prepositional phrase balancing "up the smocke" and implying hazily that Damyan pulls his great tent into a crowd of some sort. If Pope left it at that, supposing the syntax peculiar, his narrator's "not in Phrase refin'd" (to be quoted next) deflects inquiry instead from Damyan's "tent," which remained a slang term for "penis" in the nineteenth century—presumably by analogy then, as for the scribe four centuries earlier, to "tent" as a "roll or pledget, usually of soft absorbent material, often medicated . . . used to search and cleanse a wound, or to keep open or distend a wound, sore, or natural orifice." See *OED*, s.v. "tent" sb.³; and John S. Farmer and William E. Henley, *Slang and Its Analogues, Past and Present*, 7 vols. (1890–1904; reprint in 1 vol., New York: Arno, 1970), s.v. "tent."

20. *McT* l. 2081. The date is suggested by J. D. North, "Kalenderes Enlumyned Ben They. Part II," *Review of English Studies*, n.s., 20 (1969): 277.
21. Thomas Tyrwhitt, ed., *The Canterbury Tales of Chaucer*, 5 vols. (1775–78; reprint, New York: AMS Press, 1972), 2:88. Editors since have replaced Tyrwhitt's "of" with manuscripts' "er" but have tried to make sense of the passage by retaining the syntax implied by Tyrwhitt's punctuation, especially by his comma before as well as after "befill." F. N. Robinson, giving precedence to astrological accuracy, changes the line outright to "er the month of Juyn, bifil." He attempts to justify the change in the note to his second edition, page 716; Larry Benson accedes in *The Riverside Chaucer* (Boston: Houghton Mifflin, 1987). Other modern editors, disagreeing quietly, have retained the "Juyl" present in all manuscripts in various spellings.
22. The lines referred to, in Pope's *January and May*, are: "Learned Poets," l. 367, for *McT* l. 1795; "Hester," l. 343, for *McT* l. 1744; "Ovid," l. 514, for *McT* l. 2125.
23. Pope, *January and May*, ll. 375–80, for *McT* ll. 1807–11, and Tillotson's note to the lines in *Poems of Alexander Pope*, 2:33. For the errors, see "Notes by Mr. Pope," *European Magazine*, October 1787, 261, reproduced in Mack, "Pope's Books," 283–85. Mack considers the attribution plausible but not proven. Whether or not Pope wrote these notes in this copy, however, his reuse of the aphrodisiacs passage shows that he was familiar with the sloppily translated work. Perhaps he even was aware that Dryden had let the voracious publisher Jacob Tonson take his *Book One* for posthumous publication, even though "my Translation is very uncorrect: but at the same time I know no body else can do it better," as quoted in Kinsley's note to *Ovid's Art of Love. Book I*, in *Poems of John Dryden*,

4:2086. The *European Magazine* article also says that "Pope had put the name of Mr. [Thomas] Yalden as translator of the 2nd Book, which is anonymous" and which contains the aphrodisiacs passage.

24. I requote both Joseph Addison and Samuel Johnson from Ault, *New Light on Pope,* 107.

25. Pope, *Rape of the Lock,* 1714, now in *Poems of Alexander Pope,* 2:161 (canto 2, ll. 37–38).

26. Ault, *New Light on Pope,* 107–8.

27. *J&M* ll. 710–15, for *MctT* ll. 2320–23. The interplay noted here of narrative voices—those of narrator, scholar, and satirist—continues throughout Pope's works, as described extensively by Morris in *Alexander Pope: The Genius of Sense;* in *An Epistle to Dr. Arbuthnot,* for example, voices of "the historical Alexander Pope . . . the dramatic speaker of the poem . . . and the author of the poem" intertwine (28). Chaucerians will recognize the influence on Pope of the technique articulated by Donaldson, in his *Speaking of Chaucer,* 1–12, as "Chaucer the Pilgrim" distinguished from Chaucer-the-poet and Chaucer-the-man (this article reprinted from *PMLA* 69 [1954]: 928–36).

28. Pope, *January and May,* ll. 389, 524, for *MctT* ll. 1845, 1850, 2137. In my next chapter I discuss Pope's line 389 in context.

29. A floating refrain can attach itself, varying in the process, to many ballads. Another familiar floating refrain occurs in variants including, for example, "Parsley, sage, rosemary, and thyme" and "Every rose grows merry in time." On a 1946 Library of Congress recording (A.A.F.S. no. L57), Jean Ritchie sings a refrain like the one Pope knew, with her version of Child ballad no. 10, *The Twa Sisters,* one of whom drowns the other, making for such delightful juxtapositions of verse and refrain as "The oldest pushed the youngest in / I'll be true to my love if my love'll be true to me." For more about this refrain, see Bertrand Bronson, *The Ballad as Song* (Berkeley and Los Angeles: Univ. of California Press, 1969), 268–69; and *The Viking Book of Folk Ballads of the English-Speaking World,* ed. Albert B. Friedman (1956; reprint, New York: Penguin, 1976), xxi–xxiii, 165–67.

The two fullest accounts of the interest in ballads by eighteenth-century literary figures are David C. Fowler, *A Literary History of the Popular Ballad* (Durham, N.C.: Duke Univ. Press, 1968), esp. 207–331; and Albert B. Friedman, *The Ballad Revival: Studies in the Influence of Popular on Sophisticated Poetry* (Chicago: Univ. of Chicago Press, 1961), esp. 84–232. On Pope in particular, see Friedman, *Ballad Revival,* 106–9; and Ault, *New Light on Pope,* 11.

30. In *Alexander Pope: The Genius of Sense,* 40–44, Morris analyzes Pope's stylistic use of such textural binary oppositions. Among many studies of this feature of the *Merchant's Tale,* see especially Kenneth A. Bleeth, "The Image of Paradise in the Merchant's Tale," in *The Learned and the Lewd: Studies in Chaucer and Medieval Literature,* ed. Larry D. Benson (Cambridge: Harvard Univ. Press, 1974), 45–60; Douglas A. Burger, "Deluding Words in the *Merchant's Tale,*" *Chaucer Review* 12 (1977–78): 103–10; David, *Strumpet Muse,* 170–81; Germaine Dempster, *Dramatic Irony in Chaucer* (1932; reprint, New York: Humanities Press, 1959), 46–58; Don-

aldson, *Speaking of Chaucer*, 30–45; James L. Hodge, "The Marriage Group: Precarious Equilibrium," *English Studies* 46 (1965): 289–300; Paul A. Olson, "Chaucer's Merchant and January's 'Hevene in Erthe Heere,'" *English Literary History* 28 (1961): 203–14; Janette Richardson, *Blameth Nat Me: A Study of Imagery in Chaucer's Fabliaux* (The Hague: Mouton, 1970), 123–46; Paul G. Ruggiers, *The Art of the Canterbury Tales* (Madison: Univ. of Wisconsin Press, 1965), 109–20; J. S. P. Tatlock, "Chaucer's Merchant's Tale," *Modern Philology* 33 (1936): 367–81; and Gertrude M. White, "'Hoolynesse or Dotage': The Merchant's January," *Philological Quarterly* 44 (1965): 397–404.

31. Pope, *January and May*, ll. 502–3, for *MctT* ll. 2109–10. The two antithetical couplets that Pope eliminates are *MctT* ll. 1597–98, 1823–24.

32. Pope, *The Wife of Bath Her Prologue*, 1714, now in *Poems of Alexander Pope*, 2:67, 69 (ll. 214, 256, for *WBP* ll. 459, 506). On Pope's use of color, see Ault, *New Light on Pope*, 76–100. To count in such a way that "Pope adds six more colour-words to those he found in the original" of *January and May* (87), Ault apparently includes the nouns "Greensword" and "Pinks" (the flower) from the garden description (*J&M* ll. 621, 624, for *MctT* ll. 2226–31 approx.). He does not notice that Pope evens the score by eliminating two of Chaucer's color words. Pope's sad-faced January speaks without showing his "hoor" head (*J&M* l. 87, for *MctT* l. 1400); and Pope's Damian loses an imagistic link to Chaucer's "fresshe May" by perching just "among the Boughs" rather than "among the fresshe leves grene" (*J&M* l. 719, for *MctT* ll. 2327–28).

Otherwise Pope adds to the *Tale* metaphorical grays, besides the silver sound of the wedding trumpets (*J&M* l. 319, for *MctT* l. 1715 approx.). Pope's Placebo contrasts January to "grey Fools" with too little courage to wed, and would agree heartily even "if my Lord affirm'd that Black was White" (*J&M* ll. 173, 160, for *MctT* ll. 1513–15 approx., 1498–99). All the rest of Pope's colors come directly from Chaucer's carefully tinted text. Most are shades of the two natural seasons, green and white: the green and white in January's attempted denial of his proverbial leekness, the green garden entered by a silver key, the blue sky and golden sun, the green turf throne of the fairy king, and the green pears that May craves in proof of her fertility (*J&M* ll. 131–36, 461–64, 468, 614–15, 625, 722, for *MctT* ll. 1461–66, 2037–41, 2046, 2219–20, 2235, 2333).

All in all, Pope seems to be artistically developing Chaucer's patterns of green and white. Pope's added grays make even more futile January's attempt to claim the whiteness of blossoming spring rather than that of wintry old age.

33. Thomas Betterton, *Chaucer's Characters, Or The Introduction to the Canterbury Tales,* and *The Miller of Trompington, Or, The Reve's Tale from Chaucer,* both in *Miscellaneous Poems and Translations. By Several Hands* (London: Bernard Lintott [*sic*], 1712), 273–74, 262, 304, for *GP* ll. 552–64, 294, and *RvT* l. 3976.

34. Speght, fol. 34r, for *WBP* l. 386. Pope eliminates the dog images at *MctT* ll. 1438, 2014.

35. Pope, *Wife of Bath Her Prologue*, l. 152, in *Poems of Alexander Pope*, 2:64.

Concerning Pope's horseback riding, see Spence, *Observations, Anecdotes, and Characters,* 1:30–31. Concerning the periodic rediscoveries of Chaucer's final *e,* see under "Verse" in Caroline Spurgeon, *Five Hundred Years of Chaucer Criticism and Allusion, 1357–1900,* 3 vols. paginated as 6 parts (1925; reprint, New York: Russell & Russell, 1960), 3:Index.16–17.

36. Pope, *Bounce to Fop,* 1736, and *Argus,* 1709 (reworking *Odyssey* 17.290–327), both now in *Poems of Alexander Pope,* 6:366–71, 51–52. See n. 6 above for more on Pope's love of dogs.

37. Belinda's lap dog Shock, among his other activities as the day progresses toward *The Rape of the Lock,* awakens her with his tongue at canto 1, ll. 115–16, in *Poems of Alexander Pope,* 2:154. The dogs of the modernized Prioress and Monk appear in Betterton, *Chaucer's Characters,* in *Miscellaneous Poems and Translations,* 254–55, 257, for *GP* ll. 146–49, 190–92.

38. Betterton, *Miller of Trompington,* in *Miscellaneous Poems and Translations,* 301, for *RvT* ll. 3927–28.

39. Robert W. Lowe, *Thomas Betterton* (1891; reprint, New York: AMS Press, 1972), 186. Betterton's entry in the *DNB* is prepared from twenty sources, not including that by one of Pope's favorite enemies, Giles Jacob. Jacob likewise includes no Chauceriana in the three pages plus full-page portrait of Betterton in his *Poetical Register: or, the Lives and Characters of the English [Dramatick] Poets, With an Account of Their Writings,* 2 vols. (London: E. Curll, 1719–20), 1:18–20.

40. Samuel Johnson, *Lives of the English Poets,* 1779–81; and Joseph Warton, ed., *Works of Alexander Pope,* 1797; both quoted in Spurgeon, *Five Hundred Years of Chaucer Criticism,* 1:457, 500. See also Mack, *Alexander Pope: A Life,* 92–93.

41. The eighteenth-century description of Morell is Thomas Harwood's, quoted in Alderson and Henderson, *Chaucer and Augustan Scholarship,* 142; see page 147 for Henderson's explanation of the omission of Pope's name on Morell's second edition. Morell credits Pope only on the title page to the first edition, to be sure; the modernization itself, as was usual during Pope's lifetime, has "by Mr. Betterton" beneath its title. The lines skipped by Pope/Betterton, so supplied by Morell (and Ogle in 1741) are *GP* ll. 361–87, 477–528 (as Dryden's *Character of A Good Parson*), 715–858.

42. Ault, *New Light on Pope,* 27–48.

43. Ibid., 28; see also 10–12, 27–48, 242–47 for more on Pope's "love of mystification in literary matters" (28). For texts of *Chaucer* and *Capon's Tale,* see *Poems of Alexander Pope,* 6:41–42, 256–58. See my Appendix B for locations of *The Miller of Trompington* in the six Lintot's miscellanies.

44. John Caryll, letter to Pope, 1712, now in *Correspondance of Alexander Pope,* 1:142. Concerning the Bettertons, see Lowe, *Thomas Betterton,* 182–84.

45. For Lintot's account book, see Edward L. Hart, ed., *Minor Lives: A Collection of Biographies by John Nichols* (Cambridge: Harvard Univ. Press, 1971), 229–31. Concerning the onset of copyright and royalties in the eighteenth century, see Plant, *The English Book Trade,* 73–79, 98–121 (76 on Pope).

46. Ault, *New Light on Pope,* 28. Concerning Pope's friendship with Betterton,

see Spence, *Observations, Anecdotes, and Characters,* 1:15, 23, summarized in context in Sherburn, *Early Career of Alexander Pope,* 49–50; and Mack, *Alexander Pope: A Life,* 88–94.

47. Betterton, *Miller of Trompington,* in *Miscellaneous Poems and Translations,* 308, for *RvT* ll. 4078–83. Parenthetical references in my text will be to the page in this 1712 Lintot's miscellany, termed "Lintot," followed as usual by line references to Robinson's second edition of Chaucer's *Works.*

48. According to my own observations and to Mack, "Pope's Copy of Chaucer," 115, some of Pope's sparse marginal ticks occur next to *RvT* ll. 3983–84 in his 1598 Speght edition. This neatly balanced satiric couplet contains the specifically Roman Catholic sin of Mrs. Symkyn's father.

49. Mack, *Alexander Pope: A Life,* 48, 80 for quotations, and in general on education 35–52, 76–87, passim.

50. Five analogues are included in Larry D. Benson and Theodore M. Andersson, eds., *The Literary Context of Chaucer's Fabliaux: Texts and Translations* (Indianapolis: Bobbs-Merrill, 1971), 88–197, one of which duplicates the analogue in W. F. Bryan and Germaine Dempster, eds., *Sources and Analogues of Chaucer's Canterbury Tales* (1941; reprint, Atlantic Highlands, N.J.: Humanities Press, 1958), 126–47. Seven additional analogues are included in John Charles Camp, "Sources and Analogues of Chaucer's Reeve's Tale," M.A. thesis, Ohio State University, 1971. Only a few of the twelve are full analogues; most merely share motifs.

51. Donaldson, *Speaking of Chaucer,* 43.

52. William Shakespeare, *Troilus and Cressida,* 3.2.106–12.

53. Shakespeare, *Hamlet,* 1.5.91.

54. I here apply distinctions articulated in Alan Dundes, "Texture, Text, and Context," *Southern Folklore Quarterly* 28 (1964): 251–65. Although the texture of a song or story cannot be translated into another language, its text can be compared cross-culturally. Dundes urges folklorists, having spent so long in the endless collection of texts, to step up their studies of context, both of an item's immediate performance context and its meaning in broader social context—as indeed folklorists have, in the decades since this article. Dryden's remark is in *Poems of John Dryden,* 4:1452.

11: *How Pope Left the* Merchant's Tale

1. Maynard Mack, *Alexander Pope: A Life* (New Haven: Yale Univ. Press in association with W. W. Norton, 1985), 93, 152.

2. *The Workes of our Antient and Learned English Poet, Geffrey Chaucer, newly Printed,* ed. Thomas Speght (London: Adam Islip, 1598), fol. 31v, for *MctT* l. 2125. Parenthetical references in my text are to folios in this edition, termed "Speght," along with line references as usual to Robinson's second edition of Chaucer's *Works.* Pope renders the line as "Well sung sweet *Ovid,* in the Days of yore," in his *January and May; or, The Merchant's Tale: From Chaucer,* 1709, now in *The Rape of the Lock and Other Poems,* ed. Geoffrey Tillotson, 3d ed. (London: Methuen; New Haven: Yale Univ. Press, 1962), vol. 2 of *The Twickenham Edition of the Poems of Alexander Pope,* ed. John Butt, 11 vols. in 12 (1939–69), 2:40, l. 514.

3. *The Wanton Wife of Bath,* Printed and Sold at the Printing-Office in Bow-Church-Yard, London, n.d., now in the collection of Houghton Library, Harvard University, as pEB75 P4128C no. 286.

4. Pope, *January and May,* in *Poems of Alexander Pope,* 2:31, ll. 347–48, for *MctT* ll. 1753–54. Hereafter I refer to line numbers of Pope's modernization, termed *J&M,* along with the corresponding lines in Robinson's edition and, if I am specifying Pope's reuse of its text, folios in Speght's.

5. On Speght fol. 31r, for *MctT* ll. 2228–31, Proserpine gathers flowers while entering January's garden, rather than in the past when Pluto abducted her. According to Robinson's textual note on *MctT* l. 2230 (p. 893), some variant of the substitute line occurs in ten manuscripts including the Ellesmere:

> And many a lady in his company
> Folowing his wife, the quene Prosperpine
> Ech after other right as a line
> Whiles she gadred floures in a mede

Chaucer's two references to the fairy king, in *MctT* ll. 2227 and 2234, both occur on fol. 31r of Speght's edition.

6. For motif no. K1518, "The enchanted pear tree. The wife makes the husband, who has seen the adultery from the tree, believe that the tree is magic or that he has seen double," see Stith Thompson, *Motif-Index of Folk Literature,* rev. and enl. edition, 6 vols. (Bloomington: Indiana Univ. Press, 1955–58), 4:403. For references to scholarship on *MctT* analogues, see Lynn King Morris, *Chaucer Source and Analogue Criticism: A Cross-Referenced Guide* (New York: Garland, 1985), 141–44. For a collection of texts using the Christian figures in lieu of Pluto and Proserpine, see Charles A. Watkins, "Modern Irish Variants of the Enchanted Pear Tree," *Southern Folklore Quarterly* 31 (1966): 202–13. Watkins's commentary should be disregarded, however, in favor of that in Karl P. Wentersdorf, "Chaucer's Merchant's Tale and its Irish Analogues," *Studies in Philology* 63 (1966): 604–29.

7. John Quincy Adams, *Analytical Extracts* with his translation of *Oberon: A Poetical Romance,* by Christoph Martin Wieland, ed. Albert B. Faust (New York: Crofts, 1940), lxxxii, originally translated in 1800. The quarrel of William Shakespeare's Oberon and Titania begins at *Midsummer Night's Dream,* 2.1.60.

8. Pope, *J&M* ll. 626, 647–50, for *MctT* ll. 2236, 2258; Speght 32v. Speght provides the F text of *Prologue* to the *Legend of Good Women,* in which an awe-inspiring king begins to speak at *PLGW* l. F312.

9. Christoph Martin Wieland, preface to *Oberon,* 1796, quoted in Caroline Spurgeon, *Five Hundred Years of Chaucer Criticism and Allusion, 1357–1900,* 3 vols. paginated as 6 parts (1925; reprint, New York: Russell & Russell, 1960), 3:5.137.

10. [J. J. Eschenburg], *Gottfried Chaucer,* 1793, quoted in Spurgeon, *Five Hundred Years of Chaucer Criticism,* 3:5.136.

11. Werner W. Beyer, *The Enchanted Forest* (Oxford: Blackwell, 1963), 118–43. See also Beyer's *Keats and the Daemon King* (New York: Oxford Univ.

Press, 1947). Both books include the same useful plot summary of *Oberon*, 6–26 and 23–52 respectively.

12. The lines referred to, in Pope's *January and May*, are: "Paris," l. 348, for *MctT* l. 1754; "Venus," l. 5, for *MctT* ll. 1249–50; "Wife," l. 80, for *MctT* l. 1396.

13. The lines referred to, in Pope's *January and May*, are: "Fortune," ll. 300–304, for *MctT* l. 1692; "Intent," l. 310, for *MctT* l. 1702; "Bed," l. 313, for *MctT* l. 1707.

14. The lines referred to, in Pope's *January and May*, are: "Boughs," ll. 718–19, for *MctT* ll. 2326–27; deities, ll. 720, 723, 732, for *MctT* ll. 2329, 2334, 2341; powers, ll. 764, 772, 776, 780, all within *MctT* ll. 2375–87; "Oracle," ll. 809–10, for *MctT* ll. 2407–10.

15. Speght 32v, for *MctT* ll. 2284, 2276. The latter line exemplifies tonal differences created by editorial paragraphing, as I mentioned in Chapter 4, "The Eighteenth-Century Pardoner(s)." Robinson indents a paragraph at *MctT* l. 2276, so that Proserpyne's scorn for authorities functions as topic sentence for her subsequent evocation of women justly praised by men other than Solomon. On fol. 32v, Speght begins the paragraph a line later, so that refutation falls more on Solomon in particular than on authorities in general. Thus too, in Speght, *MctT* ll. 2275–76 form a closing couplet to Proserpine's promise of eternal excuses to women, a couplet that pointedly rhymes men "leude as gees" with their role as "auctoritees."

16. Pope, *Rape of the Lock*, 1714, now in *Poems of Alexander Pope*, 2:166 (canto 2, ll. 107, 109); Thomas Betterton, *The Miller of Trompington, Or, The Reve's Tale from Chaucer*, in *Miscellaneous Poems and Translations. By Several Hands* (London: Bernard Lintott [*sic*], 1712), 320, for end of *Reeve's Tale* (no equivalent speech in Chaucer).

17. Pope, *J&M* ll. 1–8, for *MctT* ll. 1245–51 (cf. Cut L); Speght 27v. Pope's pun on "Sense" echoes Chaucer's different one in *MlrT* ll. 3340–41. In *Alexander Pope: A Life*, 128, Mack remarks on the irony of this line. Note also that "Grace" could be Christian or physical, as played with by Pope/Betterton for the daughter's name in *The Miller of Trompington*.

18. Pope, *J&M* l. 58, for *MctT* l. 1318. Concerning the effect of modern editorial punctuation on interpretations of this line, see my Chapter 8, "The Merchant as Character on Tape," Cut N. January wonders whether the blessing of a wife will affect the unknown afterlife in *J&M* ll. 268–75, for *MctT* ll. 1634–54.

19. Pope, *J&M* ll. 81–86, for *MctT* ll. 1397–99; Speght 28v. The *OED*, s.v. "sad," records uses of the adjective as "serious" or "steadfast" as late as Milton.

20. Pope, *J&M* ll. 137–38, for *MctT* ll. 1467–68. January scorns Justin's advice in *J&M* ll. 220–21, for *MctT* l. 1571.

21. Pope, *J&M* ll. 148, 176–77, for *MctT* ll. 1478, 1519–20; Speght 28r. For the Pardoner discussed in my Chapter 4, "The Eighteenth-Century Pardoner(s)," see Thomas Betterton, *Chaucer's Characters, Or The Introduction to the Canterbury Tales*, in *Miscellaneous Poems and Translations*, 279, for *GP* l. 670 approx.

22. *J&M* ll. 276–77, for *MctT* ll. 1655–56; Speght 29v; *OED*, s.v. "jape."

That Speght added "jape" to his 1602 glossary is noted by Johan Kerling, *Chaucer in Early English Dictionaries: The Old-Word Tradition in English Lexicography down to 1721 and Speght's Chaucer Glossaries* (The Hague: Martinus Nijhoff, for Leiden Univ. Press; distributed in U.S. by Kluwer Boston, 1979), 36.

23. Pope adds no stage directions to *J&M* ll. 700, 705, 222, 253–54, 778, for *MctT* ll. 2311, 2316, 1572, 1618–21, 2384.

24. Pope, *J&M* l. 383, for *MctT* ll. 1821–41. Concerning this apology by Pope's narrator, see my Chapter 10, "How Pope Found the *Merchant's Tale.*"

25. Pope, *J&M* ll. 543, 565–68, for *MctT* ll. 2160, 2176, 2184; Speght 31r; Shakespeare, *Troilus and Cressida*, 3.2.122, 124–28.

26. Pope, *Wife of Bath Her Prologue, From Chaucer*, 1714, now in *Poems of Alexander Pope*, 2:64, l. 161, for *WBP* l. 401. For the proverb's medieval currency, see Bartlett Jere Whiting, *Proverbs, Sentences, and Proverbial Phrases from English Writings Mainly before 1500* (Cambridge: Harvard Univ. Press, 1958), s.v. W537, "Women can weep (and lie) at will (*varied*)."

27. See *OED*, s.v. "cry," for consistency of the alternate meanings. Chaucer's non-neutral verbs occur at *MctT* ll. 2329, 2366. Pope's neutral verbs occur in *J&M* at lines 730, 736, 758, 767, 778, 781, 783, for *MctT* ll. 2340, 2346, 2368, 2376, 2384, 2387, 2389. January speaks other than neutrally at *J&M* ll. 726, 756, 788, for *MctT* ll. 2338, 2364, 2390. May speaks other than neutrally at *J&M* ll. 720–21, 772, 795, for *MctT* ll. 2329–30, 2380, 2396.

28. Pope, *J&M* ll. 724–25, for *MctT* ll. 2335–37. Concerning the spurious passage, see my Chapter 10, "How Pope Found the *Merchant's Tale.*"

29. *MctT* ll. 2378, 2367; Speght 32r; *OED*, s.v. "swive." Someone inclined to philology or puns (preferably with access to forthcoming *MED* volumes) might want to investigate this line's redundancy. ME "stoore" basically means ModE "strong." So does ME "stronge" unless here the latter means ModE "strange." The *OED*, s.v. "stour" (adj. 5b), cites *MctT* l. 2367 in a mostly positive cluster of meanings—strong, sturdy, stalwart in bearing, countenance, speech. Robinson translates "stoore" as "bold" in his note on page 716, presumably with negative connotations; other modern editors find impudence and crudeness in its overtones.

Might other senses of the adjective "stour," as great or bulky, suggest May's pregnancy? Might the sense of the equivalent noun make January seem also to exclaim against damage to his "lady stoore," i.e., his female property? What kind of strength, or strangeness, does the "stronge" refer to anyhow? It is easy to see why scribes soon made sense of the line by means of a whore. (See note on this line in the 1987 *Riverside Chaucer*.)

30. Concerning the proverbial nature of *MctT* l. 2410, see my Chapter 12, "The Pear-Tree Scene on Tape," esp. n. 5. May's opening couplet is *MctT* ll. 2329–30, her closing one *MctT* ll. 2409–10. January ends both a speech and a couplet at *MctT* l. 2386. The couplets that span speakers are *MctT* ll. 2337–40, 2345–48, 2365–68, 2375–76, 2379–80, 2383–84, 2389–90, 2395–96.

31. *J&M* ll. 811–17, for *MctT* ll. 2411–17. Among the studies cited in n. 13 of my Introduction, see especially Katharine T. Loesch, "Literary Ambiguity

and Oral Performance," *Quarterly Journal of Speech* 51 (1965): 258–67. She and others use the transcription system proposed by George L. Trager and H. L. Smith, *An Outline of English Structure* (Norman: Univ. of Oklahoma Press, 1951).

32. George Lyman Kittredge, *Chaucer and His Poetry* (Cambridge: Harvard Univ. Press, 1915), 202; J. S. P. Tatlock, "Chaucer's Merchant's Tale," *Modern Philology* 33 (1936): 367.

12: *The Pear-Tree Scene on Tape*

1. Monroe C. Beardsley, "Right Readings and Good Readings," *Literature in Performance* 1 (1980): 20–21, discussed in my Introduction.

2. As one example, with further references, see George List,"The Boundaries of Speech and Song," *Ethnomusicology* 7 (1963): 1–16. Here I account for twenty-four performances in that two readers begin the scene after *MctT* l. 2323. Later I will account for twenty-five readings of the *Tale's* closing, likewise because Utley read only *MctT* ll. 2348–96 for his Ohio State students.

3. "The enchanted pear tree" is motif no. K1518 in Stith Thompson, *Motif-Index of Folk Literature,* rev. and enl. ed., 6 vols. (Bloomington: Indiana Univ. Press, 1955–58), 4:403. For references to collections and discussions of analogues, see Lynn King Morris, *Chaucer Source and Analogue Criticism: A Cross-Referenced Guide* (New York: Garland, 1985), 141–44.

4. Alan Dundes, the foremost proponent of "Freudian" symbolic interpretation of folklore, admits the methodological problem that no informant (i.e., no actual active bearer of the item under consideration) is likely to proffer the symbolic interpretation. Often Dundes does supply evidence that he interprets as awareness by the folk of the symbolic interpretation he is proposing. Among many examples, see his "Here I Sit—A Study of American Latrinalia," *Kroeber Anthropological Society Papers,* no. 34 (1966): 101; "Into the Endzone for a Touchdown: A Psychoanalytic Consideration of American Football," *Western Folklore* 37 (1978): 86–87; "Wet and Dry, the Evil Eye: An Essay in Indo-European and Semitic Worldview," in Dundes's *Interpreting Folklore* (Bloomington: Indiana Univ. Press, 1980), 102; and "Life Is Like a Chicken Coop Ladder: A Study of German National Character through Folklore," *The Journal of Psychoanalytic Anthropology* 4 (1981): 354–55.

5. On the binary structure of proverbs see Roger D. Abrahams, "Proverbs and Proverbial Expressions," in his *Folklore and Folklife: An Introduction* (Chicago: Univ. of Chicago Press, 1972), 117–27; Alan Dundes, "On the Structure of the Proverb," *Proverbium* 25 (1975): 961–73; and Robert A. Rothstein, "The Poetics of Proverbs," in *Studies Presented to Professor Roman Jakobson by His Students,* ed. Charles E. Gribble (Cambridge, Mass.: Slavica, 1968), 265–74. Dan Ben-Amos suggests briefly that "the saying of a proverb may involve a shift in intonation," in "Toward a Definition of Folklore in Context," *Journal of American Folklore* 84 (1971): 11.

Bartlett Jere Whiting includes *MctT* l. 2410 in *Chaucer's Use of Proverbs* (1934; reprint New York: AMS, 1973), 107. It does not appear in proverb dictionaries, however, not even Whiting's own *Proverbs, Sentences, and Proverbial Phrases from English Writings Mainly before 1500* (Cambridge: Harvard Univ. Press, 1958). It may be that Chaucer is here creating a proverblike line. Concerning analogous proverblike lines and their function in defining a cultural subgroup, see Betsy Bowden, *Performed Literature: Words and Music by Bob Dylan* (Bloomington: Indiana Univ. Press, 1982), 77–78.

6. Concerning the shift from oral to written literature in ancient Greece, see Eric Havelock, "The Alphabetic Mind: A Gift of Greece to the Modern World," *Oral Tradition* 1 (1986): 134–50; idem, *The Literate Revolution in Greece and Its Cultural Consequences* (Princeton: Princeton Univ. Press, 1982); and idem, *Preface to Plato* (Cambridge: Harvard Univ. Press, 1963). For a survey of the oral/written issue in general, with bibliography, see Walter J. Ong, *Orality and Literacy: The Technologizing of the Word* (New York: Methuen, 1982).

7. Helge Kökeritz can be heard on side 2 of the recording *Beowulf-Chaucer,* KE 90395, formerly LE 5055 (1956), available from Educational Audio Visual, Inc., Pleasantville, NY 10570. It accompanies his *Guide to Chaucer's Pronunciation* (1961; reprint, Toronto: Univ. of Toronto Press, for the Mediaeval Academy of America, 1978). Concerning the aesthetics of performance on this and other commercially available recordings, see my forthcoming *Teachers' Guide to Chaucer Read Aloud: An Annotated Discography.*

BIBLIOGRAPHY

1. Chaucer Editions, Modernizations, and Imitations

Bell, John, ed. *The Poetical Works of Geoffrey Chaucer.* 14 vols. in 7. In *Bell's Edition. The Poets of Great Britain.* Edinburgh: Apollo Press, 1782–83.

Betterton, Thomas [and/or Alexander Pope]. *Chaucer's Characters, Or The Introduction to the Canterbury Tales; and The Miller of Trompington, Or, The Reve's Tale from Chaucer.* Both in *Miscellaneous Poems and Translations. By Several Hands,* [edited by Alexander Pope], 247–82, 301–20. London: Bernard Lintott [*sic*], 1712.

Clarke, Charles Cowden, ed. *The Riches of Chaucer: In Which His Impurities Have Been Expunged; His Spelling Modernised; His Rhythm Accentuated; And His Obsolete Terms Explained.* 2 vols. London: Effingham Wilson, 1835.

Dryden, John. *Palamon and Arcite: Or, The Knight's Tale, from Chaucer; The Cock and the Fox: or, The Tale of the Nun's Priest, from Chaucer; The Wife of Bath Her Tale; and The Character of A Good Parson; Imitated from Chaucer, And Inlarg'd.* All four originally in his *Fables Ancient and Modern; Translated Into Verse,* 1700. Now in vol. 4 of *The Poems of John Dryden,* edited by James Kinsley, 1468–1529, 1605–26, 1703–17, 1736–40. 4 vols. Oxford: Clarendon, 1958.

Furnivall, Frederick J., and W. G. Stone, eds. *The Tale of Beryn, with A Prologue of the merry Adventure of the Pardoner with a Tapster at Canterbury.* Edited from Northumberland ms. 455, ca. 1450. Originally published in 1887 by The Chaucer Society, then in 1909 by Early English Text Society, extra ser., no. 105. Reprint. Millwood, N.Y.: Kraus Reprints, 1975.

Horne, Richard H., ed. *The Poems of Geoffrey Chaucer modernised.* London: Whittaker, 1841.

Hunt, Leigh. *Death and the Ruffians. Modernized from Chaucer;* and *Cambus Khan. A Fragment.* Both in his *Stories in Verse,* 262–73, 274–93. London: George Routledge & Co., 1855.

———. *The Pardoner's Way of Preaching.* In his *Wit and Humour, Selected from the English Poets,* 114–16. London: Smith, Elder, & Co., 1846.

Lipscomb, William. *The Canterbury Tales of Chaucer, completed in a Modern Version.* 3 vols. London: J. Cooke & G. G. & J. Robinson, 1795.

Manly, John M., and Edith Rickert, eds. *The Text of The Canterbury Tales, Studied on the Basis of All Known Manuscripts.* 8 vols. Chicago: Univ. of Chicago Press, 1940.

Morell, Thomas, ed. *The Canterbury Tales of Chaucer, in the Original, From the*

Most Authentic Manuscripts; And as they are Turn'd into Modern Language by Mr. Dryden, Mr. Pope, and Other Eminent Hands. London: For the Editor, 1737.

Ogle, George, ed. *The Canterbury Tales of Chaucer, Modernis'd by several Hands.* 3 vols. London: J. & R. Tonson, 1741.

Pope, Alexander. *January and May; or, The Merchant's Tale: From Chaucer,* 1709; *The Wife of Bath Her Prologue, From Chaucer,* 1714; and *The Temple of Fame,* 1715. All three now in *The Rape of the Lock and Other Poems,* edited by Geoffrey Tillotson. 3d ed. London: Methuen; New Haven: Yale Univ. Press, 1962. Vol. 2 of *The Twickenham Edition of the Poems of Alexander Pope,* edited by John Butt. 11 vols. in 12 (1939–69), 2:13–54, 55–78, 249–89.

————. *Imitations of English Poets. I. Chaucer,* 1727. Now in *Minor Poems,* edited by Norman Ault and John Butt. London: Methuen; New Haven: Yale Univ. Press, 1954. Vol. 6 of *The Twickenham Edition of the Poems of Alexander Pope,* edited by John Butt. 11 vols. in 12 (1939–69), 6:41–42.

Robinson, F. N., ed. *The Works of Geoffrey Chaucer.* 2d ed. Boston: Houghton Mifflin, 1957.

Skeat, William Walter, ed. *The Complete Works of Geoffrey Chaucer.* 7 vols. Oxford: Clarendon, 1894–97.

Speght, Thomas, ed. *The Workes of our Antient and Learned English Poet, Geffrey Chaucer, newly Printed.* London: Adam Islip, 1598.

Tyrwhitt, Thomas, ed. *The Canterbury Tales of Chaucer.* 5 vols. 1775–78. Reprint. New York: AMS Press, 1972.

Urry, John, ed. *The Works of Geoffrey Chaucer.* London: Bernard Lintot, 1721.

Wordsworth, William. *Selections from Chaucer, modernised,* 1820; and "Chaucer Modernised: II. The Manciple," translated in 1801 and never published. Both now in vol. 4 of *The Poetical Works of William Wordsworth,* edited by E. de Selincourt and Helen Darbishire, 209–33, 358–65. 5 vols. Oxford: Clarendon, 1940–49.

Wright, Herbert G., ed. *A Seventeenth-Century Modernisation of the First Three Books of Chaucer's "Troilus and Criseyde."* The Cooper Monographs on English and American Language and Literature, no. 5. Bern: A. Francke, 1960.

Wright, Thomas, ed. *The Canterbury Tales of Chaucer.* 3 vols. London: Percy Society, 1847–51.

2.   *Reference Works and Frequently Cited Chaucer Commentary*

Alderson, William L. Unpublished papers, now in my possession.

Alderson, William L., and Arnold C. Henderson. *Chaucer and Augustan Scholarship.* Berkeley and Los Angeles: Univ. of California Press, 1970.

Baird, Lorrayne Y. *A Bibliography of Chaucer, 1964–1973.* Boston: G. K. Hall, 1977.

Benson, Larry D., and Theodore M. Andersson, eds. *The Literary Context of Chaucer's Fabliaux: Texts and Translations.* Indianapolis: Bobbs-Merrill, 1971.

Blake, William. *A Descriptive Catalogue of Pictures, Poetical and Historical Inventions,* 1809. Now in *Blake: Complete Writings,* edited by Geoffrey Keynes,

563–86. London: Oxford Univ. Press, 1966. [Concerning use of this edition, see my Chap. 1, n. 27.]

Bowden, Betsy. "The Artistic and Interpretive Context of Blake's 'Canterbury Pilgrims.'" *Blake: An Illustrated Quarterly* 13 (1980): 164–90.

———. *Teachers' Guide to Chaucer Read Aloud: An Annotated Discography.* Forthcoming.

Brathwait, Richard. *A Comment Upon the Two Tales of our Ancient . . . Poet Sr Jeffray Chaucer,* 1665. Edited by Caroline F. E. Spurgeon, under the title *Richard Brathwait's Comments, in 1665, upon Chaucer's Tales of the Miller and the Wife of Bath.* The Chaucer Society, 2d ser., no. 33. London: Kegan Paul, Trench, Trübner & Co., 1901.

Bryan, W. F., and Germaine Dempster, eds. *Sources and Analogues of Chaucer's Canterbury Tales.* 1941. Reprint. Atlantic Highlands, N.J.: Humanities Press, 1958.

Carey, William Paulet. *Critical Description of the Procession of Chaucer's Pilgrims to Canterbury, painted by Thomas Stothard, Esq. R.A.* 2d ed. London: Glindon, 1818.

Case, Arthur C. *A Bibliography of English Poetical Miscellanies, 1521–1750.* Oxford: Oxford Univ. Press for the Bibliographical Society, 1935 for 1929.

Chaucer Review. Perodical providing annual bibliography of criticism, 1966–.

The Compact Edition of the Oxford English Dictionary. 2 vols. New York: Oxford Univ. Press, 1971.

Crawford, William R. *Bibliography of Chaucer, 1954–63.* Seattle: Univ. of Washington Press, 1967.

Crow, Martin M., and Clair C. Olson, eds. *Chaucer Life-Records.* From materials assembled by John M. Manly and Edith Rickert, with the assistance of Lilian J. Redstone and others. Austin: Univ. of Texas Press, 1966.

Curry, Walter Clyde. *Chaucer and the Mediaeval Sciences.* 2d ed. New York: Barnes & Noble, 1960.

Dent, R. W. *Proverbial Language in English Drama Exclusive of Shakespeare, 1495–1616: An Index.* Berkeley and Los Angeles: Univ. of California Press, 1984.

Dictionary of National Biography. Edited by Leslie Stephen and Sidney Lee. 22 vols. 1885–1901. Reprint. London: Oxford Univ. Press, 1937–38.

Donaldson, E. Talbot. *Speaking of Chaucer.* New York: Norton, 1970.

Dryden, John. *Preface* to his *Fables Ancient and Modern; Translated into Verse,* 1700. Now in vol. 4 of *The Poems of John Dryden,* edited by James Kinsley, 1444–63. 4 vols. Oxford: Clarendon, 1958.

Farmer, John S., and William E. Henley. *Slang and Its Analogues, Past and Present.* 7 vols. 1890–1904. Reprint in 1 vol., with introduction by Theodore M. Bernstein. New York: Arno Press, 1970.

Foxon, David F. *English Verse, 1701–1750.* 2 vols. Cambridge: Cambridge Univ. Press, 1975.

Gibaldi, Joseph. *Approaches to Teaching Chaucer's Canterbury Tales.* New York: Modern Language Association of America, 1980.

Griffith, Dudley David. *Bibliography of Chaucer, 1908–1953.* Seattle: Univ. of Washington Press, 1955.

Grose, Francis. *A Classical Dictionary of the Vulgar Tongue.* Originally published in 1785. 3d ed. 1796. Reprint, edited by Eric Partridge. 3d ed. of reprint. New York: Barnes & Noble, 1963.

Hammond, Eleanor P. *Chaucer: A Bibliographical Manual.* 1908. Reprint. New York: Peter Smith, 1933.

Howard, Donald R. *The Idea of the Canterbury Tales.* Berkeley and Los Angeles: Univ. of California Press, 1976.

Kittredge, George Lyman. *Chaucer and His Poetry.* Cambridge: Harvard Univ. Press, 1915.

Lounsbury, Thomas R. *Studies in Chaucer, His Life and Writings.* 3 vols. 1892. Reprint. New York: Russell & Russell, 1962.

Lumiansky, Robert M. *Of Sondry Folk: The Dramatic Principle in the Canterbury Tales.* Austin: Univ. of Texas Press, 1955.

Mann, Jill. *Chaucer and Medieval Estates Satire: The Literature of Social Classes and the General Prologue to the Canterbury Tales.* Cambridge: Cambridge Univ. Press, 1973.

Middle English Dictionary. Edited by Hans Kurath. 10 vols. to date. Ann Arbor: Univ. of Michigan Press,1952–.

Morris, Lynn King. *Chaucer Source and Analogue Criticism: A Cross-Referenced Guide.* New York: Garland, 1985.

Muscatine, Charles. *The Book of Geoffrey Chaucer.* San Francisco: Book Club of California, 1963.

Nichols, John. *Literary Anecdotes of the Eighteenth Century.* 9 vols. 1812–16. Edited in excerpts, along with other of Nichols's works, by Edward L. Hart, under the title *Minor Lives: A Collection of Biographies by John Nichols.* Cambridge: Harvard Univ. Press, 1971.

Sampson, George. *The Concise Cambridge History of English Literature,* 3d ed. Cambridge: Cambridge Univ. Press, 1972.

Spence, Joseph. *Observations, Anecdotes, and Characters of Books and Men.* First published 1820, from Spence's mss. ca. 1726–68. Edited, along with other of Spence's papers, by James M. Osborn. 2 vols. Oxford: Clarendon, 1966.

Spurgeon, Caroline F. E. *Five Hundred Years of Chaucer Criticism and Allusion, 1357–1900.* Originally published in 1908–17 by The Chaucer Society. Collected in 1925. Reprint. 6 parts in 3 vols. New York: Russell & Russell, 1960. [References to collections of addenda to Spurgeon's compilation are provided by James D. Johnson, "Identifying Chaucer Allusions, 1953–1980: An Annotated Bibliography," *Chaucer Review* 19 (1984–85): 62–86.]

Studies in the Age of Chaucer. Periodical providing annual annotated bibliography of criticism. 1979–.

Thompson, Stith. *Motif-Index of Folk Literature.* Rev. and enl. ed. 6 vols. Bloomington: Indiana Univ. Press, 1955–58.

Tilley, Morris Palmer. *A Dictionary of the Proverb in England in the Sixteenth and Seventeenth Centuries.* Ann Arbor: Univ. of Michigan Press, 1950.

Tobler, Alfred. *Geoffrey Chaucer's Influence on English Literature.* 1905. Reprint. New York: AMS Press, 1973.

Whiting, Bartlett Jere. *Chaucer's Use of Proverbs.* 1934. Reprint. New York: AMS Press, 1973.

———. *Proverbs, Sentences, and Proverbial Phrases from English Writings Mainly before 1500*. Cambridge: Harvard Univ. Press, 1958.

3. Works (Not Necessarily Cited) from the Fields of Medieval Literature and Culture, Literary Theory, Printing History, Oral Interpretation, and Folklore

Alcheringa/Ethnopoetics. Journal on oral poetics, 1970–80.

Alden, Raymond Macdonald. "The Mental Side of Metrical Form." *Modern Language Review* 9 (1914): 297–308.

Bakhtin, Mikhail. *Rabelais and His World*. Translated by Hélène Iswolsky. 1968. Reprint. Bloomington: Indiana Univ. Press, 1984. Originally published as *Tvorchestvo Fransua Rable i narodnaia kul'tura srednevekov'ia i Renessansa* (Moscow: Khudozhestvennia literatura, 1965).

Bäuml, Franz H. "Varieties and Consequences of Medieval Literacy and Illiteracy." *Speculum* 55 (1980): 237–65.

Beardsley, Monroe C. "Right Readings and Good Readings." *Literature in Performance* 1 (1980): 10–22.

Ben-Amos, Dan, and Kenneth S. Goldstein, eds. *Folklore: Performance and Communication*. The Hague: Mouton, 1975.

Bennett, H. S. *English Books and Readers, 1475 to 1557*. Cambridge: Cambridge Univ. Press, 1952.

Bleich, David. *Subjective Criticism*. Baltimore: Johns Hopkins Univ. Press, 1978.

Booth, Mark W. *The Experience of Songs*. New Haven: Yale Univ. Press, 1981.

Bowden, Betsy. "The Art of Courtly Copulation." *Medievalia et Humanistica*, n.s., 9 (1979): 67–85.

———. *Performed Literature: Words and Music by Bob Dylan*. Bloomington: Indiana Univ. Press, 1982.

Boyd, Beverly. *Chaucer and the Medieval Book*. San Marino, Calif.: Huntington Library, 1973.

Bronson, Bertrand. *Printing as an Index of Taste in Eighteenth Century England*. New York: New York Public Library, 1958.

Burke, Peter. *Popular Culture in Early Modern Europe*. New York: Harper & Row, 1978.

Clair, Colin. *A History of Printing in Britain*. New York: Oxford Univ. Press, 1966.

Crews, Frederick C. *The Pooh Perplex: A Freshman Casebook*. New York: Dutton, 1963.

Crosby, Ruth C. "Oral Delivery in the Middle Ages." *Speculum* 11 (1936): 88–110.

———. "Chaucer and the Custom of Oral Delivery." *Speculum* 13 (1938): 413–32.

Crystal, David. *The English Tone of Voice: Essays in Intonation, Prosody and Paralanguage*. New York: St. Martin's Press, 1975.

Dundes, Alan. "Texture, Text, and Context." *Southern Folklore Quarterly* 28 (1964): 251–65.

Eagleton, Terry. *Literary Theory: An Introduction*. Oxford: Blackwell, 1983.

Ellis, John M. *The Theory of Literary Criticism: A Logical Analysis.* Berkeley and Los Angeles: Univ. of California Press, 1974.

Empson, William. *Seven Types of Ambiguity: A Study of Its Effects in English Verse.* 3d ed. 1953. Reprint. New York: Meridian, 1955.

Fairbanks, Grant. "Recent Experimental Investigations of Vocal Pitch in Speech." *Journal of the Acoustical Society of America* 11 (1940): 457–66.

Febvre, Lucien, and Henri-Jean Martin. *The Coming of the Book: The Impact of Printing, 1450–1800.* Translated by David Gerard. Edited by Geoffrey Nowell-Smith and David Wootton. 1976. Reprint. London: Verso, 1984. Originally published under the title *L'Apparition du Livre* (Paris: Editions Albin Michel, 1958).

Fine, Elizabeth. *The Folklore Text: From Performance to Print.* Bloomington: Indiana Univ. Press, 1984.

Finnegan, Ruth. *Oral Poetry: Its Nature, Significance and Social Context.* Cambridge: Cambridge Univ. Press, 1977.

Fish, Stanley E. *Is There a Text in This Class? The Authority of Interpretive Communities.* Cambridge: Harvard Univ. Press, 1980.

Fowler, David C. *A Literary History of the Popular Ballad.* Durham, N.C.: Duke Univ. Press, 1968.

Gaylord, Alan T. "Scanning the Prosodists: An Essay in Metacriticism." *Chaucer Review* 11 (1976–77): 22–82.

Gellrich, Jesse M. *The Idea of the Book in the Middle Ages.* Ithaca, N.Y.: Cornell Univ. Press, 1985.

Georges, Robert A. "Toward an Understanding of Storytelling Events." *Journal of American Folklore* 82 (1969): 313–28.

Handover, P. M. *Printing in London, from 1476 to Modern Times.* London: Allen & Unwin, 1960.

Havelock, Eric. *The Literate Revolution in Greece and Its Cultural Consequences.* Princeton: Princeton Univ. Press, 1982.

Hohendahl, Peter Uwe. *The Institution of Criticism.* Various translators. Ithaca, N.Y.: Cornell Univ. Press, 1982.

Holub, Robert C. *Reception Theory: A Critical Introduciton.* New York: Methuen, 1984.

Iser, Wolfgang. *The Act of Reading: A Theory of Aesthetic Response.* Translated by David Henry Wilson. Baltimore: Johns Hopkins Univ. Press, 1978. Originally published under the title *Der Akt des Lesens* (Munich: Wilhelm Fink, 1976).

Jacobs, Melville. *The Content and Style of an Oral Literature: Clackamas Chinook Myths and Tales.* Chicago: Univ. of Chicago Press, 1959.

Jauss, Hans Robert. *Aesthetic Experience and Literary Hermeneutics.* Translated by Michael Shaw. Introduction by Wlad Godzich. Theory and History of Literature, vol. 3. Minneapolis: Univ. of Minnesota Press, 1982. Originally published under the title *Ästhetische Erfahrung und literarische Hermeneutik I* (Munich: Wilhelm Fink, 1977).

Johnson, Paula. *Form and Transformation in Music and Poetry of the English Renaissance.* New Haven: Yale Univ. Press, 1972.

Juhl, P. D. *Interpretation: An Essay in the Philosophy of Literary Criticism.* Princeton: Princeton Univ. Press, 1980.

Kintgen, Eugene R. *The Perception of Poetry.* Bloomington: Indiana Univ. Press, 1983.

Lam, George L., and Warren H. Smith. "George Vertue's Contributions to Chaucerian Iconography." *Modern Language Quarterly* 5 (1944): 303–22.

Leavis, F. R. *The Living Principle: "English" as a Discipline of Thought.* New York: Oxford Univ. Press, 1975.

Levin, Richard L. *New Readings vs. Old Plays: Recent Trends in the Reinterpretation of English Renaissance Drama.* Chicago: Univ. of Chicago Press, 1979.

Lindahl, Carl. *Earnest Games: Folkloric Patterns in The Canterbury Tales.* Bloomington: Indiana Univ. Press, forthcoming.

Literature in Performance. Journal on oral interpretation, 1980–.

Loesch, Katharine T. "Literary Ambiguity and Oral Performance." *Quarterly Journal of Speech* 51 (1965): 258–67.

Meyer, Leonard B. *Emotion and Meaning in Music.* Chicago: Univ. of Chicago Press, 1956.

Miskimin, Alice. "The Illustrated Eighteenth-Century Chaucer." *Modern Philology* 77 (1979): 26–55.

———. *The Renaissance Chaucer.* New Haven: Yale Univ. Press, 1975.

Mitchell, W. J. T., ed. *Against Theory: Literary Studies and the New Pragmatism.* Chicago: Univ. of Chicago Press, 1985. Originally published as articles in *Critical Inquiry,* 1982–85.

Murphy, James J. *Rhetoric in the Middle Ages: A History of Rhetorical Theory from Saint Augustine to the Renaissance.* Berkeley and Los Angeles: Univ. of California Press, 1974.

Muscatine, Charles. *Chaucer and the French Tradition: A Study in Style and Meaning.* Berkeley and Los Angeles: Univ. of California Press, 1957.

New Literary History 8 (spring 1977): 335–535. Issue on Oral Cultures and Oral Performances.

New Literary History 10 (winter 1979): 181–416. Issue on Medieval Literature and Contemporary Theory.

New Literary History 16 (autumn 1984): 1–206. Issue on Oral and Written Traditions in the Middle Ages.

Olson, Glending. *Literature as Recreation in the Later Middle Ages.* Ithaca, N.Y.: Cornell Univ. Press, 1982.

Ong, Walter J. *Orality and Literacy: The Technologizing of the Word.* New York: Methuen, 1982.

Opland, Jeff. *Anglo-Saxon Oral Poetry: A Study of the Traditions.* New Haven: Yale Univ. Press, 1980.

Oral Tradition. Journal with annual annotated bibliography, 1986– .

Paredes, Americo, and Richard Bauman, eds. *Toward New Perspectives in Folklore.* American Folklore Society Bibliographical and Special Series, vol. 23. Austin: Univ. of Texas Press for the American Folklore Society, 1972.

Pearsall, Derek. "Chaucer and the Modern Reader: A Question of Approach." *Dutch Quarterly Review of Anglo-American Letters* 11 (1981): 258–66.

Plant, Marjorie. *The English Book Trade: An Economic History of the Making and Sale of Books.* 3d ed. London: Allen & Unwin, 1974.

Pratt, Mary Louise. *Toward a Speech Act Theory of Literary Discourse.* Bloomington: Indiana Univ. Press, 1977.

Quinn, William A., and Audley S. Hall. *Jongleur: A Modified Theory of Oral Improvisation and Its Effects on the Performance and Transmission of Middle English Romance*. Washington, D.C.: University Press of America, 1982.

Ridley, Florence. "Chaucerian Criticism: The Significance of Varying Perspectives." *Neuphilologische Mitteilungen* 81 (1980): 131–41.

Robertson, D. W., Jr. *A Preface to Chaucer: Studies in Medieval Perspectives*. Princeton: Princeton Univ. Press, 1962.

Rosenblatt, Louise M. *The Reader, the Text, the Poem: The Transactional Theory of the Literary Work*. Carbondale: Southern Illinois Univ. Press, 1978.

Rowland, Beryl. "Chaucer's Speaking Voice and Its Effect on His Listeners' Perception of Criseyde." *English Studies in Canada* 7 (1981): 129–40.

———. "*Pronuntiatio* and its Effect on Chaucer's Audience." *Studies in the Age of Chaucer* 4 (1982): 33–51.

Ruggiers, Paul G., ed. *Editing Chaucer: The Great Tradition*. Norman, Okla.: Pilgrim Books, 1984.

Sebeok, Thomas A., ed. *Style in Language*. Cambridge: Massachusetts Institute of Technology Press, 1960.

Shattuck, Roger. "How to Rescue Literature." *New York Review of Books*, 17 April 1980, 29–35.

Smith, Barbara Herrnstein. *On the Margins of Discourse: The Relation of Literature to Language*. Chicago: Univ. of Chicago Press, 1978.

Sontag, Susan. *Against Interpretation and Other Essays*. New York: Dell, 1966.

Steiner, George. *On Difficulty and Other Essays*. New York: Oxford Univ. Press, 1978.

Suleiman, Susan R., and Inge Crosman, eds. *The Reader in the Text: Essays on Audience and Interpretation*. Princeton: Princeton Univ. Press, 1980.

Toelken, Barre. *The Dynamics of Folklore*. Boston: Houghton Mifflin, 1979.

Tompkins, Jane P., ed. *Reader-Response Criticism, from Formalism to Post-Structuralism*. Baltimore: Johns Hopkins Univ. Press, 1980.

Utley, Francis Lee. "Boccaccio, Chaucer, and the International Popular Tale." *Western Folklore* 33 (1974): 181–201.

Ward, Donald. "The Performance and Perception of Folklore and Literature." *Fabula* 20 (1979): 256–64.

Wimsatt, W. K., Jr. "One Relation of Rhyme to Reason: Alexander Pope." *Modern Language Quarterly* 5 (1944): 323–38.

———, and Monroe C. Beardsley. "The Intentional Fallacy." *Sewanee Review* 54 (1946): 468–88.

Winters, Yvor. "The Audible Reading of Poetry." In his *Function of Criticism: Problems and Exercises*, 81–100. Denver: Alan Swallow, 1957.

Wood, Chauncey. "Affective Stylistics and the Study of Chaucer." *Studies in the Age of Chaucer* 6 (1984): 21–40.

Yates, Frances A. *The Art of Memory*. Chicago: Univ. of Chicago Press, 1966.

INDEX

(including Appendix B and substantive endnotes)

University of Pennsylvania Press
MIDDLE AGES SERIES
Edward Peters, General Editor

Edward Peters, ed. *Christian Society and the Crusades, 1198–1229*. Sources in Translation, including The Capture of Damietta by Oliver of Paderborn. 1971

Edward Peters, ed. *The First Crusade: The Chronicle of Fulcher of Chartres and Other Source Materials*. 1971

Katherine Fischer Drew, trans. *The Burgundian Code: The Book of Constitutions or Law of Gundobad and Additional Enactments*. 1972

G. G. Coulton. *From St. Francis to Dante: Translations from the Chronicle of the Franciscan Salimbene (1221–1288)*. 1972

Alan C. Kors and Edward Peters, eds. *Witchcraft in Europe, 1110–1700: A Documentary History*. 1972

Richard C. Dales. *The Scientific Achievement of the Middle Ages*. 1973

Katherine Fischer Drew, trans. *The Lombard Laws*. 1973

Henry Charles Lea. *The Ordeal*. Part III of Superstition and Force. 1973

Henry Charles Lea. *Torture*. Part IV of Superstition and Force. 1973

Henry Charles Lea (Edward Peters, ed.). *The Duel and the Oath*. Parts I and II of Superstition and Force. 1974

Edward Peters, ed. *Monks, Bishops, and Pagans: Christian Culture in Gaul and Italy, 500–700*. 1975

Jeanne Krochalis and Edward Peters, ed. and trans. *The World of Piers Plowman*. 1975

Julius Goebel, Jr. *Felony and Misdemeanor: A Study in the History of Criminal Law*. 1976

Susan Mosher Stuard, ed. *Women in Medieval Society*. 1976

James Muldoon, ed. *The Expansion of Europe: The First Phase*. 1977

Clifford Peterson. *Saint Erkenwald*. 1977

Robert Somerville and Kenneth Pennington, eds. *Law, Church, and Society: Essays in Honor of Stephan Kuttner*. 1977

Donald E. Queller. *The Fourth Crusade: The Consquest of Constantinople, 1201–1204*. 1977

Pierre Riché (Jo Ann McNamara, trans.). *Daily Life in the World of Charlemagne*. 1978

Charles R. Young. *The Royal Forests of Medieval England*. 1979

Edward Peters, ed. *Heresy and Authority in Medieval Europe*. 1980

Suzanne Fonay Wemple. *Women in Frankish Society: Marriage and the Cloister, 500–900*. 1981

R. G. Davies and J. H. Denton, eds. *The English Parliament in the Middle Ages.* 1981

Edward Peters. *The Magician, the Witch, and the Law.* 1982

Barbara H. Rosenwein. *Rhinoceros Bound: Cluny in the Tenth Century.* 1982

Steven D. Sargent, ed. and trans. *On the Threshold of Exact Science: Selected Writings of Anneliese Maier on Late Medieval Natural Philosophy.* 1982

Benedicta Ward. *Miracles and the Medieval Mind: Theory, Record, and Event, 1000–1215.* 1982

Harry Turtledove, trans. *The Chronicle of Theophanes: An English Translation of anni mundi 6095–6305 (A.D. 602–813).* 1982

Leonard Cantor, ed. *The English Medieval Landscape.* 1982

Charles T. Davis. *Dante's Italy and Other Essays.* 1984

George T. Dennis, trans. *Maurice's Strategikon: Handbook of Byzantine Military Strategy.* 1984

Thomas F. X. Noble. *The Republic of St. Peter: The Birth of the Papal State, 680–825.* 1984

Kenneth Pennington. *Pope and Bishops: The Papal Monarchy in the Twelfth and Thirteenth Centuries.* 1984

Patrick J. Geary. *Aristocracy in Provence: The Rhône Basin at the Dawn of the Carolingian Age.* 1985

C. Stephen Jaeger. *The Origins of Courtliness: Civilizing Trends and the Formation of Courtly Ideals, 939–1210.* 1985

J. N. Hillgarth, ed. *Christianity and Paganism, 350–750: The Conversion of Western Europe.* 1986

William Chester Jordan. *From Servitude to Freedom: Manumission in the Sénonais in the Thirteenth Century.* 1986

James William Brodman. *Ransoming Captives in Crusader Spain: The Order of Merced on the Christian-Islamic Frontier.* 1986

Frank Tobin. *Meister Eckhart: Thought and Language.* 1986

Daniel Bornstein, trans. *Dino Compagni's Chronicle of Florence.* 1986

James M. Powell. *Anatomy of a Crusade, 1213–1221.* 1986

Jonathan Riley-Smith. *The First Crusade and the Idea of Crusading.* 1986

Susan Mosher Stuard, ed. *Women in Medieval History and Historiography.* 1987

Avril Henry, ed. *The Mirour of Mans Saluacioune.* 1987

María Menocal. *The Arabic Role in Medieval Literary History.* 1987

Margaret J. Ehrhart. *The Judgment of the Trojan Prince Paris in Medieval Literature.* 1987

Betsy Bowden. *Chaucer Aloud: The Varieties of Textual Interpretation.* 1987

Felipe Fernández-Armesto. *Before Columbus: Exploration and Colonization from the Mediterranean to the Atlantic, 1229–1492.* 1987

Michael Resler, trans. *EREC by Hartmann von Aue.* 1987

Alastair J. Minnis, *Medieval Theory of Authorship.* 1987